300
MASON
JARS

Preserving History

300

MASON JARS

JOANNE
THOMSON

Heritage House Publishing Company Ltd.
heritagehouse.ca

Cataloguing information available from Library and Archives Canada
978-1-77203-516-2 (hardcover)
978-1-77203-517-9 (e-book)

Edited by Lara Kordic
Cover and interior book design by Setareh Ashrafologhalai
Artwork by Joanne Thomson
Cover images: *Mason Jar with Cosmos*, 2015 (*front*); *Mason Jar with Dragonfly*, 2014 (*back*)

The interior of this book was produced on FSC®-certified, acid-free paper, processed chlorine free, and printed with vegetable-based inks.

Heritage House gratefully acknowledges that the land on which we live and work is within the traditional territories of the Lkwungen (Esquimalt and Songhees), Malahat, Pacheedaht, Scia'new, T'Sou-ke, and W̱SÁNEĆ (Pauquachin, Tsartlip, Tsawout, Tseycum) Peoples.

We acknowledge the financial support of the Government of Canada through the Canada Book Fund (CBF) and the Canada Council for the Arts, and the Province of British Columbia through the British Columbia Arts Council and the Book Publishing Tax Credit.

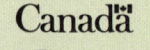 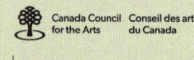
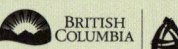

28 27 26 25 24   1 2 3 4 5

Printed in China

To Werner, Eva, and
their descendants

CONTENTS

"The men and women . . . were now an
image in the minds of their descendants. They
had acquired the mystery and the stability of
the past. They had attained a kind of complete
incompleteness. They were waiting to be
completed by the knowledge and the actions of
their descendants. And, at the same time, they
were complete for they had completed them-
selves: they could do no more."

JOHN BERGER

And Our Faces, My Heart, Brief as Photos
(New York: Vintage International, 1984, 20)

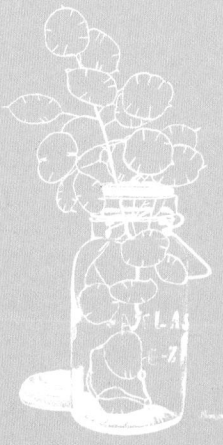

INTRODUCTION

I AM often asked how I came up with the idea of using Mason jars for this series. I thank Fred Marshall and his trusty tape recorder. When Fred purchased the property "up Kerr Creek," where my grandparents Werner and Eva lived and raised their daughters between 1926 and 1946, he sought out my grandmother and recorded her stories. Years later, he contacted me and asked me to transcribe them. In one of the stories, Eva described how she had 300 Mason jars "on the go at all times" to preserve food.

At the time, I had been trying to create a monumental work of art expressing the family history. Frustrated with my attempts, I decided I may just as well do something useful. My students were always asking me to teach them how to paint glass, so I'd learn how to paint glass. I put an egg in a jar and painted it, then a pear, knitting needles, wool, and bone. I quickly became fascinated with painting glass, and the distortions glass causes to the objects seen through it. It was while painting *Mason Jar with Barking Dog* (April 5, 2014) that I realized I had a series emerging and that the series was about my relationship with family and my quest to claim a lost legacy. When I finished the painting, I recognized that the dog was me and I was barking out the secrets and stories. I had unconsciously chosen a wide mouth Kerr Mason jar:

Wide mouth open
She barks out the family secrets
Refusing to put a lid on it!

The lids are off the jars in all the paintings, so the secrets can circulate; the stories can join with other stories and become ordinary.

An unanticipated joy of this series has been how it resonates with individuals far removed from my birth family. So many of us grew up with secrets and poverty. So many had root cellars full of Mason jars. I discovered that the joys and the sorrows of my heritage are shared human experiences. It seems we all live extraordinarily ordinary human lives.

THE MOTIVATION to explore my family history and legacy was a dark one. My grandfather

Werner Preetzman immigrated from Halle, Germany, when he was 17. He travelled by himself to Saskatchewan and worked for relatives until he earned enough to purchase a procurement of 160 acres near Kerrobert. That procurement failed during the drought of 1914–18 and remains community pasture land today.

My mother never spoke about her father, except when showing photographs of his ancestors. I had three different stories of his death. It was at my aunt's kitchen table that the secret finally slipped out. I didn't understand the reason for the secret until I was halfway through this series. My mother was protecting me. She believed if I had known Werner had taken his own life, I may have done the same when times were tough, as they often were. It explained why my ambitions were so actively discouraged and why I was advised to be content with where I was. I must have worried her tremendously with my refusal to stop striving and learning and trying and failing and trying again.

The incremental nature of this series, the small steps toward completion of the narrative, the gathering together of fragments of joy and sorrow helped her to see how I navigate the world and that my way was okay. Before I started the series, I had asked my mother to take me to her childhood home and she reluctantly agreed. When we went *up Kerr Creek,* she shared stories of her mother and the neighbours and yet did not mention her father. As I approached the middle of the series, my mother asked me to take her *up Kerr Creek* again. On that trip, she talked about her father. She recounted how he would drive her and her sister to dances, how he was called on to break horses, how he worked two farms so they could have cattle and milk. She pointed out the roads and fences he built, the gate he invented, and where she helped him build the chimney for the new house. She reclaimed his legacy and wove him back into her narrative. This is the greatest gift of the series.

During the painting of the series I became a matriarch. My mother passed away suddenly, a vigorous 89 years old, and I thank this series for allowing the truth of our family history to be communicated before she passed. Mom and

I had always loved each other, but we didn't understand each other. The secrets kept us guarded and distant. Once the secrets were freed and the truth was seen to be just ordinary tragic human stuff, Mom and I had a wonderful few years, adding to our love, seeing and respecting each other. I have come to own my family in all its ups and downs. All of my family: The living, the dead, and the yet to come.

THE IMAGES in this series were painted in watercolour on paper, in season, and most were created in studio from still-life arrangements on my drawing table. A few were done outdoors when the artifacts were too large to bring inside (cabin, wheelbarrow, etc.). The poems emerged as the images were being painted. In this book, the images and poems have been organized into chapters: Women's Work, Men's Work, Food Security, Hope and Renewal, Heirlooms and Artifacts, and Hidden and Suppressed. I hope that you will find some of your own story on these pages and find new ways to connect to the legacy of your ancestors.

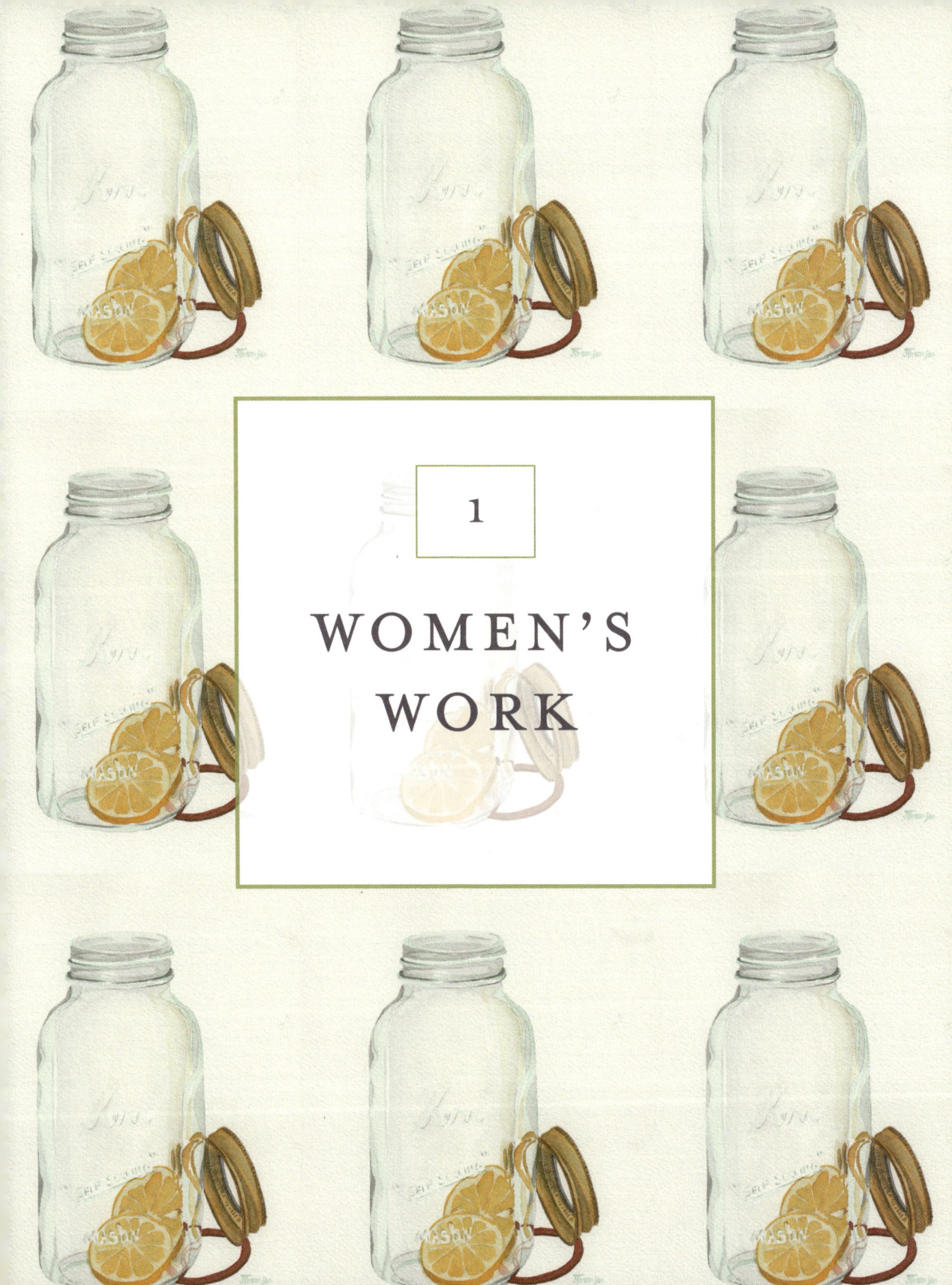

1

WOMEN'S
WORK

I DO LOVE "women's work." I love to take string and make it into lace, pick berries and make them into jam, use a needle and thread to mend or make a garment, tend a vegetable garden, cook a meal, pick flowers and then paint them. As a child, I was privileged to be introduced to women's work by matriarchs who also loved it. I did not do any "men's work" until I left home and found it necessary to use a hammer, pliers, and staple gun.

My grandmother Eva Moncrief Preetzman grew up with women's work. She was the seventh of 13 children and helped to run the house and care for her siblings. As a young woman, she prepared a hope chest for her future marriage. I still have some of the lace she made. She continued to crochet and knit until her eyes didn't allow it. Then, when she was 80, I set her up with paper and watercolour paints. She won an award for her painting at the Pacific National Exhibition in 1983.

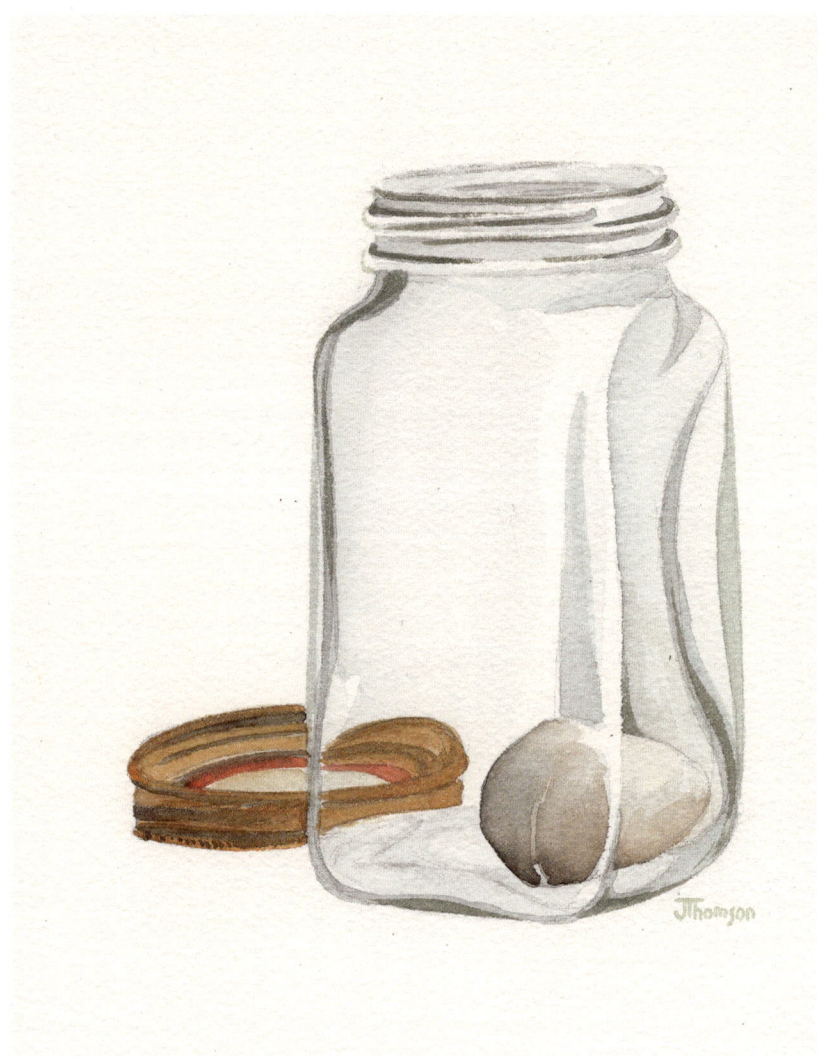

MASON JAR   Eggs in a jar
WITH EGG   I don't know why.
2014   Give me a riddle and I'll reply,
       Issinglass, Issinglass, Issinglass eggs.

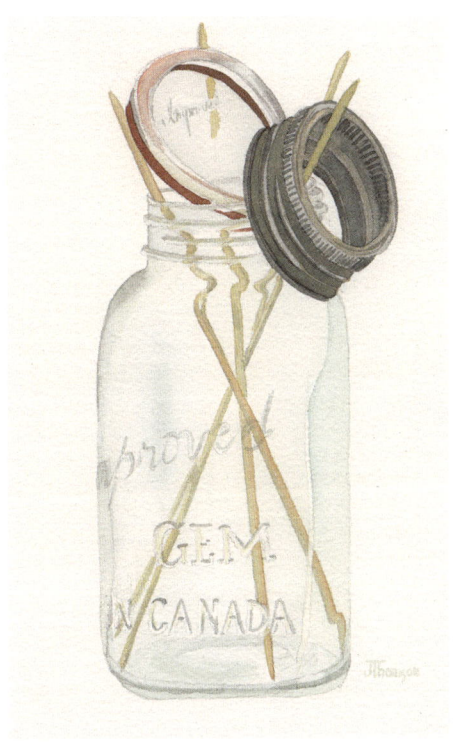

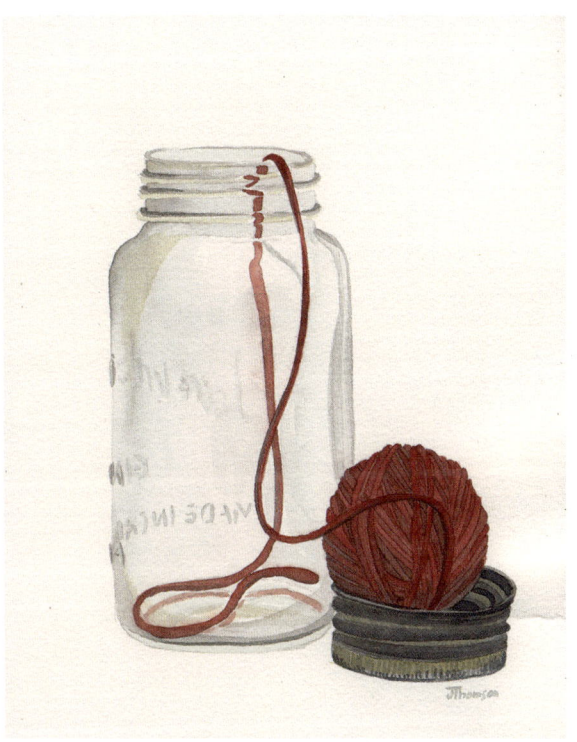

MASON JAR WITH Long winter nights
KNITTING NEEDLES Low light and fire
2014 Rhythmic click of needles
Stories and conversation.

MASON JAR WITH Shearing sheep
HOMESPUN WOOL Carding wool
2014 Spinning wheel
Lumpy Winter warmth.

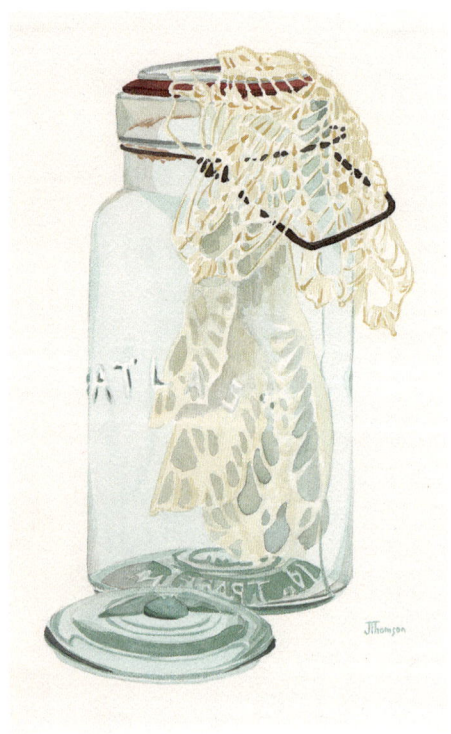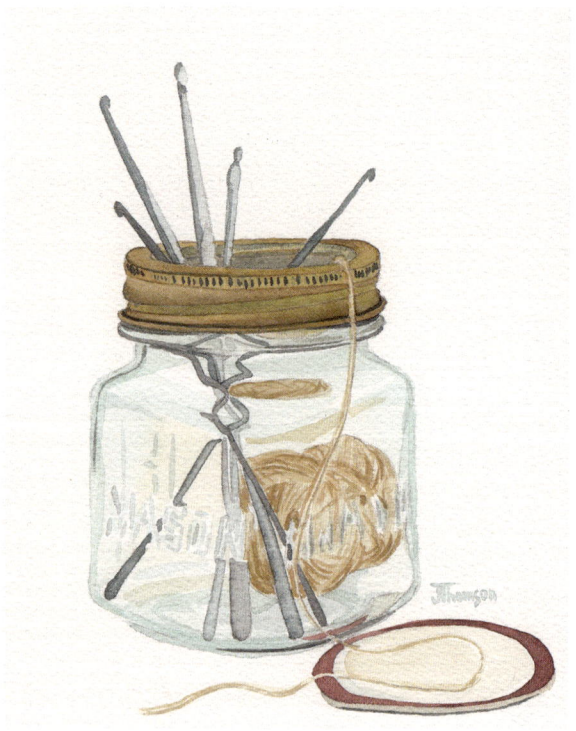

MASON JAR WITH
CROCHET DOILY
2014

Women's work
Women's pleasure
Something beautiful
Made of string.

MASON JAR WITH
CROCHET HOOKS AND
COTTON FOR LACE
2014

One must sit still
When making lace,
Listening and musing,
A welcome quiet disguised as productivity.

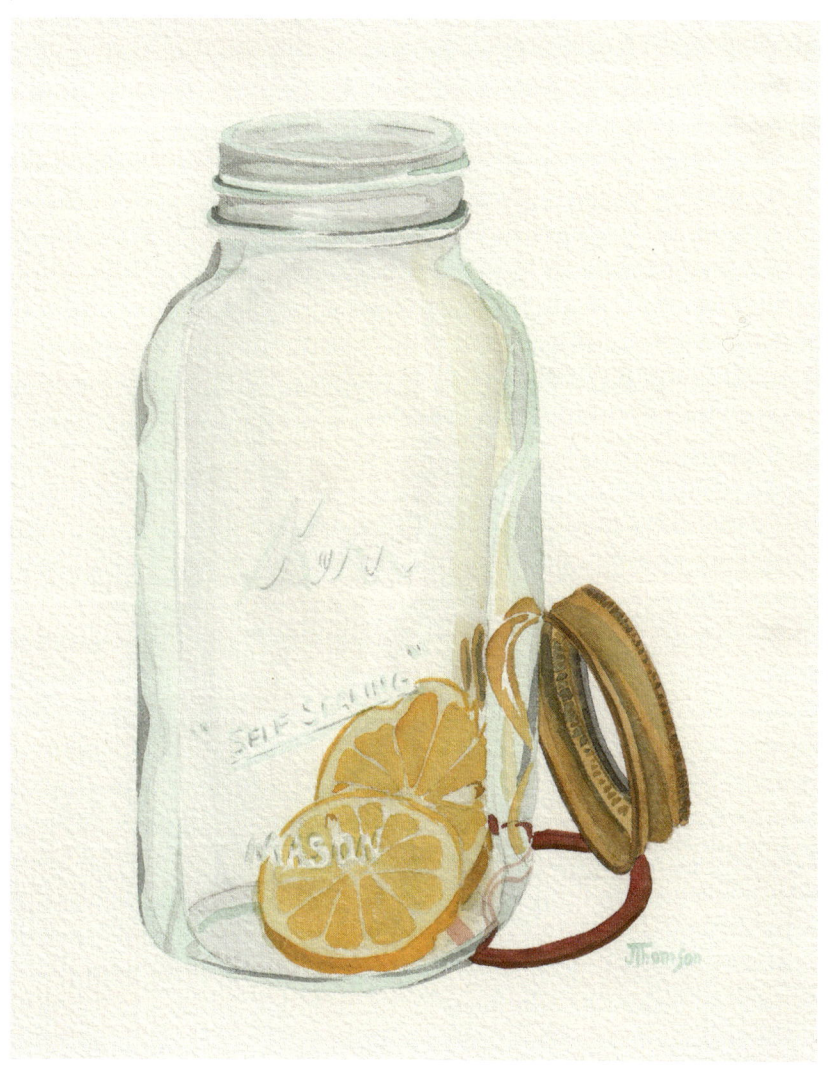

MASON JAR WITH
LEMON SLICES

2014

Where did the lemons come from?
For the making of
Elderflower champagne
To delight young and old?

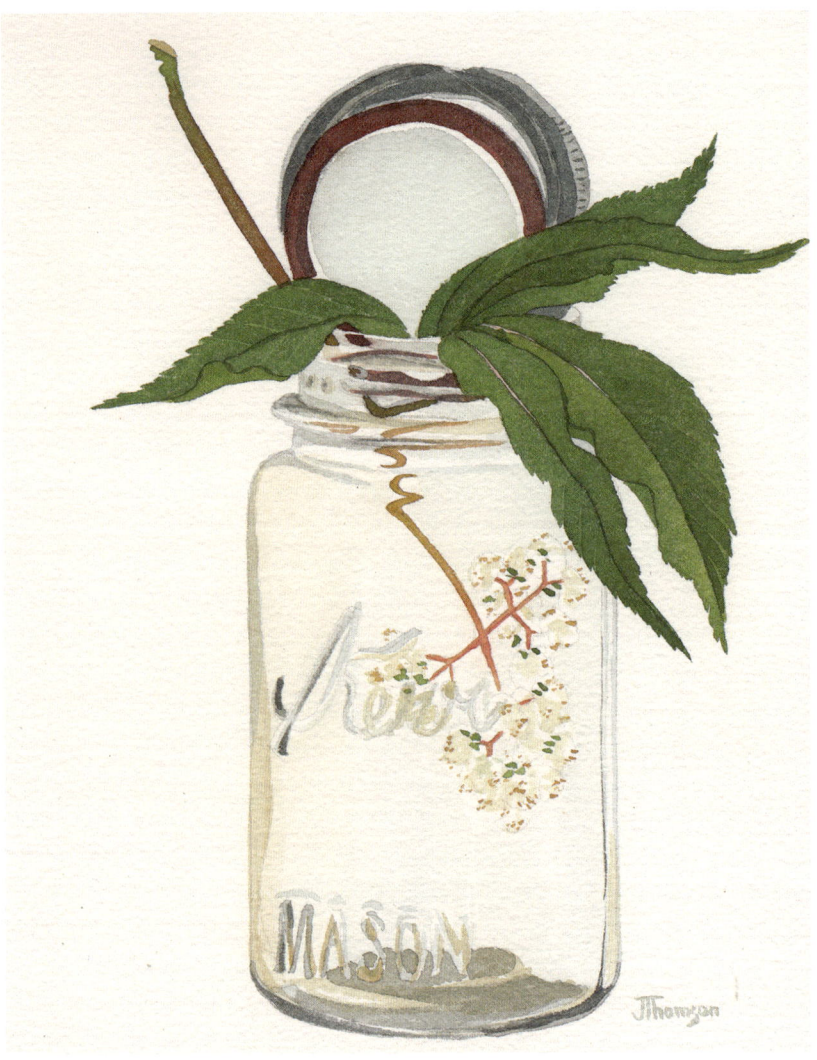

MASON JAR WITH   The making of elderflower champagne,
ELDERFLOWER   The joy of anticipation

2014   Weeks waiting for
         Sweet fragrant bubbles.

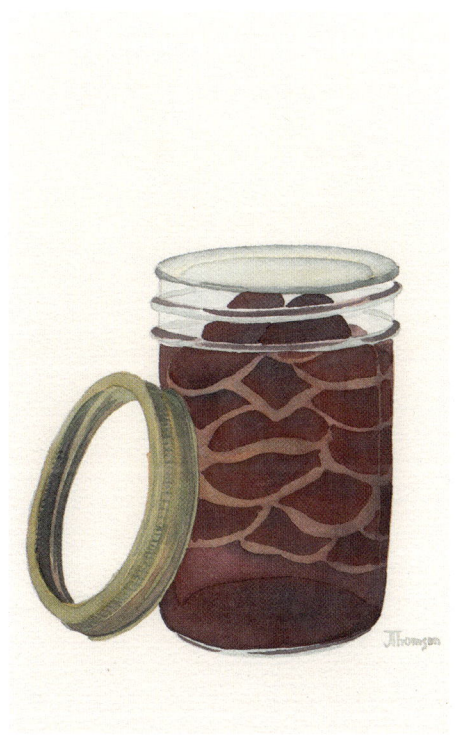 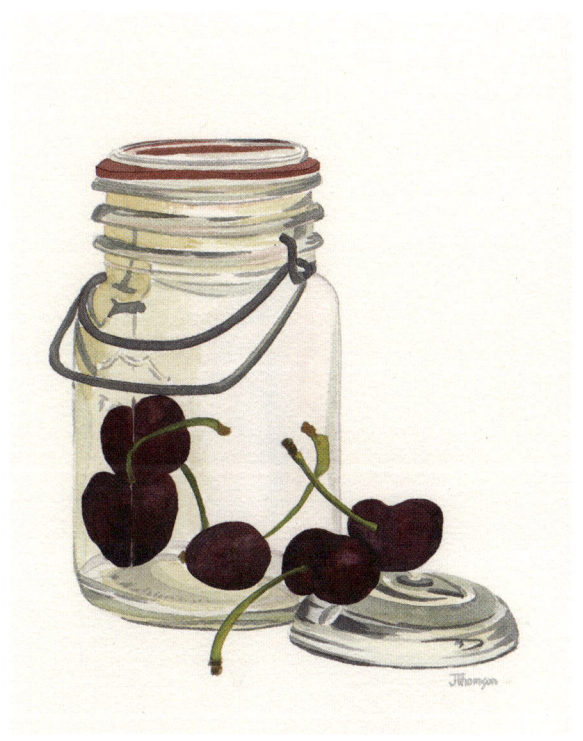

MASON JAR WITH	Italian prune plums
LAST YEAR'S PLUMS	Coffee cake with plums
2014	Custard and plums
	Plum syrup on pancakes.

MASON JAR WITH	Bing cherries
BING CHERRIES	Bing Crosby
2014	Taste and sound
	Resonant with pleasure.

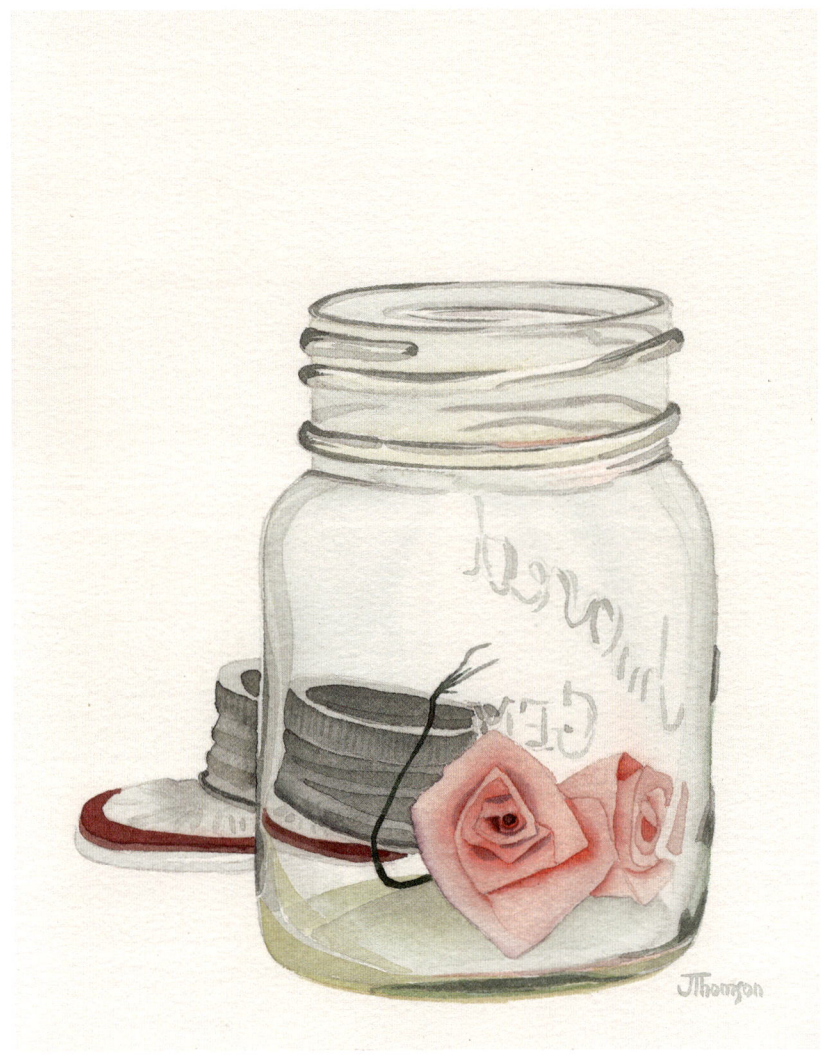

MASON JAR WITH
RIBBON ROSE
2014

My mother's wish for me
Ribbon roses
For a fairy tale wedding
Only the roses remain.

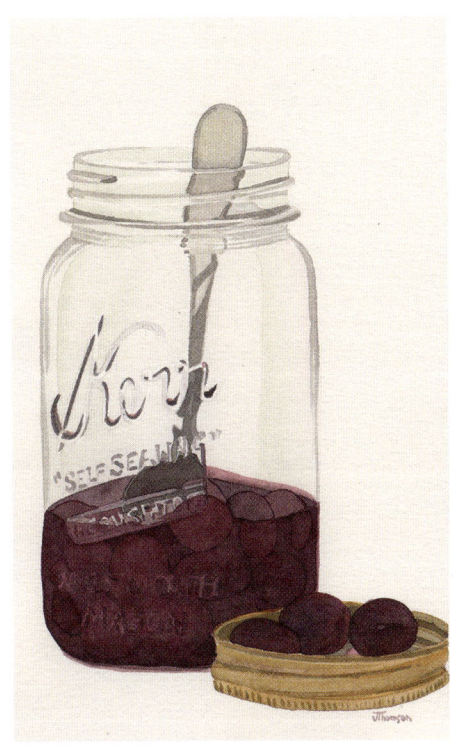
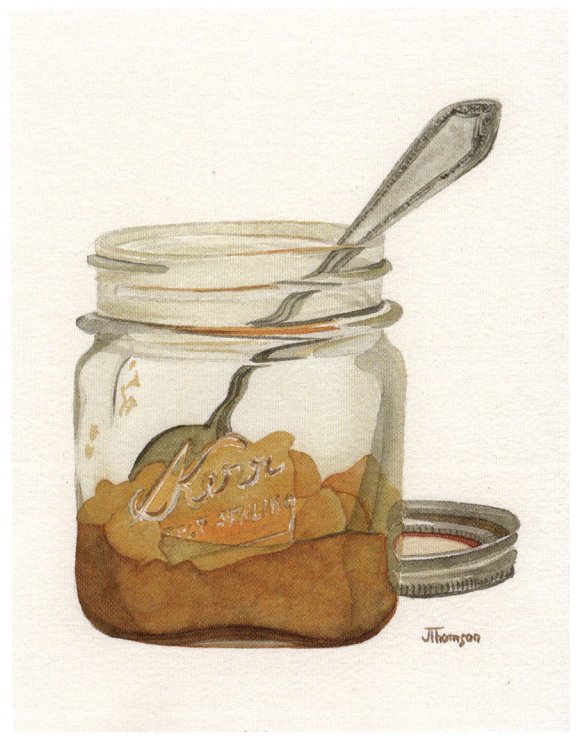

**MASON JAR WITH
CANNED CHERRIES
AND SPOON**

2015

The taste of summer in January
Perhaps the myth,
The silver spoon,
Is real.

**MASON JAR WITH
APPLESAUCE**

2015

A warm gingersnap
A cup of tea
A bowl of applesauce
A complete afternoon.

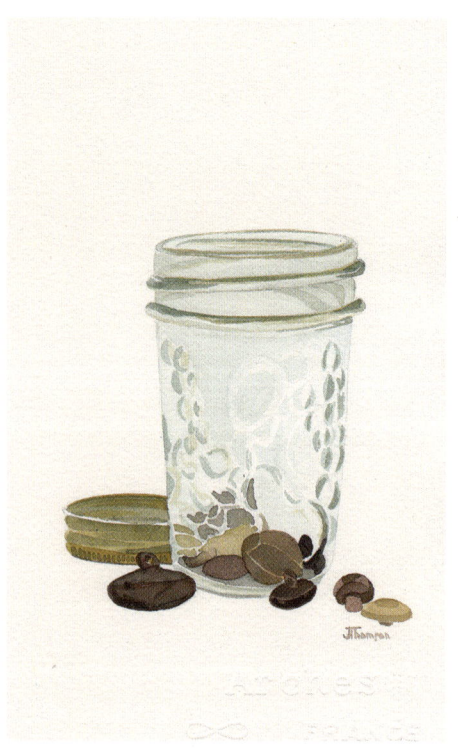 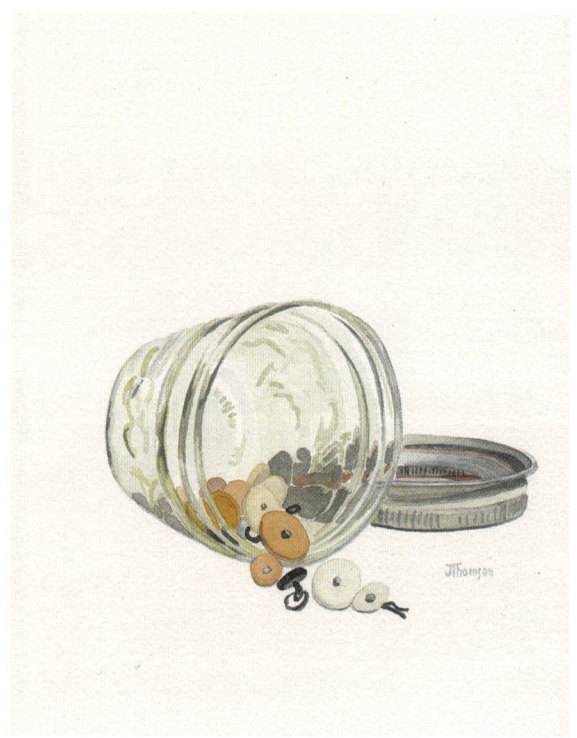

MASON JAR WITH
LEATHER BUTTON
2015

Where do they come from
These odd buttons?
One of each, rarely two.

MASON JAR WITH
DETACHABLE BUTTONS
2015

Footnotes from the past
Change your appearance
Change your look
As simple as one, two, three.

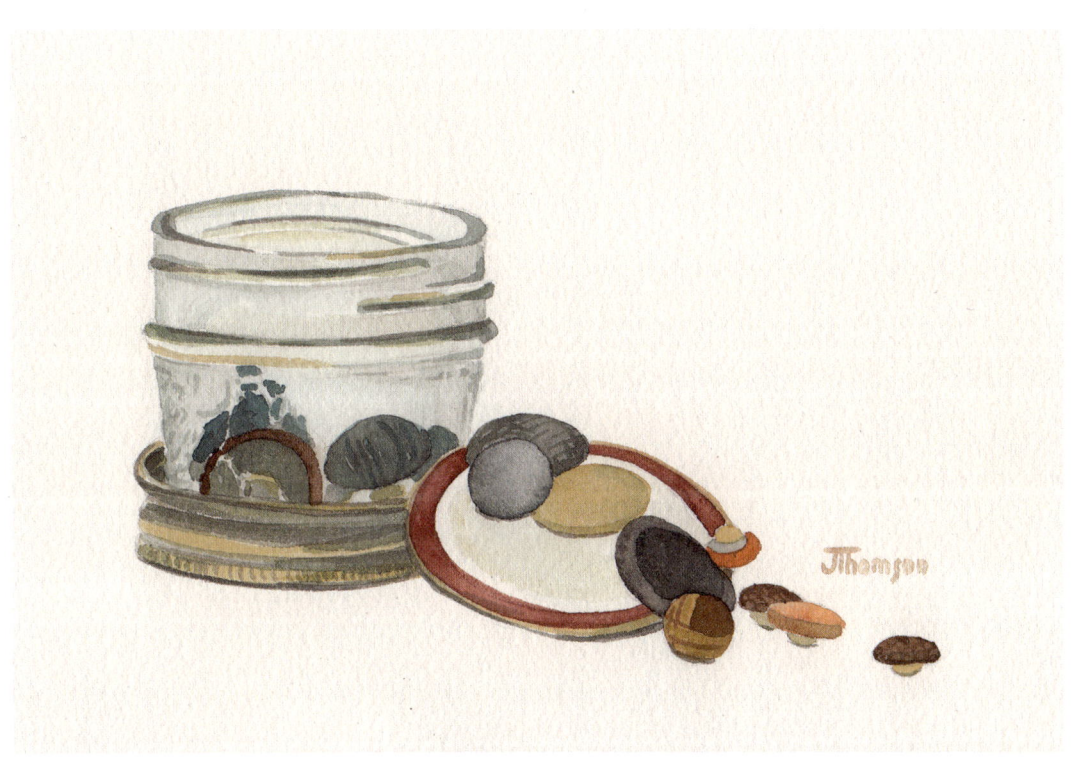

MASON JAR WITH
CLOTH BUTTONS
2015

I wonder where they are now.
All those buttons I made
To match the jackets and the pants
Fashioning impermanence.

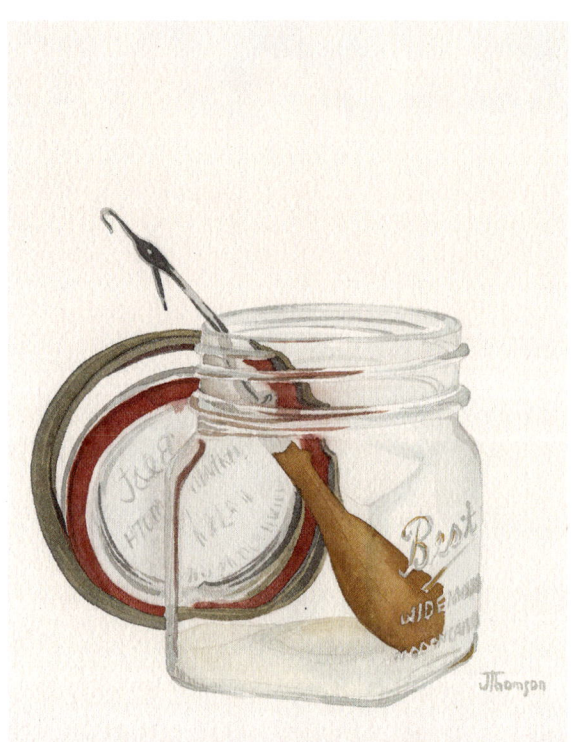
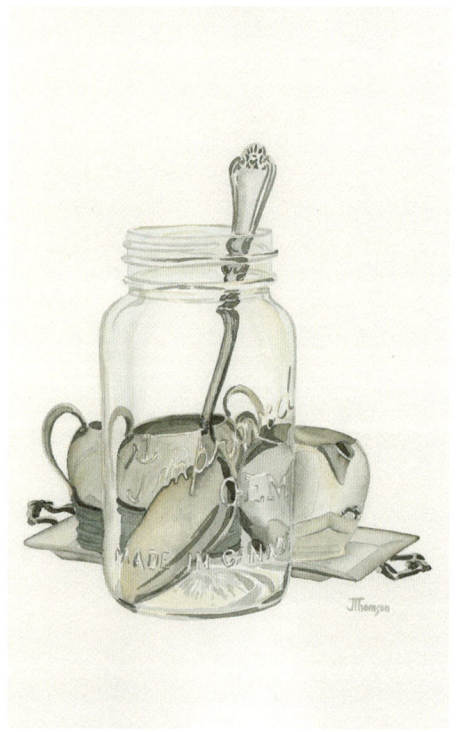

MASON JAR   The firstborn suffered
WITH RUG HOOK   Slivered knees from floorboards
2015   Yet to be covered by rag rugs.

MASON JAR WITH   The silver polished
SILVER CREAM   The play began
AND SUGAR   "Ladies of Leisure"
2015   Tea in china cups.

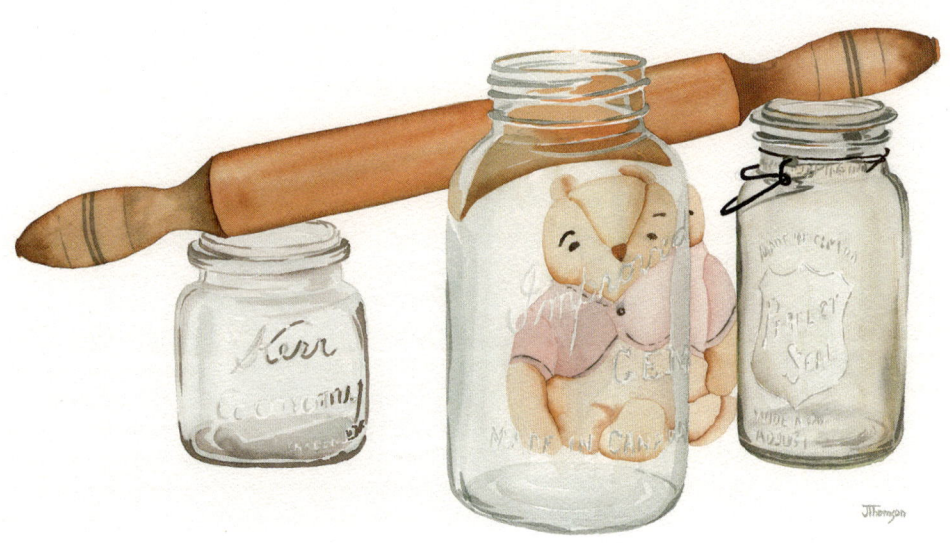

MASON JAR WITH
HOMAGE TO
GRANDMOTHERS
2016

Grandmothers hold the secrets,
Distribute discipline and treats,
Tell us stories
To help us escape reality.

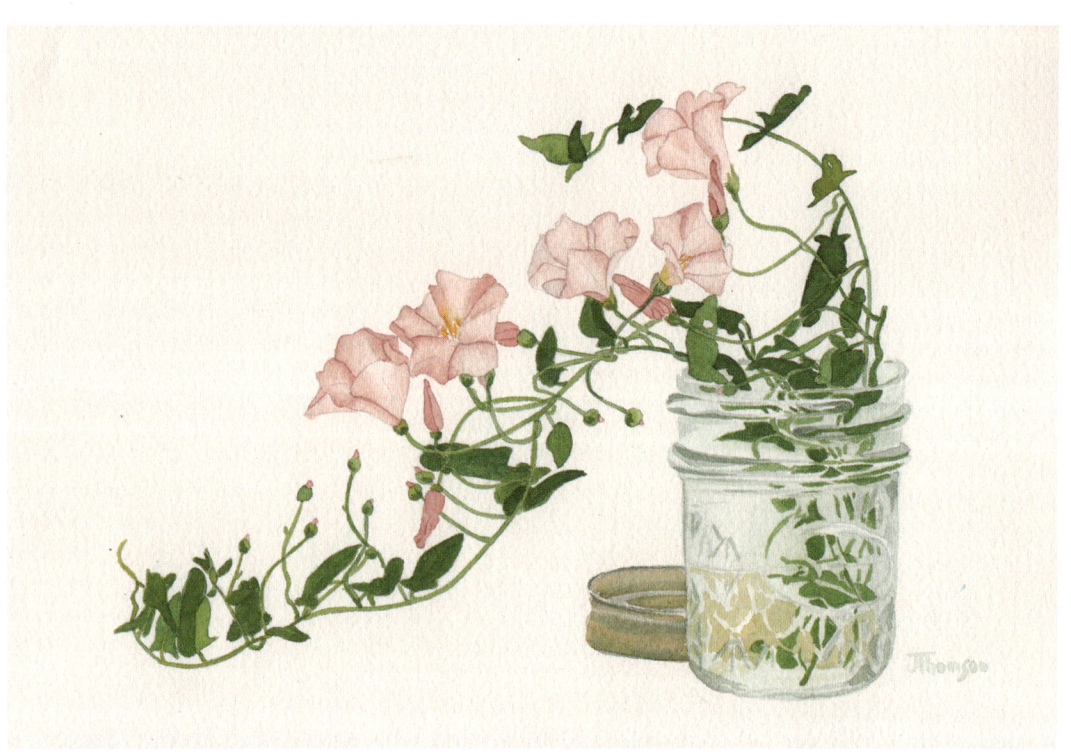

MASON JAR WITH
BINDWEED
2016

A capable foe
Creeping beneath mulch and cloth
Invading from the dark
A wonder.

MASON JAR WITH
ECHINACEA
2016

Ancient, medicinal beauties,
Often underestimated.

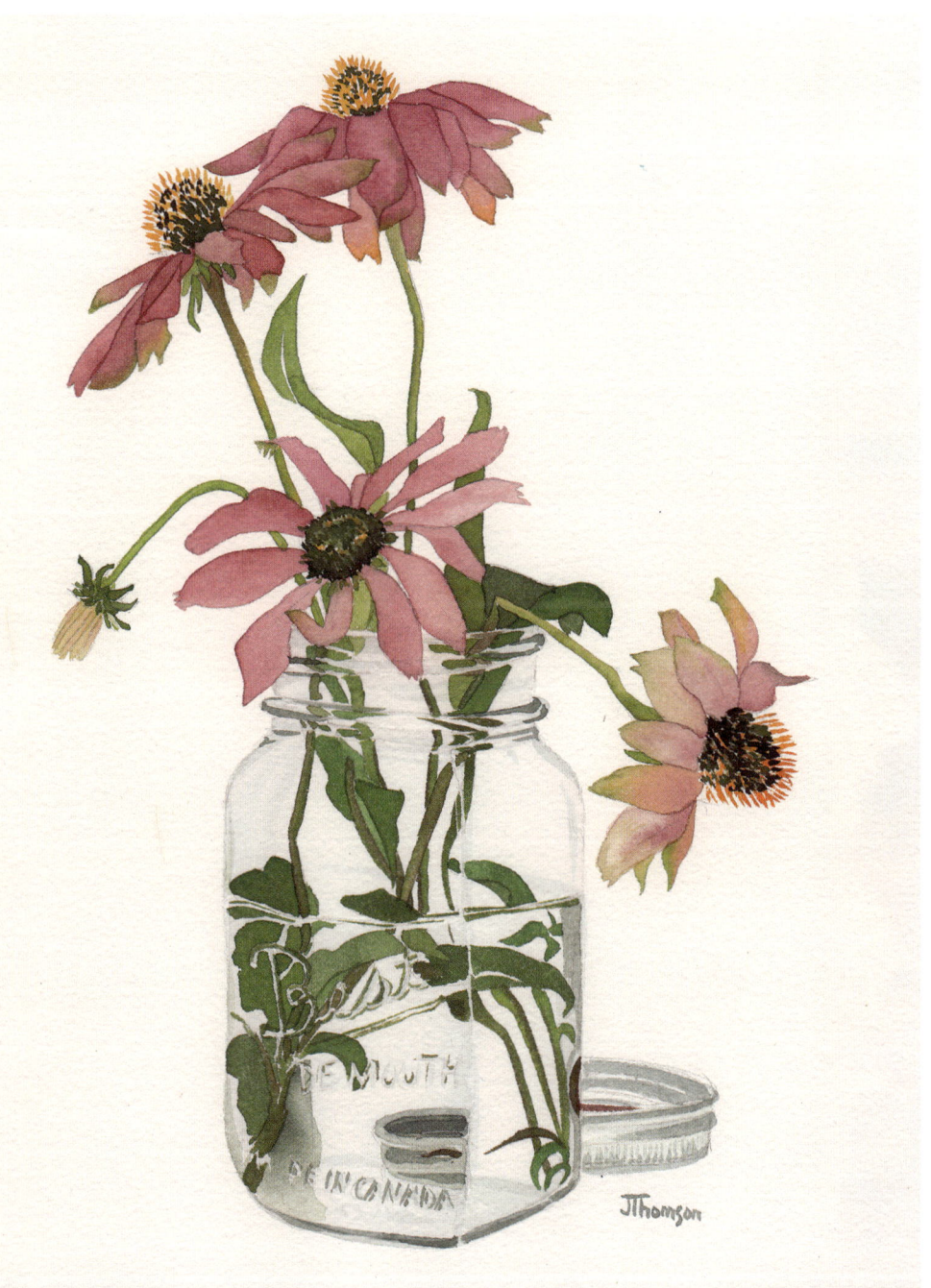

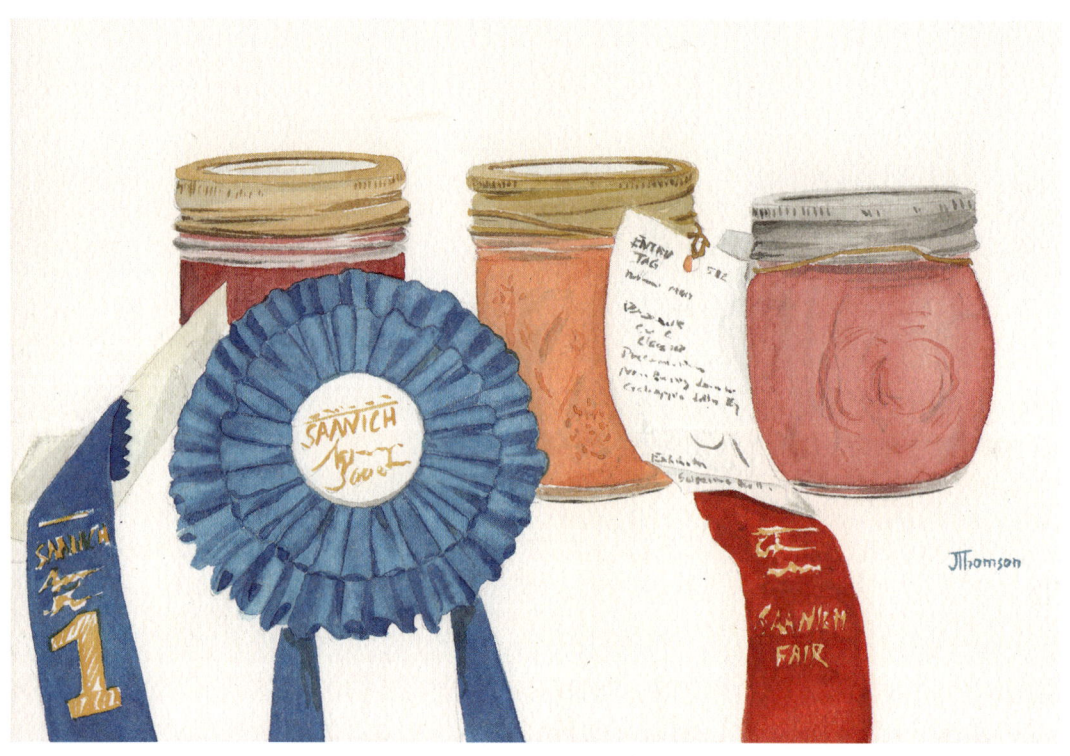

MASON JARS WITH The 149th Saanich Fall Fair
PRIZE WINNING Preserving traditions
CRAB APPLE JELLY All decked out with ribbons!

2016

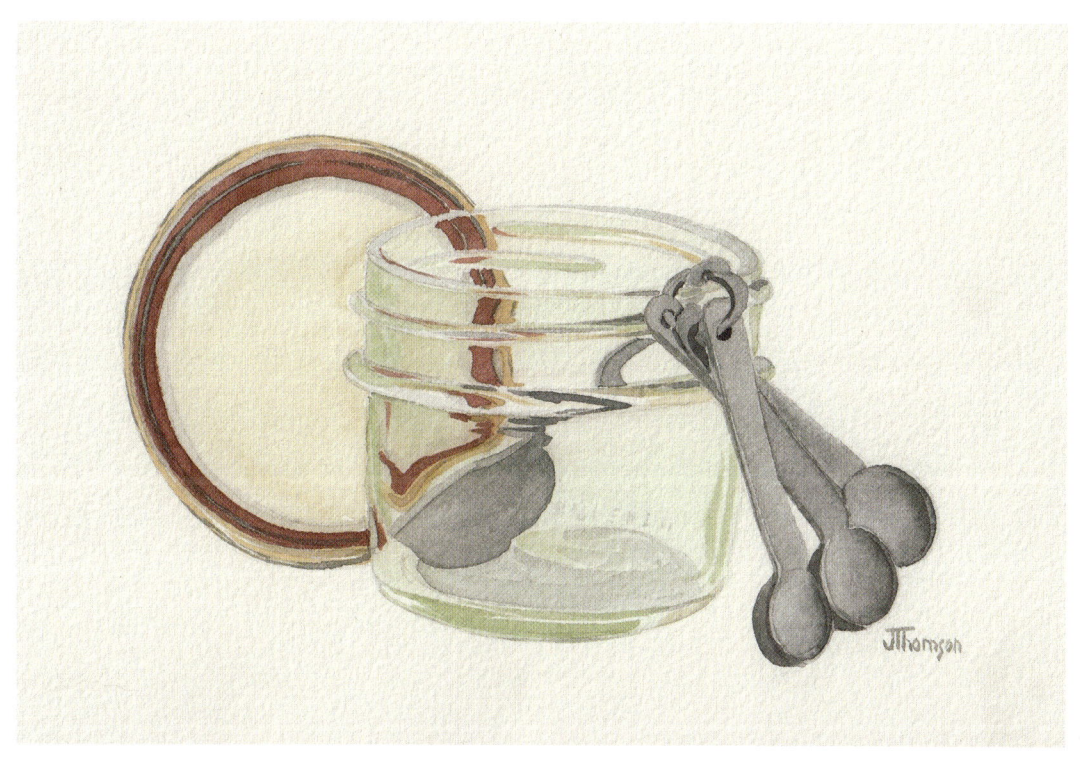

**MASON JAR WITH
MEASURING SPOONS**

2018

This is how you fill the spoon
Careful now, not too much
Tip it in and stir, don't spill
Many lessons to remember.

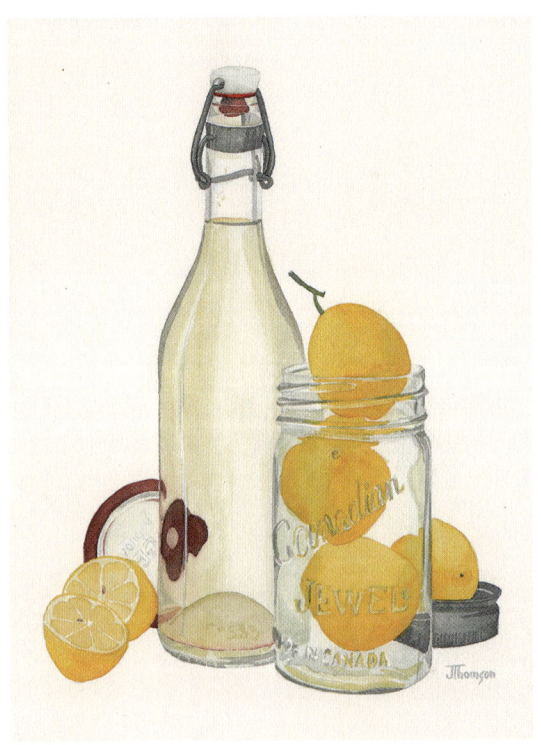
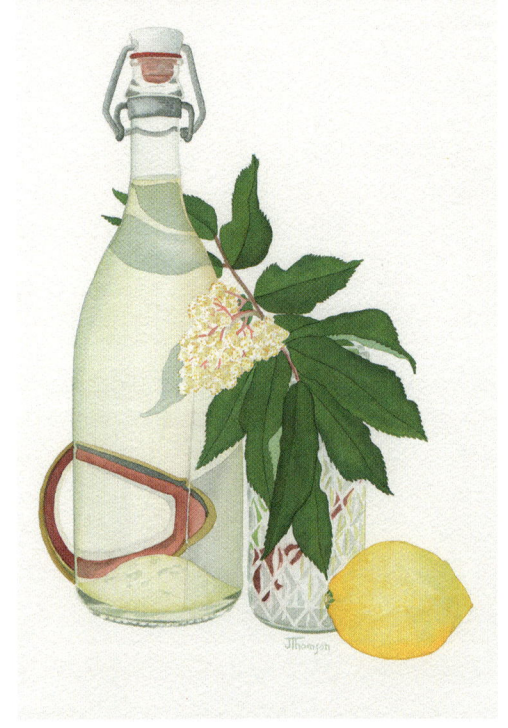

MASON JAR WITH LEMONS AND ELDERFLOWER CHAMPAGNE

2017

Lemons in winter
Dedicated grower
Sweet-sour reward.

MASON JAR WITH ELDERFLOWER CHAMPAGNE

2019

Grandmother's love remembered
With each sip of "champagne"
A traditional pleasure.

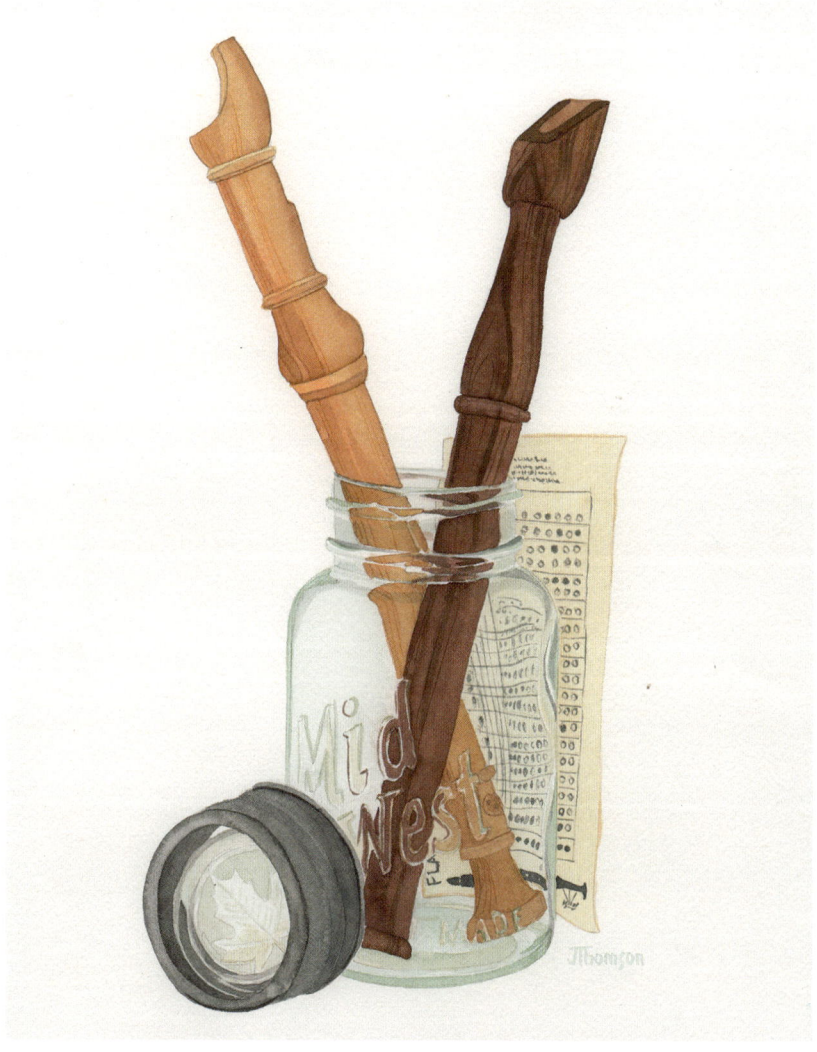

MASON JAR WITH
RECORDER
AND WHISTLE

2019

Wind and wood make music
Private sounds in rooms with doors
Someday they will escape.

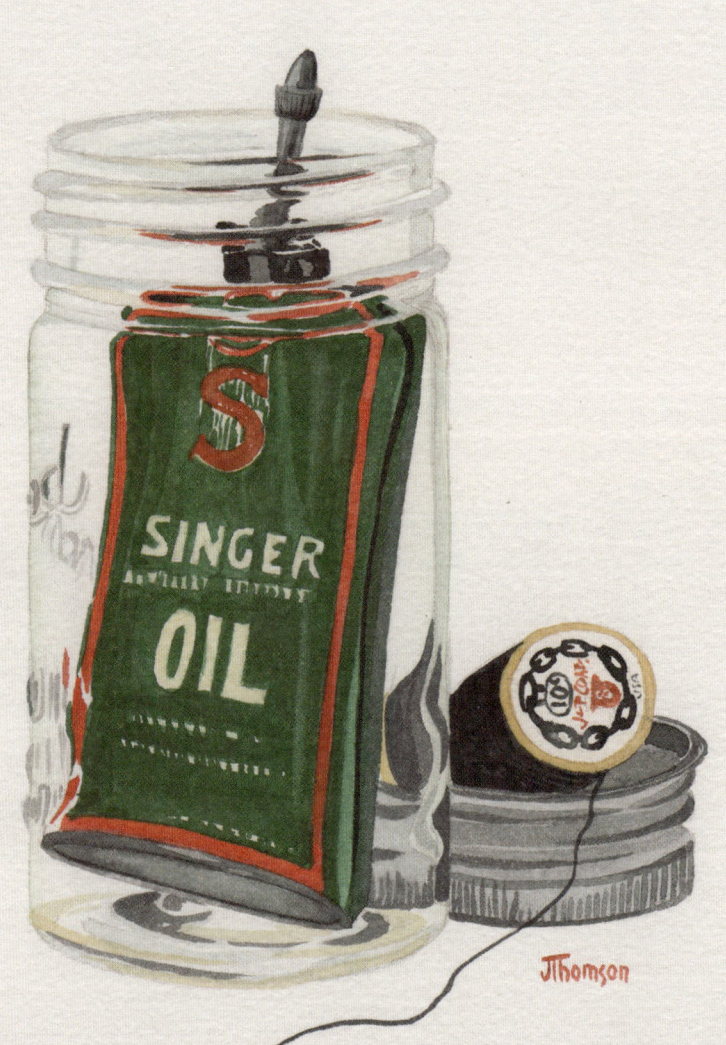

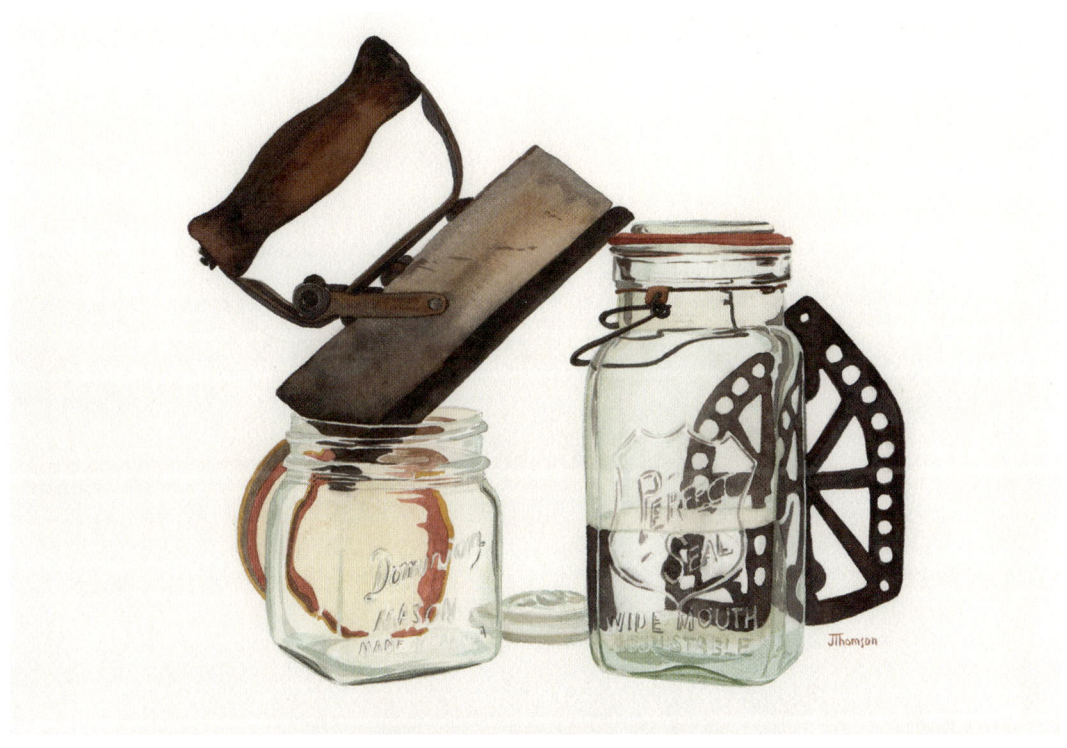

MASON JAR WITH SINGER SEWING MACHINE OIL

2019

The machine was rarely put away
Clothing, napkins, curtains.
The oil was always handy
Though rarely used.

MASON JAR WITH IRON AND STAND

2019

Eva came to Canada with high hopes
Thought she could leave service behind her
Live like a lady.
But the work multiplied.

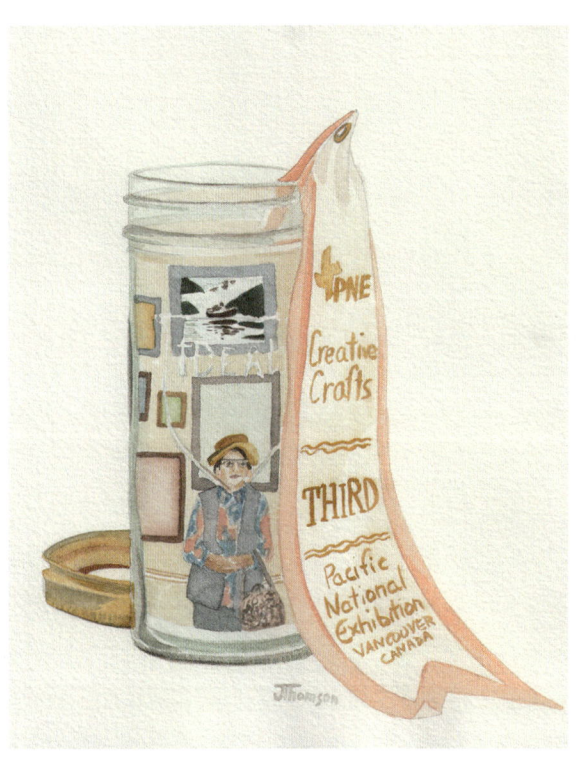

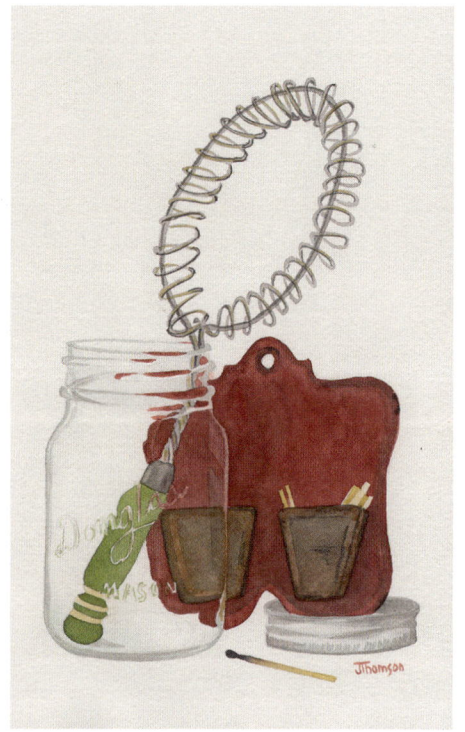

MASON JAR WITH
EVA AND AWARD
2019

Eighty years young
A ribbon at the fair
A cruise remembered
Fame enjoyed.

MASON JAR WITH
WHISK AND
MATCH HOLDER
2019

The kitchen matches always near
Light for the school papers
Long into the evening
While Mom cooked.

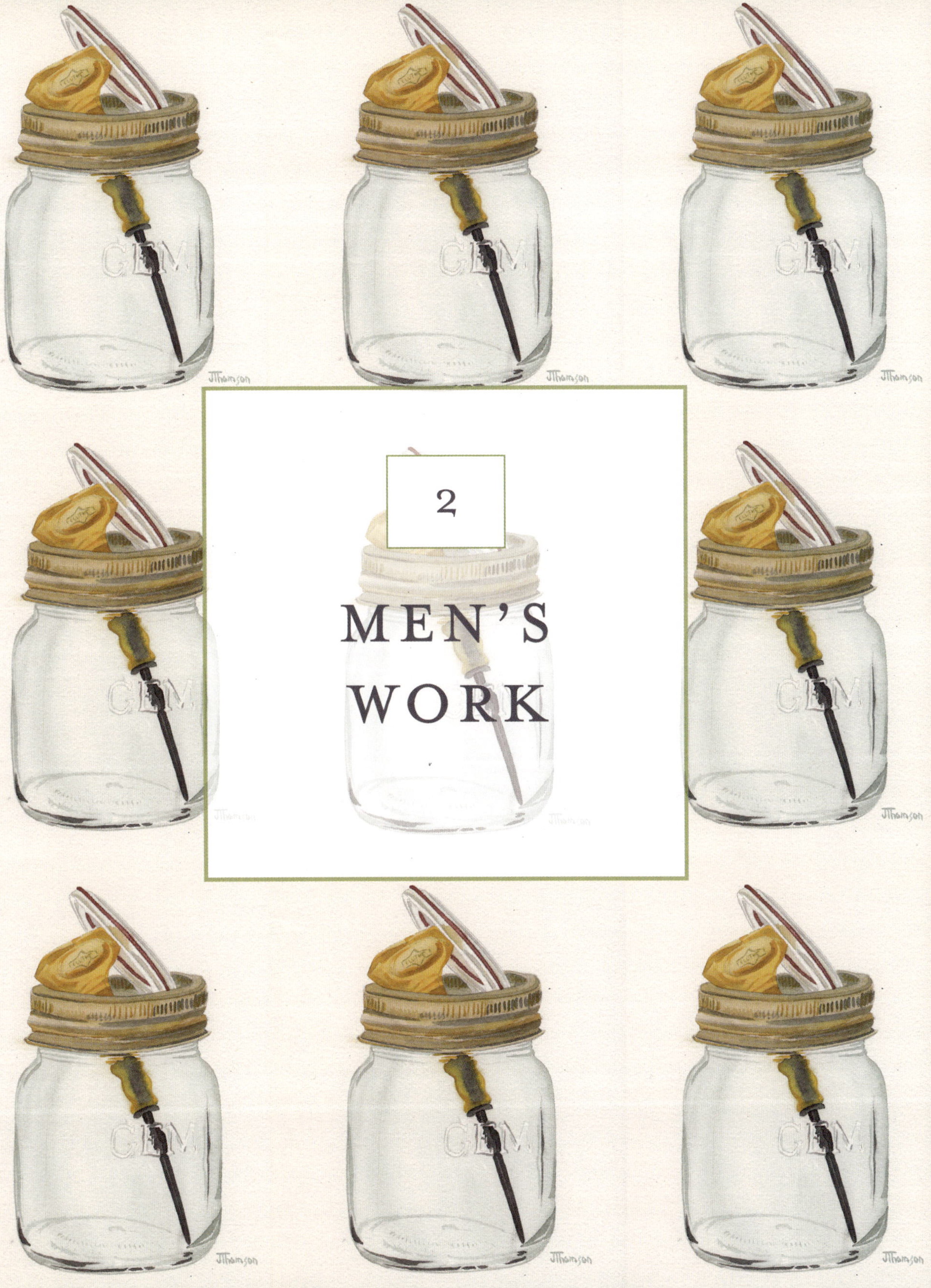

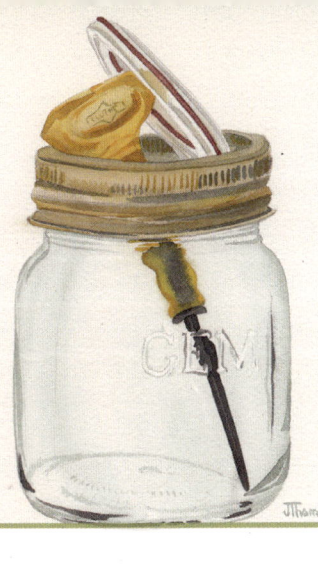
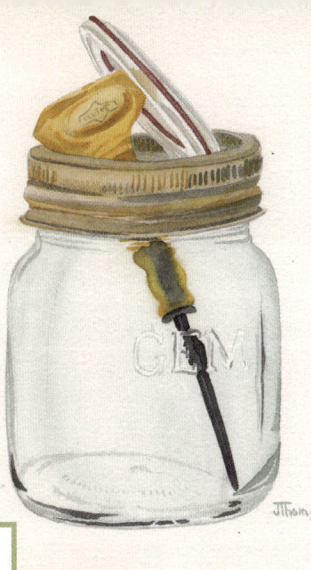
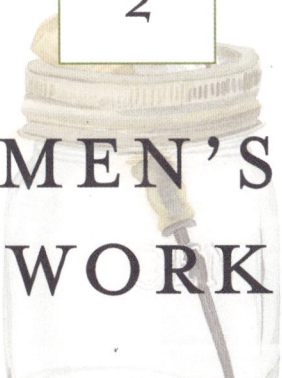

2

MEN'S
WORK

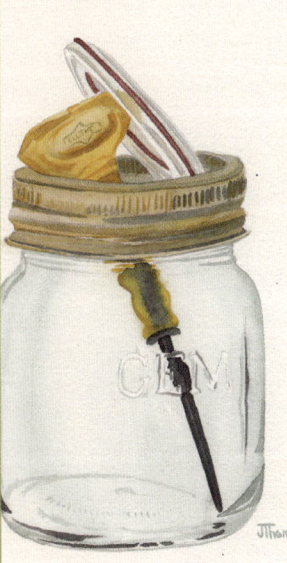
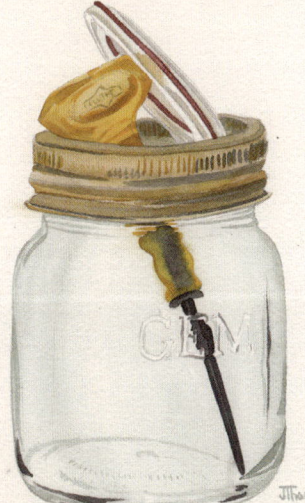
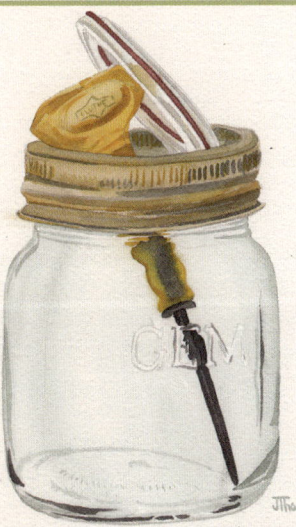
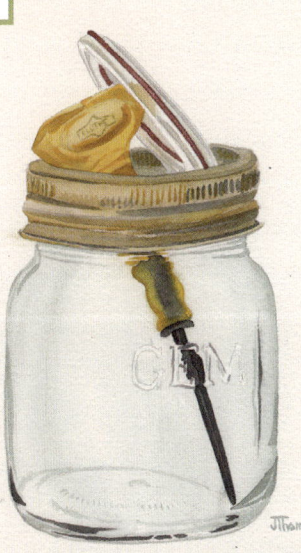

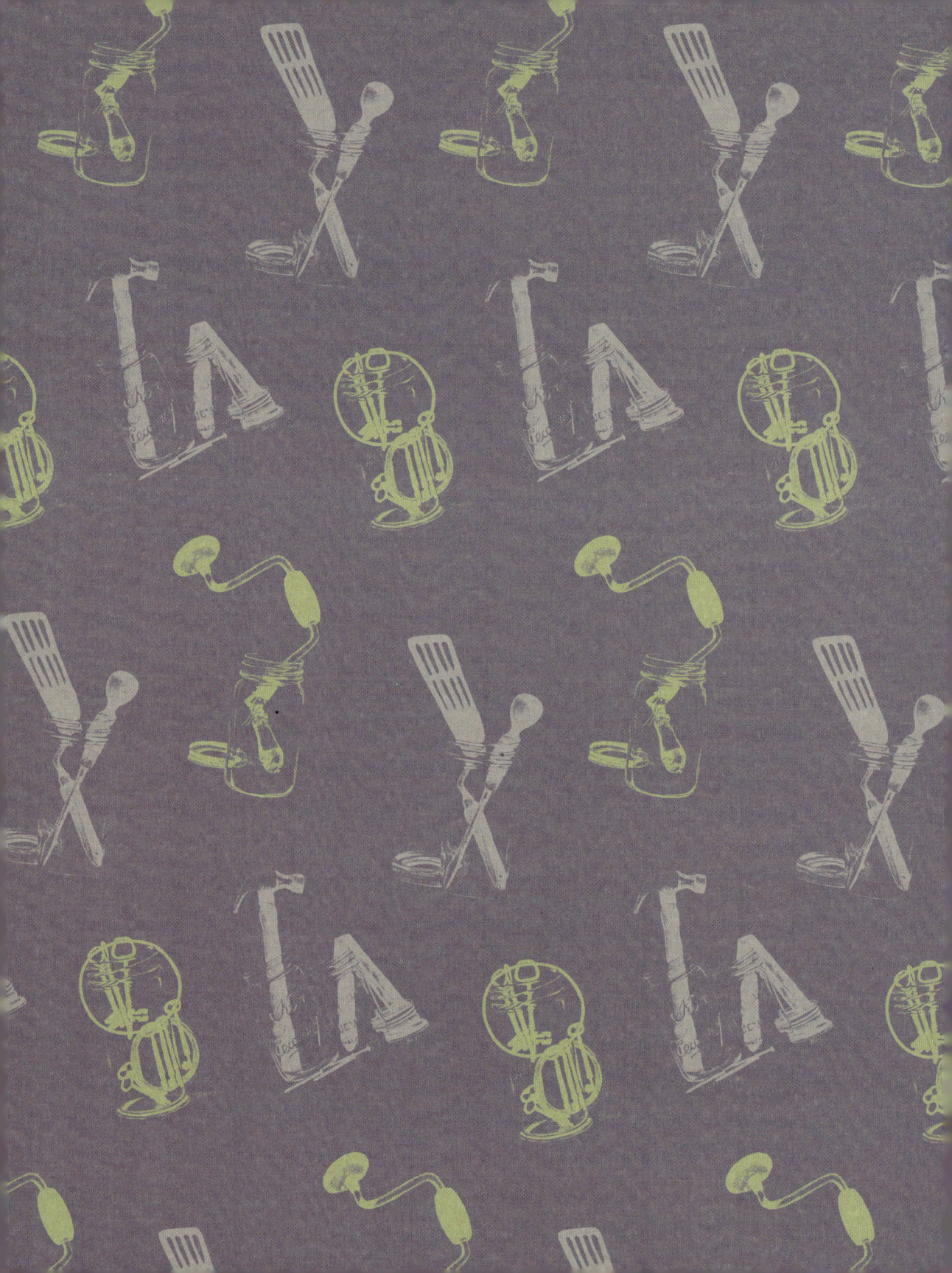

THIS CHAPTER is my effort to reinsert men's contributions into the predominantly female narrative of my family. When Werner, my grandfather, took his own life, he disappeared from the family stories. He immigrated to Canada at 17 and worked to purchase a procurement in Mariposa, Saskatchewan, when he was 19. The land was dry and he lost the rights to it during the drought of 1914–19. He became a naturalized Canadian citizen months before Canada declared war with Germany in 1914. We have a photograph of Werner in a Canadian army uniform—he was likely a volunteer with the home guard. In 1924, he purchased the Kerr Creek procurement near Midway, BC. He worked the land, clearing fields; building a house, outbuildings, and a barn; raising cattle; haying; road building; fencing; repairing machinery; and more. He was inventive and resilient. My father, Don Thomson, also inhabits this chapter. I cherish his quiet, gentle treatment of my children and myself.

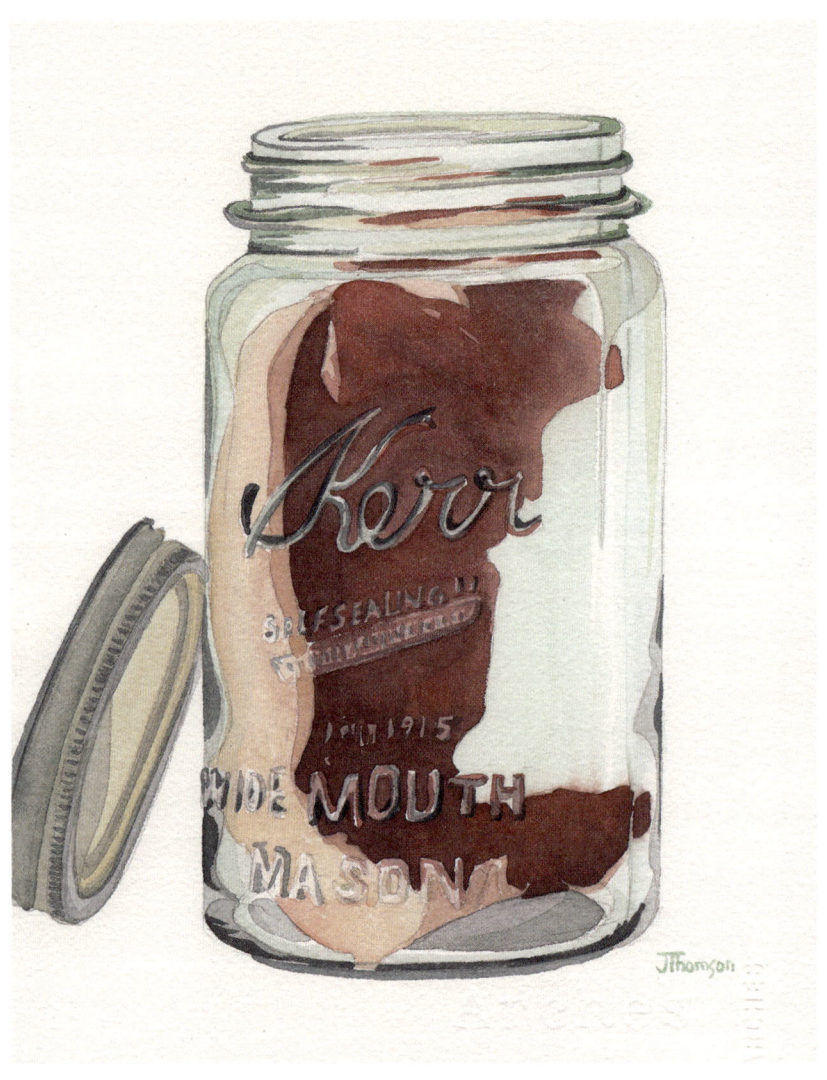

MASON JAR I cannot imagine
WITH STEAK Wood fire, copper kettles, jars, rings
2014 An entire steer
Preserved for winter.

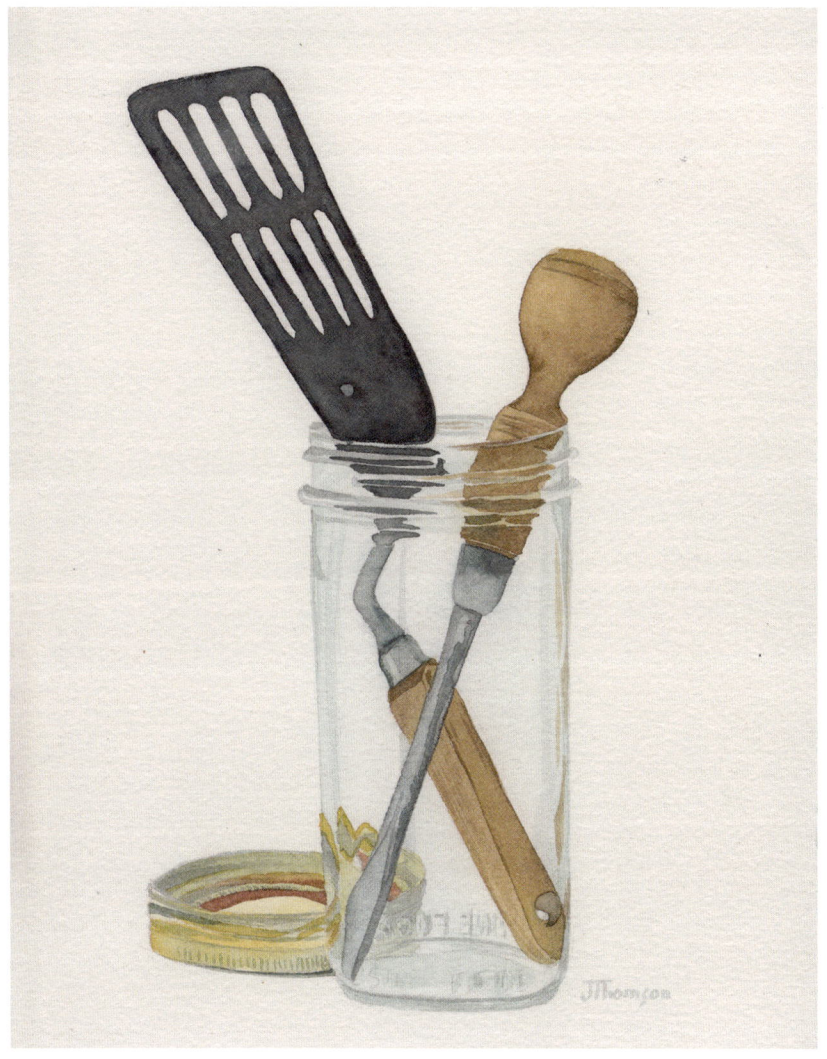

MASON JAR WITH
DAD'S TOOLS
2019

So many pancake mornings
So many eggs and bacon
He must have had a screw loose
To take on these children.

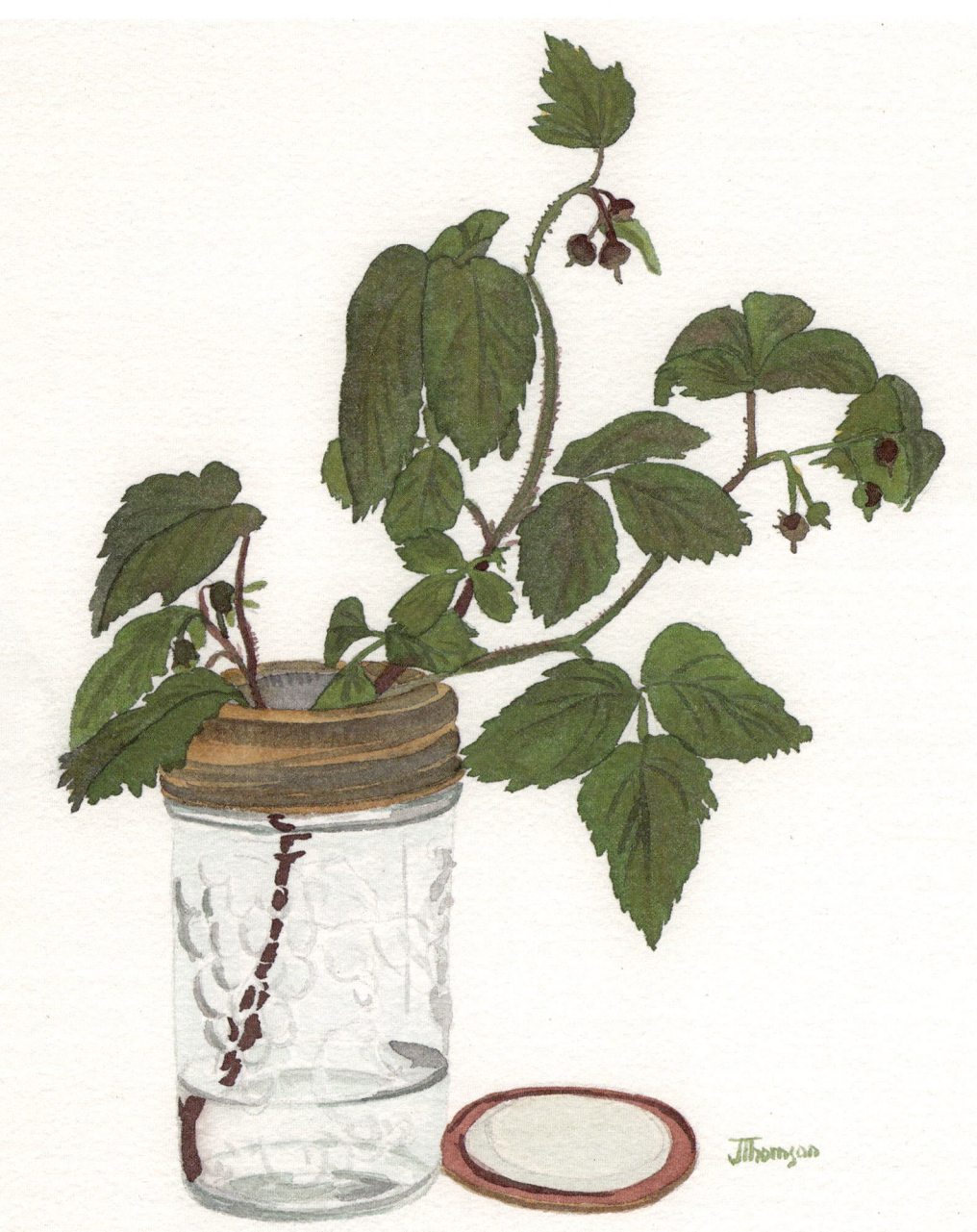

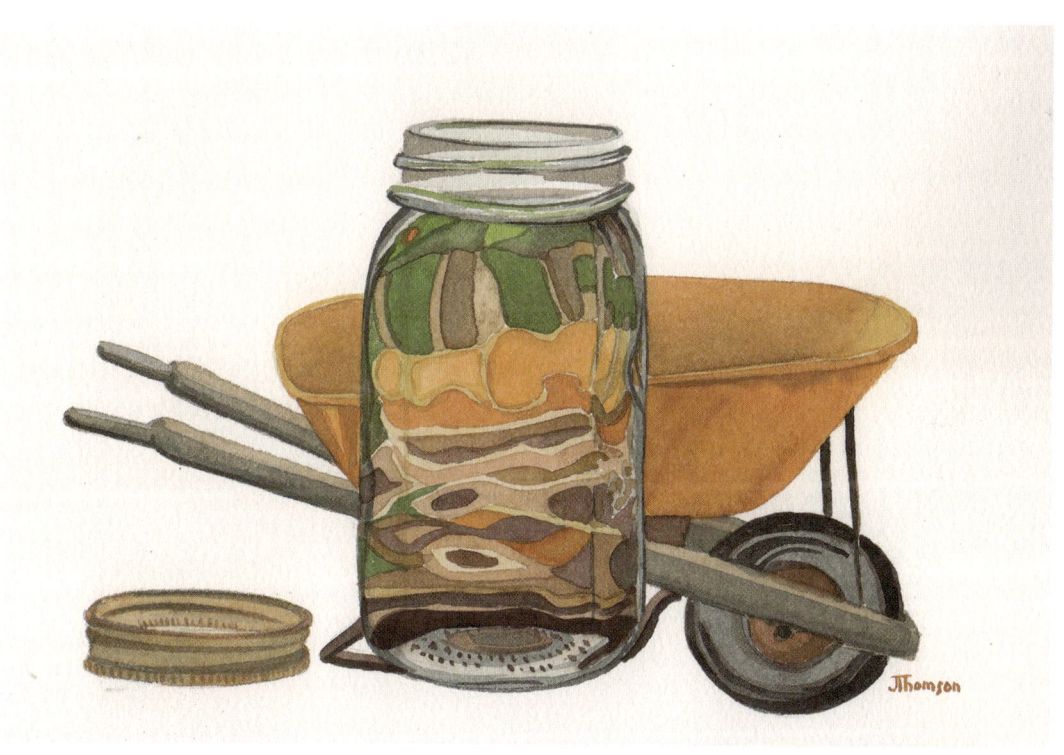

MASON JAR WITH
RASPBERRY CANE
2014

Thinning out the raspberry patch
Removing healthy stalks
To make room for larger berries
Feels like ingratitude.

MASON JAR WITH
WHEELBARROW
AND FRESHLY
PLANTED GARDEN
2014

We can imagine
Yet cannot know
What the lives of others contain
A jar of garden
Is but an illusion.

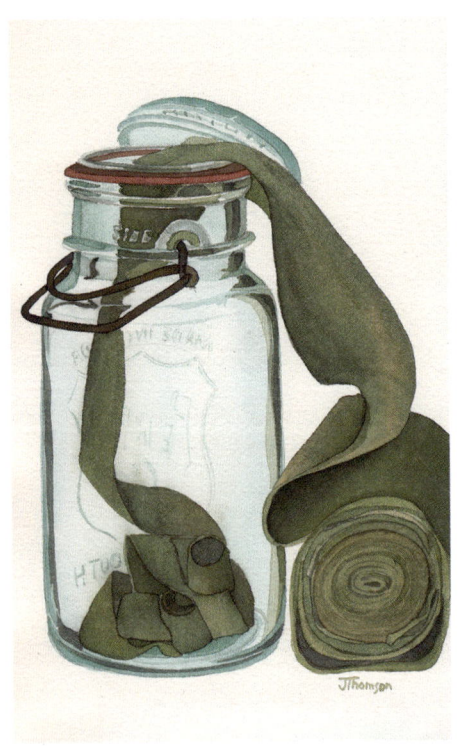 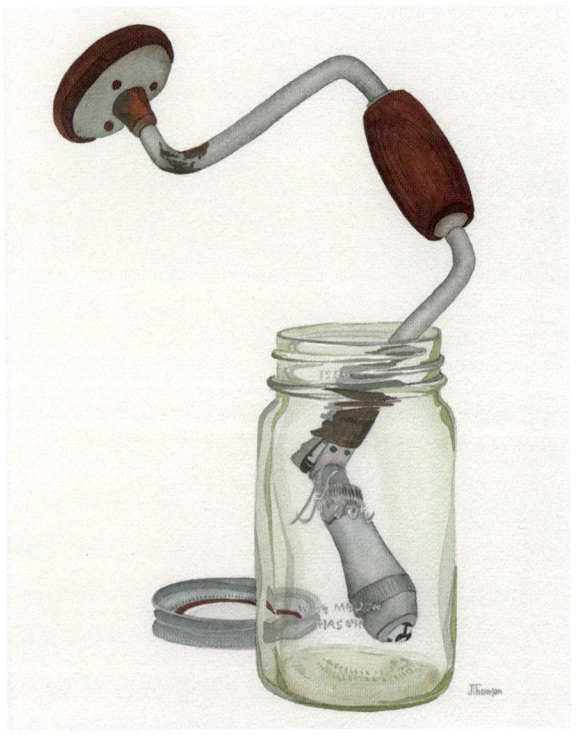

**MASON JAR
WITH PUTTEE**

2014

He wasn't a soldier
There is no record
Yet he wore the puttee for a portrait.
What is the rest of the story?

**MASON JAR WITH
HAND DRILL**

2014

Too large to be contained
The evidence effort spills out.

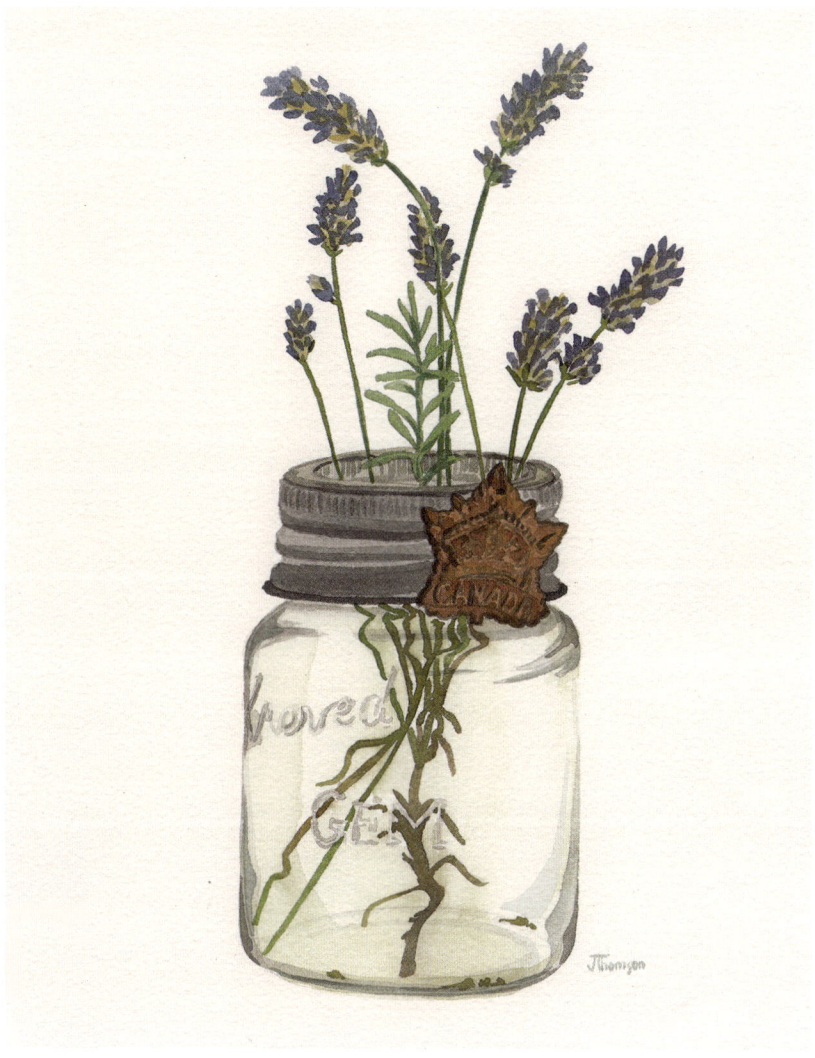

MASON JAR WITH　　What really happened
CANADIAN ARMY HAT　　In the land he adopted
BADGE AND LAVENDER　　While his brother flew planes for Germany
2014　　To crash and die at 19?

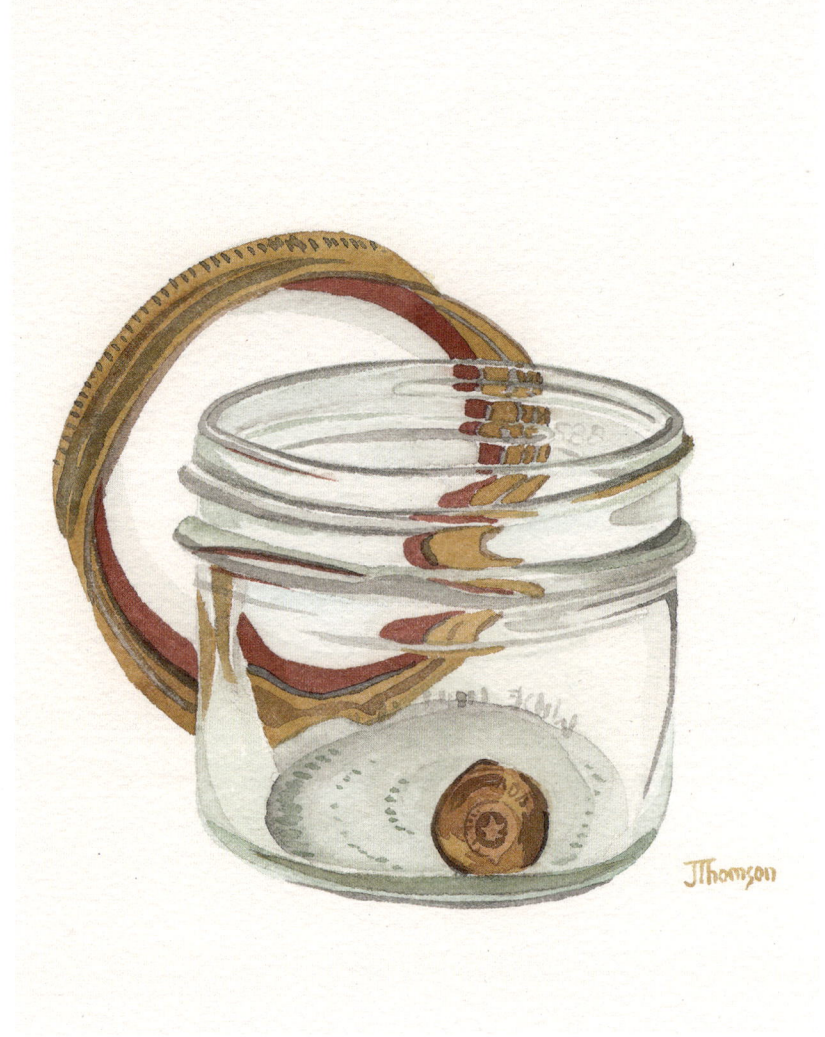

MASON JAR Centuries of military heritage
WITH CANADIAN The Von before Preetzman awarded.
ARMY BUTTON Who was the man who left it all
2014 To become a farmer?

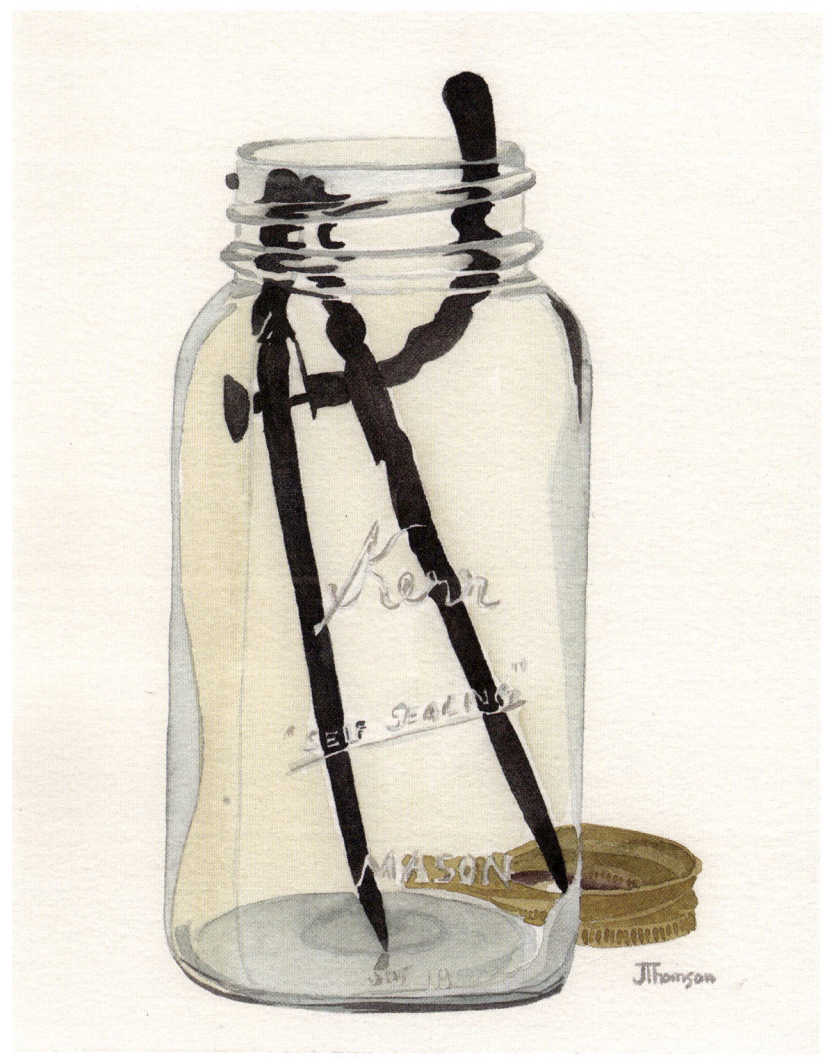

MASON JAR   The land gives up her treasures
WITH COMPASS   Reluctantly tells her story
2014   The compass tells
    Of one man trying to find his way.

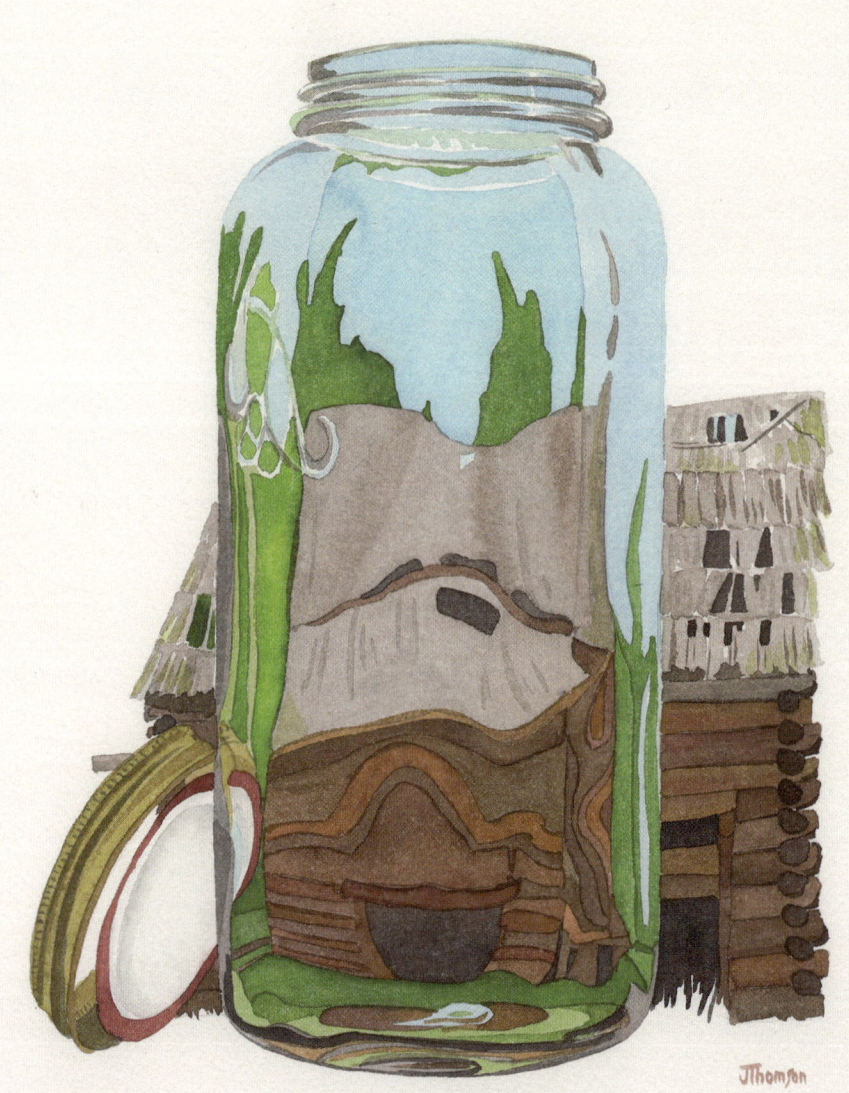

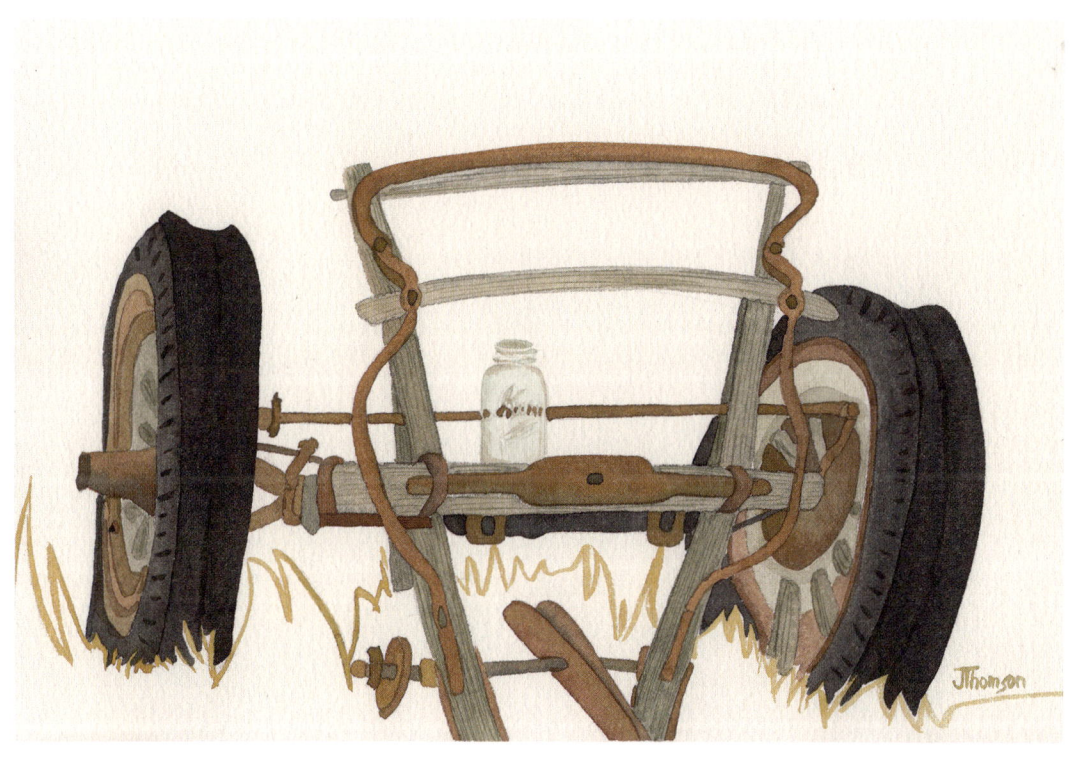

MASON JAR WITH
SETTLER'S CABIN

2014

A promise of shelter,
Hardwood floors,
Shattered brick chimney,
Home to pack rats and owls.

MASON JAR WITH
WAGON INVENTION

2015

Compassion for hardworking horses
Brakes for the downhill ride
As they pull full loads of change.

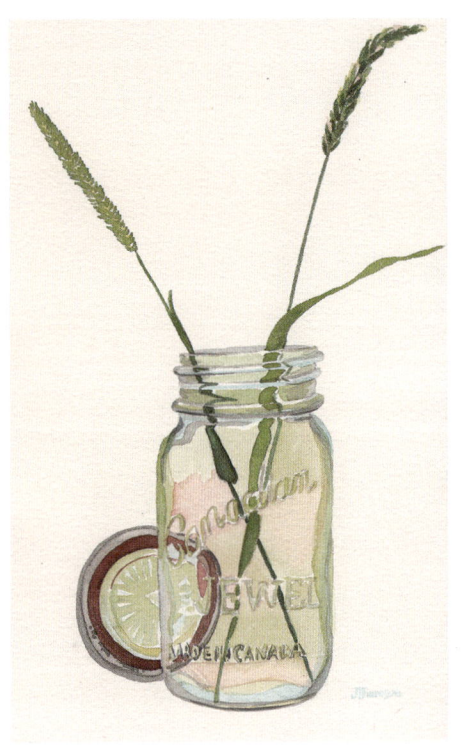 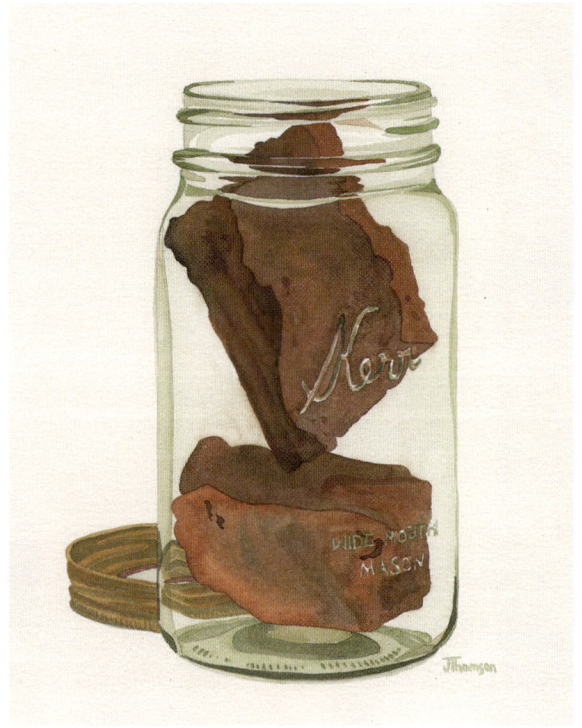

MASON JAR WITH Sweet smell on the breeze
HAY FROM BAUER A cabin full of memories
CREEK RANCH A window without glass
2014 Many years we kept horses.

MASON JAR WITH Firebricks
BRICKS FROM Fragmented by winter rain and frost
BAUER RANCH They once kept a family safe.
2014

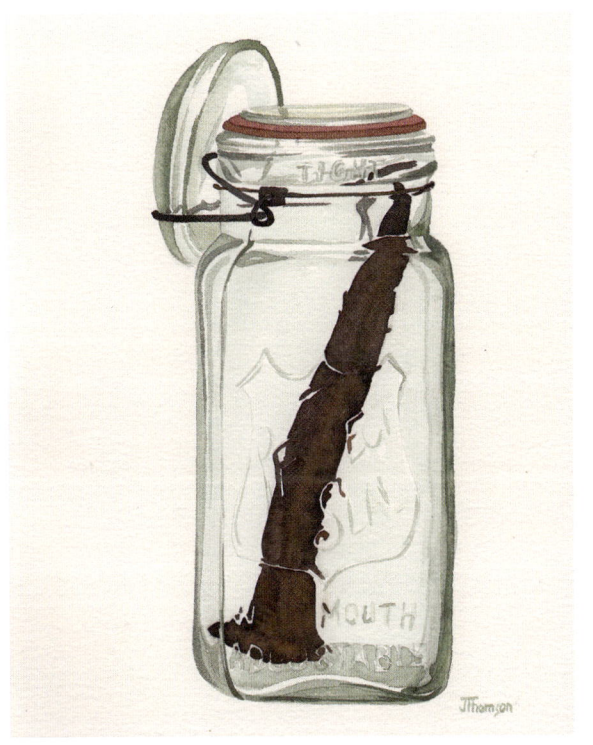
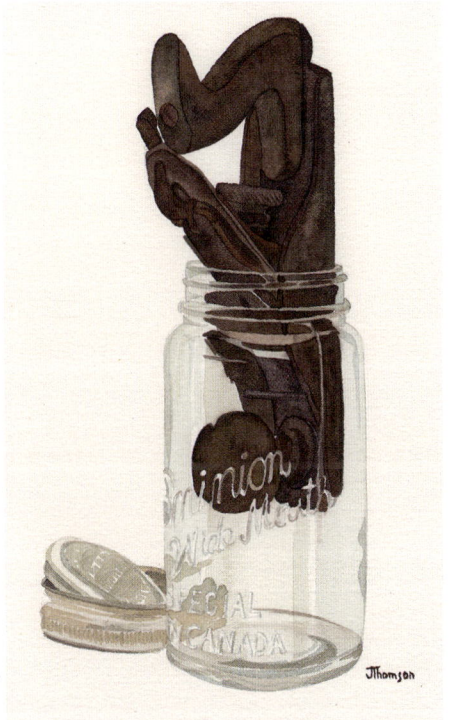

MASON JAR WITH
RAILROAD SPIKE

2014

The land was lost to drought
Still the railroad moves on
Hammer in hand
He dreams of land with more water.

MASON JAR
WITH PLANER

2015

Every man had a planer
When the homestead was built
To make the parts fit
To fit to the part.

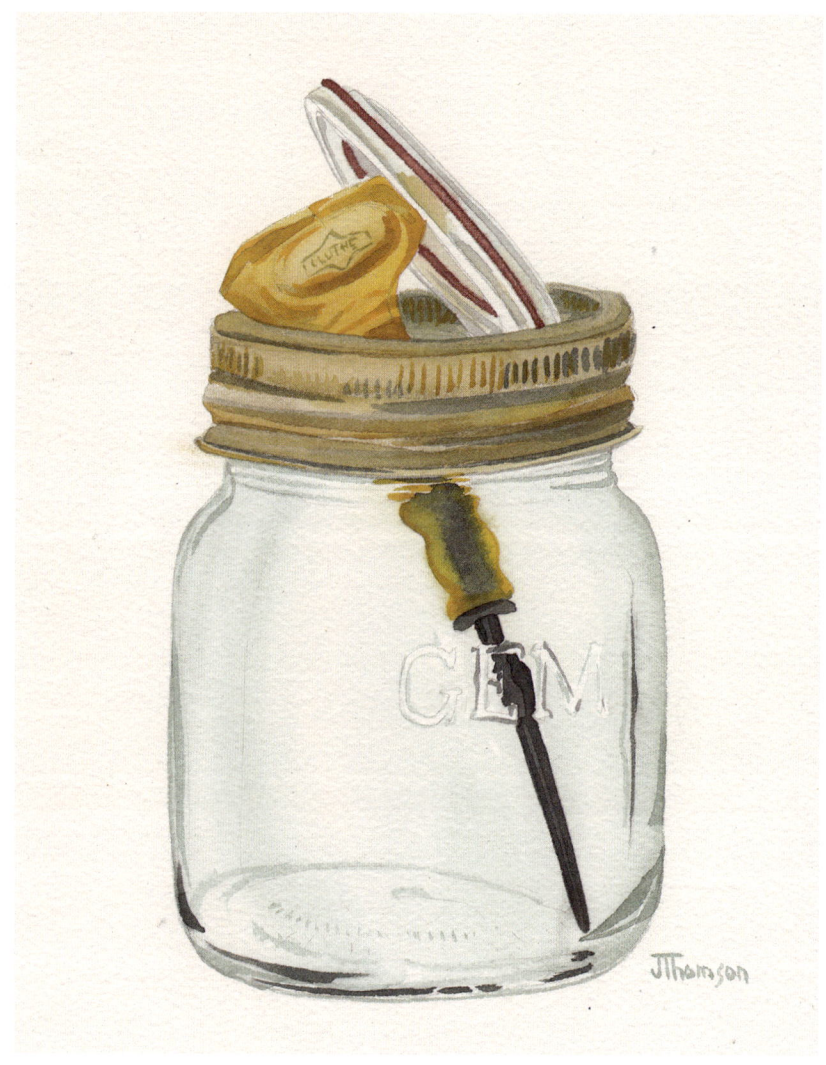

MASON JAR   When balancing on timbers
WITH PUNCH   This little starter for screws
2015   Offers welcome assistance.

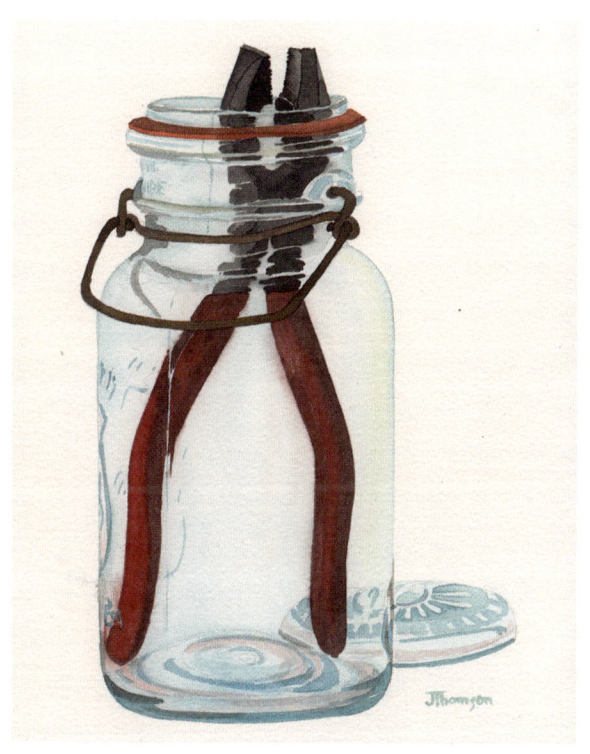
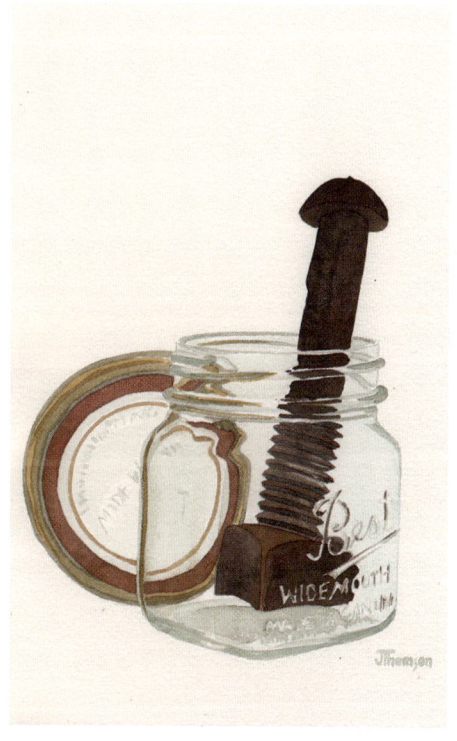

MASON JAR Wire fences
WITH PLIERS Cut and spliced and repaired.
2015 Miles and miles of them.

MASON JAR WITH Along the rails in southern Saskatchewan
RAILROAD BOLT A young man runs from his past
2015 I reach out to embrace him.

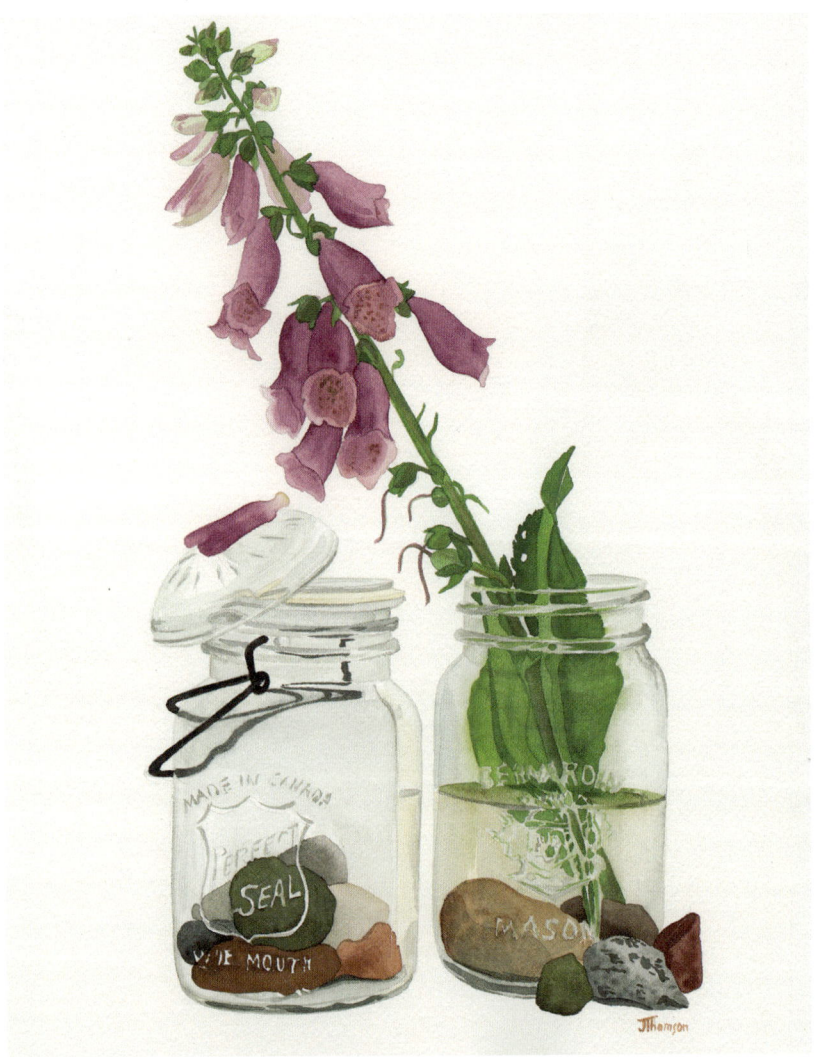

MASON JAR WITH FOXGLOVE AND SASKATCHEWAN RAILROAD STONES

2016

Saskatchewan railroad stones
British Columbia foxglove
The tracks stretch across Canada.

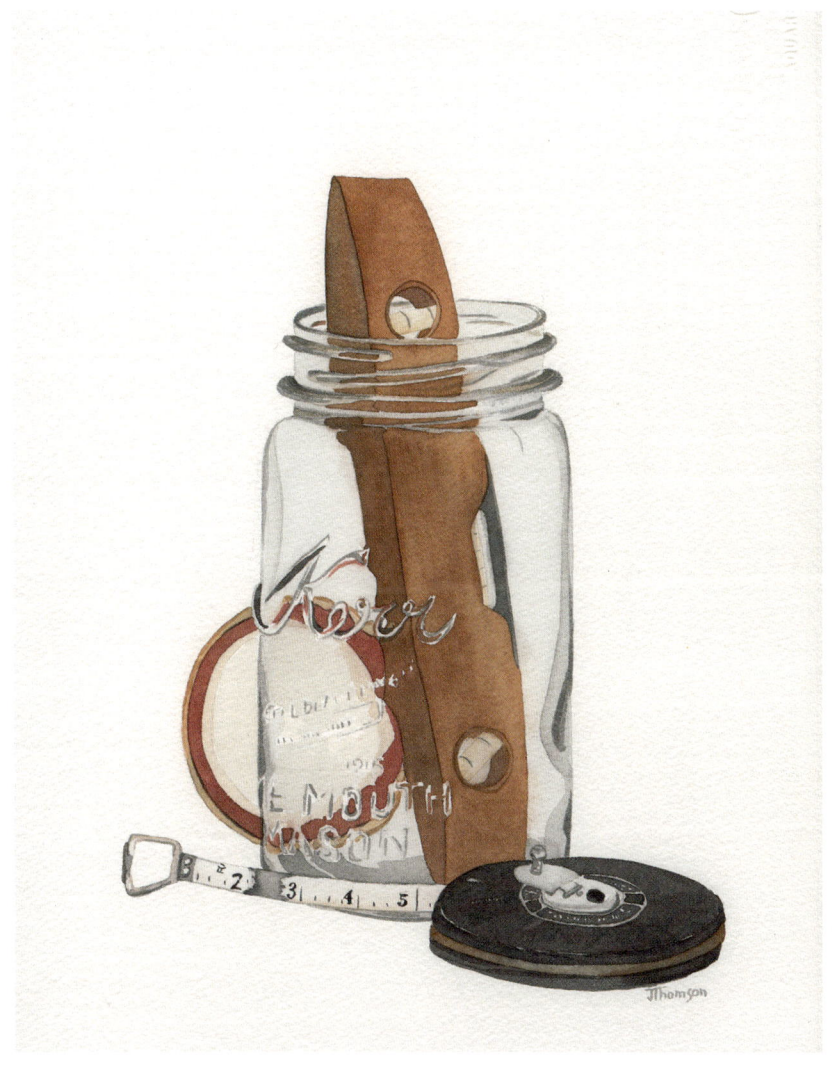

MASON JAR WITH   Dad liked to keep things level
LEVEL AND   With three women in the home
MEASURING TAPE   It wasn't always easy.
2019   Careful measuring out of territory helped.

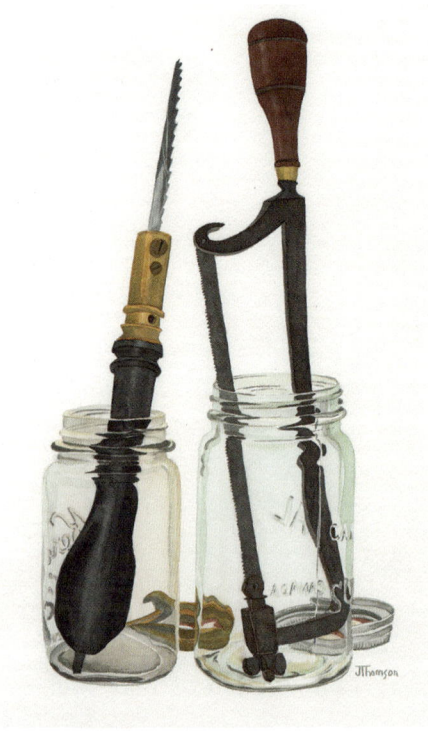 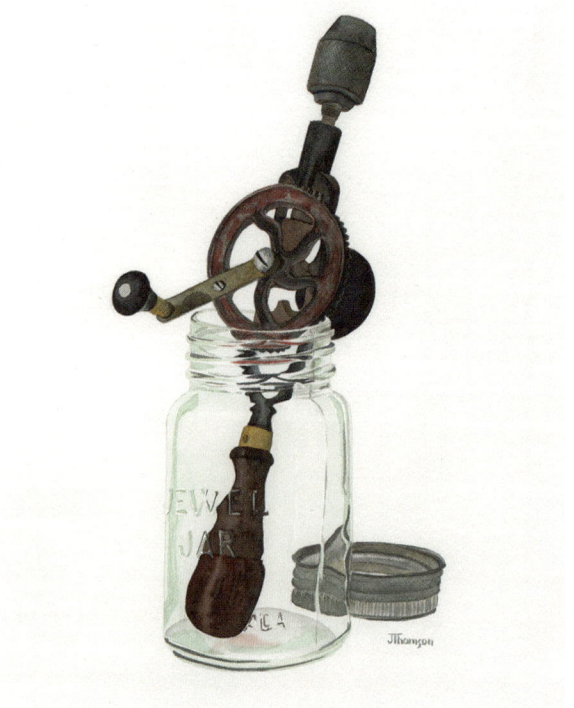

MASON JARS WITH
VICTORIAN HACK
AND KEY SAWS
2019

What beauty was created
When craftsmen made their own tools and
Stores were few and far between.

MASON JAR WITH
HAND DRILL
2019

How many grandchildren have learned to drill
With Grandpa's hands
And the smell of heated wood
Embracing them?

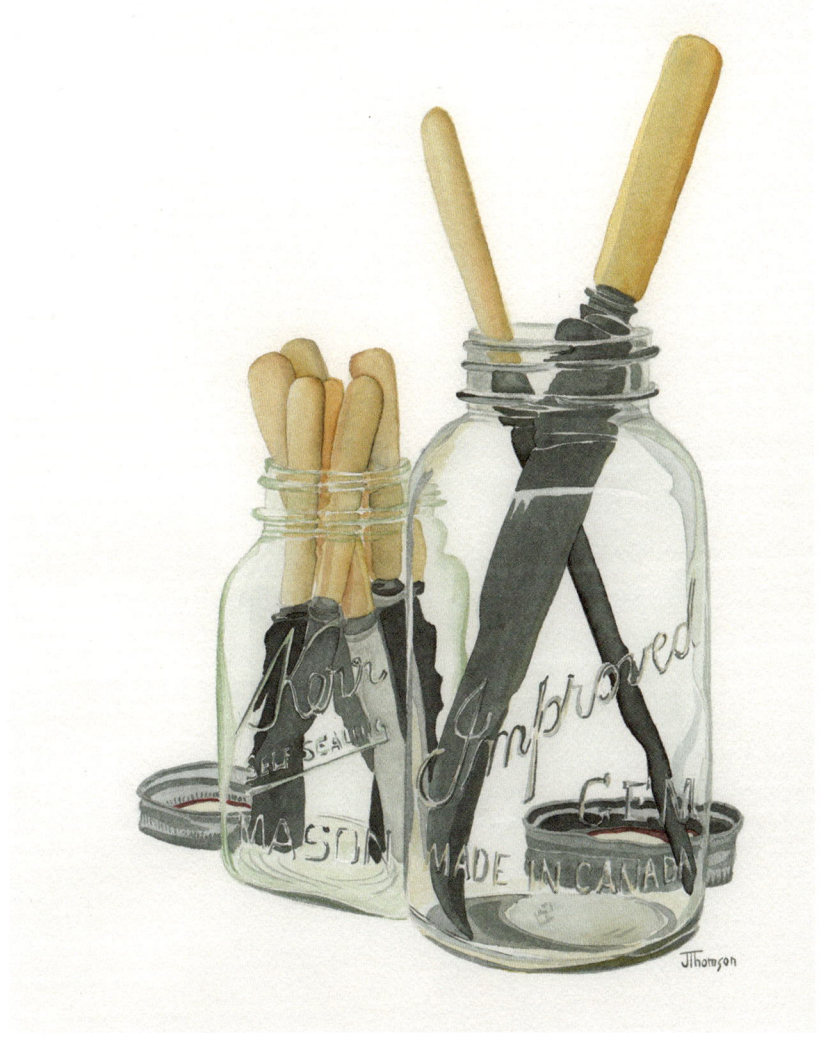

MASON JARS WITH
CARVING KNIFE
AND SHARPENER

2019

So many Christmas dinners
Dad sharpening the knife at the table.
Mom wishing he had done it earlier.
They are both gone now so I can chuckle about it.

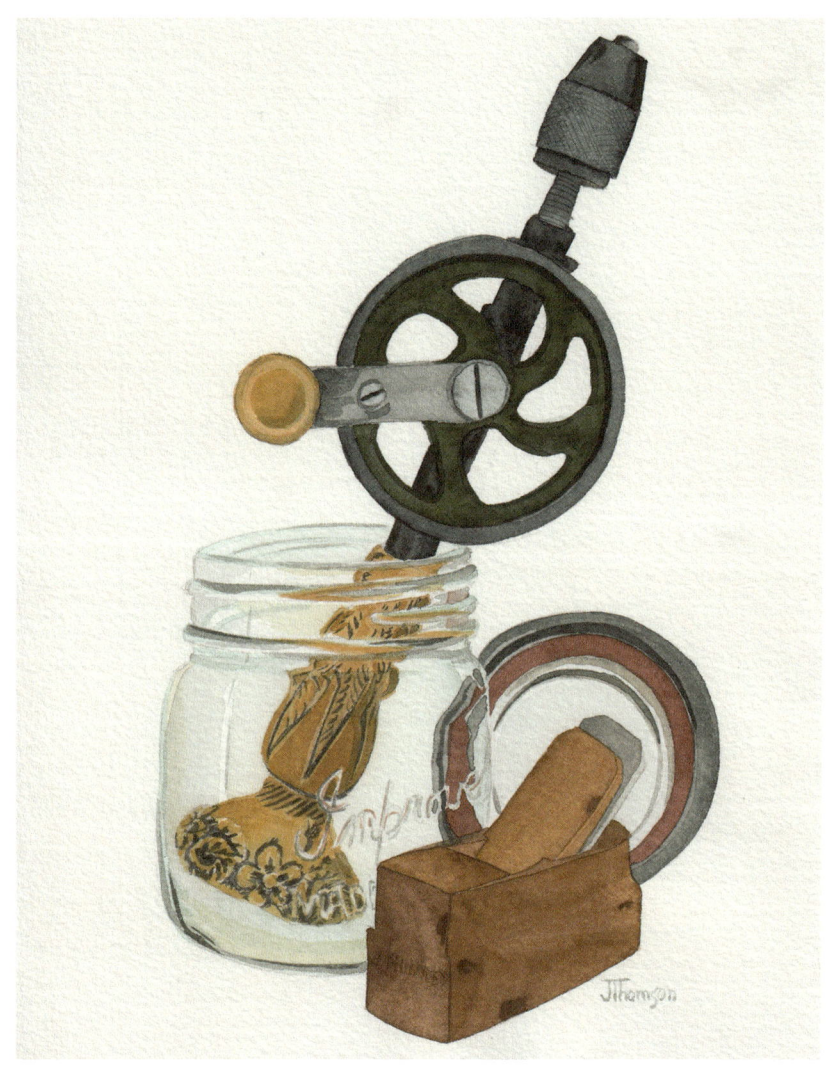

MASON JAR WITH
IMPROVED DRILL

2019

If Mary Poppins were to use a drill
It would look like this one
Another toy to teach children
Lessons in practical imaginings.

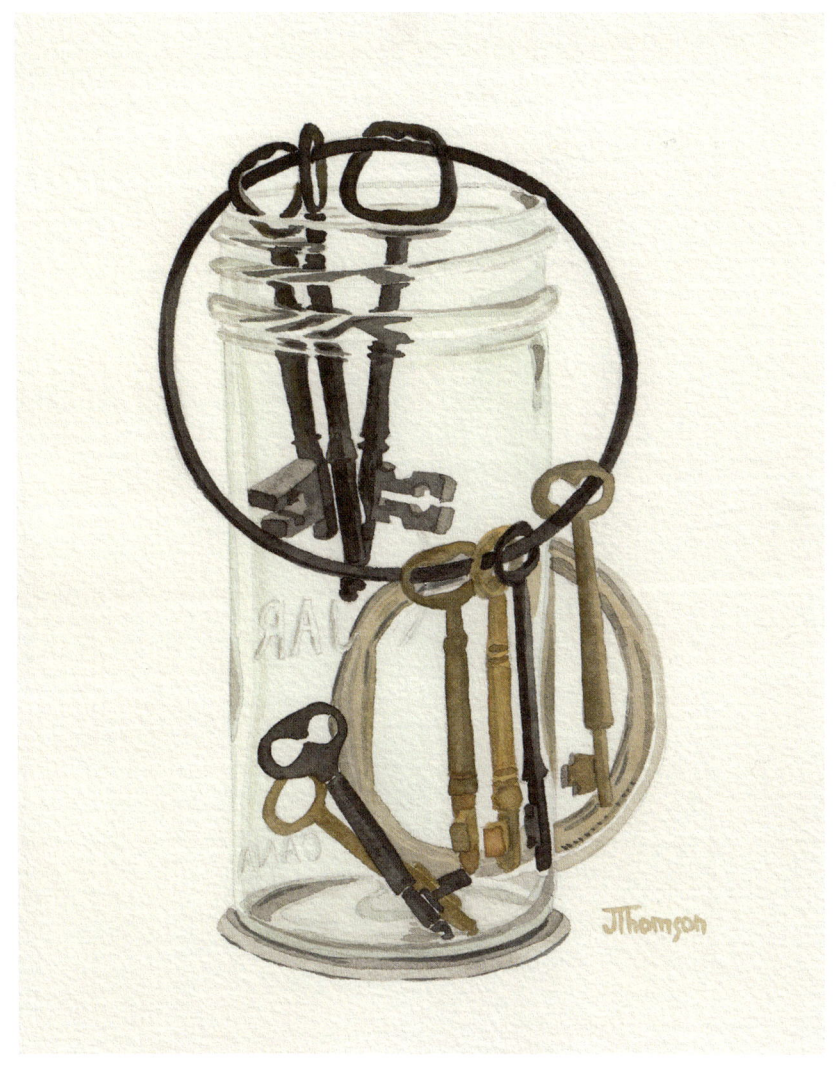

MASON JAR WITH Keys for doors
VINTAGE KEYS Now past existence
2019 Objects that remind
But do not open.

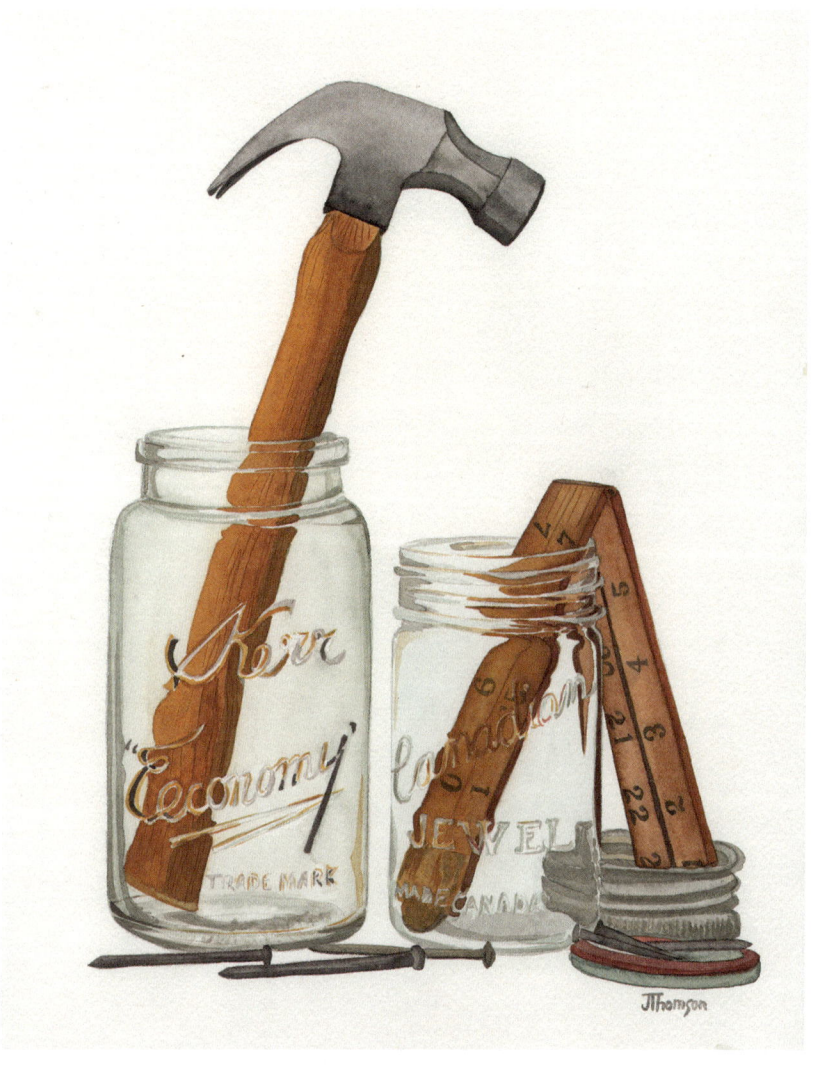

MASON JAR WITH   Tools of generations
HAMMER   Masculine and feminine
AND RULER   Embracing each other
2019   Remembering work shared.

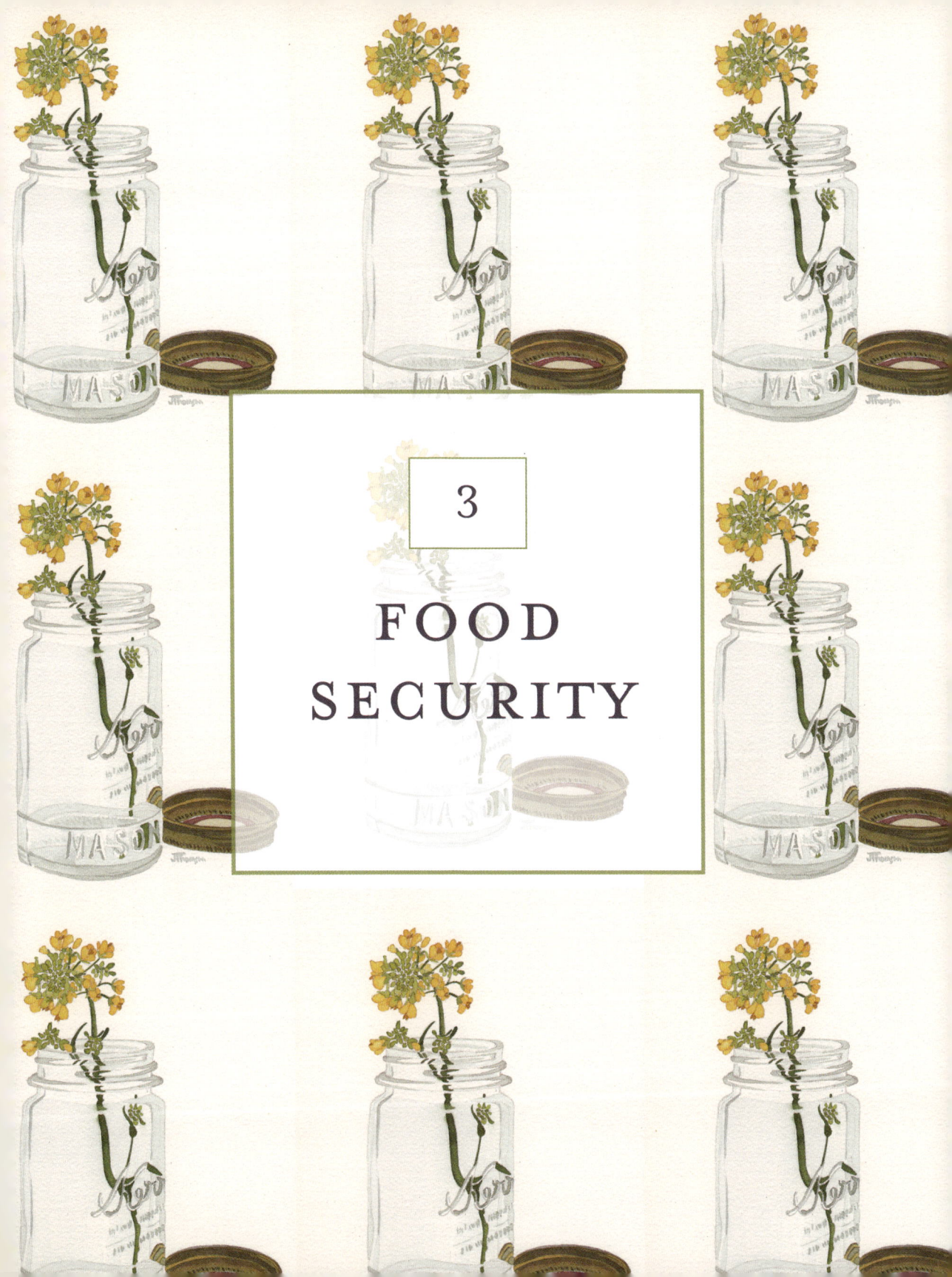

3

FOOD SECURITY

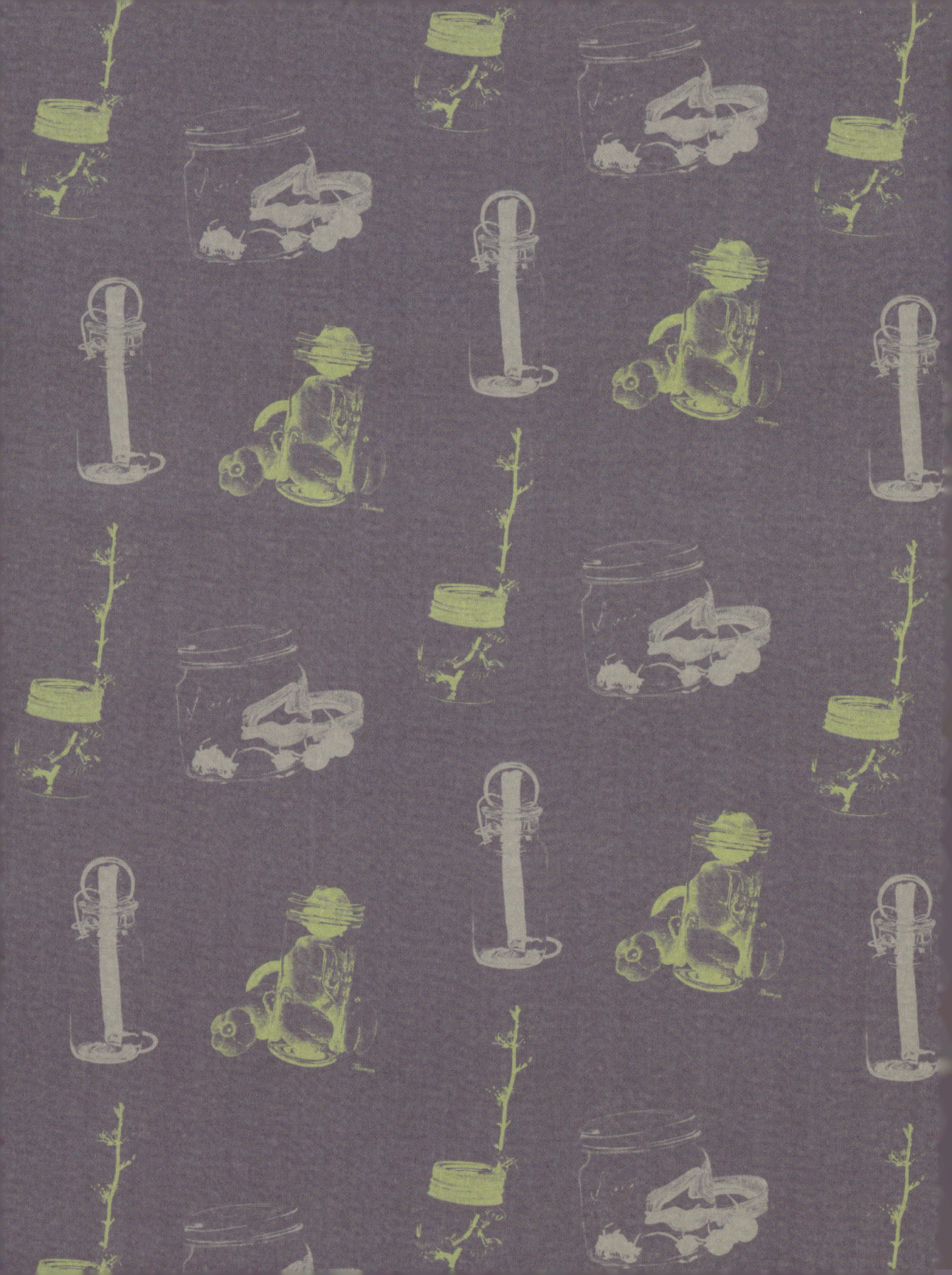

VEGETABLE GARDENS, berry bushes, and fruit trees filled the backyard of my childhood. We took foraging trips to gather wild berries and waited eagerly for the fabulous elderflowers to bloom so we could make "champagne." Our family was low income, yet I experienced a childhood of abundance.

Growing food and preserving it was how we knit our family together and then enjoyed the memory of those times in the winter months. Trips down the stairs to the cold room to retrieve fruit from the past summer or to the freezer to retrieve peas for our supper gave me a sense of accomplishment and belonging. I had helped to pick and preserve, or watched the food being picked and preserved. (I have a clear memory of my mother shelling peas over her battered old aluminum colander.) The acts of growing, gathering, and preserving are rich acts of caring.

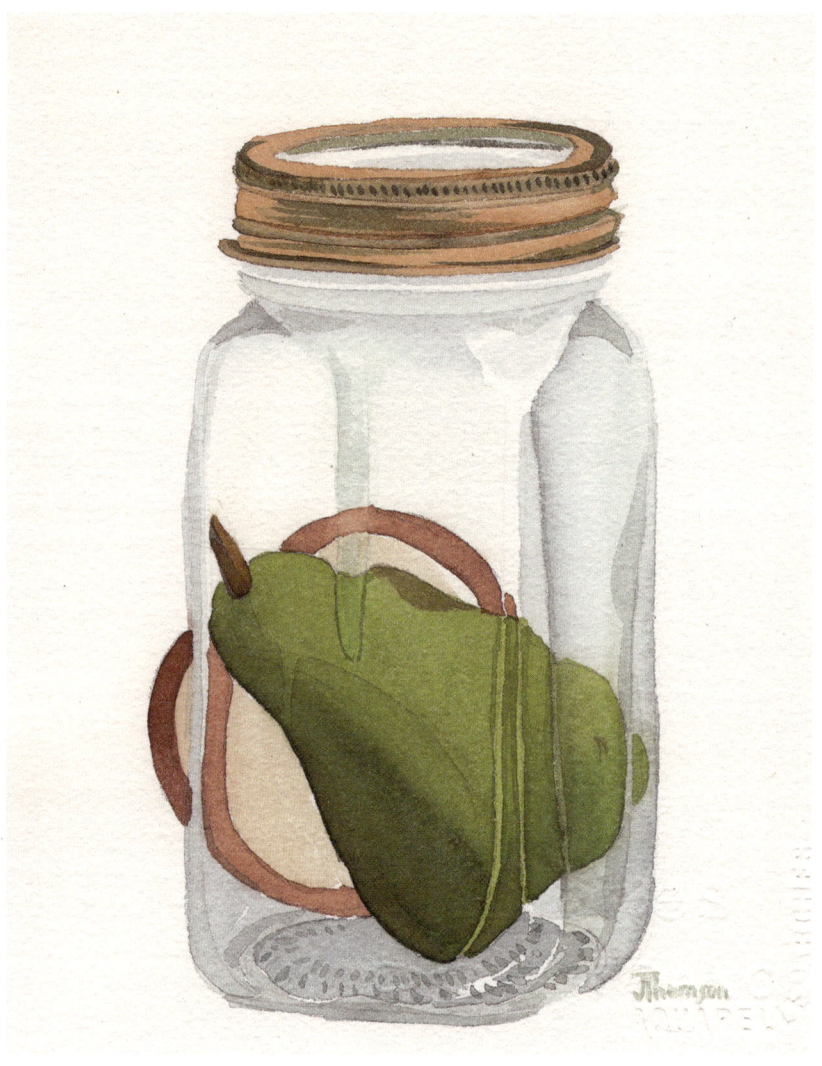

MASON JAR WITH	I wonder
ANJOU PEAR	Winter pear
2014	What you can see
	From your side of the glass.

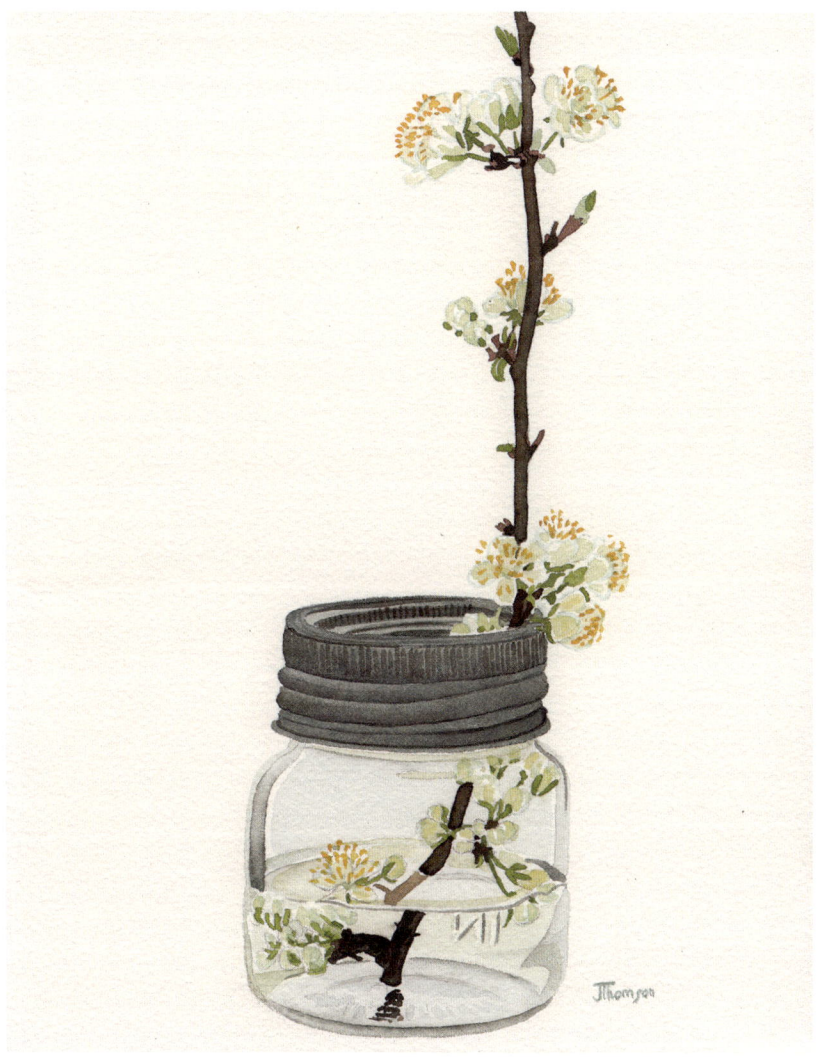

MASON JAR WITH
PLUM BLOSSOM
2014

Depression jar
Generations of use
The blossom promises
Fruit to fill.

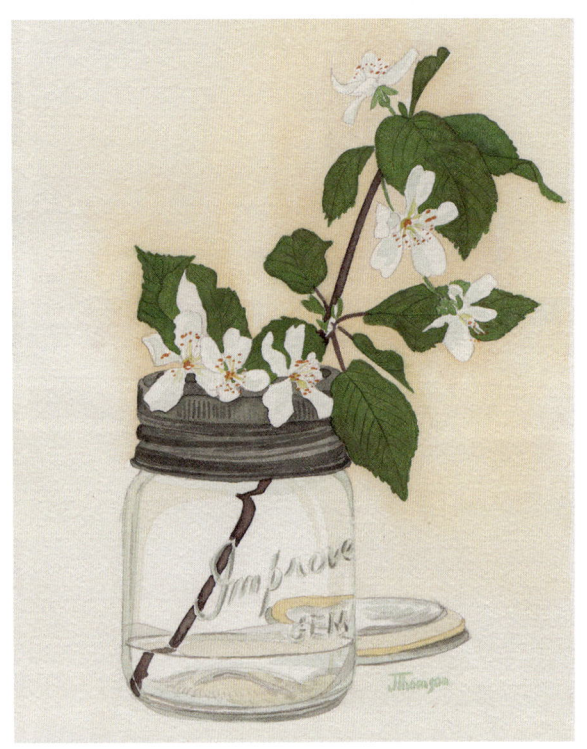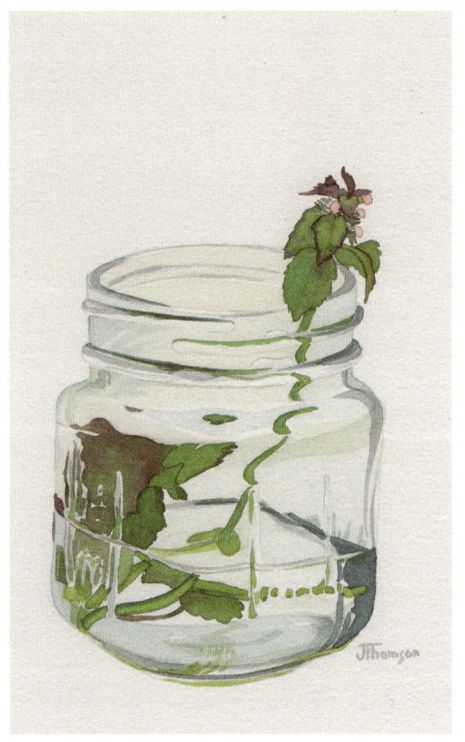

MASON JAR WITH
CHERRY BLOSSOM
2014

The bees will help make cherries
We will get what the birds leave us
Can them for winter
Eat them with ice-cream and custard.

MASON JAR WITH
YERBA BUENA
2014

A light summer tea when brewed
I pull masses of them out of my garden
Enjoying the fresh scent
Imagining someone in Spain doing the same.

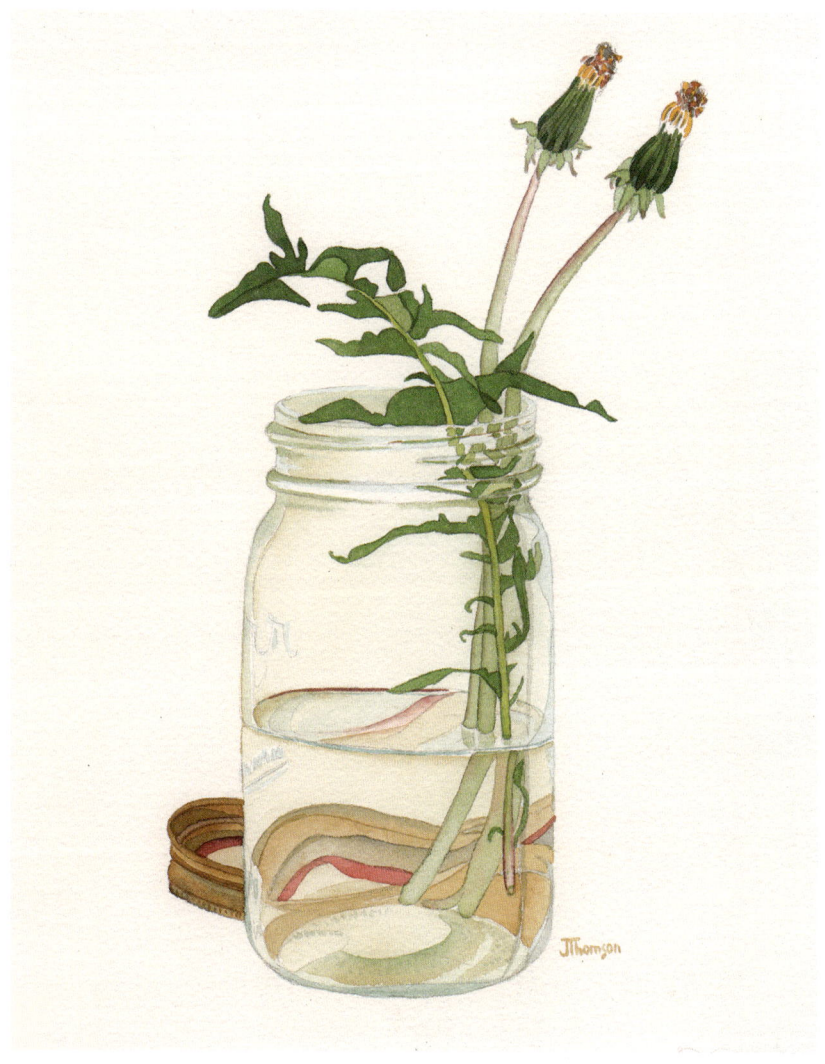

MASON JAR WITH
DANDELIONS
2014

Long winter ends
With welcome bitterness
Dandelion greens
Taste of spring.

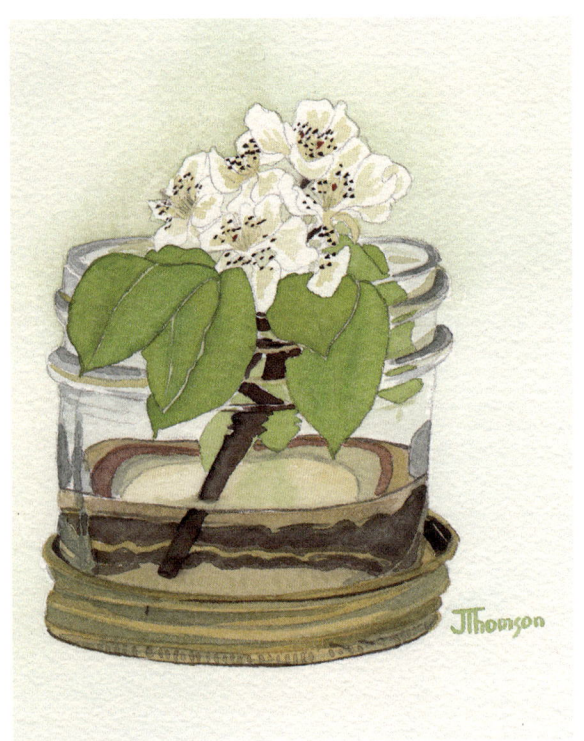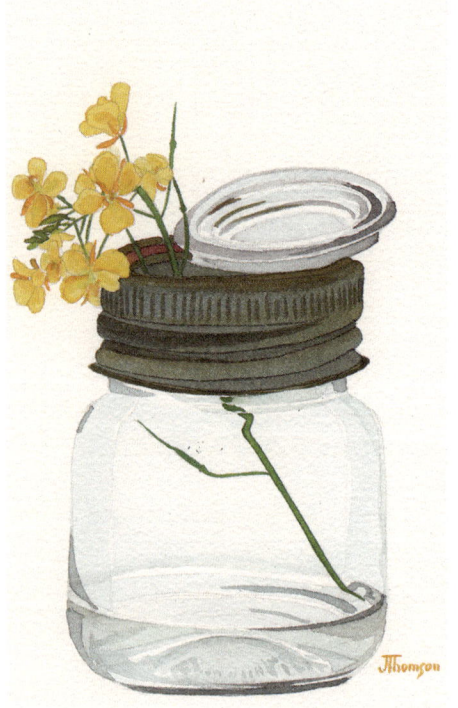

MASON JAR WITH
PEAR BLOSSOMS

2014

Pear blossoms hardly evoke
The pleasures of the fruit they will become
Canned or fresh
An abundance of white flesh on my tongue.

MASON JAR WITH
NOT CANOLA

2014

Not canola,
Not yellow button,
The inaccuracy of my imagination
Is, yet again, laid bare.

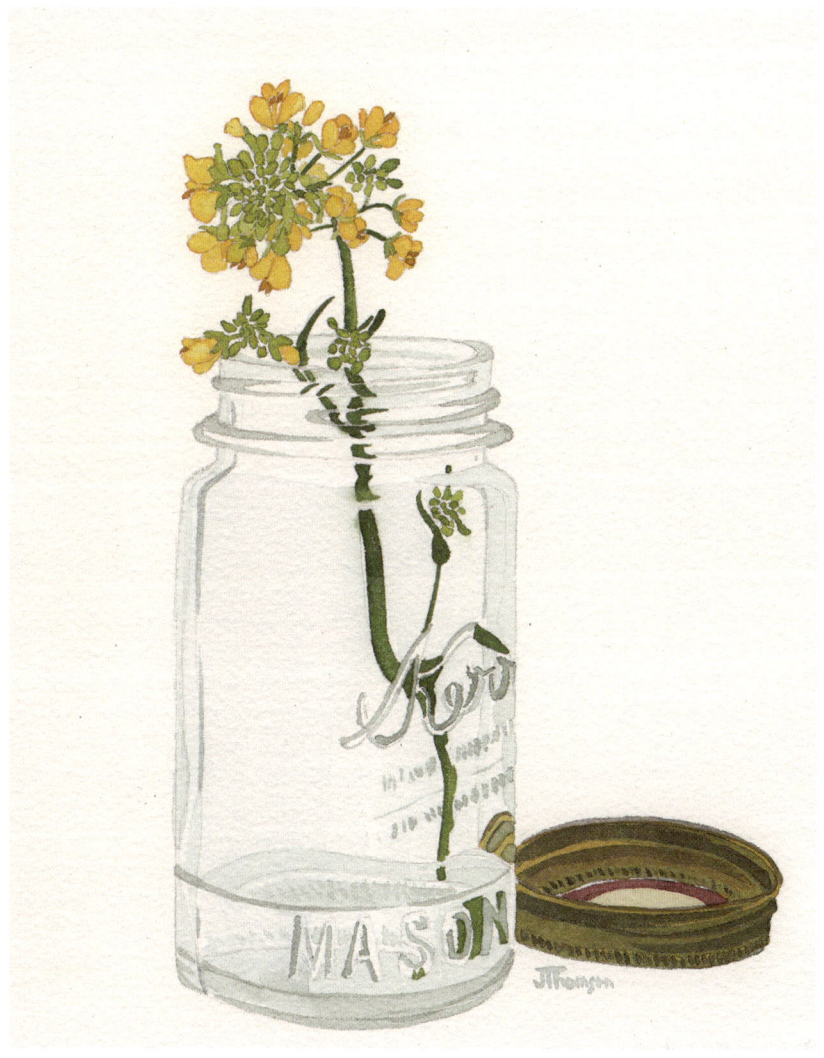

MASON JAR A beautiful field of yellow
WITH CANOLA Canola tastes good to deer
2014 Planted for dairy cows and rabbits
Sometimes deer end up on the table too.

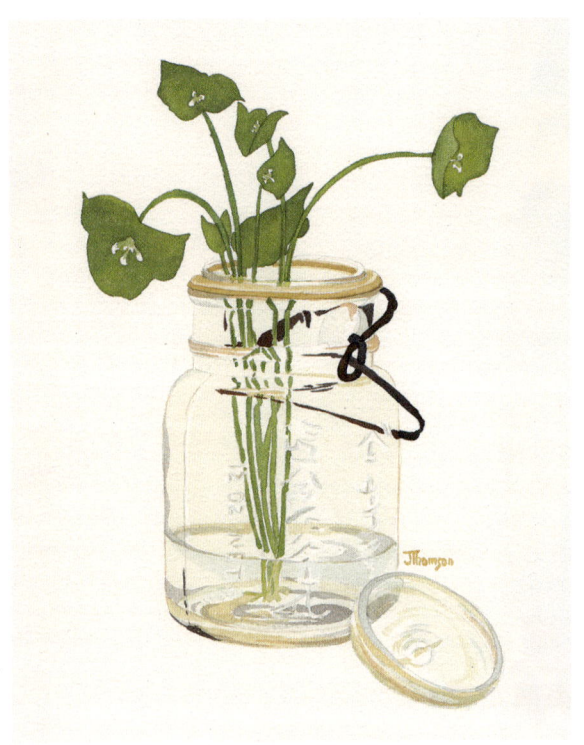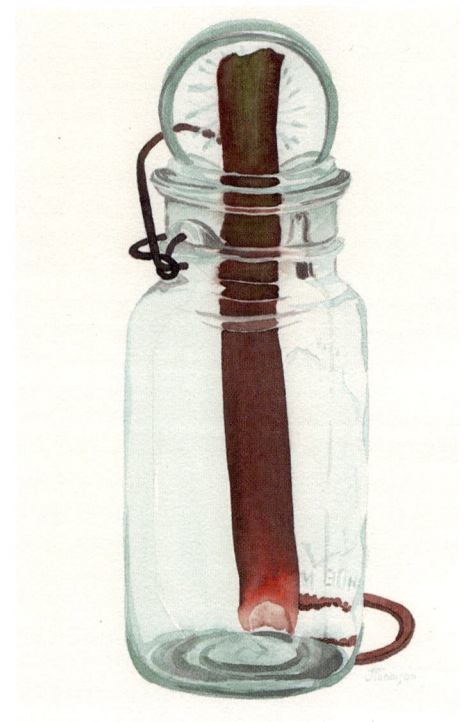

MASON JAR WITH MINER'S LETTUCE

2014

The long winter ends
Green a welcome site
Green a welcome taste
Green a welcome bite.

MASON JAR WITH RHUBARB

2014

Raw with sugar
To stop the mouth inverting
Stewed on ice cream
Baked in pies.

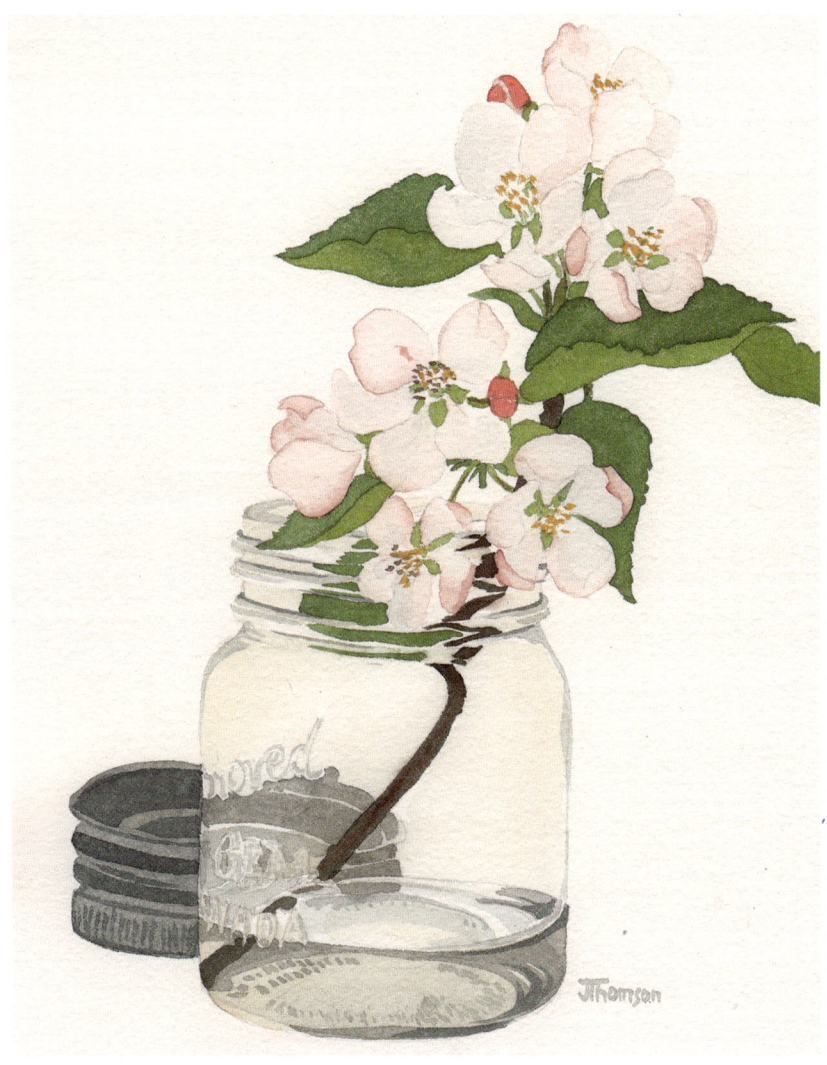

MASON JAR WITH Promise of apples
APPLE BLOSSOMS the blooms cry out
2014 "we are, we are and we will be."

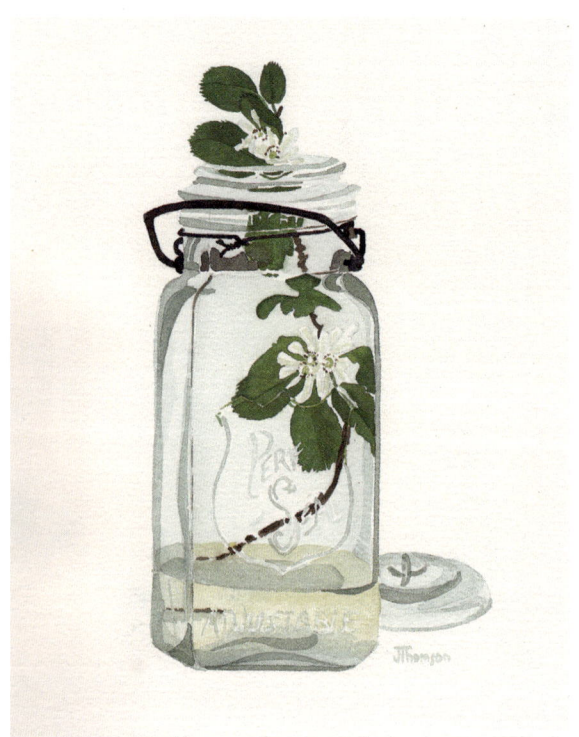

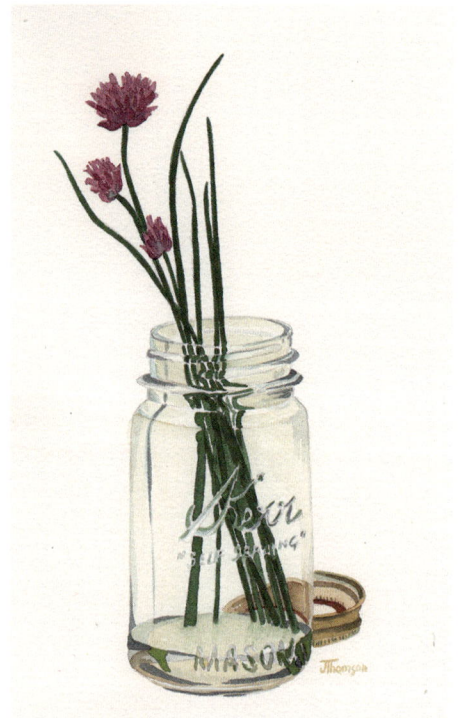

MASON JAR WITH
SASKATOON FLOWER

2014

The fruit anticipated,
The location noted
White flowers and saw tooth leaves
Predicting an August of abundance.

MASON JAR
WITH CHIVES

2014

Strong like a successful pioneer
Lucky to land on fertile ground
Free to bloom and grow
With an abundance that outreaches harvest.

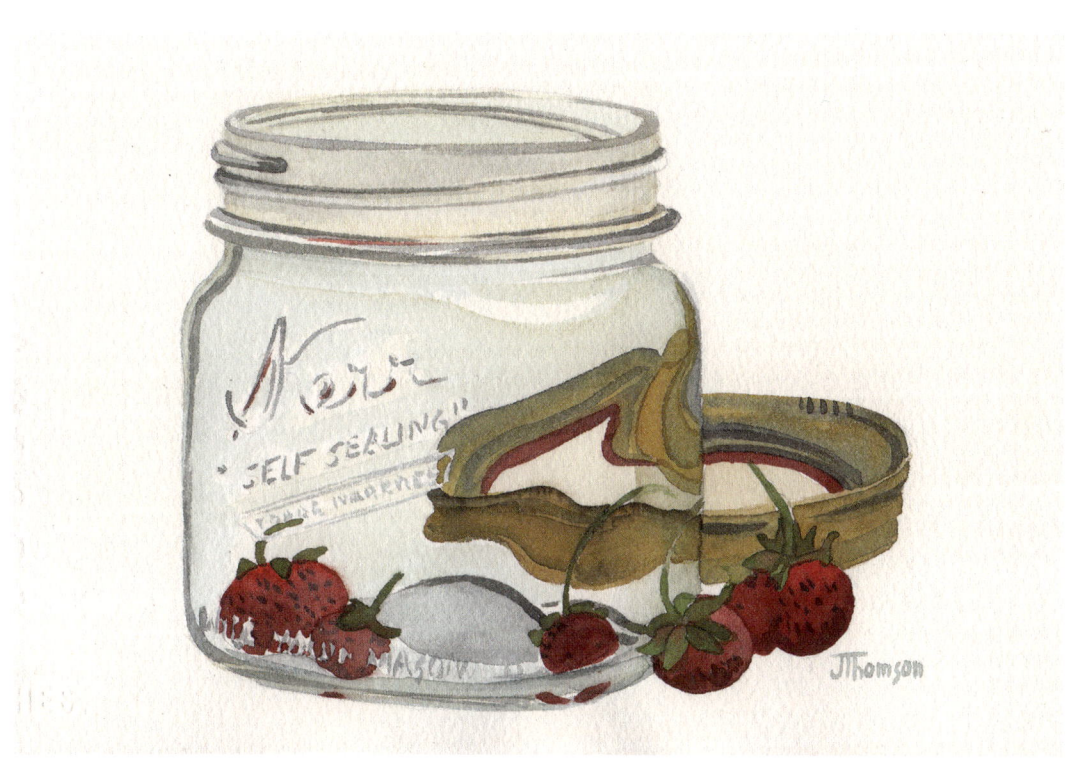

MASON JAR WITH
WILD STRAWBERRIES
2014

Guilty pleasures
Tiny treasures
Stolen from mice and rabbits.

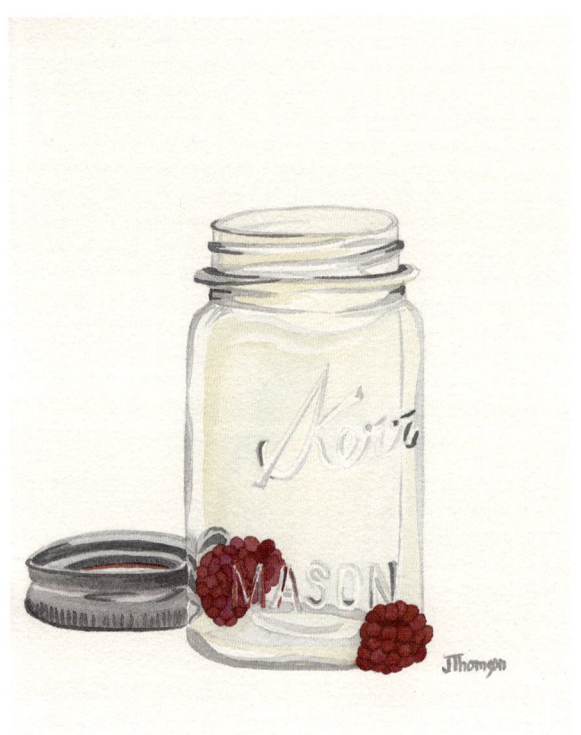
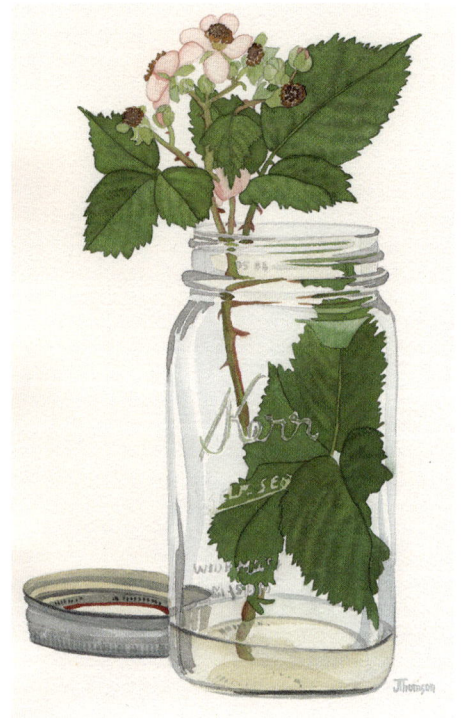

MASON JAR WITH **RASPBERRIES** *2014*	Such abundance can be cursed When the ripening is fast and furious The canning and jam making onerous Forgiven on fresh bread in the dead of winter…
MASON JAR WITH **BLACKBERRY** **BLOSSOMS** *2014*	Rose sisters corrupt the hedgerows Battle with gardens Resist clippers and shears Stubbornly offering flowers and fruit.

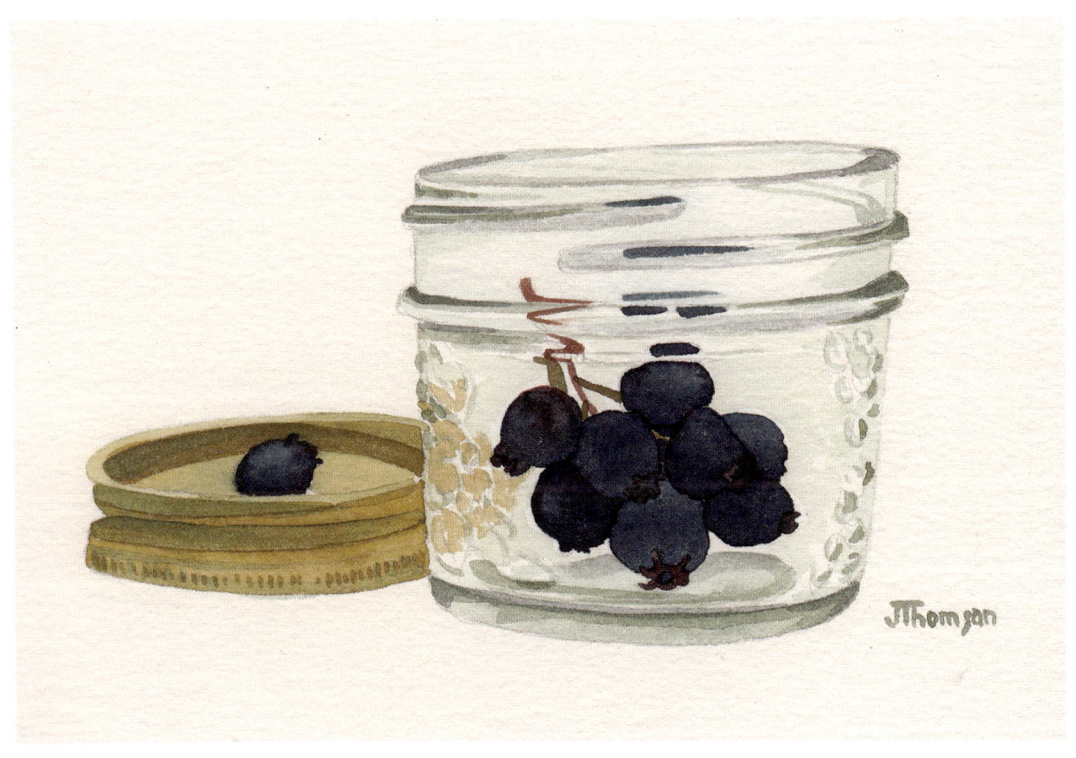

MASON JAR WITH
SASKATOON BERRIES

2014

Sweet delights
Warmed by the sun
No anxiety in my life
To collect and save them for winter
I enjoy them now.

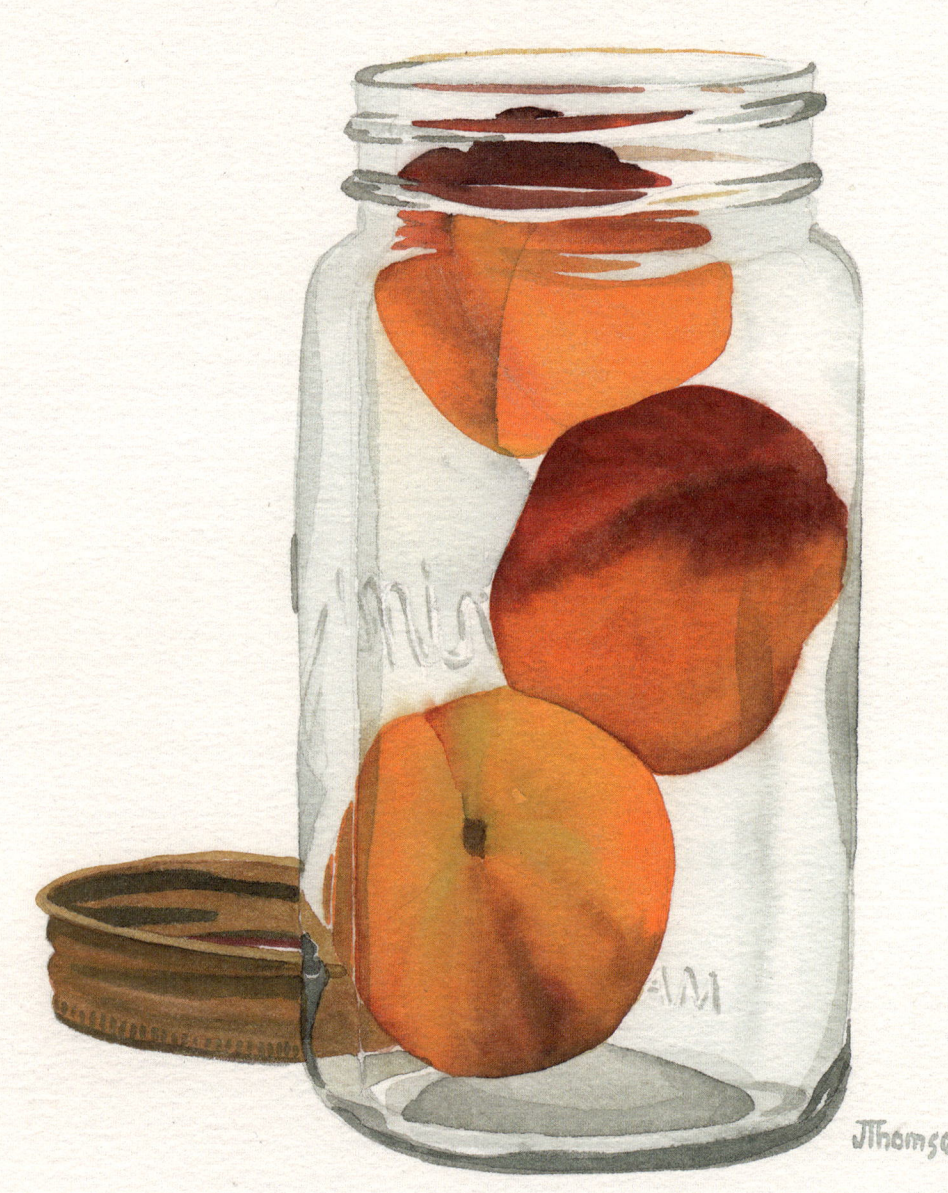

JThomson

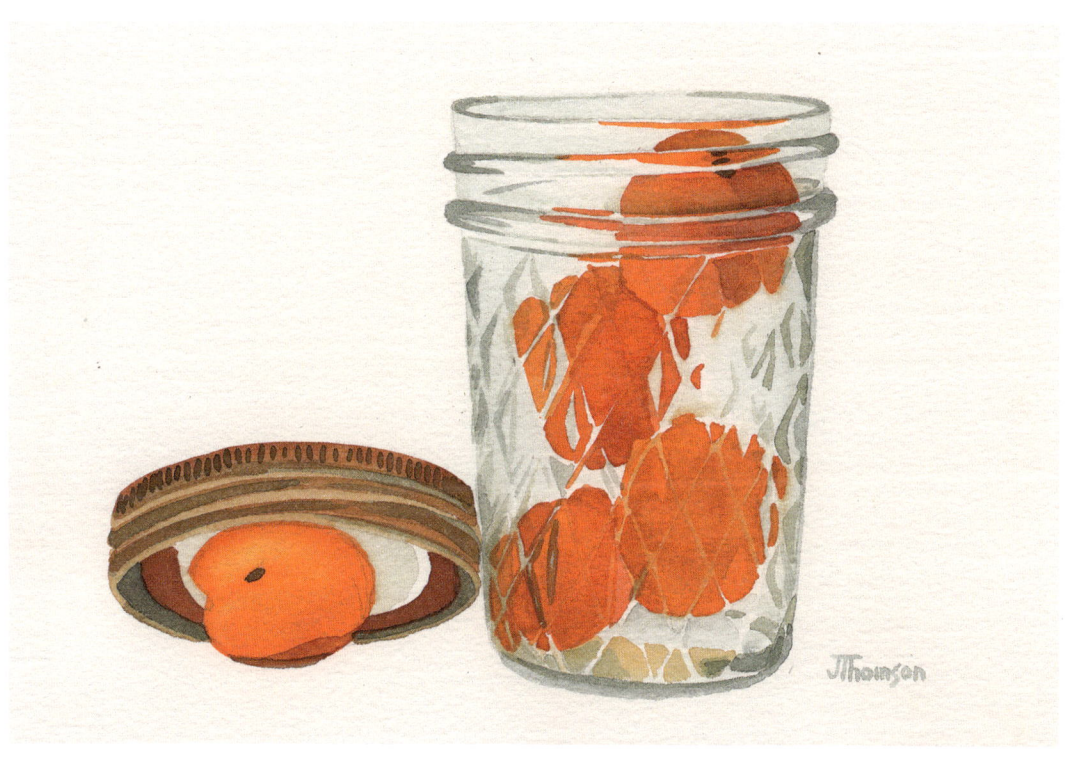

MASON JAR Fragrant freshness
WITH PEACHES Calls out for tasting
2014 Eat those who cling to their pits
    Save the freestones for winter.

MASON JAR Decisions, decisions
WITH APRICOTS Beauty waits for me to decide
2014 Jam . . . Preserves . . .
    Pleasure now without restraint?

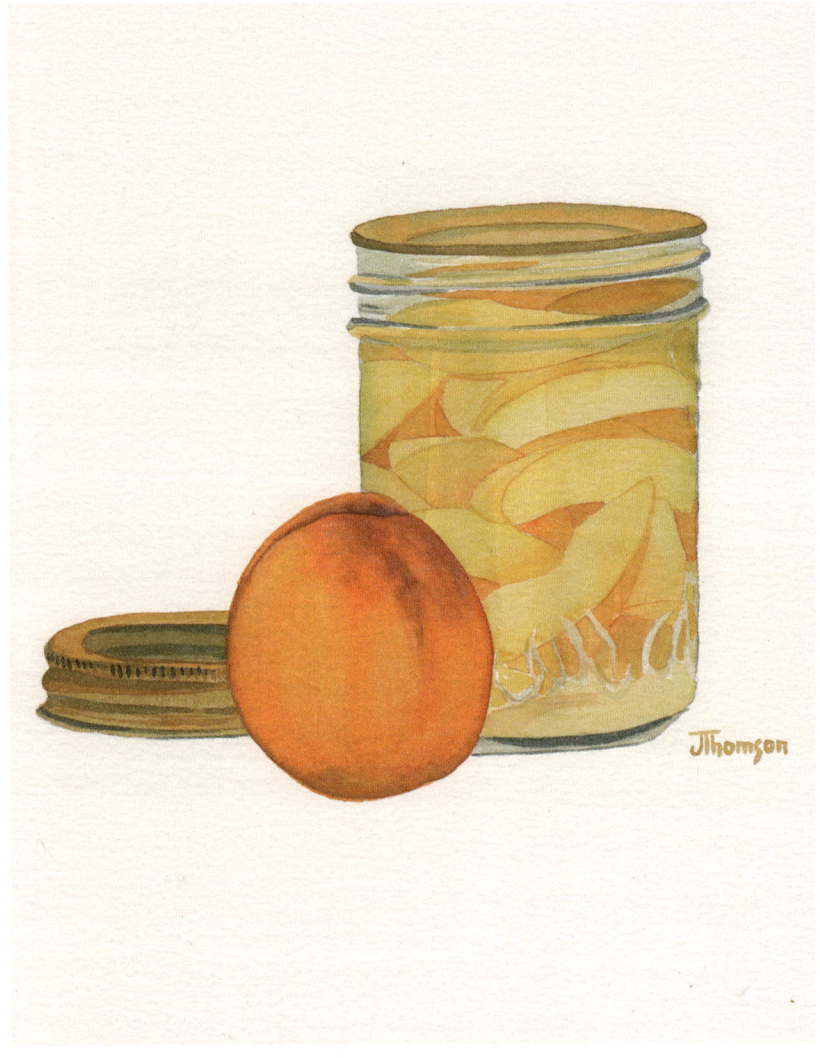

MASON JAR WITH
CANNED AND FRESH
CLINGSTONE PEACHES

2014

Ahhh … winter dreams of
Peaches and ice cream
Warm peach cake
Drizzled with brandy.

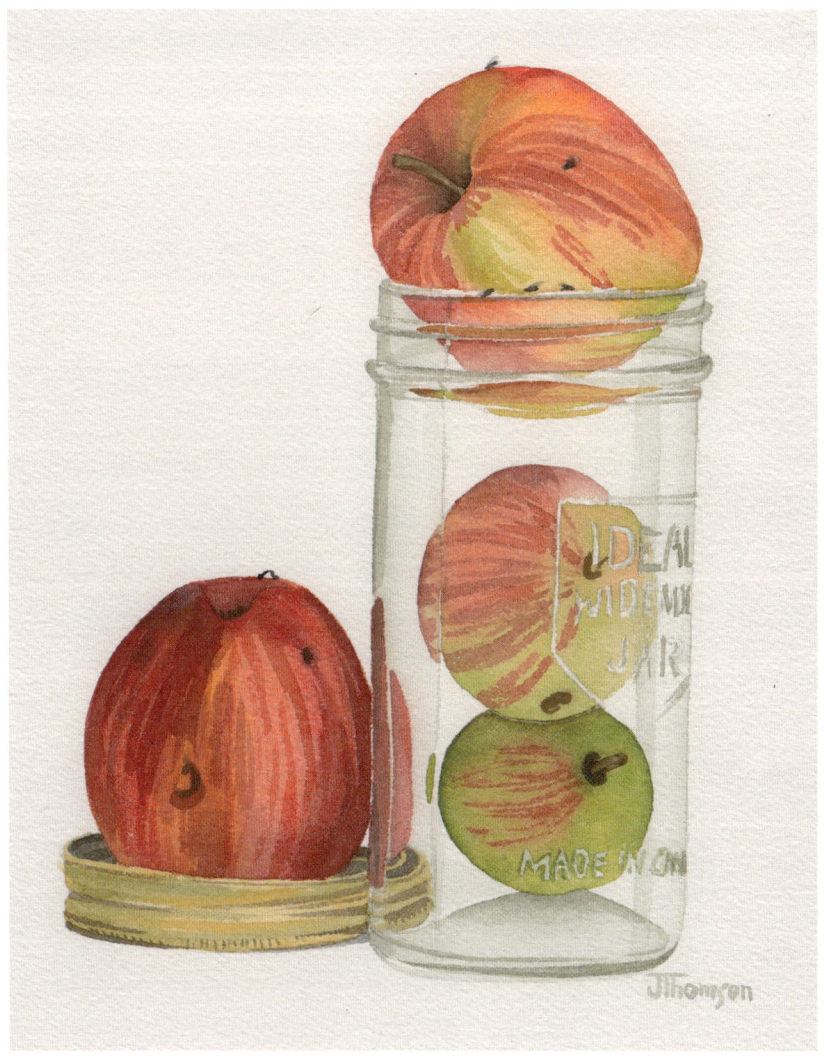

**MASON JAR WITH
WORM AND APPLES**

2015

Every year there is a battle
Between the worm and the apple
The deer and the farmer
Sharing is not always voluntary.

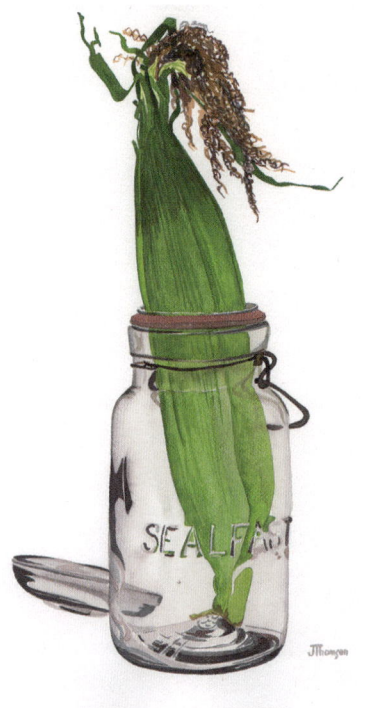
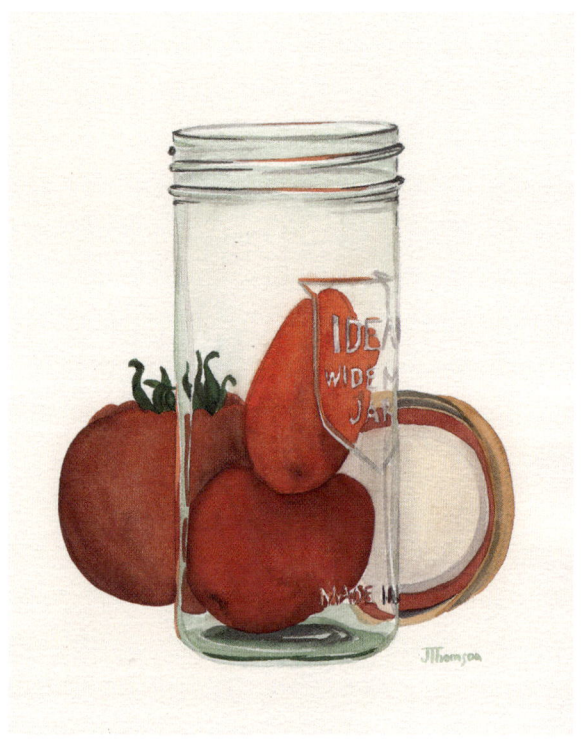

MASON JAR WITH
CORN ON THE COB
2014

Slow to be realized
Pleasure in sweet corn
We are not animals after all
Then, we realize that we are.

MASON JAR
WITH TOMATOES
2014

Wishing for tomatoes
Everyday of the year
Fresh and flavourful
As they are now.

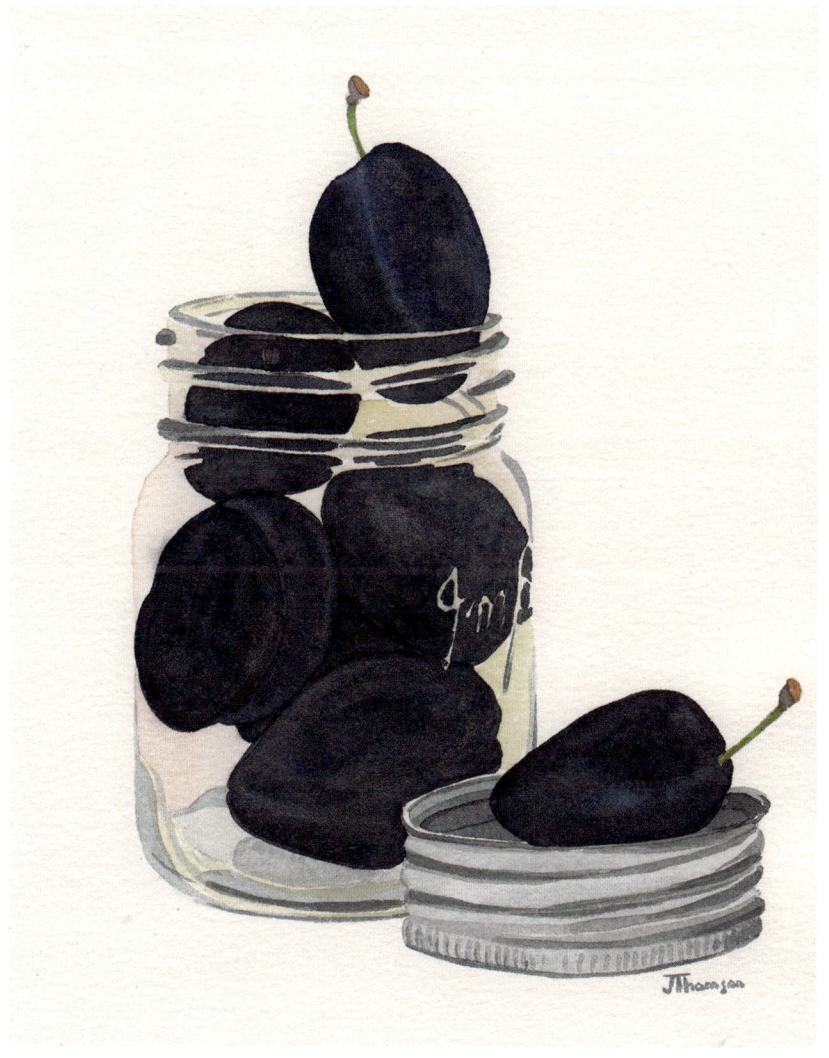

MASON JAR WITH
PRUNE PLUMS

2014

The blush of plums
Rubbed to reveal shining blue
Soft, forgiving flesh
As delicious as sex.

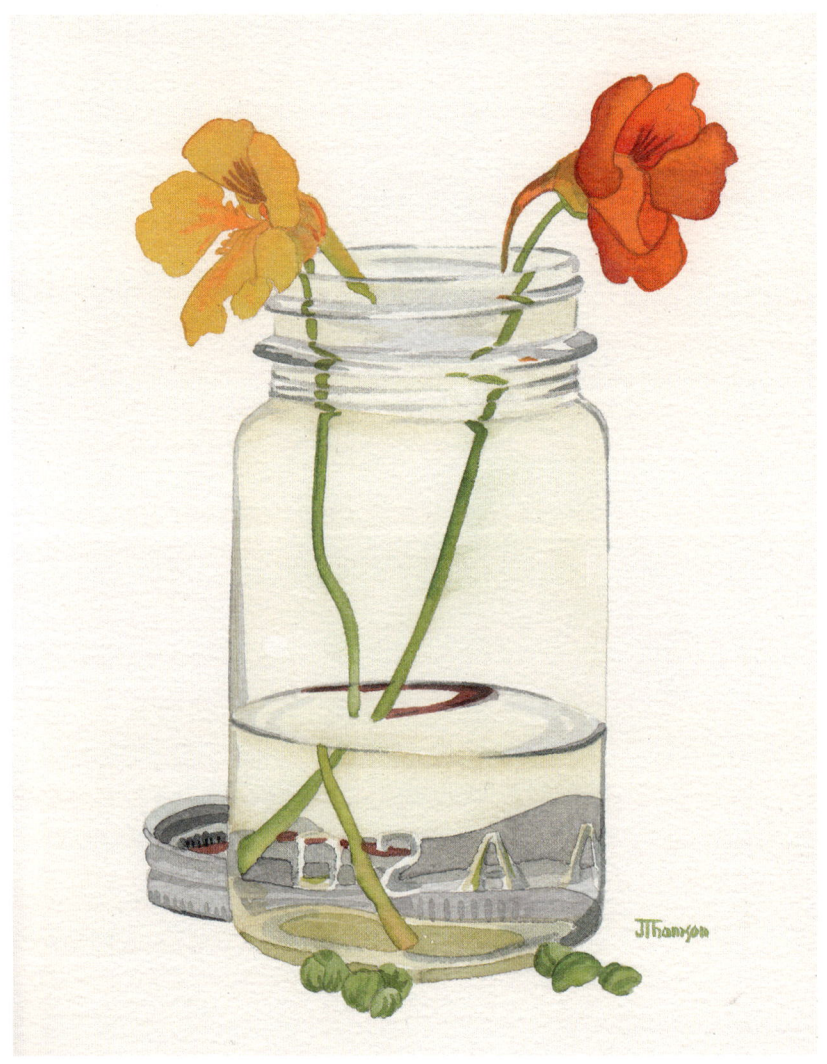

MASON JAR WITH
NASTURTIUMS
AND CAPERS
2014

Bright bites of pepper
Soft scent of morning
Bees' friend and feast
A wealth of gifting.

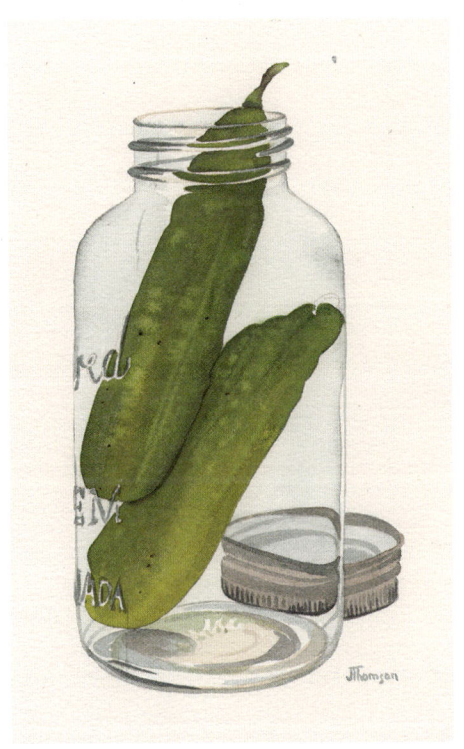

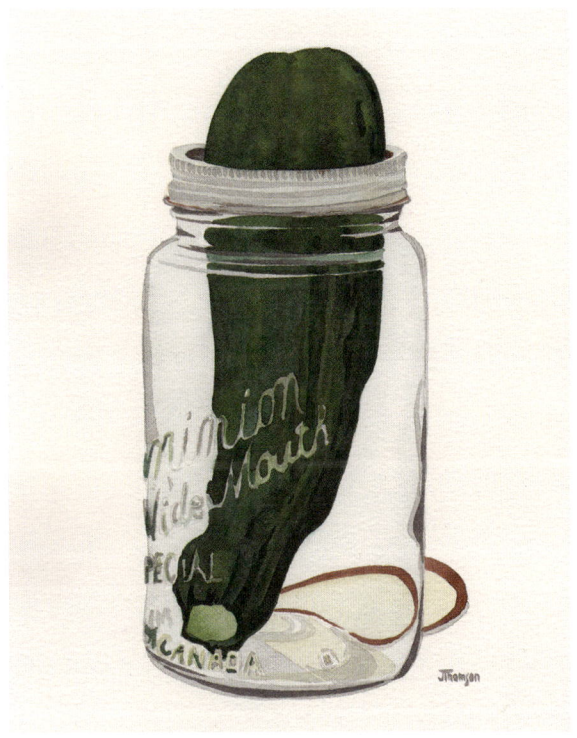

MASON JAR WITH
CUCUMBERS
2014

Ahhh... Freida has a garden
Wins ribbons at the Fall Fair
Fresh and canned and tested
They prove their worth.

MASON JAR
WITH ZUCCHINI
2014

What to do,
What to do
What to do.
Does no one want another zucchini?

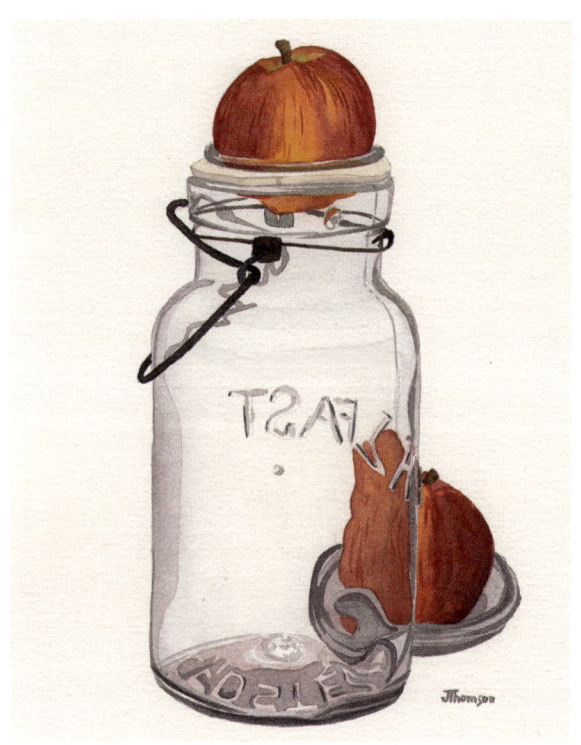
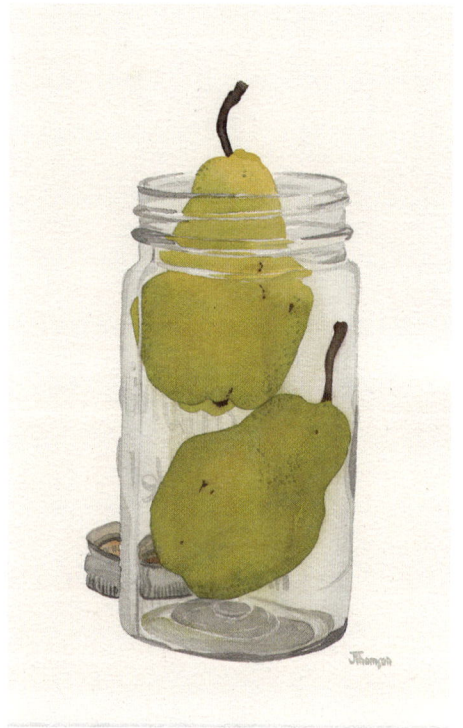

MASON JAR WITH
WINDFALL APPLES
2014

Windfalls for applesauce
And apple crisp
And apple chips
Much wealth from the fallen ones.

MASON JAR WITH
BARTLETT PEARS
2014

Delicate smell of pears
Fragile and easily bruised
Paint them quickly to preserve them.
Before they rot from the inside.

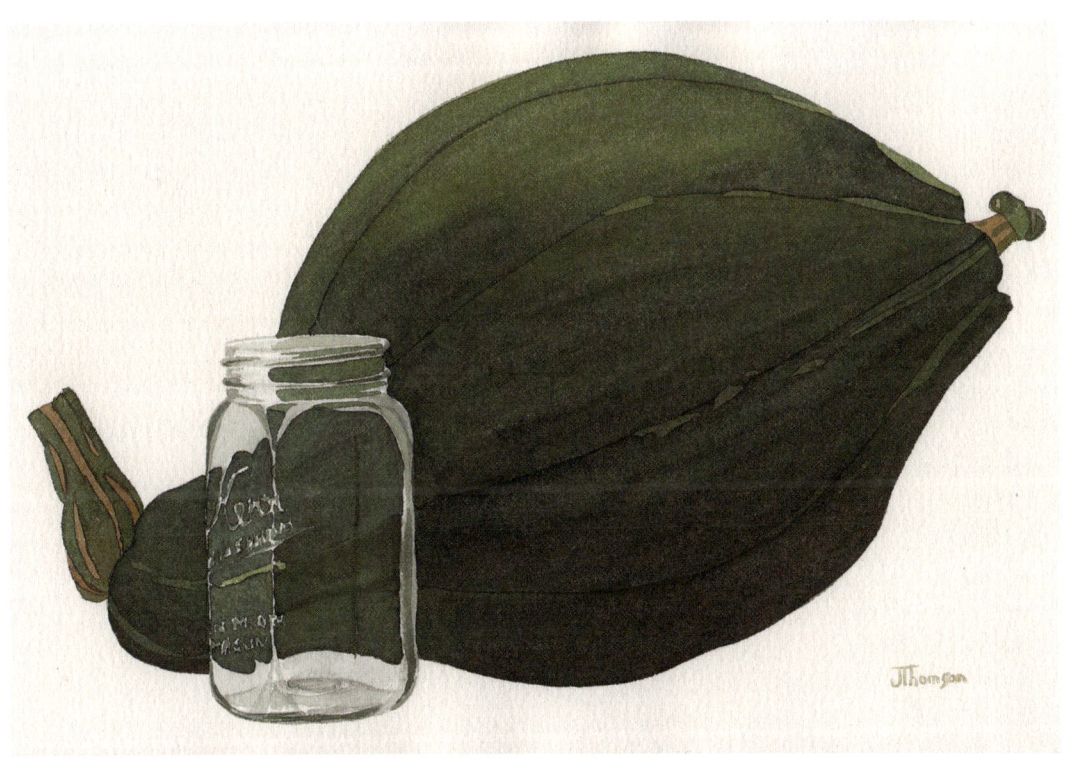

MASON JAR WITH   A wealth of winter squash!

HUBBARD SQUASH   A treasure for winter eating

2014   They ramble and climb and bloom and produce!

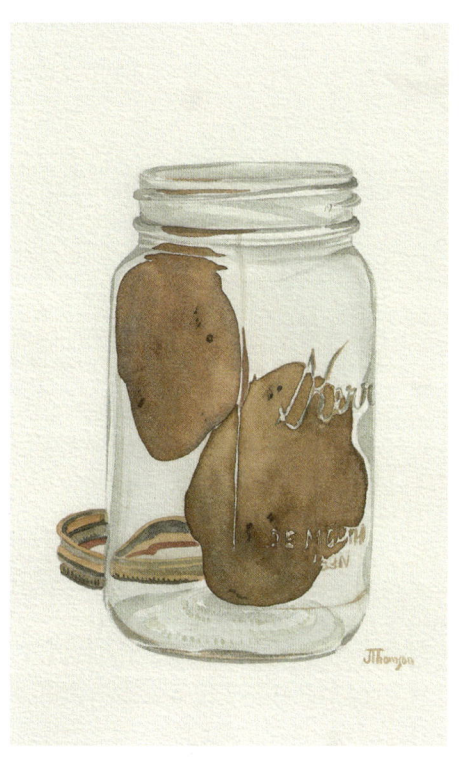
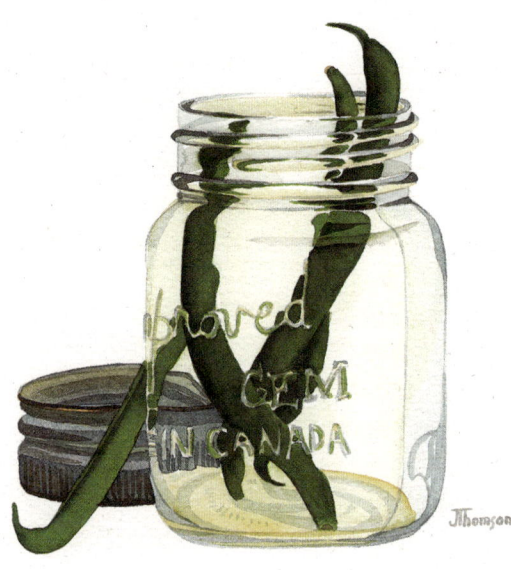

MASON JAR   Versatile potatoes
WITH POTATOES   Root cellar delegates
2014   Companions at breakfast,
Lunch and supper.

MASON JAR WITH   Dried in winter
GREEN BEANS   Fresh spring, summer, and fall
2014   Raw is best.

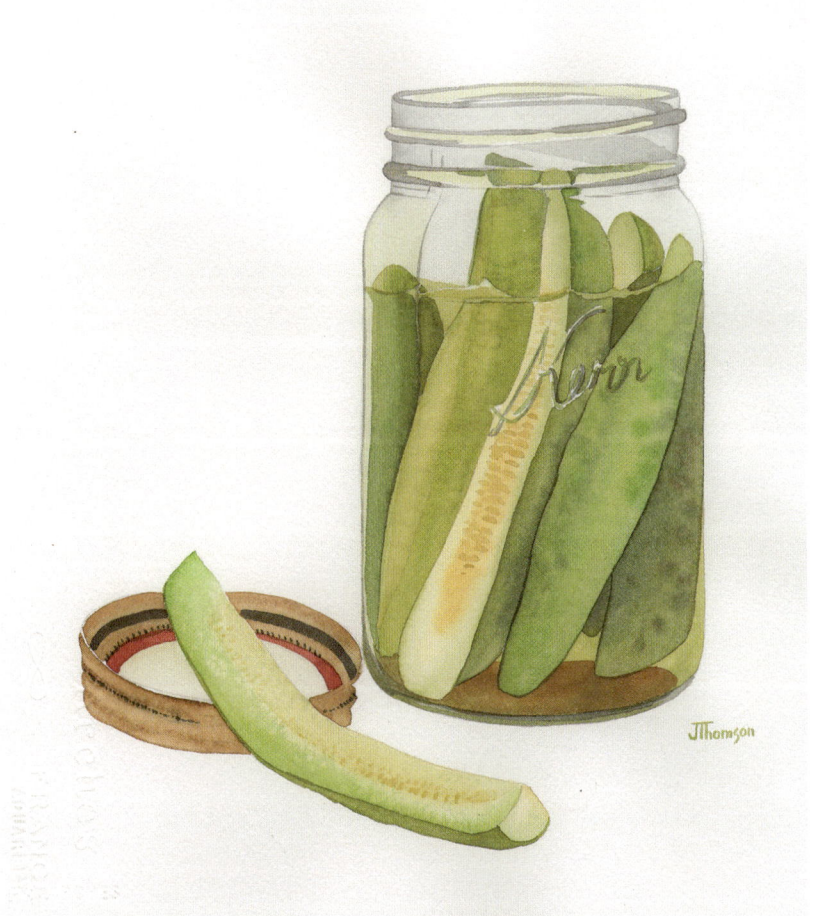

MASON JAR
WITH PICKLES
2014

Large simple pickles
Fingers of summer heat
Cooled in vinegar
Deceive the eater and
Bite the tongue.

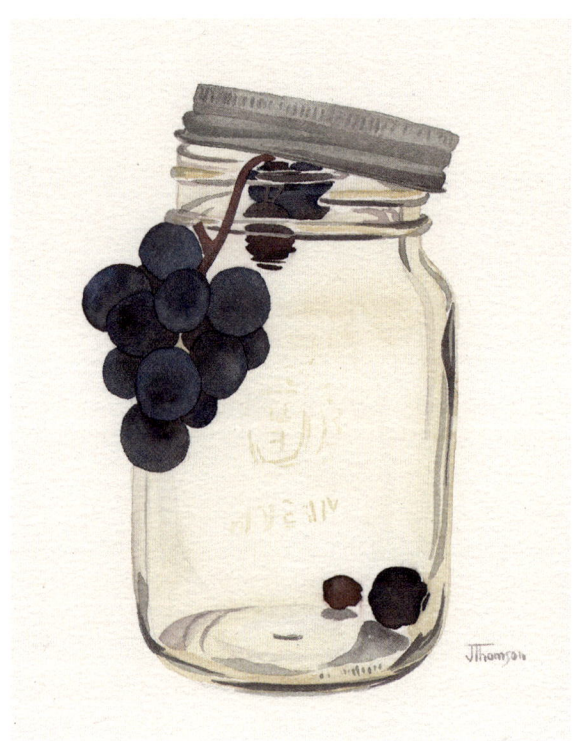
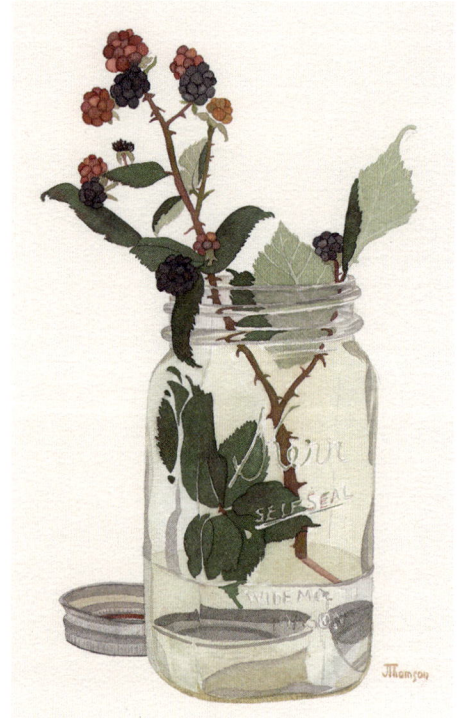

MASON JAR
WITH GRAPES
2014

The raccoons found too many
Left a few for me
They are quite delicious.
Juice, jelly, and jam.

MASON JAR WITH
BLACKBERRY FRUIT
AND LEAVES
2014

The offered bribes of brambles
Sun sweetened mouthfuls
Jam, crumble, and pie.

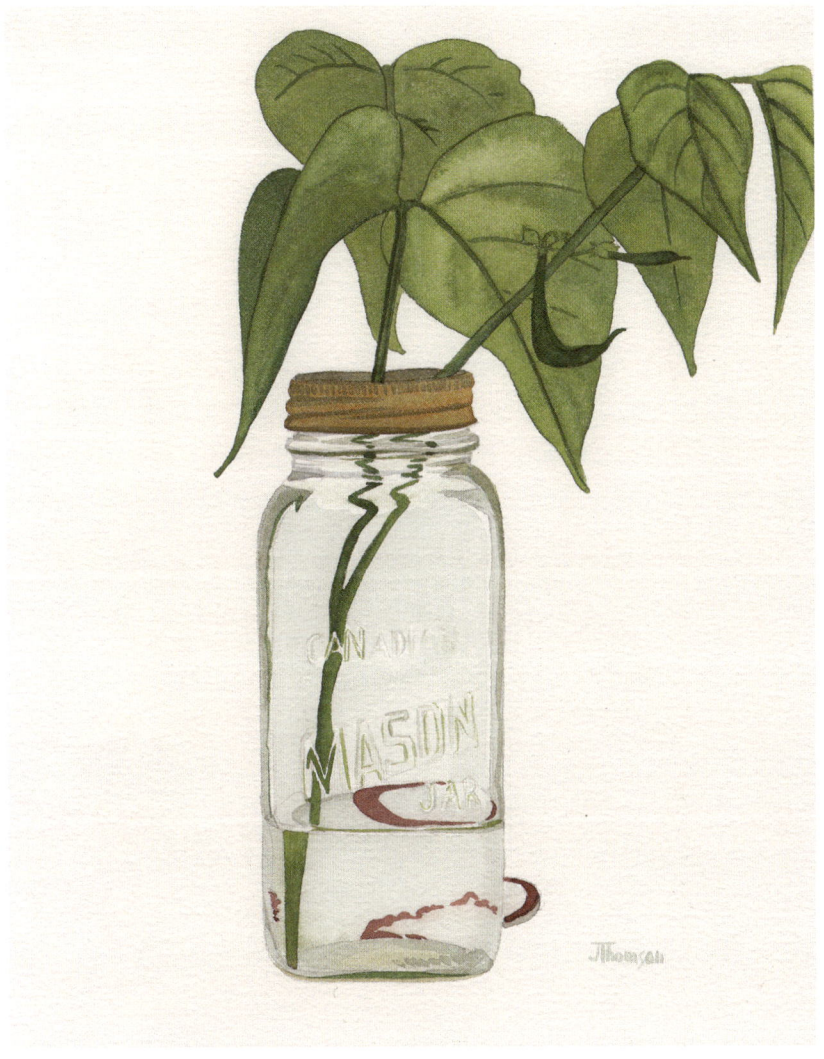

MASON JAR WITH
GREEN BEANS
AND LEAVES

2014

Second crop of beans
Hoping to fruit before the frost
Not all hopes are realized.

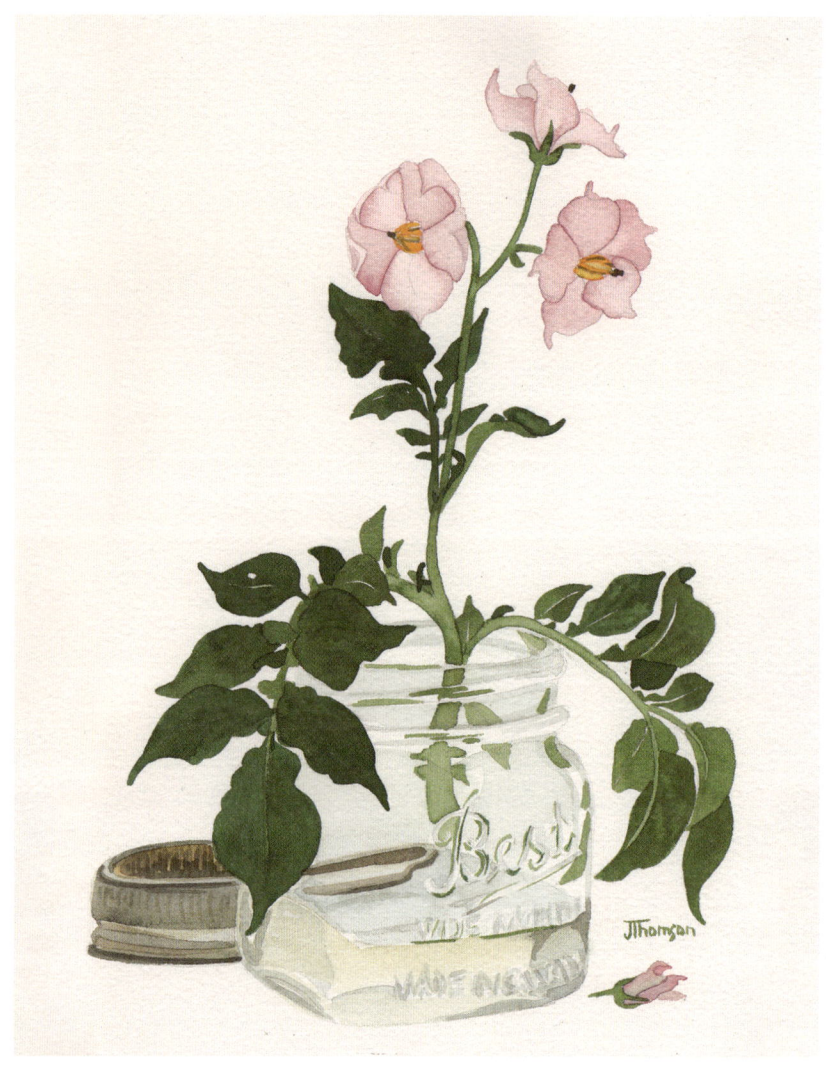

MASON JAR WITH Flowers pink, white and purple
POTATO FLOWER   Compete with green
2015   Over a promise of potatoes
                Boiled, fried, and mashed.

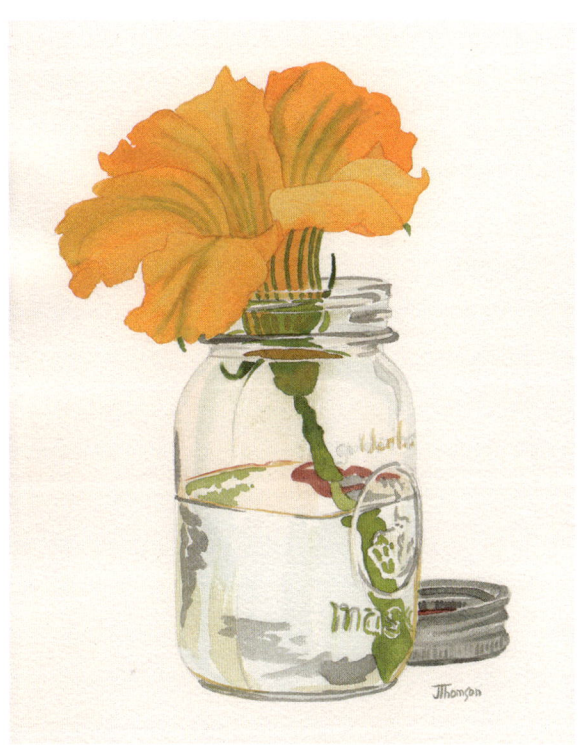
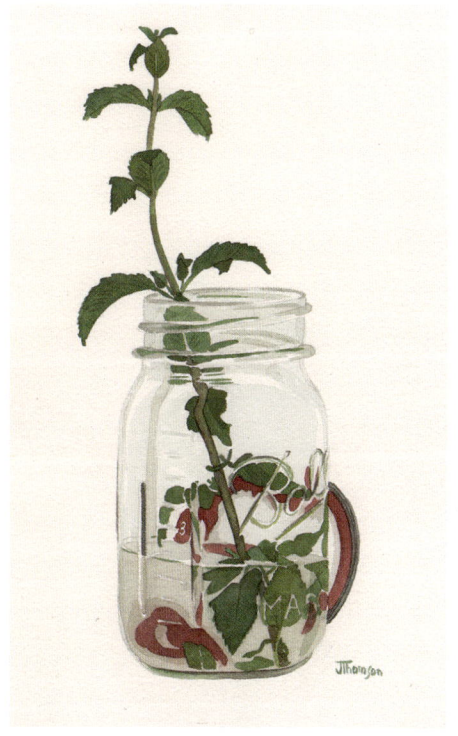

MASON JAR WITH	We are not alone as humans
LONELY MALE	To need male and female to create fruit
SQUASH FLOWER	Squash have bees to mediate
2015	We use letters and words.
MASON JAR	I moved the mint into the grass
WITH MINT	Now I walk through the scent of Christmas
2015	In summer heated air.

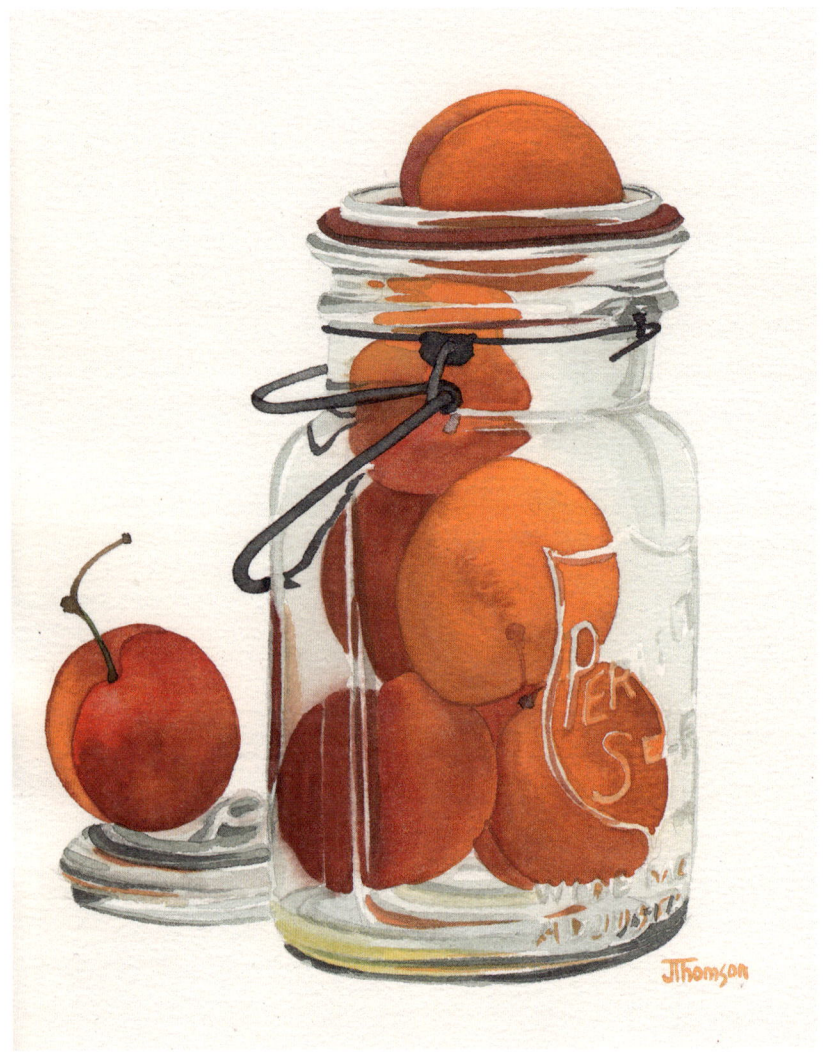

MASON JAR WITH
ORANGE PLUMS

2015

Waiting for my paintbrush
They ripen from yellow,
  to gold, to rich orange and red
Then meet their demise.

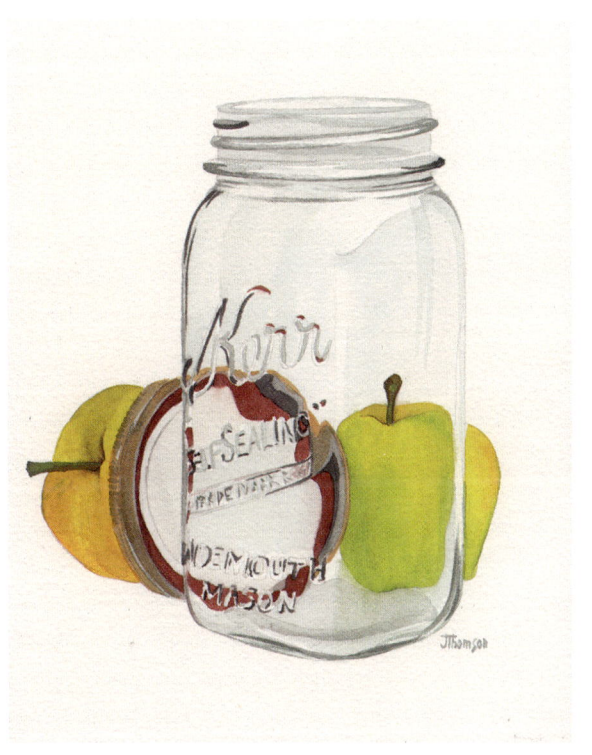

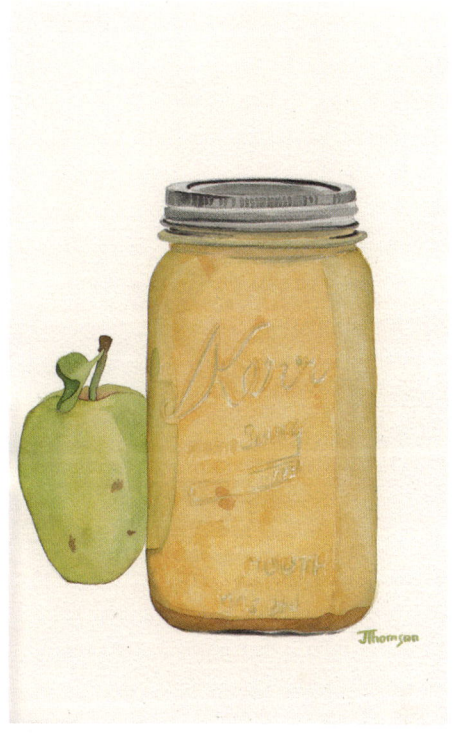

**MASON JAR WITH YELLOW
TRANSPARENT APPLES**

2015

Transparent apples
Transparent glass
But not completely
Some remain unseen.

**MASON JAR WITH
APPLES AND
APPLESAUCE**

2015

They melt into applesauce,
Only heat required,
Heat and jars and water,
And a little time.

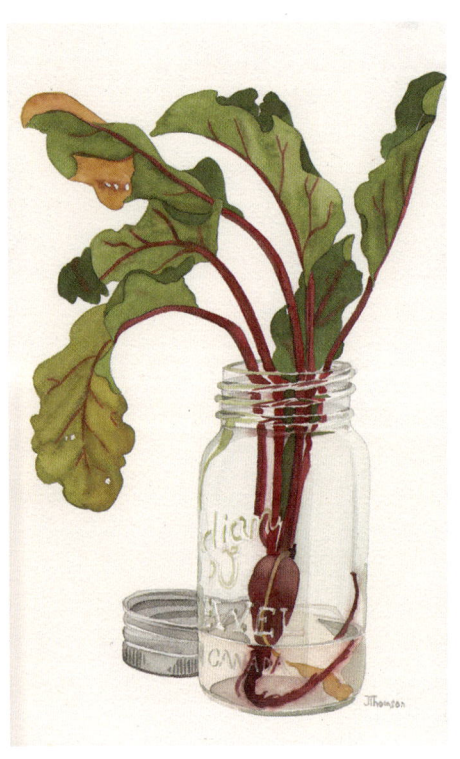

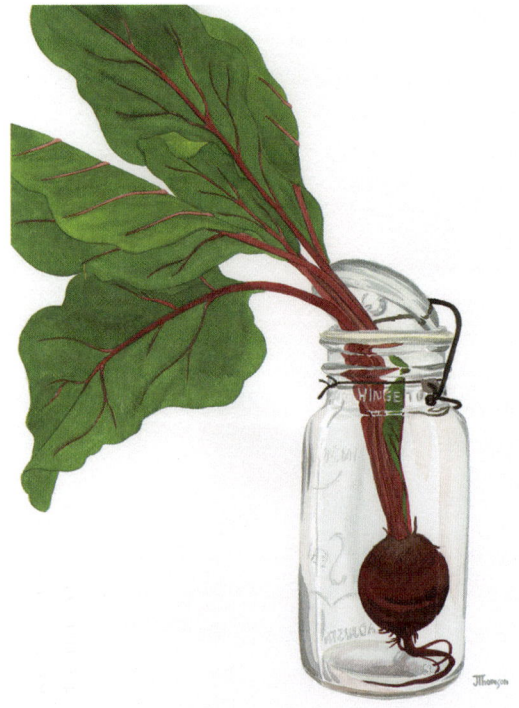

MASON JAR The rabbits are after my beets this year.

WITH BEET I wonder if their pee is red too.

2015

MASON JAR Sweet greens and flesh

WITH BEET Evoking the taste of autumn

2014 Soon to be pickled

For winter pleasure.

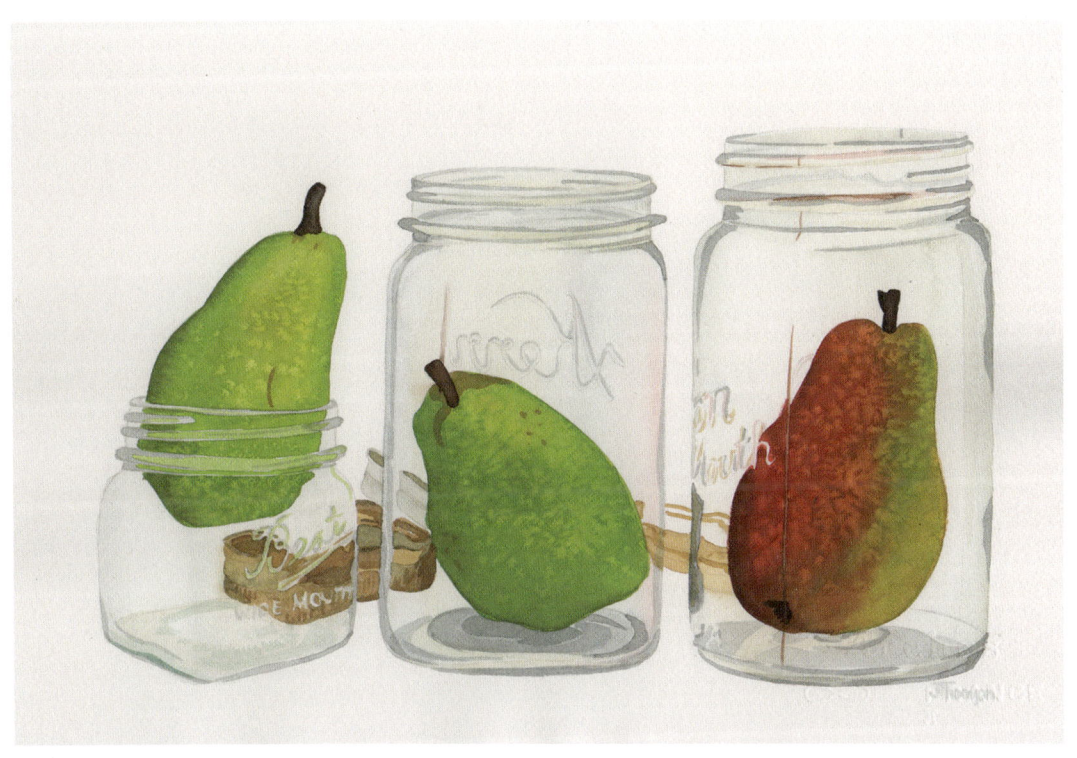

MASON JARS WITH   Such a warm year this was
SCHAU ANJOUS   Winter keepers fall from the trees
2015   To be preserved in jars.

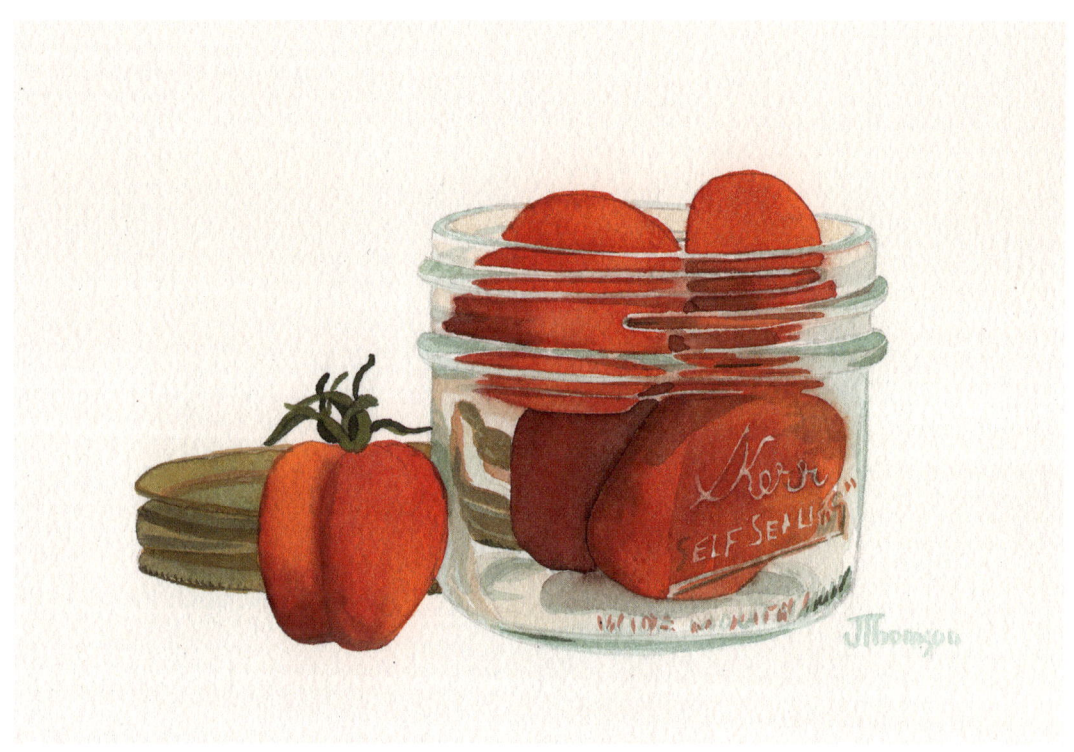

MASON JAR WITH   Surprising hybrid volunteers
SMALL TOMATOES   Part roma
2015   Part cherry
Beautifully disappointing.

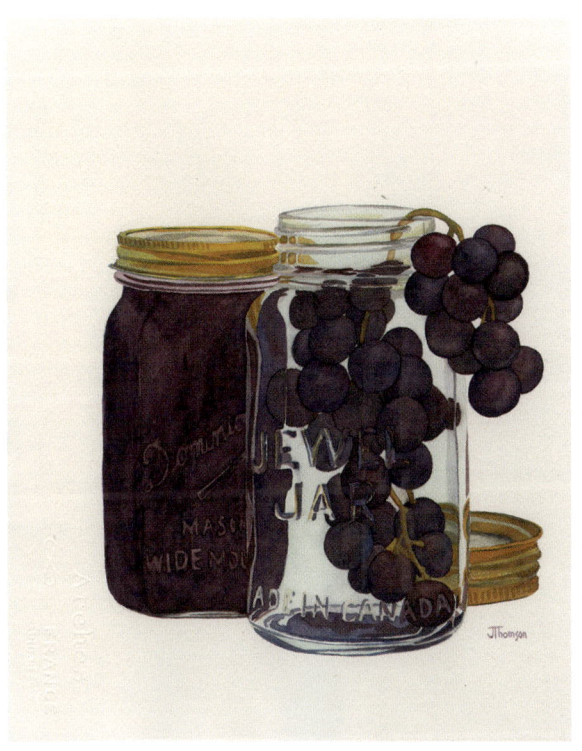
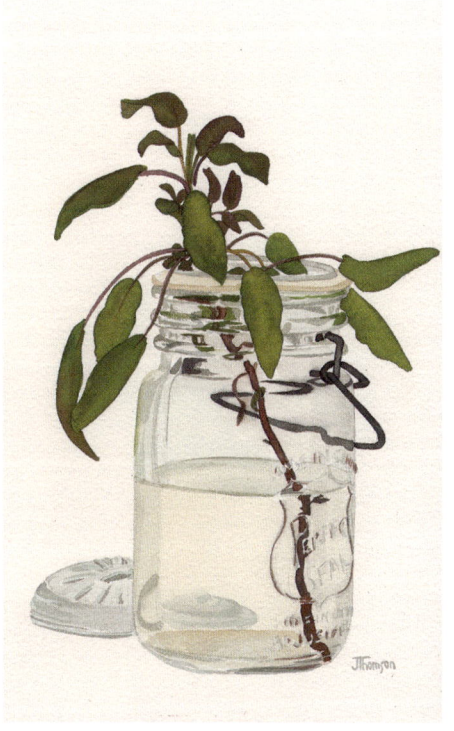

MASON JAR WITH
CONCORD GRAPES
AND JUICE

2015

Too many this year for the raccoons to consume
Troubling me with abundance
Time being less so.

MASON JAR
WITH SAGE

2015

White woman's healing herb
Rub it
Air-wash yourself
In fragrance.

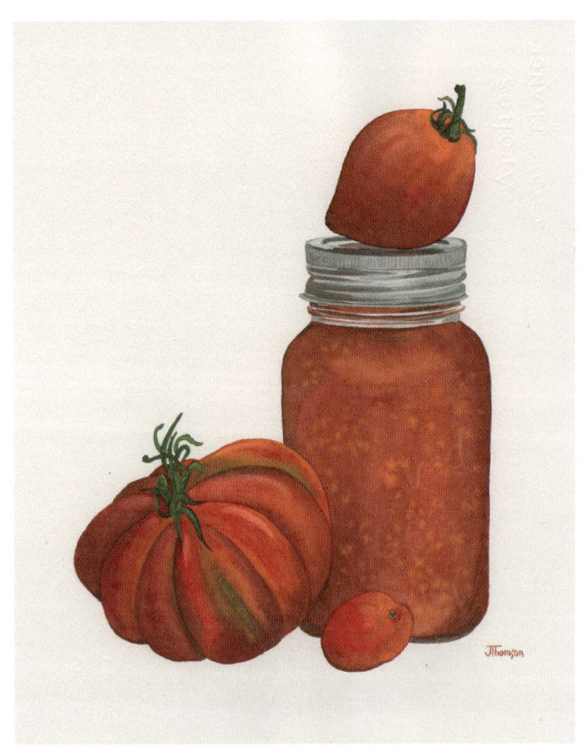
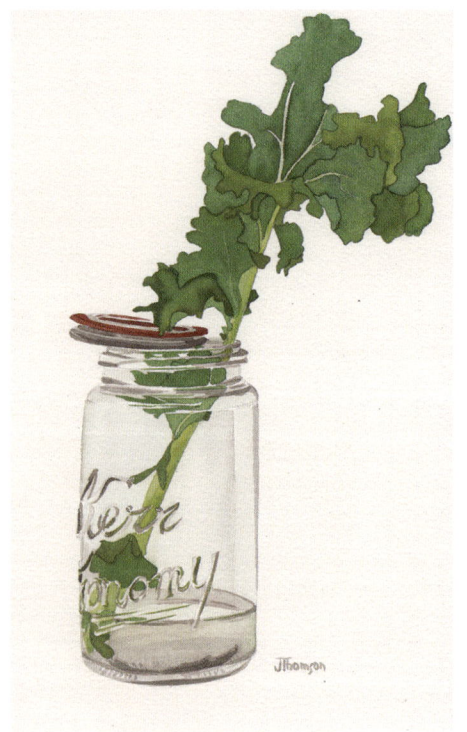

MASON JAR WITH
BEEFSTEAK TOMATO AND
CANNED TOMATOES

2015

Glass and zinc and rubber rings.
Saved seeds and free plants
Who can ask for more?

MASON JAR
WITH KALE
2015

An old food renewed
A fad
A fashion
Prepared in ways old claimed new.

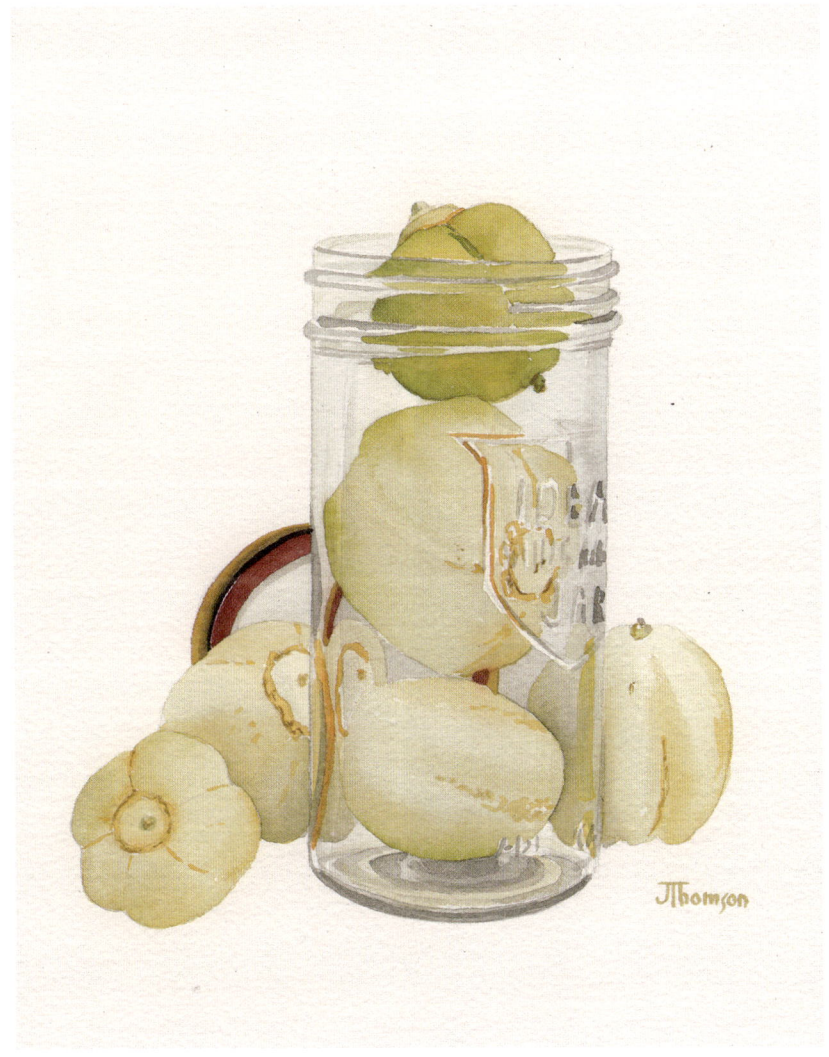

MASON JAR WITH
LEMON CUCUMBERS
2015

Delicious to look at
Bitter to the tongue
They are greedy for heat
Yet clouds block the sun.

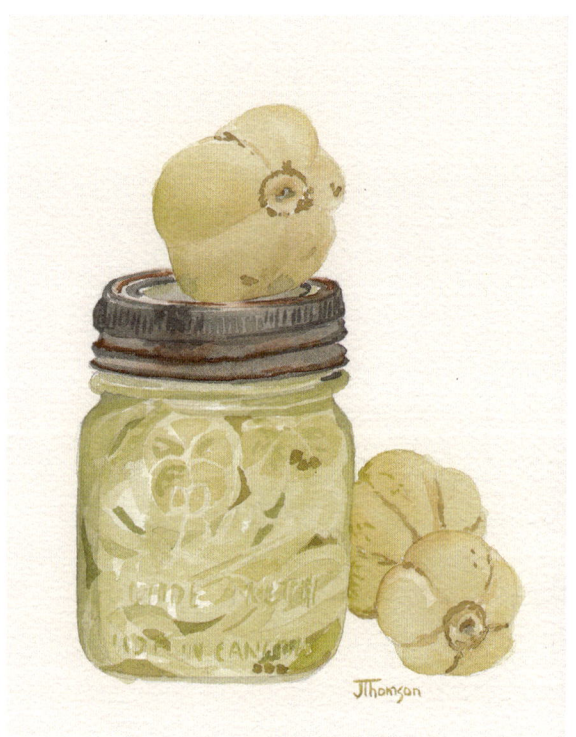

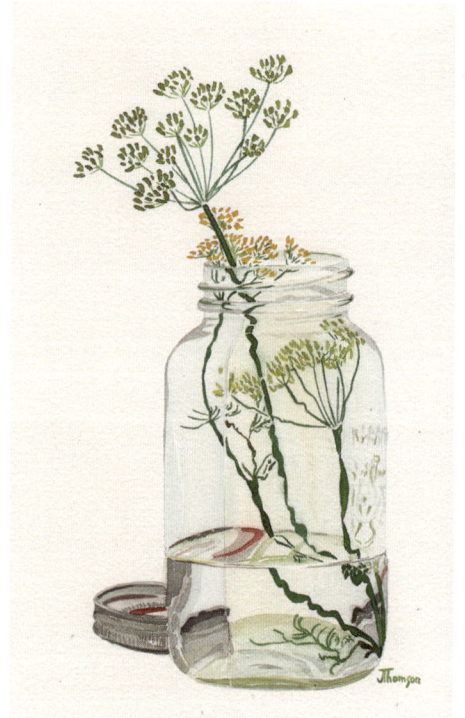

MASON JAR WITH   Vinegar and sugar,

PICKLED LEMON   Some spice and onion too,

CUCUMBERS   In winter they remind us of

2015   What summer couldn't do.

MASON JAR   I plant this weed

WITH DILLWEED   To bring memories to my garden

2015   Its fragrance keeps them fresh.

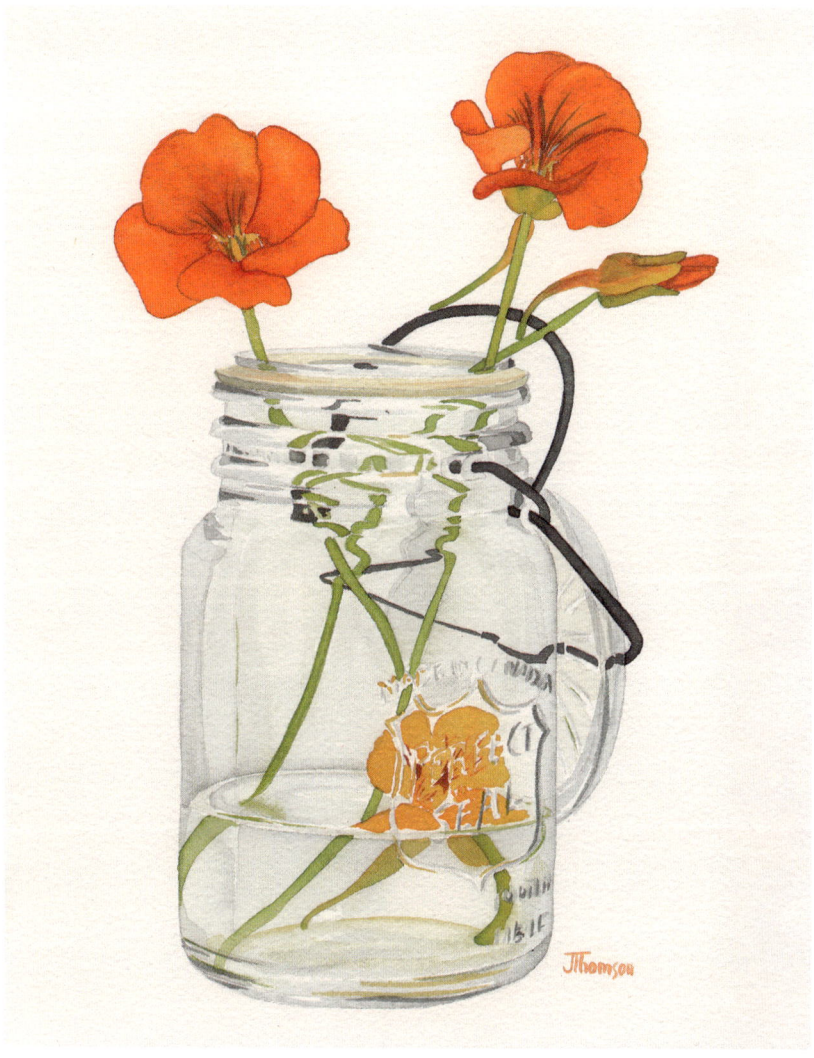

MASON JAR WITH
NASTURTIUM
2015

As winter approaches the nasturtiums march
Claiming the garden
Careless vines climbing
Without knowledge of the coming frost.

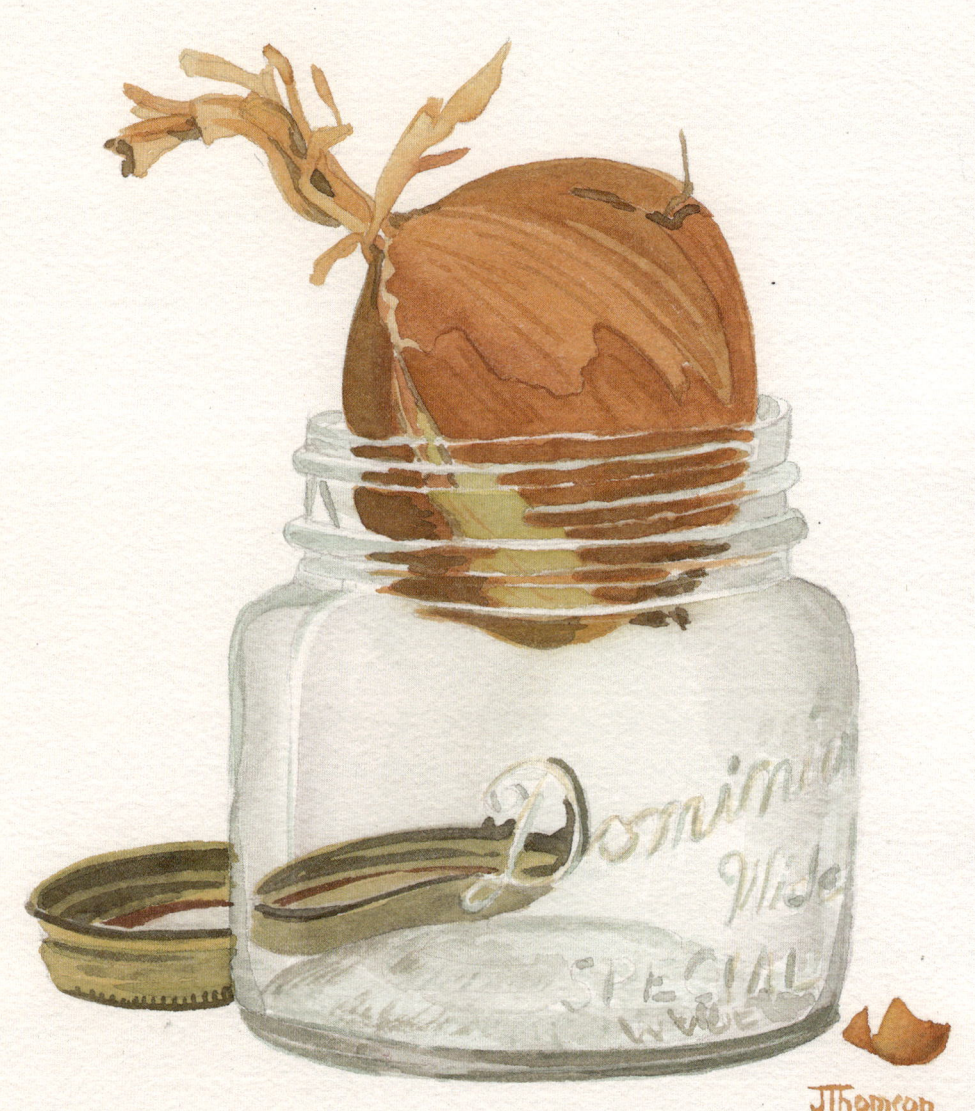

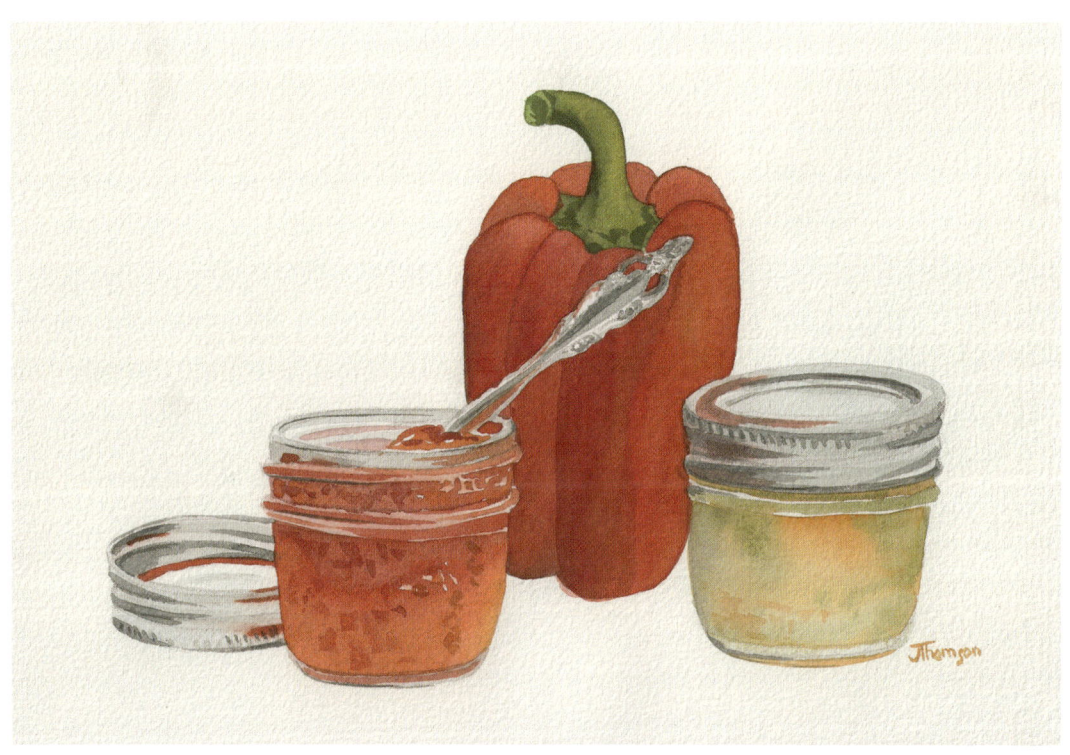

MASON JAR
WITH ONION
2015

Fried with potatoes, tomatoes, and ham
Stewed with beef and bay leaf
Royalty of the root cellar
Enriches food in all seasons.

MASON JARS WITH
PEPPER JELLY
2024

Pepper jelly Christmas giving
Another generation embraces
The making and gifting of
Edible beauty.

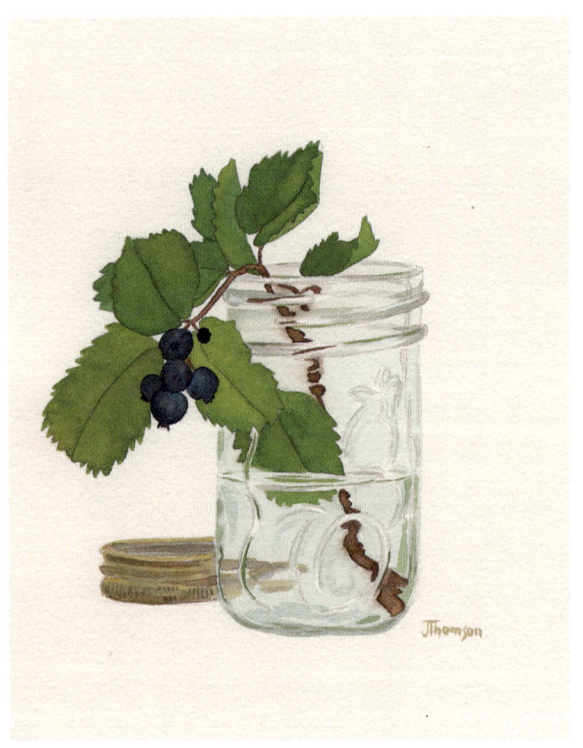 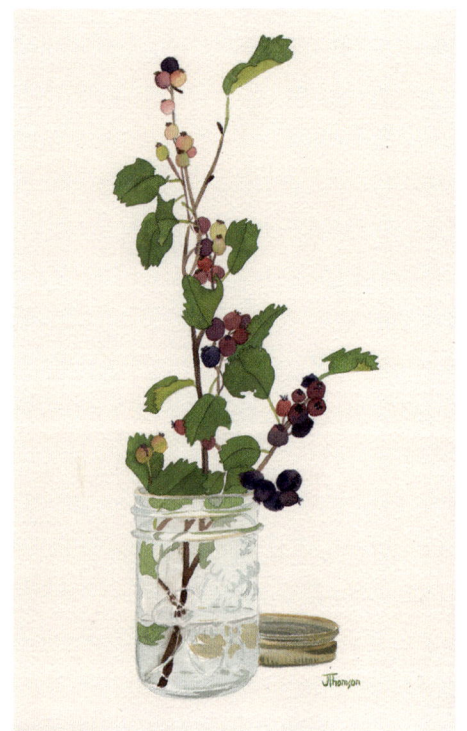

MASON JAR WITH
SMALL SASKATOONS
2016

On an island
Plump berries rest
In the shade of pines
Listening to the river.

MASON JAR WITH
SASKATOON BRANCH
2016

On the road side
They reach up and away
Pithy and tart
Well populated with caterpillars.

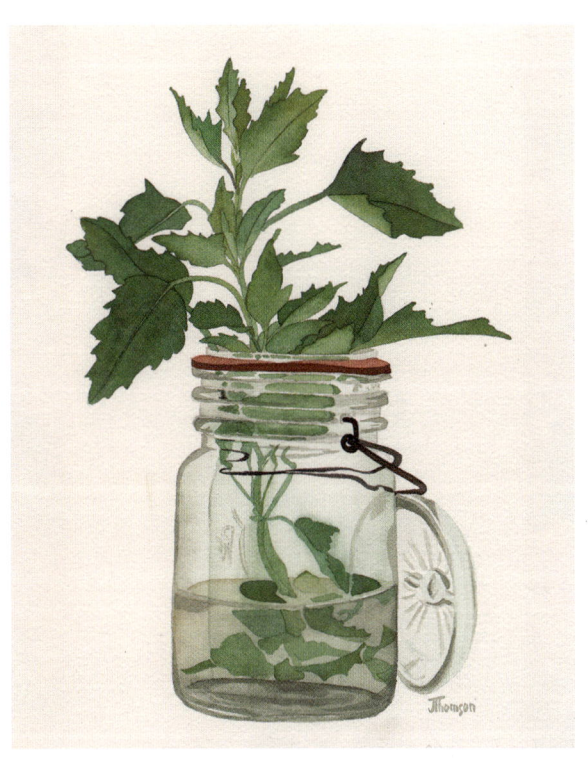 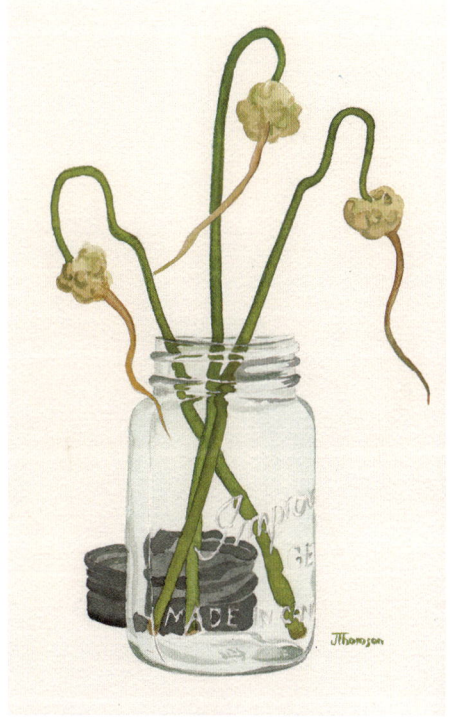

MASON JAR WITH
LAMB'S QUARTERS
2016

Tasty volunteers
Friends of pioneers
Encouraged in their opportunism
Foraged for salads.

MASON JAR WITH
GARLIC SCAPES
2016

The bloom bears fruit
Becoming next year's harvest.

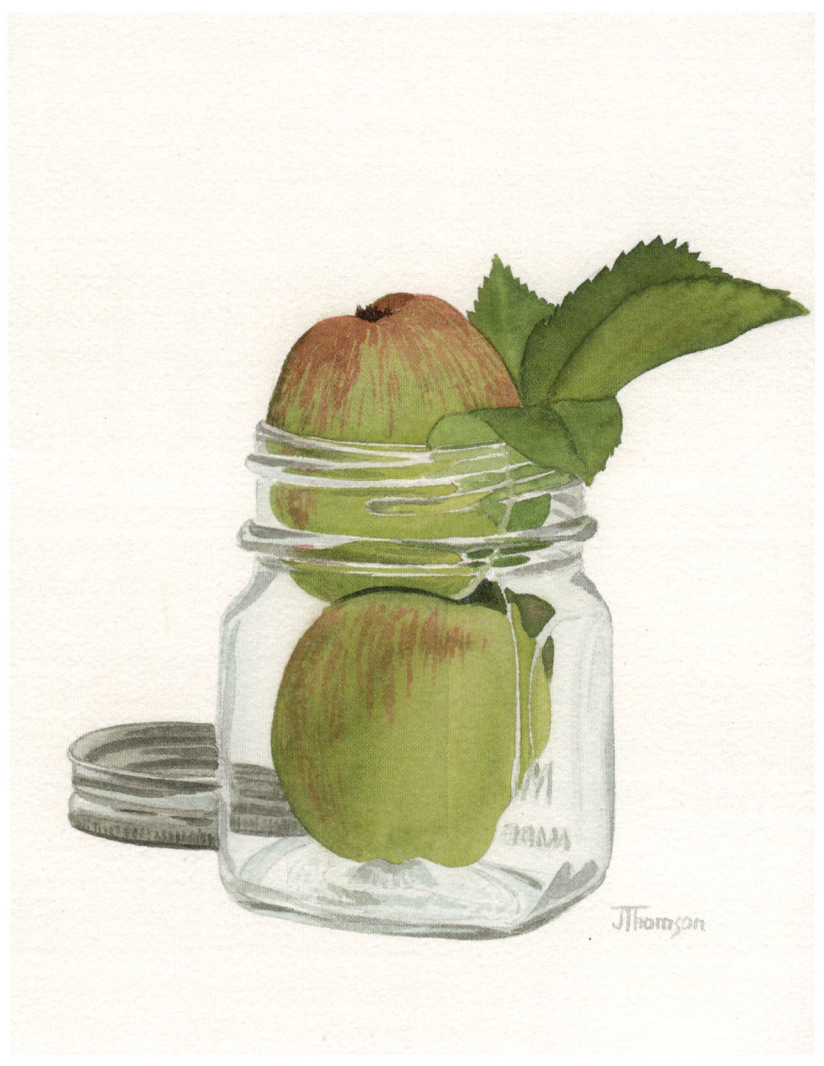

MASON JAR WITH
GREEN APPLES
2016

Branches overladen
Snap and release the artist's models
Too young for use.

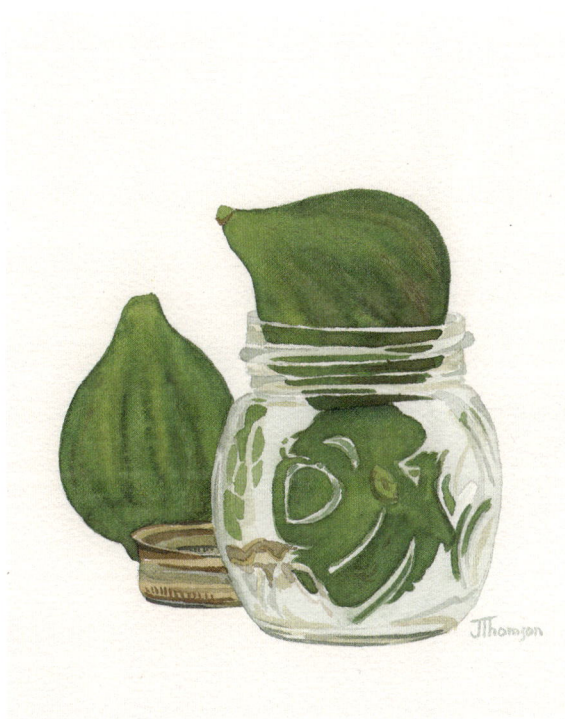 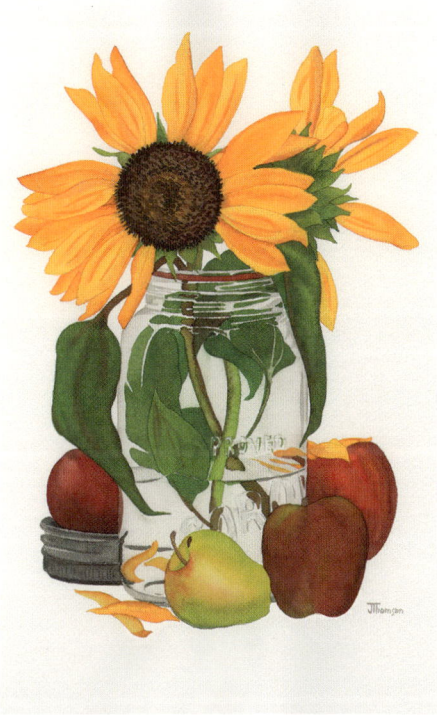

MASON JAR   A season of sweet delights
WITH FIGS   Figs fresh from the branch
2016   Abundant in the heat of July.

MASON JAR WITH   Fruits enjoyed by
SUNFLOWERS   Deer and red-winged blackbirds
AND APPLES   So good to have plenty.
2016

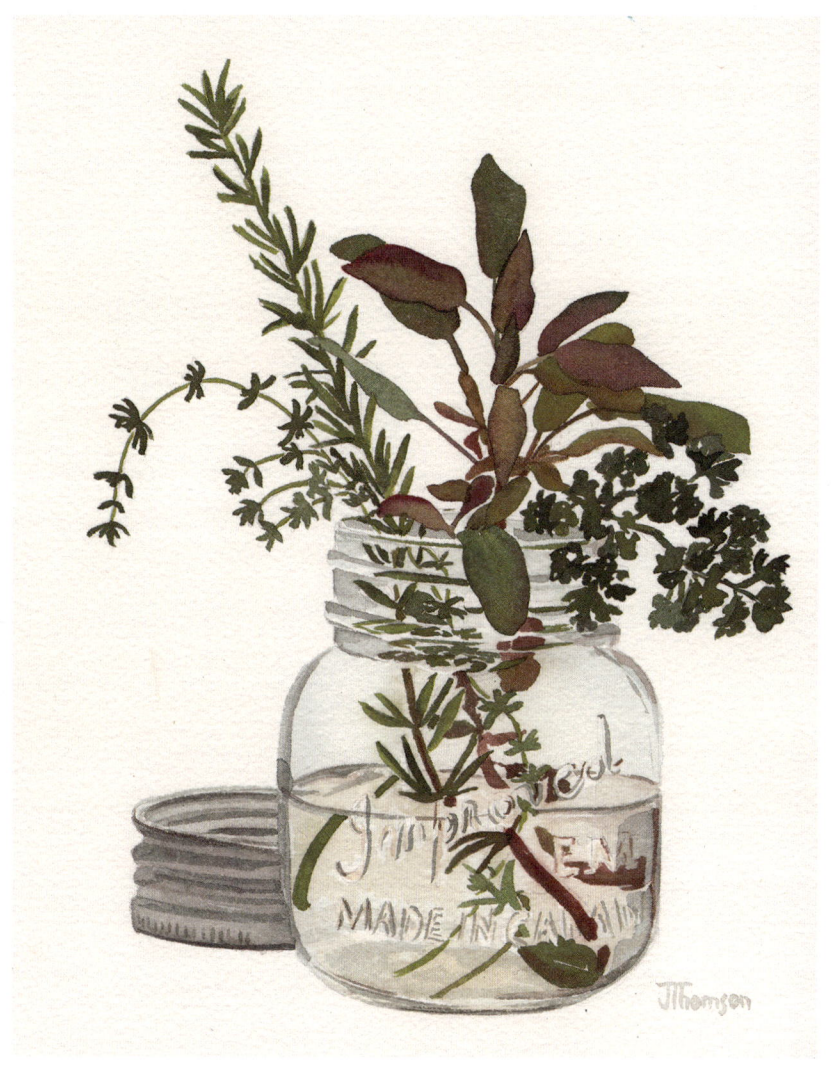

**MASON JAR WITH
PARSLEY, SAGE,
ROSEMARY, AND THYME**

2016

Have you been to Scarborough Fair
Around campfires singing
Imagining lost loves?

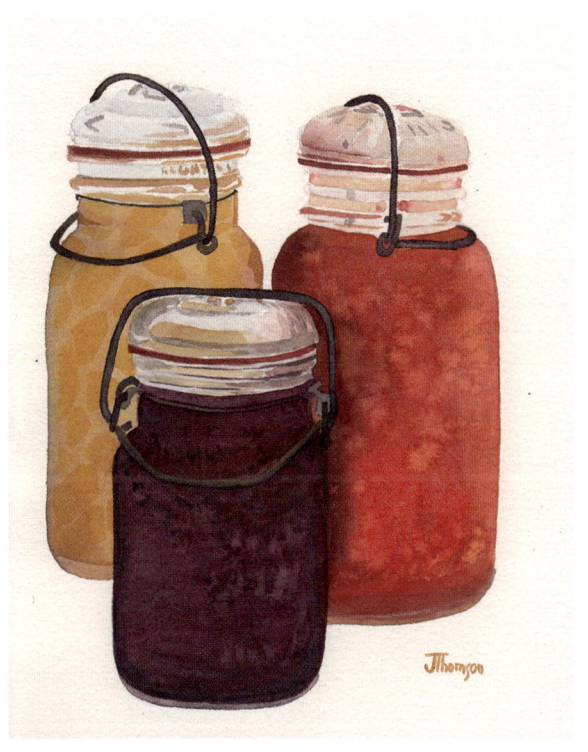

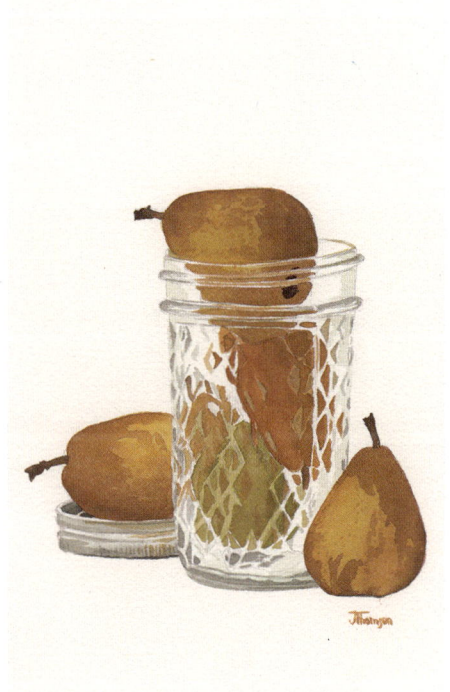

MASON JARS WITH CANNED
PEARS, CANNED TOMATOES
AND BLACKBERRY JAM
2016

Harvest trio
Heritage glass
An imitation created without wood,
Sealed on an electric range.

MASON JAR WITH
CONFERENCE PEARS
2016

Honey in a skin
Small packets reward patience.

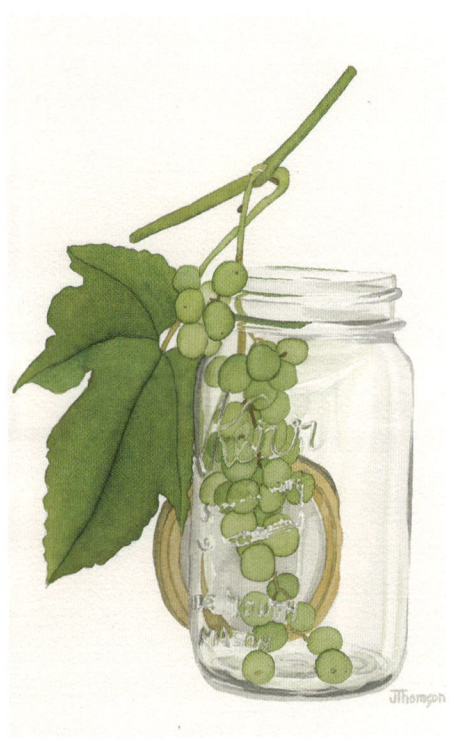

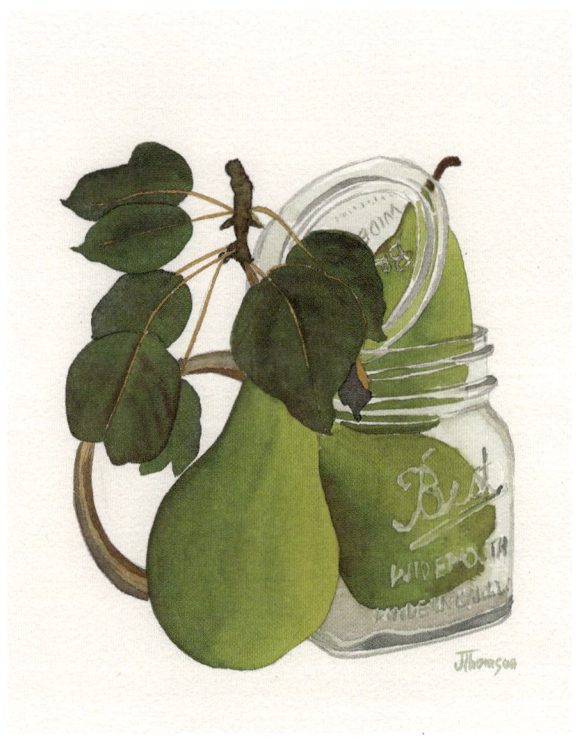

MASON JAR WITH
GREEN GRAPES
2016

They drop on the unsuspecting
And reward the daring
With transient sticky sweetness.

MASON JAR WITH
WINTER PEARS
2016

A laden tree
A gift of fruit
Awaiting January for enjoyment.

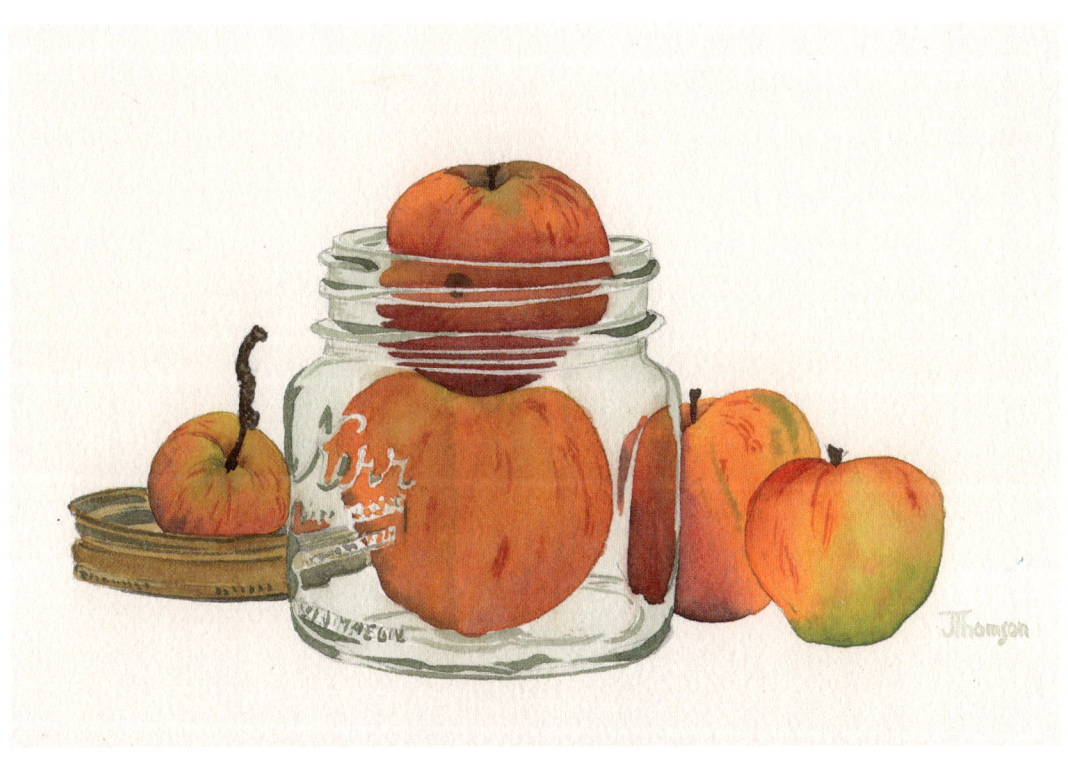

MASON JAR WITH
SMALL APPLES
2016

A ladder and a basket,
A bounty of small sweet fruit
Winter keepers for winter nights.

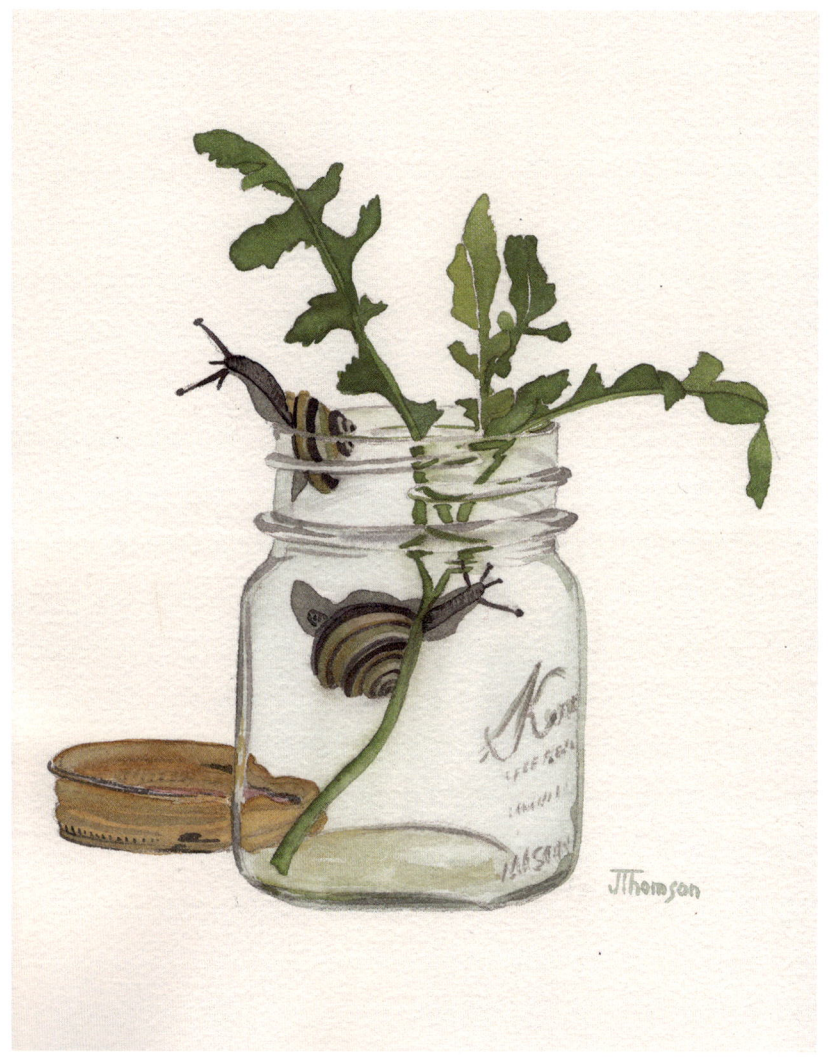

MASON JAR
WITH ARUGULA
AND SNAILS

2016

Children leave home
Sometimes encouraged by a
Peppery environment.

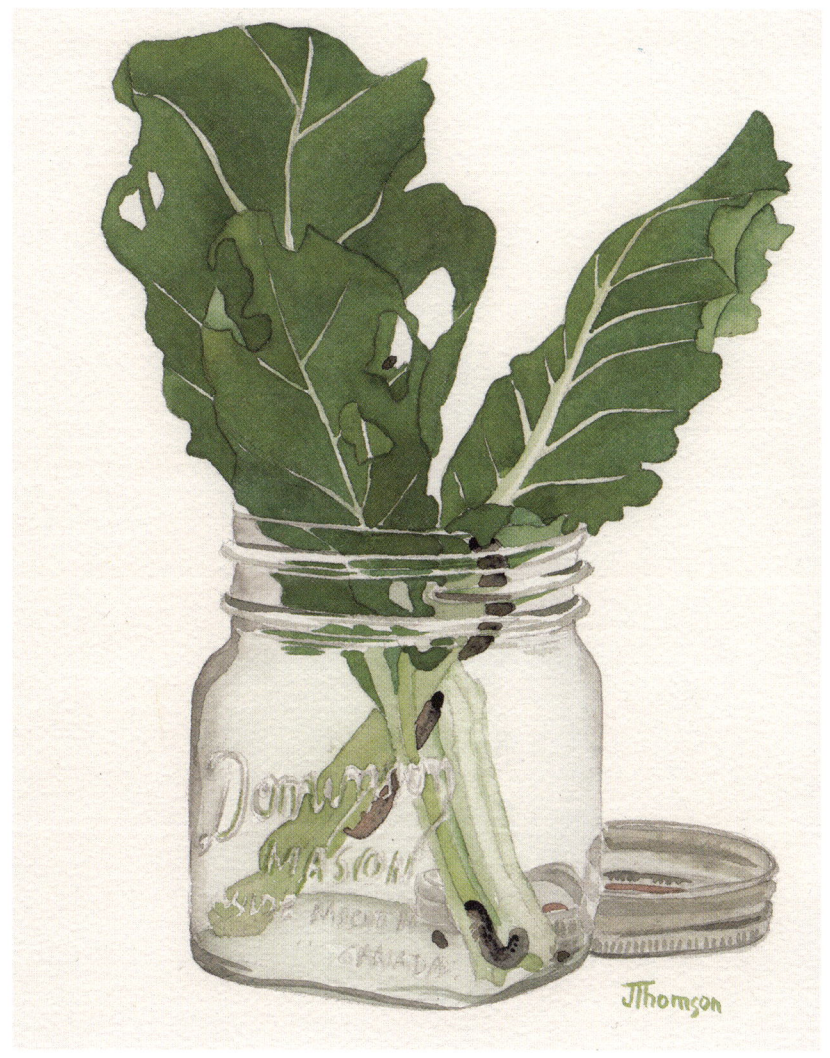

MASON JAR WITH
CHARD AND
THREE GRUBS

2016

A late harvest of spotty chard
Made lacey by grubs
Sometimes I tire of sharing.

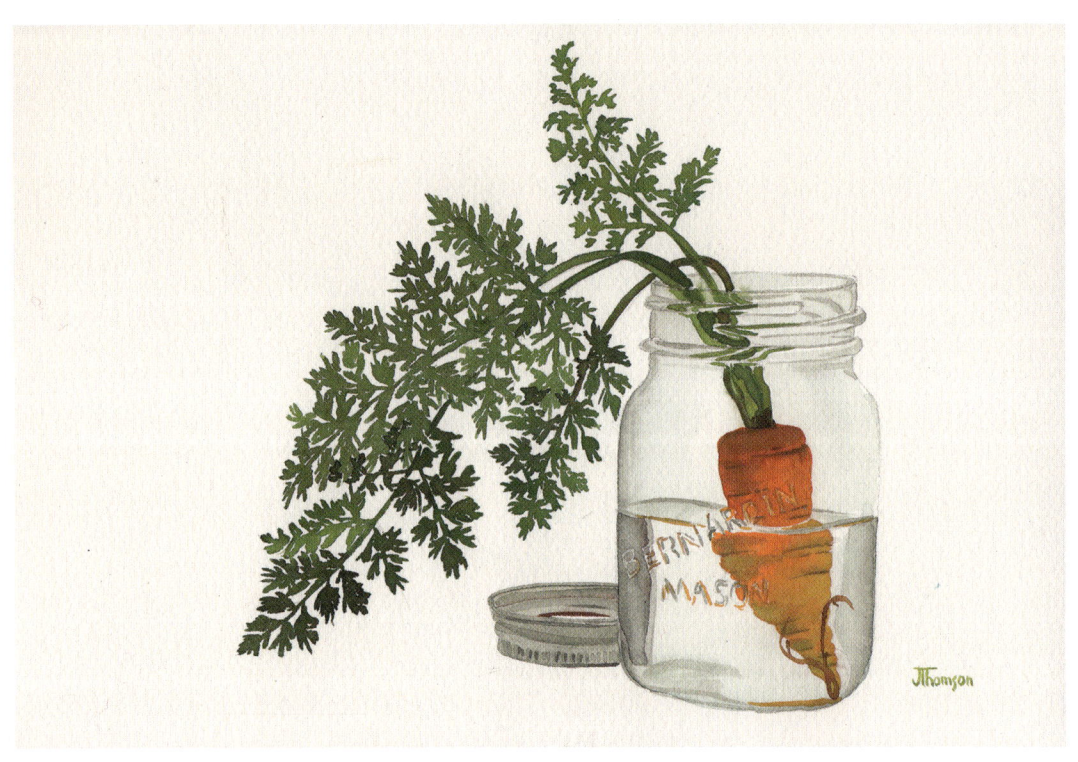

MASON JAR WITH
LAST CARROT OF
THE SEASON
2016

Carrots are difficult here
Flies and worms and wet
Deer and rabbits and mice
This is my share of the crop.

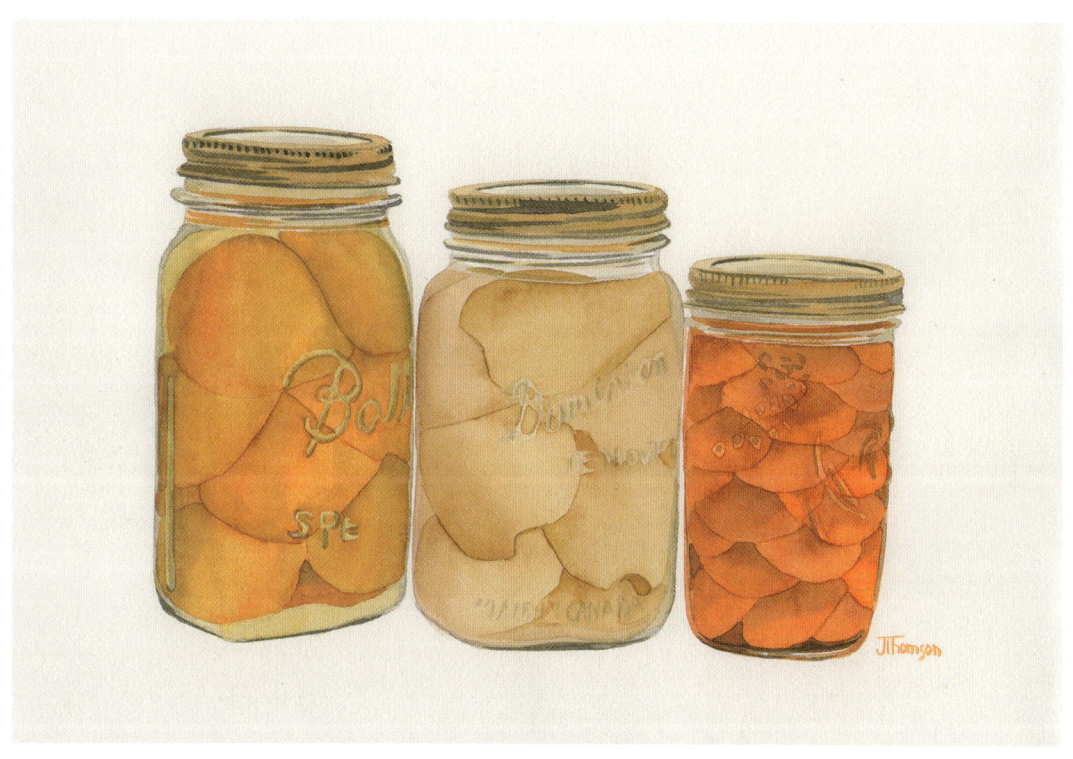

MASON JARS WITH
PEACHES, PEARS
AND APRICOTS

2017

The wealth of our lives
Remembered
Summer in jars on the table.

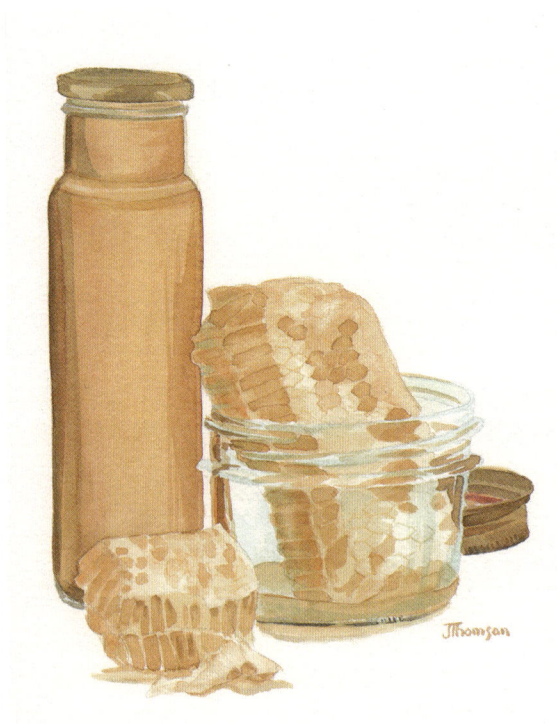

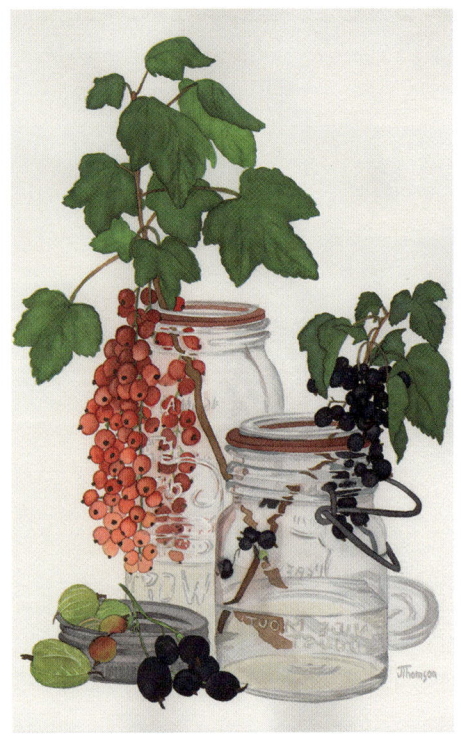

MASON JAR WITH
HONEY AND
HONEYCOMB
2017

All summer they labour
So we may have honey
To sweeten our brandy
When winter arrives

MASON JAR WITH
RED AND BLACK
CURRANTS
2017

Under a shade tree
On a hot summer day
Currant cordial and good company
Nothing is finer.

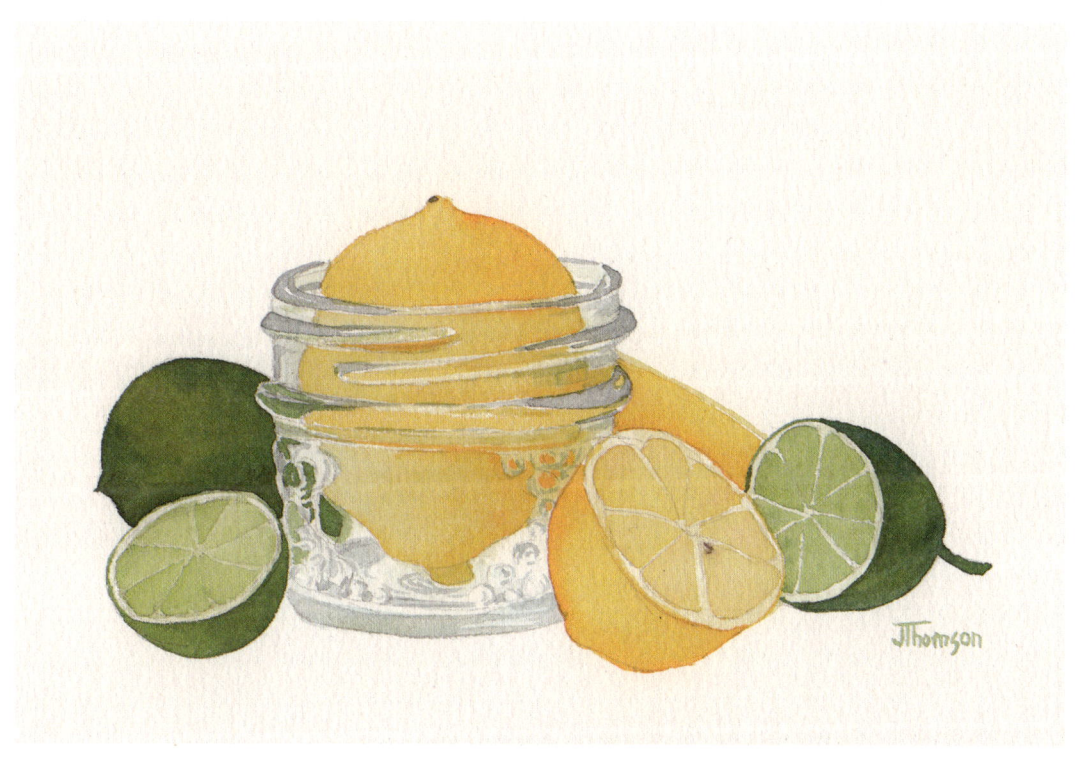

MASON JAR WITH
LIMES AND LEMONS
2017

Small fruit from the island
Our island
In a greenhouse over winter
Such wealth.

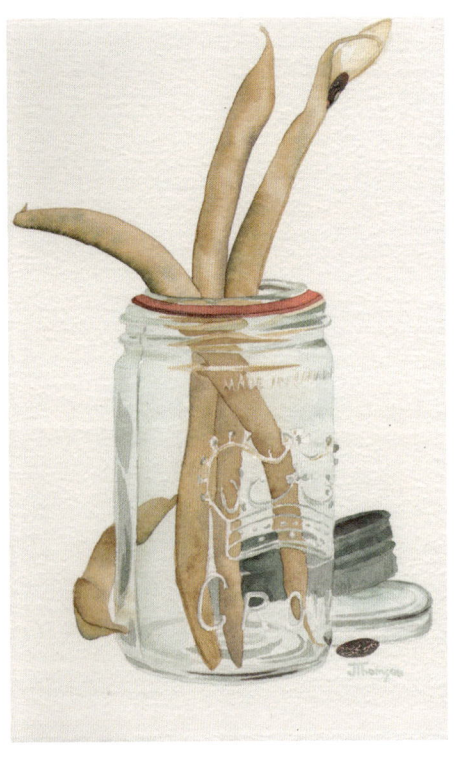
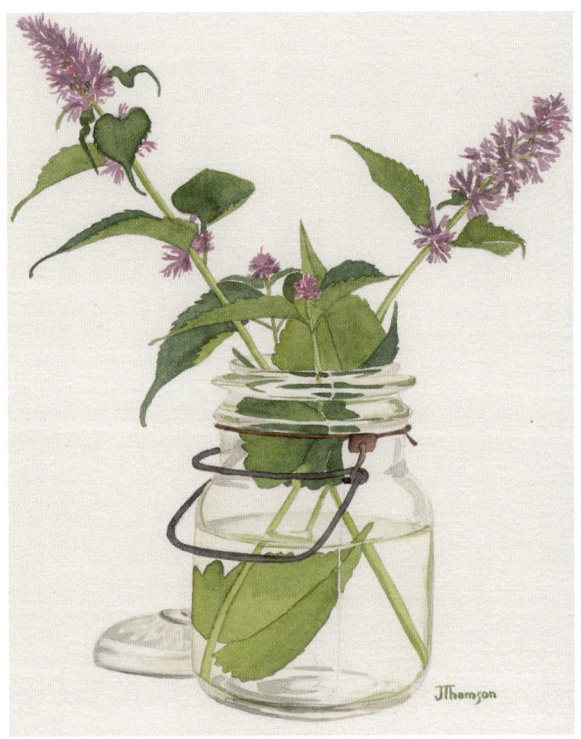

MASON JAR　　Not all the beans
WITH SCARLET　　Make soup and stew
RUNNER BEANS　　Some are saved as seed
2023　　For next year's crop.

MASON JAR WITH　　Brushing past
LICORICE MINT　　I always smile
2019　　A burst of licorice scented air.
　　Hummingbirds love them.

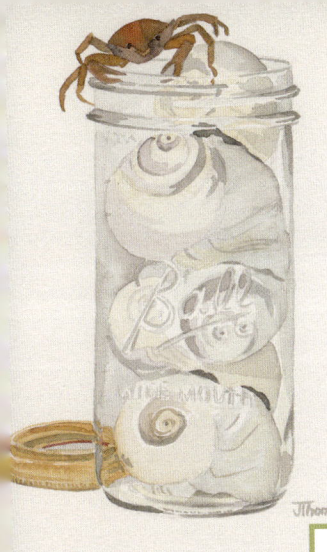
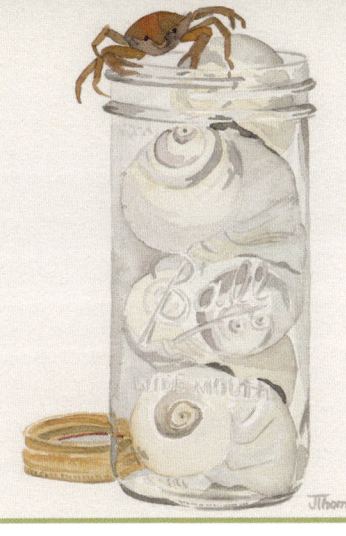
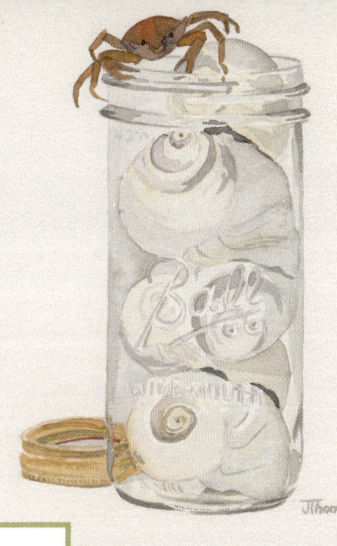
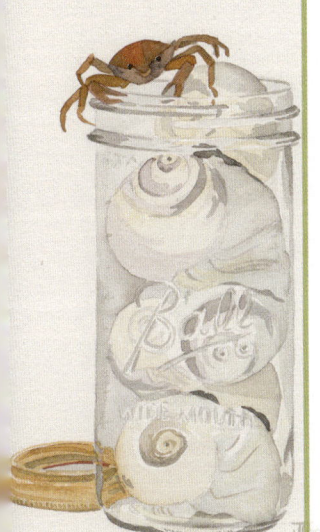
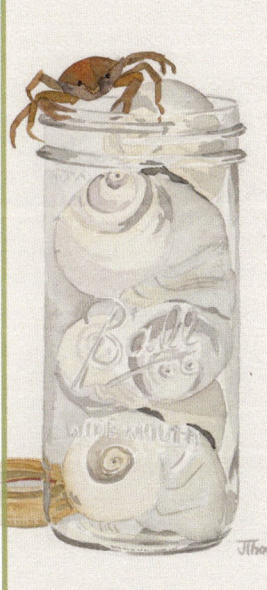
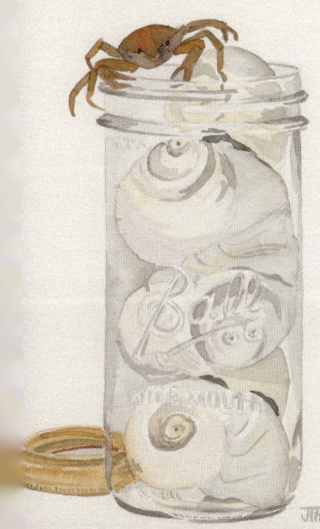
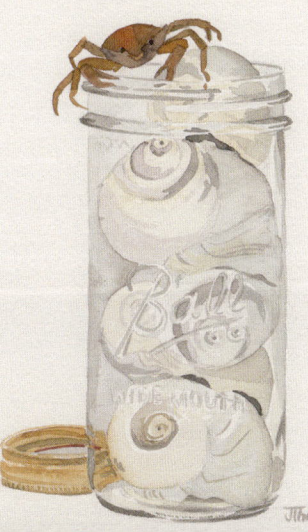
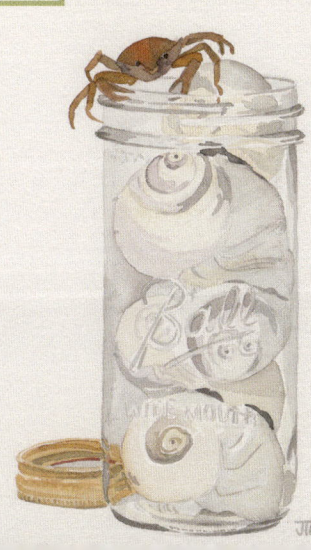

4

RENEWAL
AND HOPE

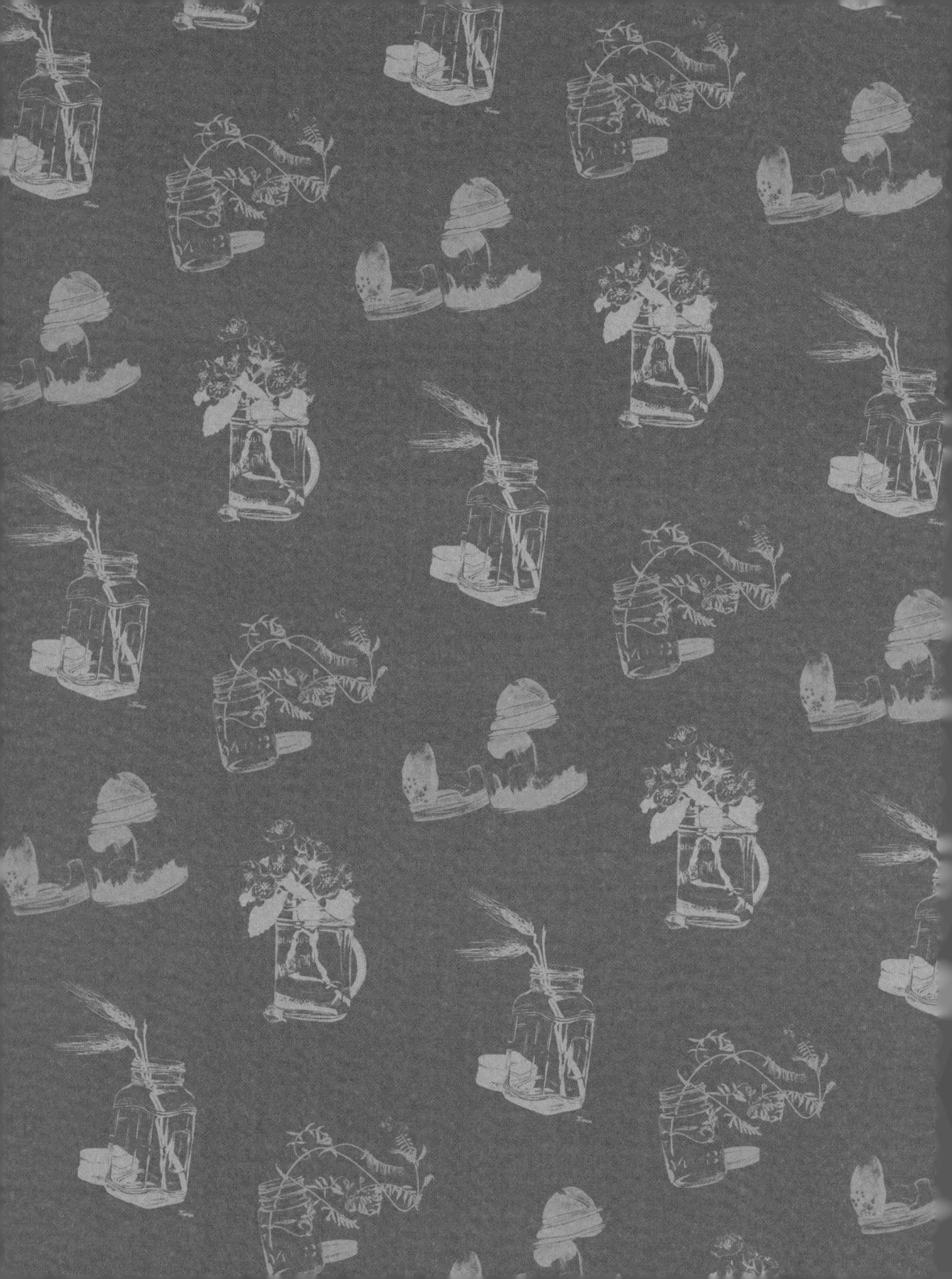

WERNER LOVED the land and the life on it. He passed this love on to his children, and they passed it on to theirs. He was a sustainable logger before it was called that. My mother encouraged my fascination with wild plants and wild places. I was allowed to wander and collect plants, pressing them in old telephone books and mounting them in scrap books. In painting these moments of hope and renewal, I was struck by the way glass and water distort. I spent hours pondering the realization that beauty is not constant. It moves from the original, creating insights into resilience. In setting up the still lifes for these works, I played with these variations, experimenting with the jars and objects to create distortions that supported the narrative I was creating. I hope you will also find renewal in these images and discover a new way to connect with beauty.

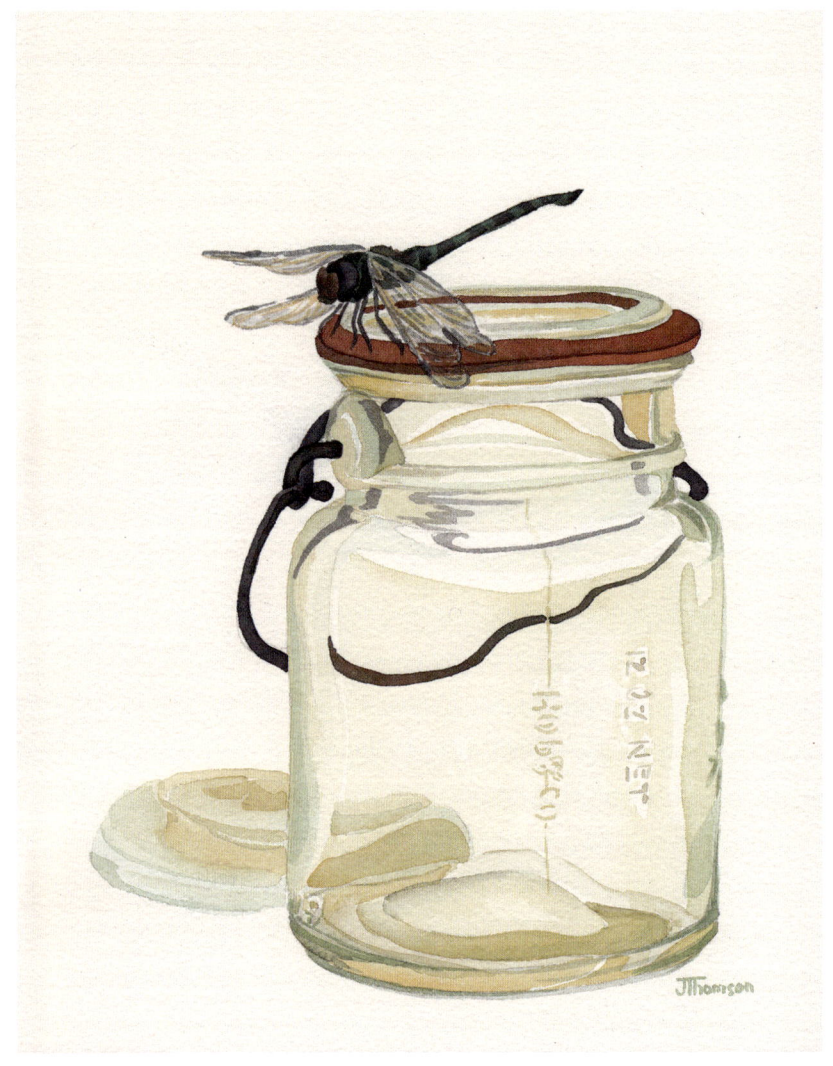

MASON JAR WITH
DRAGONFLY
2014

If wishes could be retroactive
I'd wish my Mother's childhood
To have more dragonflies to eat insects.

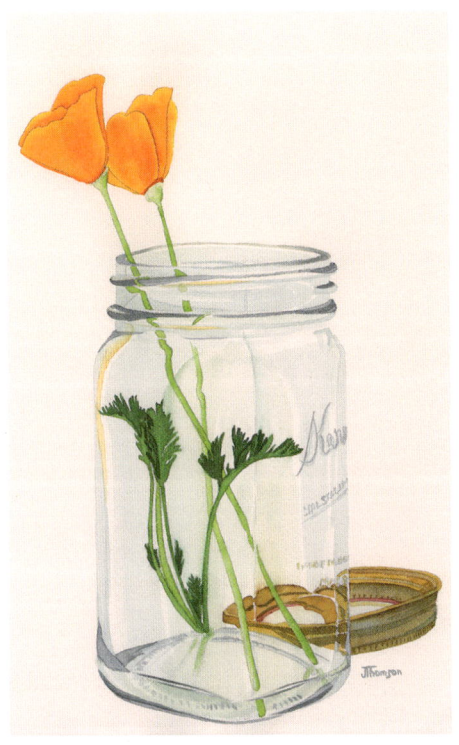

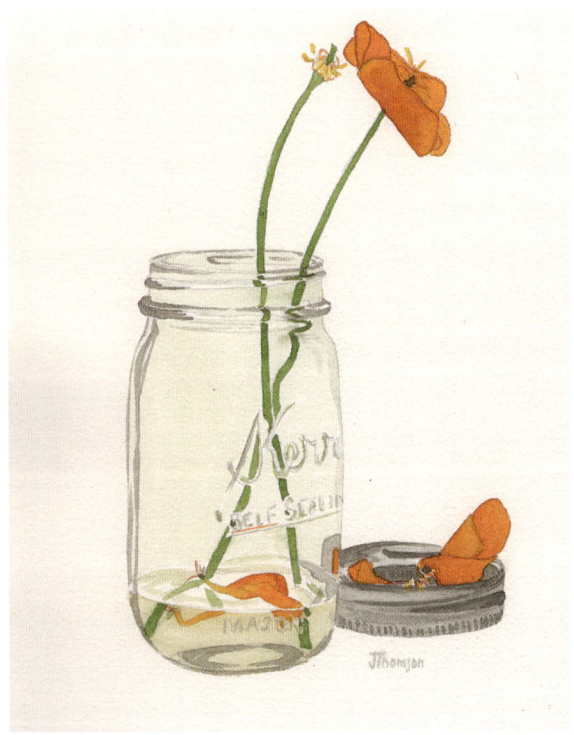

MASON JAR WITH
CALIFORNIA POPPY

2014

I remember my first time
A rural girl trapped in an urban land
Longing for wild things
This orange offered remembrance of freedom.

MASON JAR WITH
CALIFORNIA POPPIES
PAST THEIR PRIME

2014

Time passes
Youthful beauty becomes
Mature beauty
And is preserved.

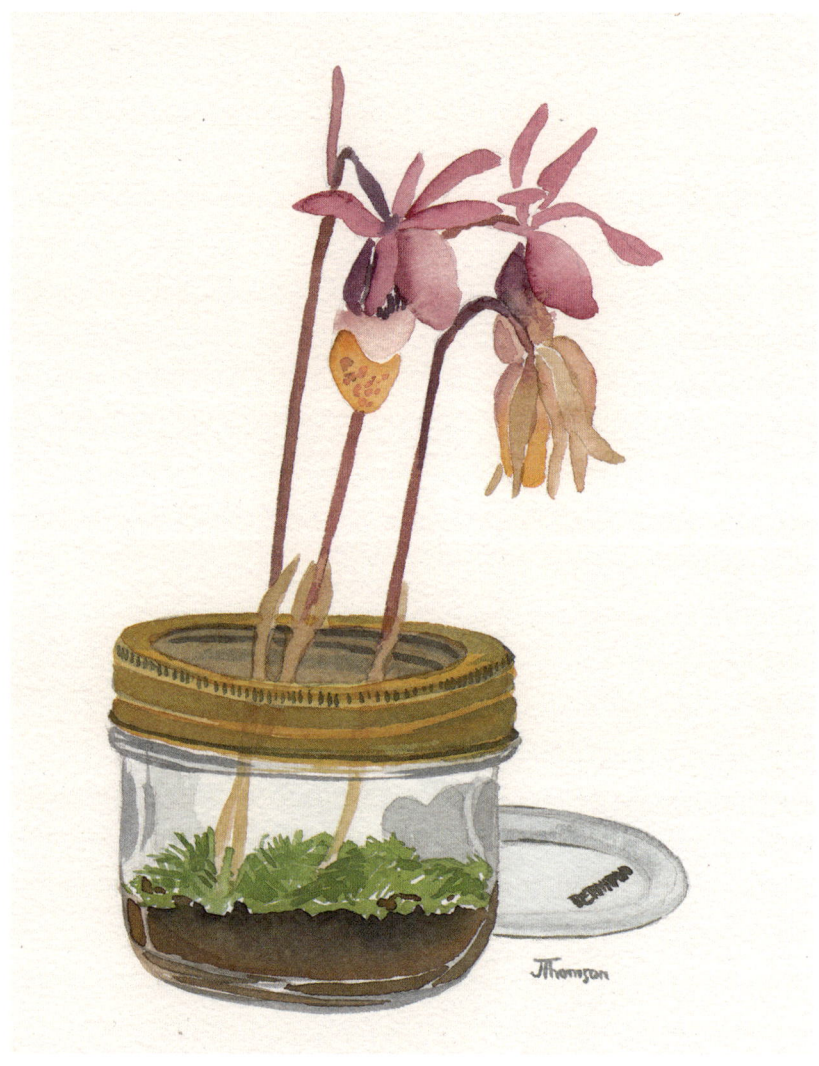

MASON JAR WITH Rare beauty in the forest
CALYPSO ORCHID Two in their prime and one past it.
2014 My Mother, my Aunt, and their Mother.
Matriarchs of my life.

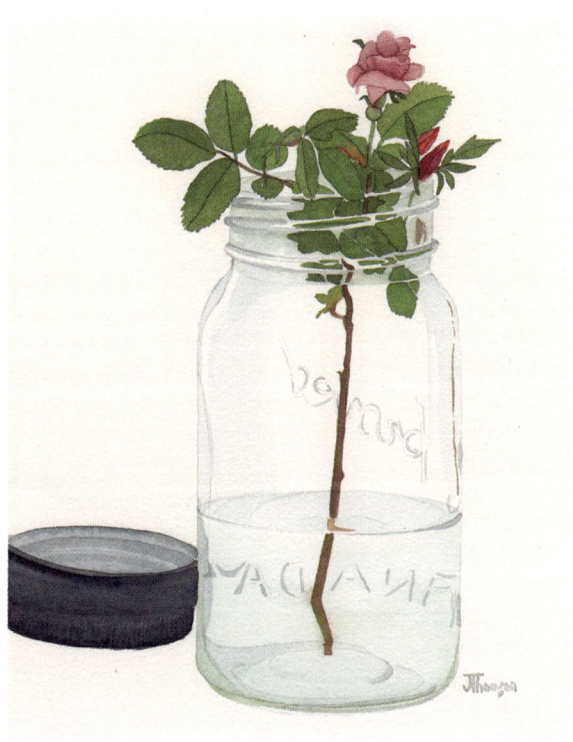 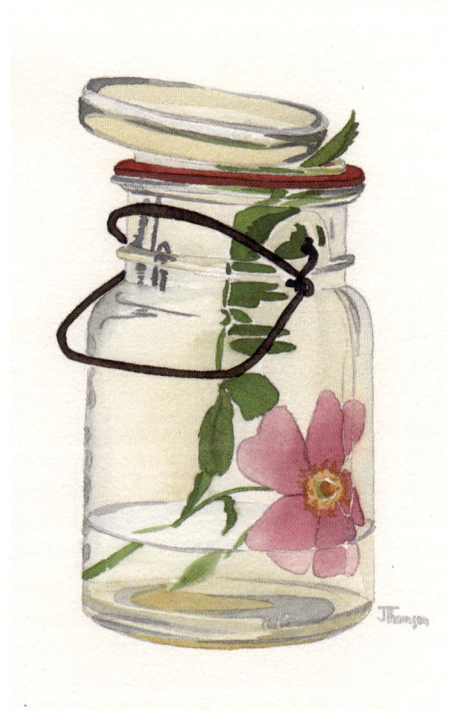

MASON JAR WITH
WILD ROSE BUDS
2014

Potential
Simple and wild
Promises unspoken
Fulfilled in the moment.

MASON JAR WITH
WILD ROSE
2014

Mature and wild
Beauty fades fast
Yet remains
In memory.

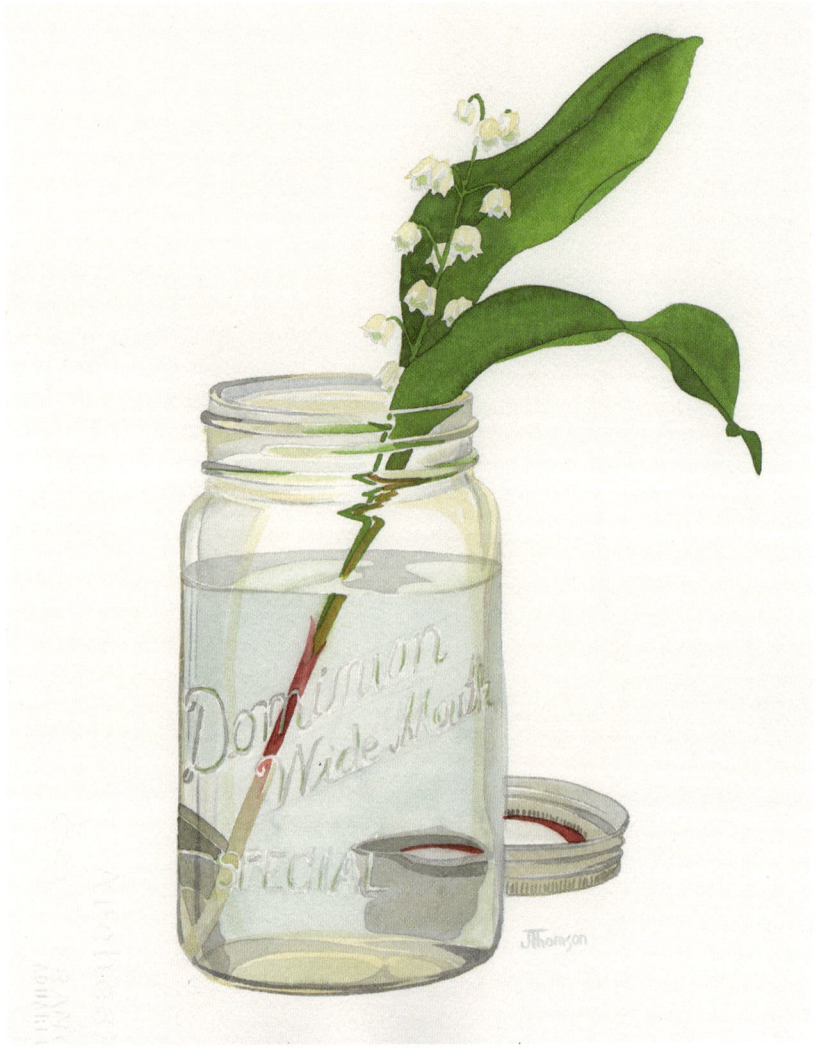

**MASON JAR WITH
LILY OF THE VALLEY**

2014

Can you smell them?
The fragrance of memories
Embedded in strong stock
Suspended in firm resolve?

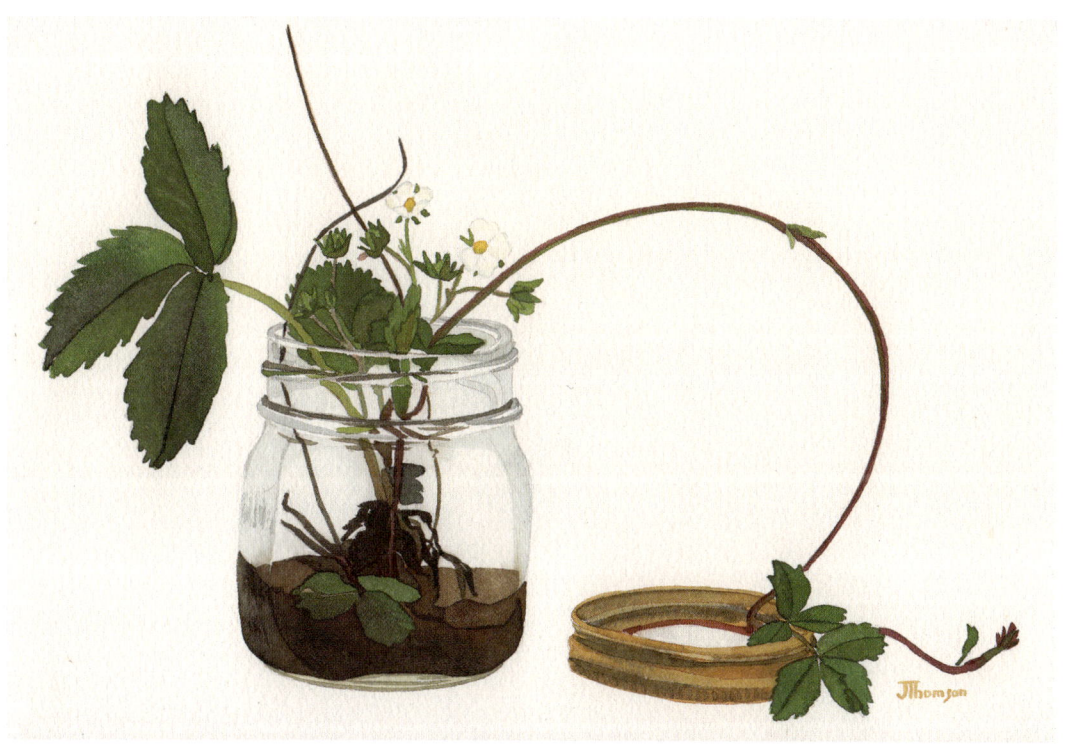

MASON JAR WITH
STRAWBERRY PLANT

2014

We work so hard to launch our young
to greener pastures
sometimes forgetting
how good our homes are.

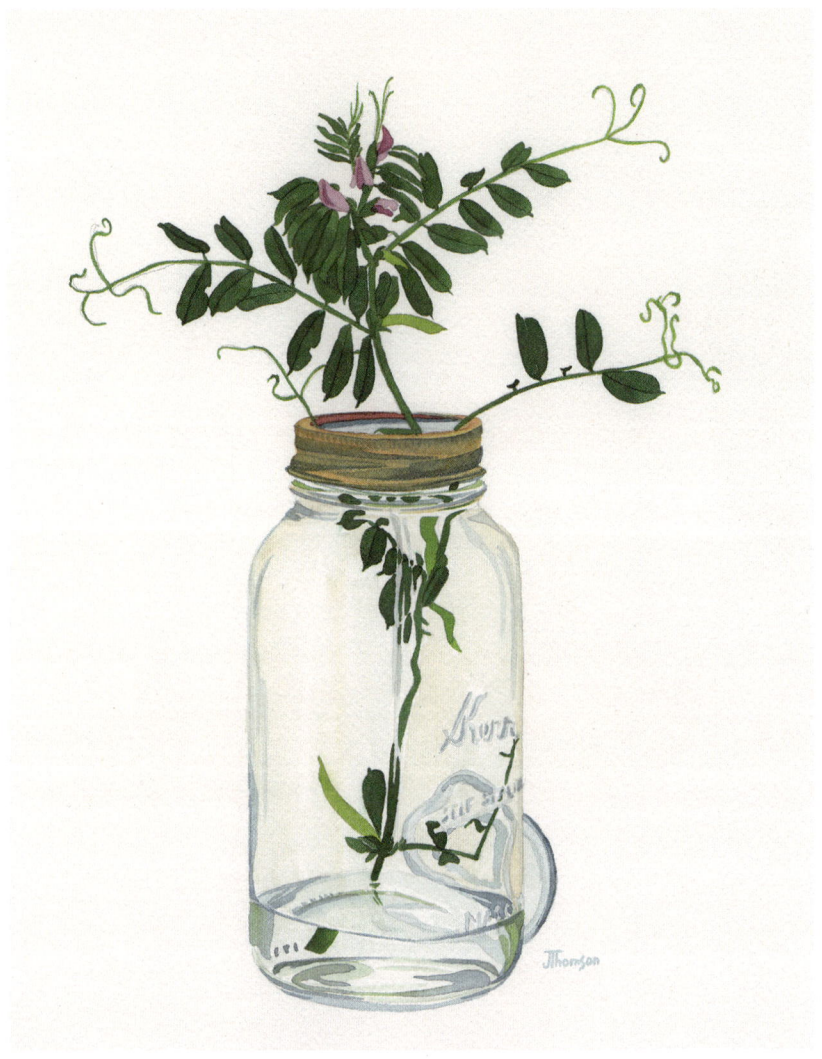

MASON JAR   Vetch,
WITH VETCH   If it were a verb
2014   It would mean "to complain,"
                  Such beautiful complaining
                  Pulls me into ditches.

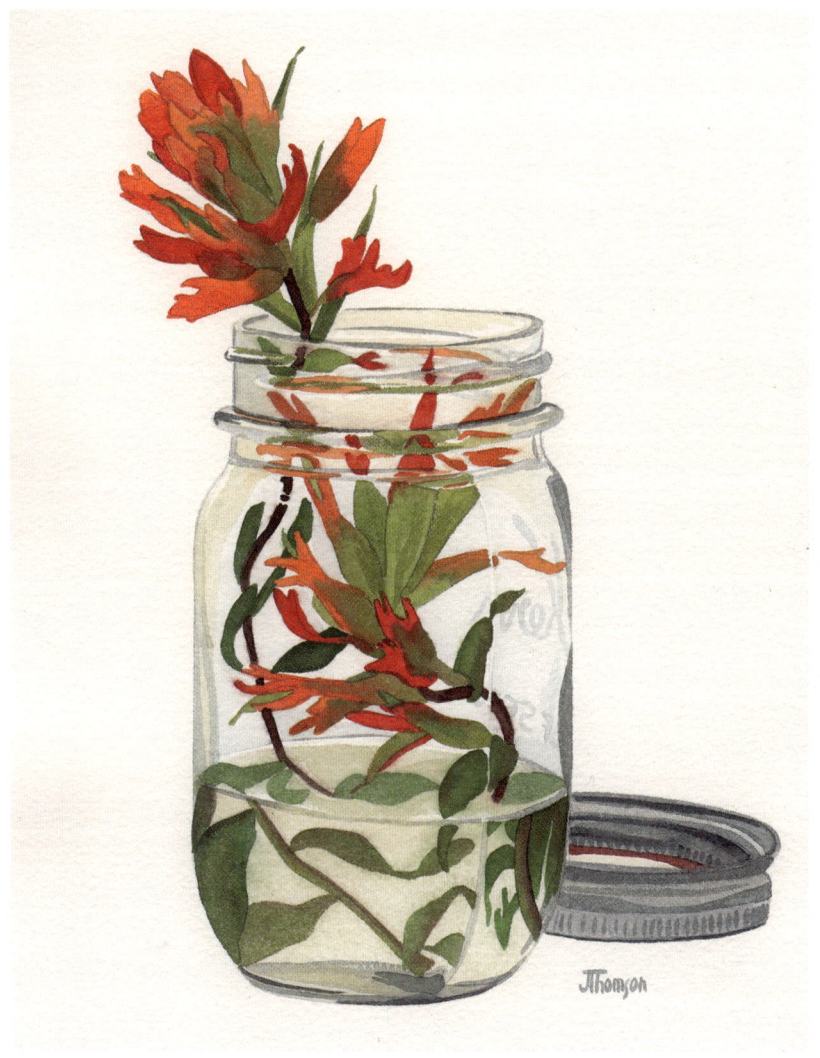

MASON JAR
WITH INDIAN
PAINTBRUSH
2014

Spilling out the edges
form and colour
refuse to comply
with the expected.

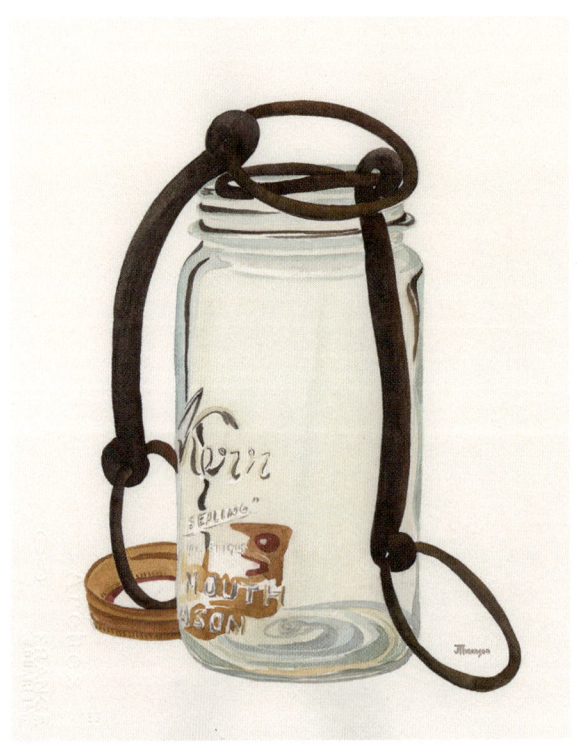
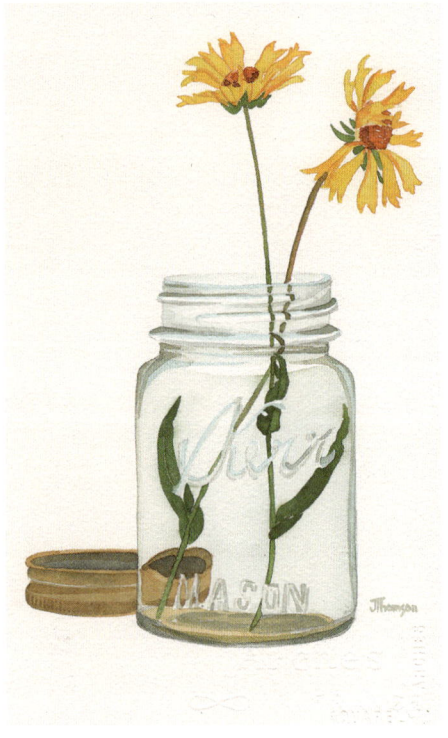

MASON JAR
WITH TWO BITS
2014

A taste of freedom
Escape from work and poverty
To range the hills on horses
Well-earned pleasure.

MASON JAR WITH
BROWN-EYED SUSAN
2014

Winking along the trail edge
On a lazy summer afternoon
No reason to be
Other than to be.

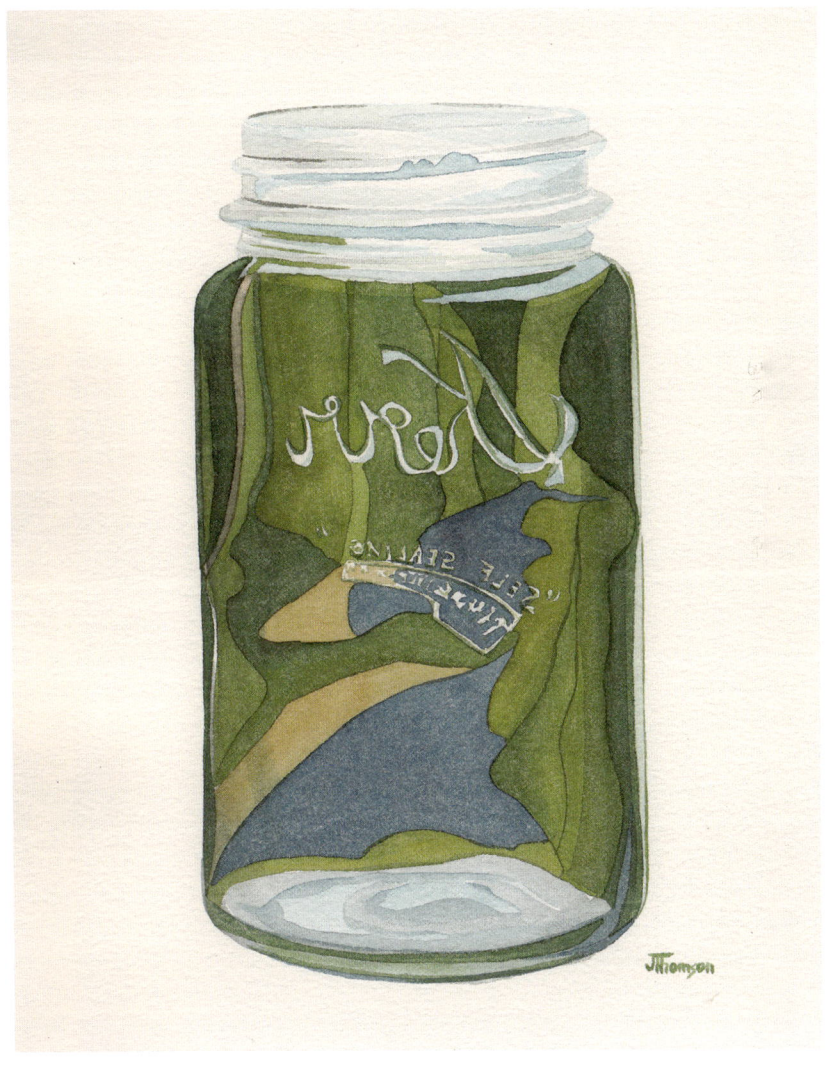

MASON JAR WITH
BOUNDARY CREEK

2014

He died at Boundary Creek
Not here but further up,
At a camp, in a fire,
Alone with his story.

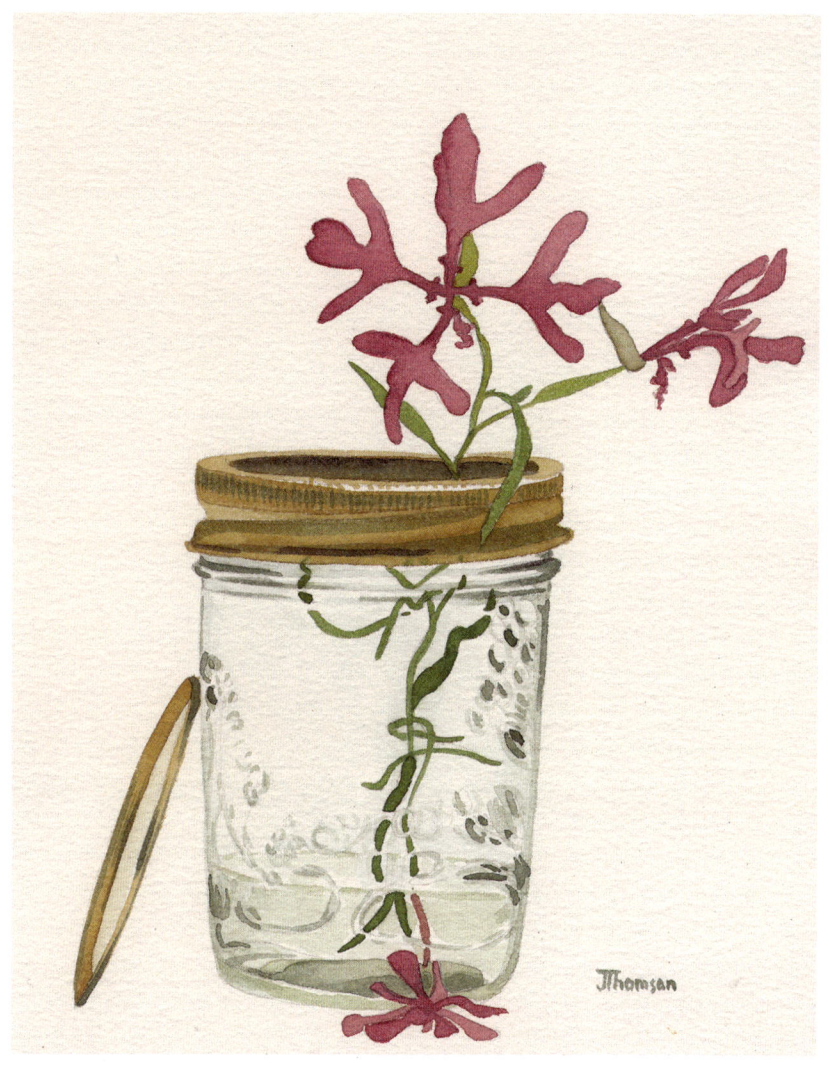

MASON JAR WITH
STAGHORN FLOWER

2014

A flower for memory
Diminutive, pink, on the dry slope
Suspended in pine scented air
Claiming their places beautifully.

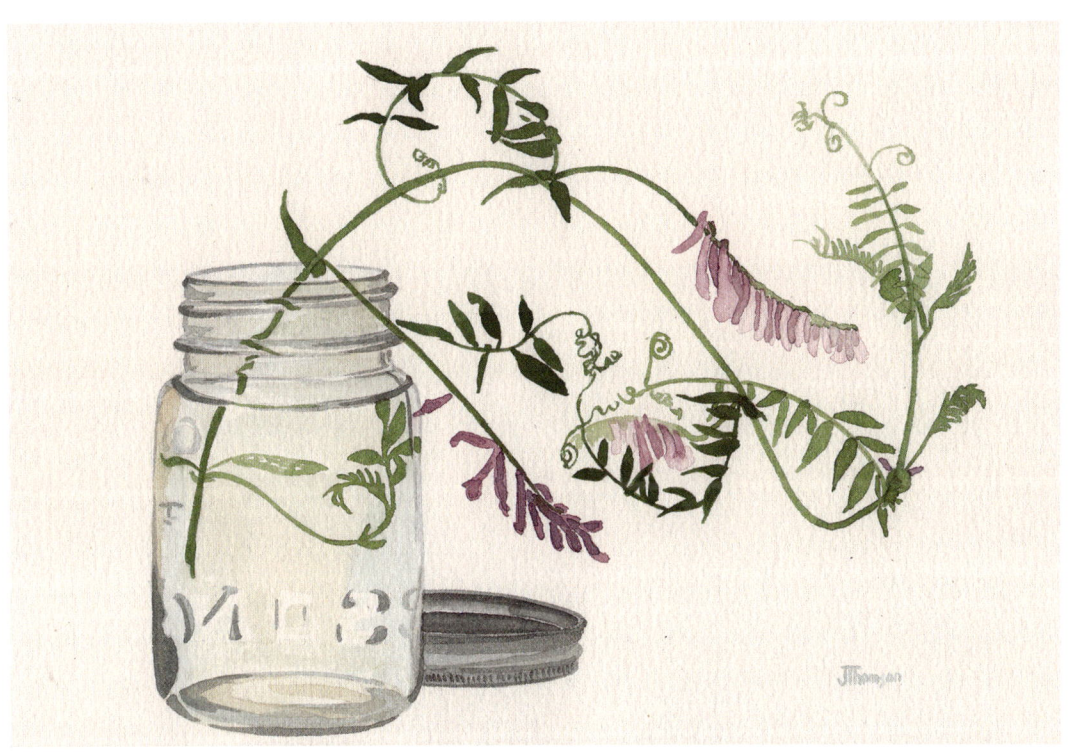

MASON JAR WITH
PURPLE VETCH
2014

Real and imagined memories
Of others enjoying these blooms
Weeds on window ledges
In jars with other destinies.

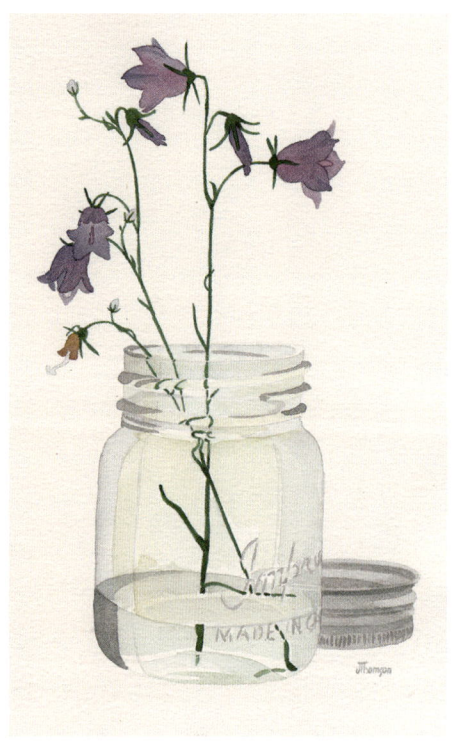
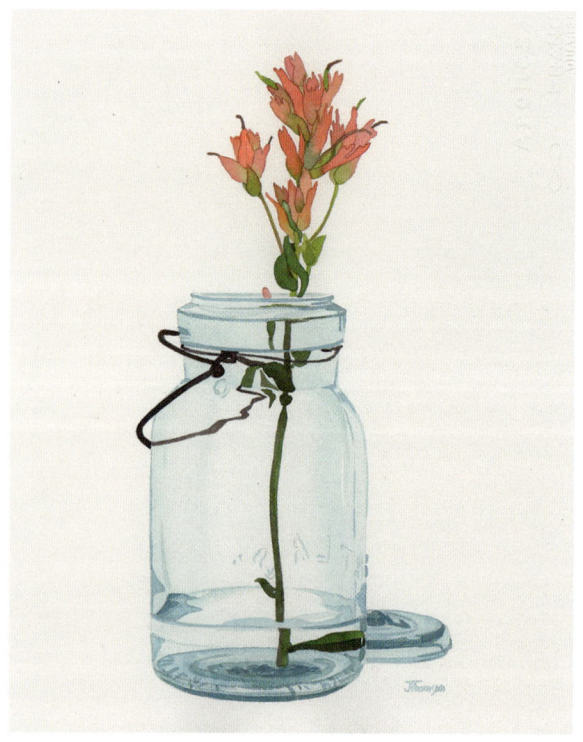

MASON JAR WITH	Imagine the ringing of bells
HAREBELLS	As hares dance by moonlight
2014	In fields decorated with pieces of sky.
MASON JAR WITH	A more subtle brush,
PALE INDIAN	A keeper of secrets
PAINTBRUSH	Guarding what cannot be known
2014	From those who cannot know it.

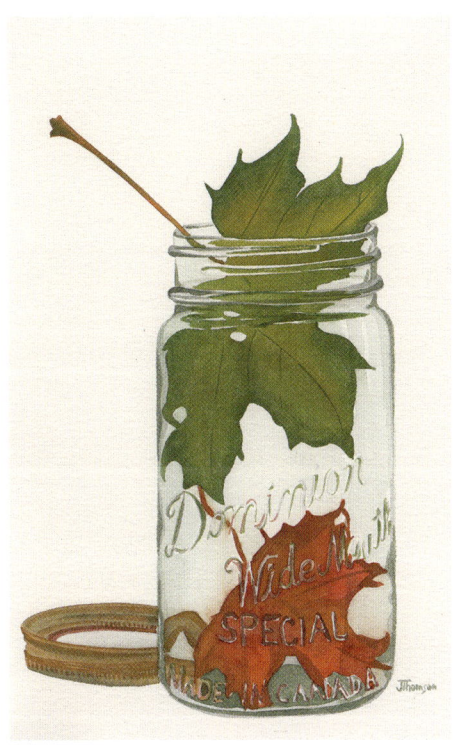
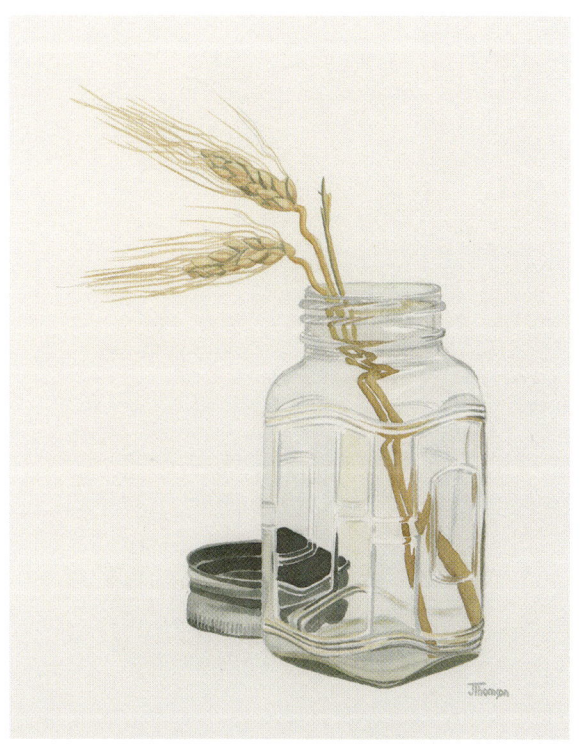

MASON JAR WITH
MAPLE LEAVES
2014

It is complicated,
Being Canadian
Distilled from other
Not quite fitting.

MASON JAR
WITH WHEAT
2014

Wheat from a ditch in Alberta
Escaping from a field
Making its way to a table
In a place where wheat does not grow.

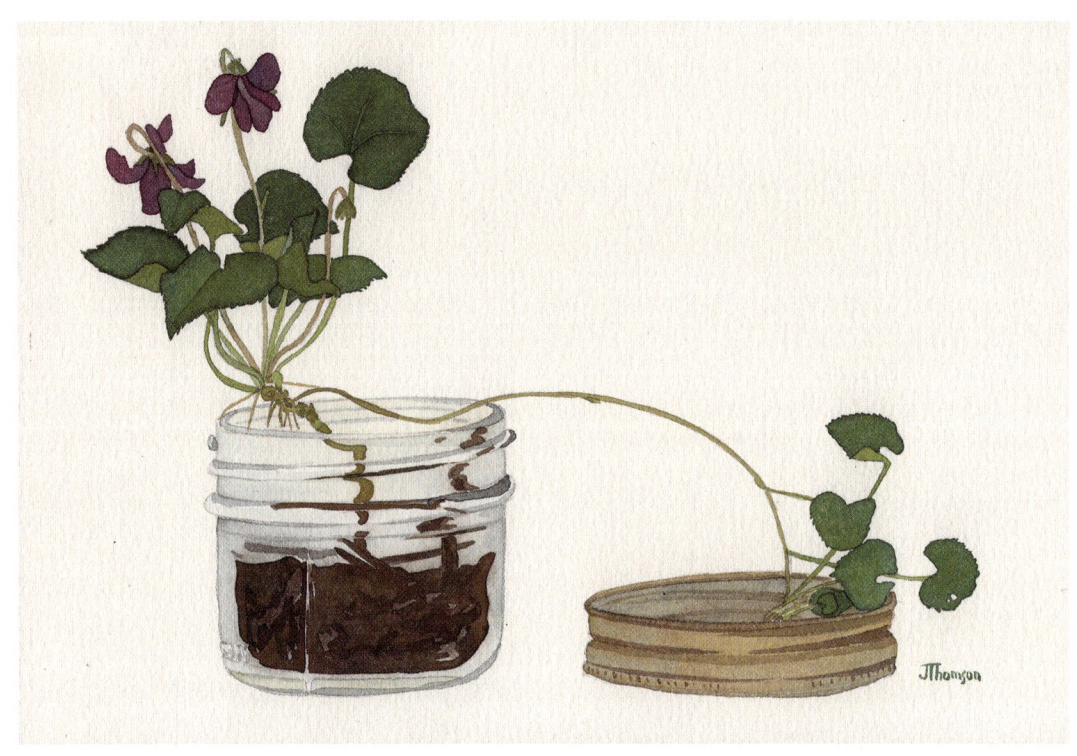

MASON JAR Do they know
WITH EARLY They are remarkable
SPRING VIOLETS As they freeze each night
2015 Thawing into blooms each morning?

MASON JAR WITH Meek and hardy
CALENDULA FLOWERS Prolific and easily uprooted
2015 Resilient and persistent
They beat the odds.

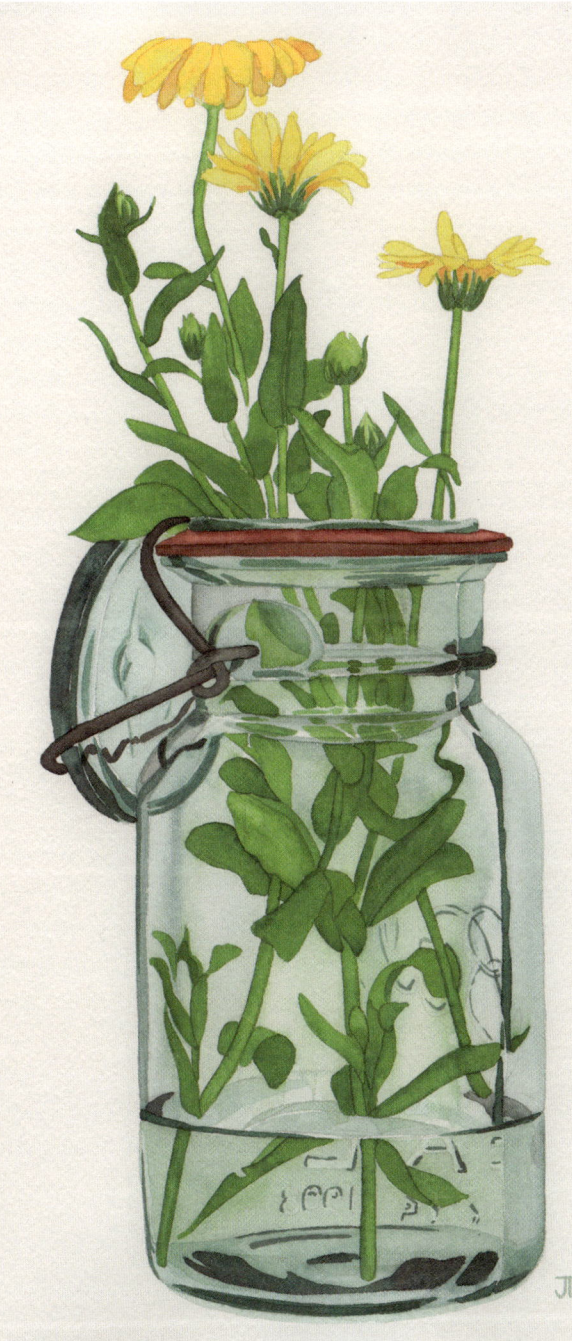

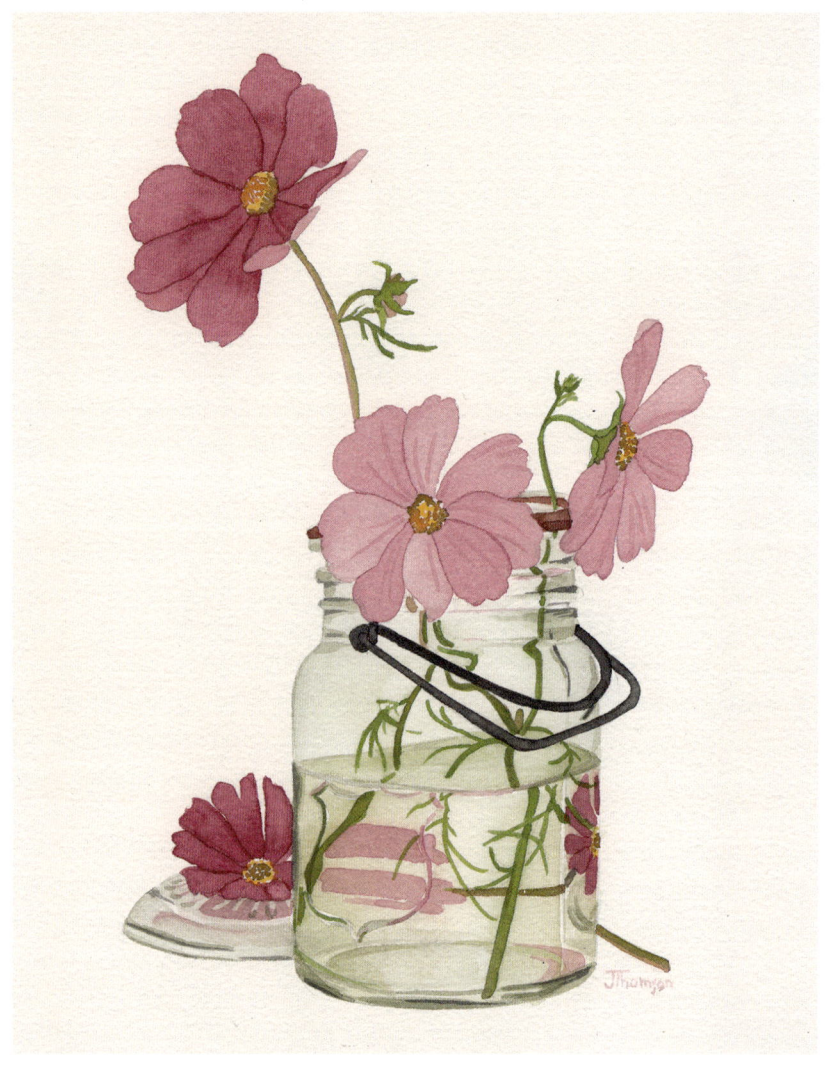

MASON JAR Ohhh, such pleasure for bees
WITH COSMOS Mason, bumble, honey, false
2015 They gather here to feast.

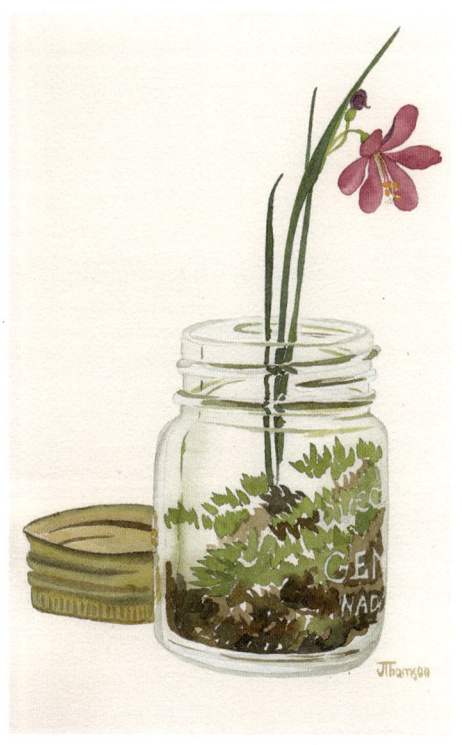 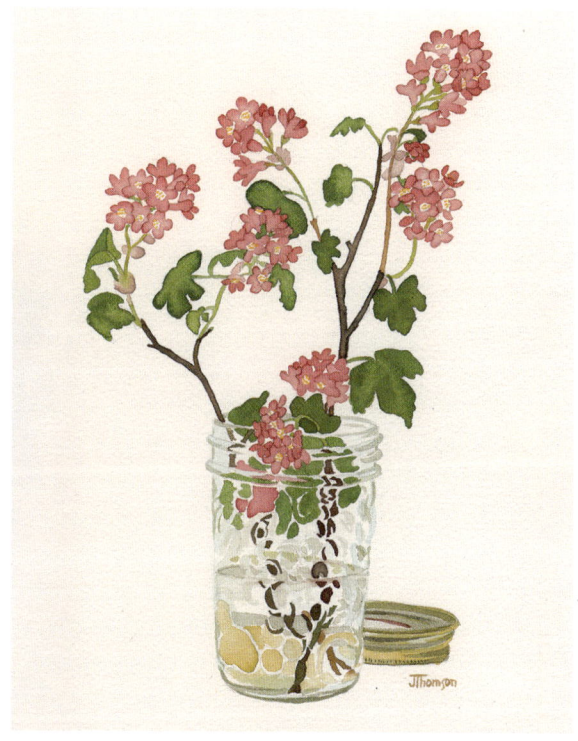

MASON JAR WITH
SATIN FLOWER
2016

They break the earth
Disguised as grass
Awoken by sunlight
Delightful colour on quiet slopes.

MASON JAR WITH RED
FLOWERING CURRANT
2016

Resilient and drought tolerant
The red flowering currant is in style again
Celebrated by hummingbirds
Bright blooms hurrying Spring.

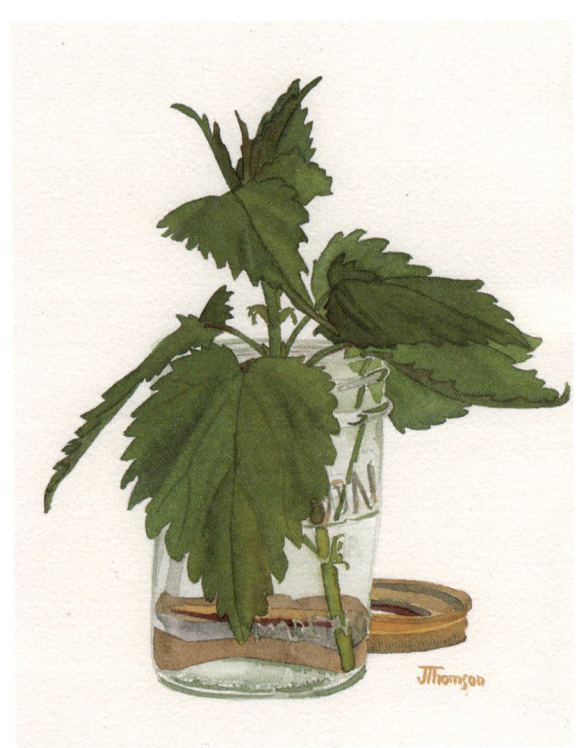

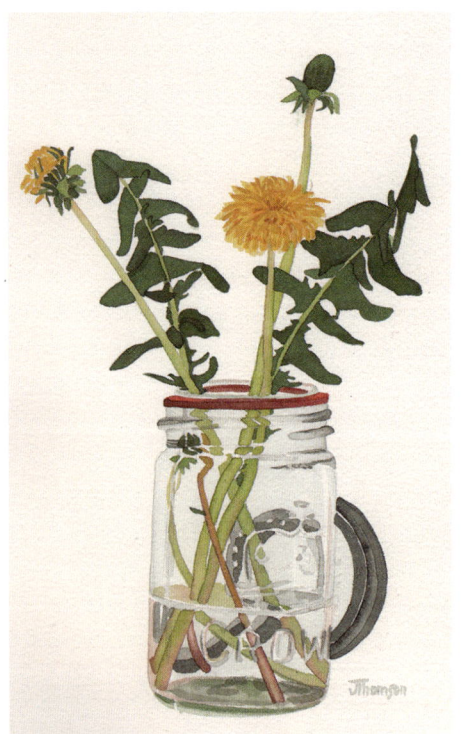

MASON JAR
WITH NETTLE
2016

Early greens for settlers
Now a boon for foragers
Harvest with caution and enjoy.

MASON JAR WITH
BLOOMING
DANDELION
2016

Bouquets of dandelions
Dripping white onto clothing
Leave the mark of their demise
On little hands and shirts.

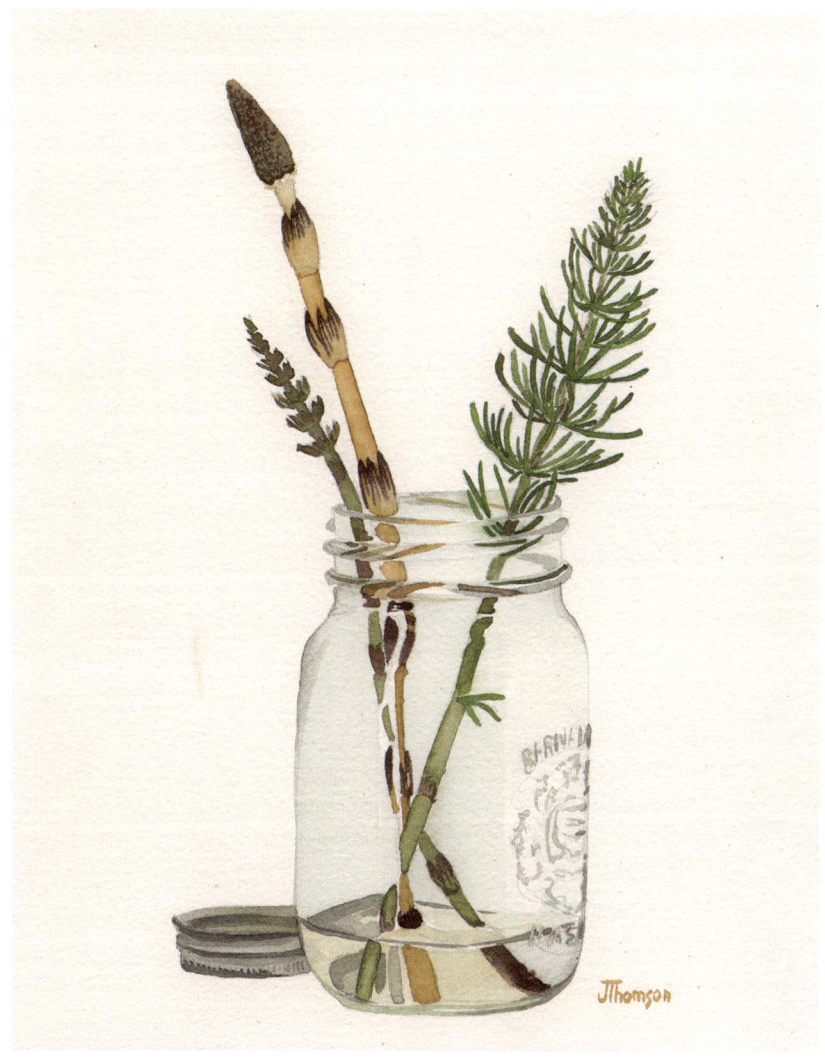

MASON JAR WITH   Ancient soldiers of water and mud
HORSETAILS   Slopes, mountains, ditches
2016   Before us, with us, and beyond us too.

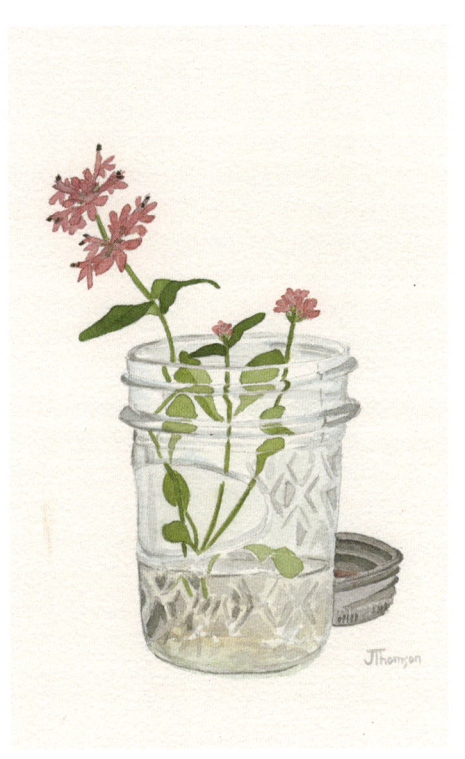

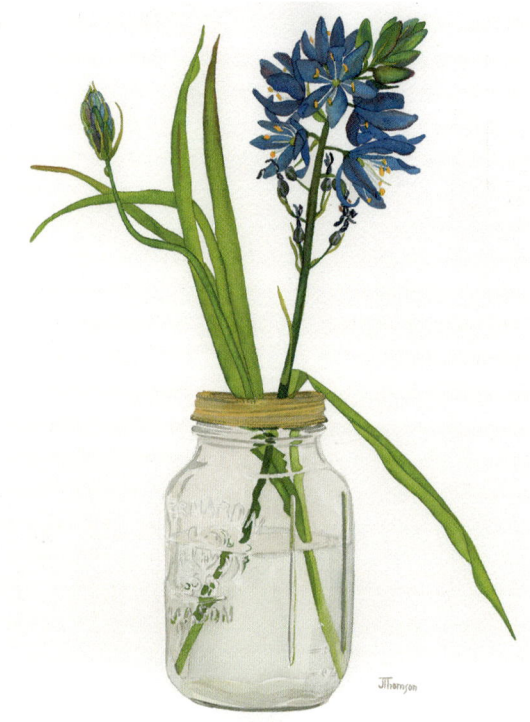

MASON JAR
WITH SEA BLUSH
2016

Slopes near the ocean
Rose glow in the Spring
Simple, stubborn, and glorious!

MASON JAR WITH
GRAND CAMAS
2016

The Garry oaks just budding golden
These majestic beauties claim the ground
These unfortunates plucked for a nature lesson.

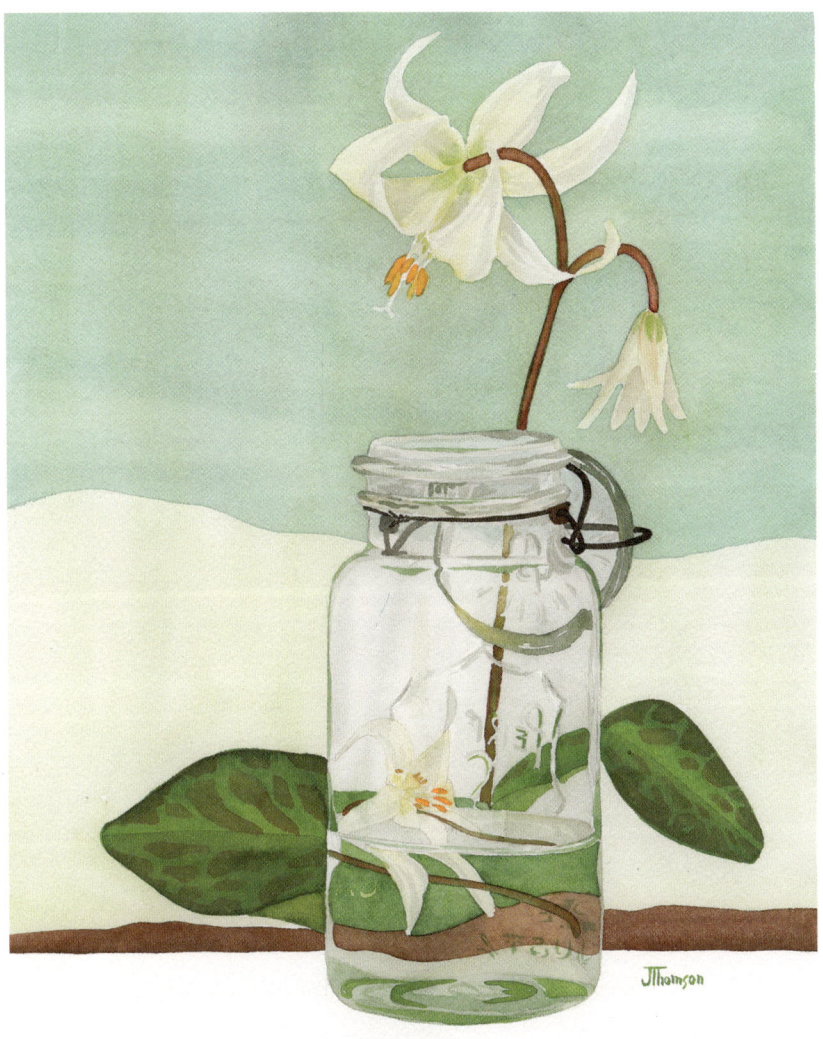

MASON JAR
WITH FAWN LILY
(ERYTHONIUM)
2016

In the shade of oak trees
Abundant lilies bloom
Fawn spotted leaves
Fade as their youth passes.

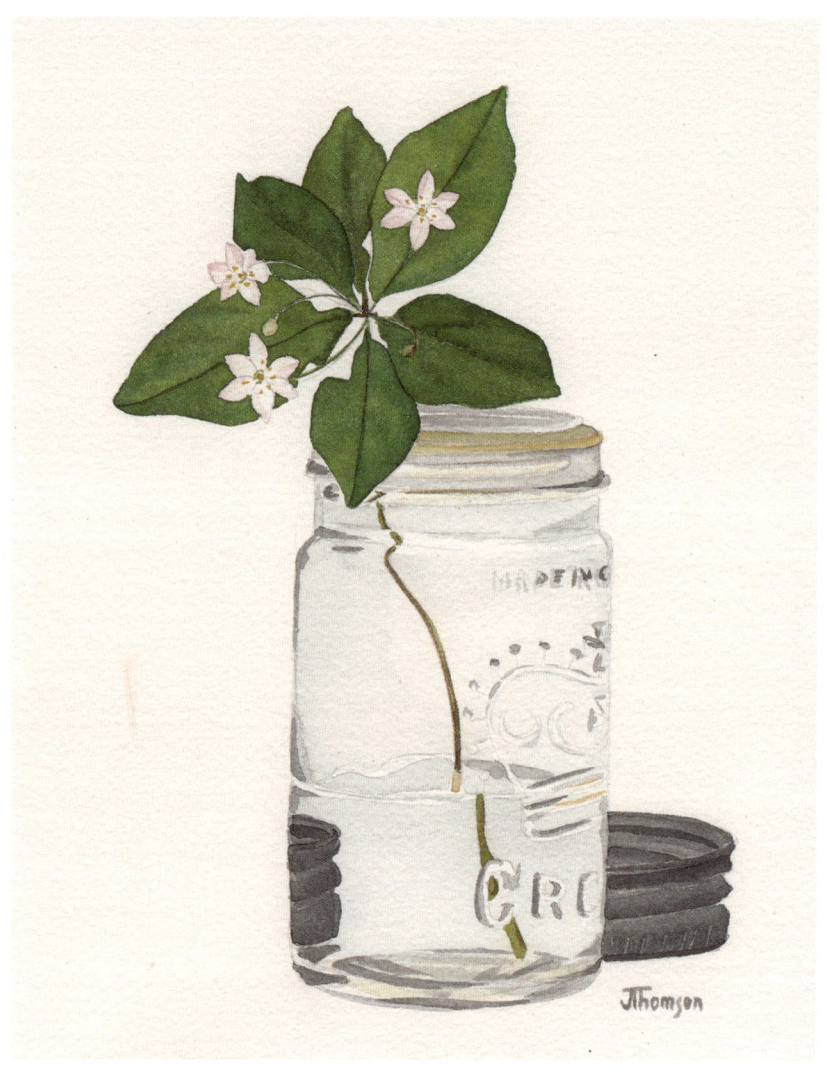

MASON JAR WITH   Beneath the fir trees
STAR FLOWER   A carpet of leaves and stars
2016   Walkers slow down to marvel.

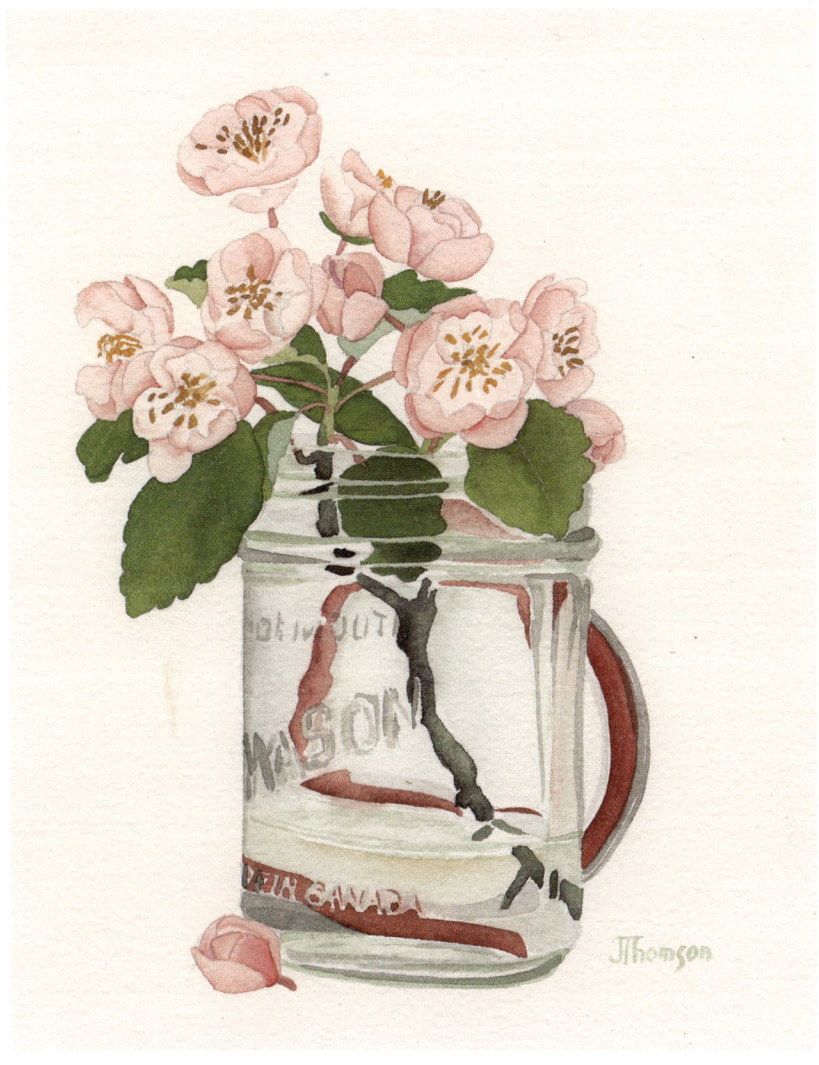

MASON JAR WITH　　Blossoms within blossoms
ORNAMENTAL　　They offer gentle beauty in the spring
APPLE BLOSSOM　　And no fruit in the fall.

2016

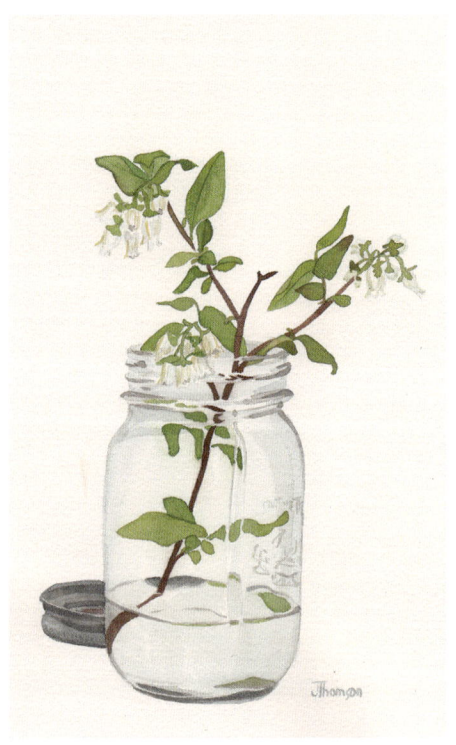 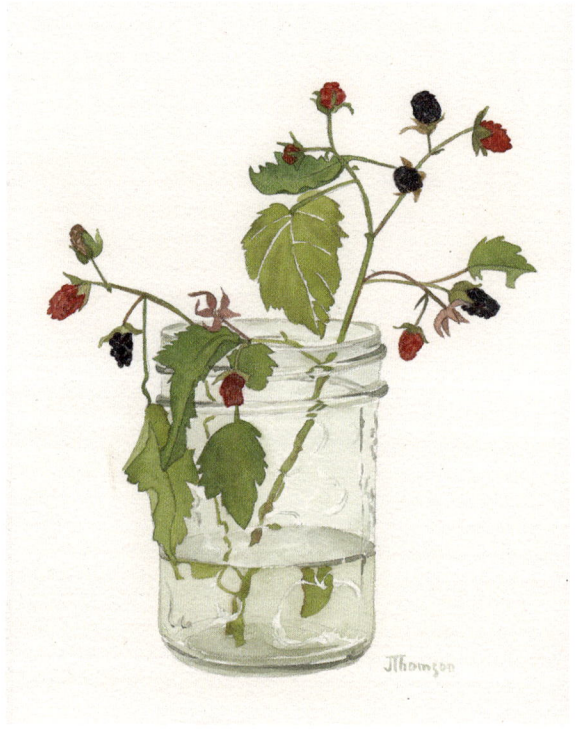

MASON JAR WITH
BLUEBERRY BLOSSOM
2016

So many blossoms like bells
Salal, huckleberry, twin flower
These offer succulent berries
When they are not plucked from the branch.

MASON JAR
WITH TRAILING
BLACKBERRIES
2016

They hold the flowers within them
These fragrant fruits
Taste of summer and spring combined.

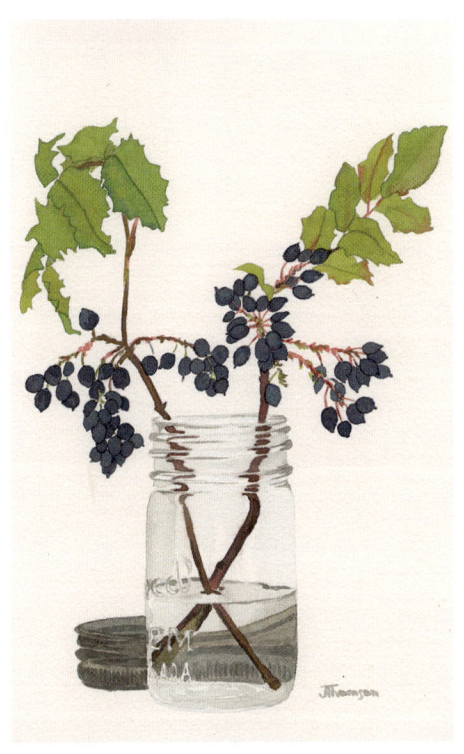

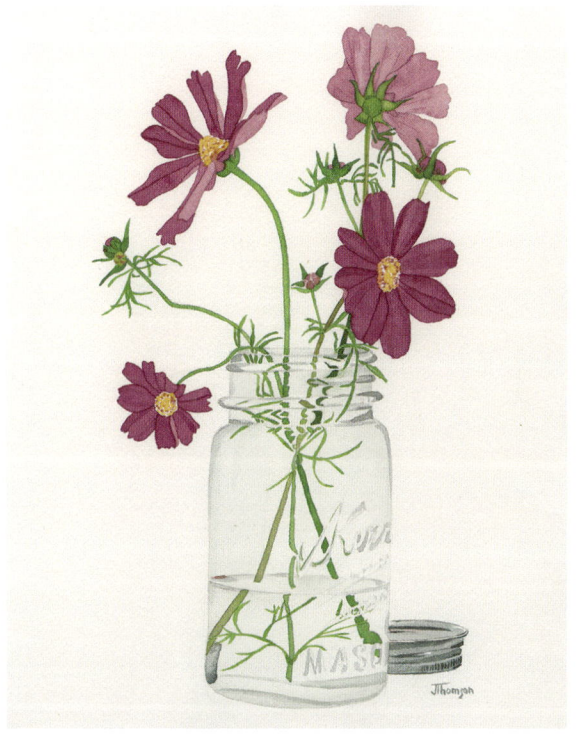

MASON JAR WITH
OREGON GRAPES
2016

Jelly, dye, decorative borders
Oregon grapes experience
A surge of drought resistant popularity!

MASON JAR WITH
MAGENTA COSMOS
2016

Self seeding beauties
They arrive each year
Just as I begin to fear
They have forgotten me.

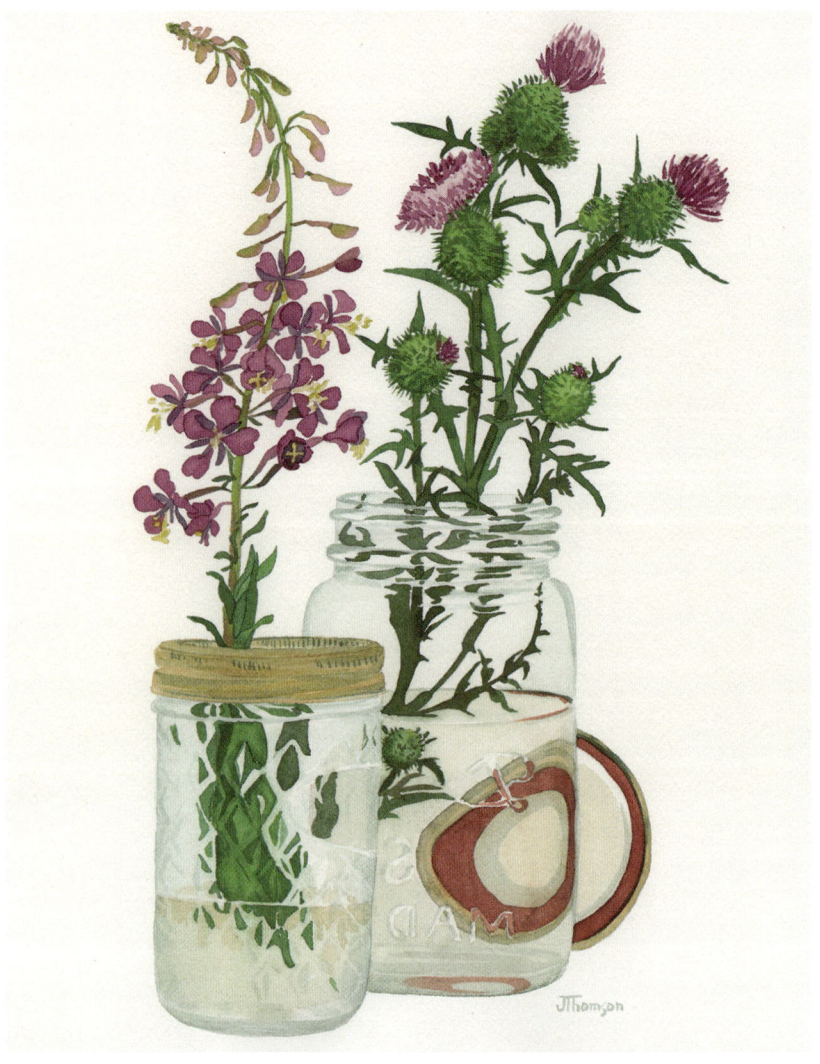

MASON JARS
WITH FIREWEED
AND THISTLE
2016

Just a step from the garden
These wild ones abound
The fireweed more welcome.
It knows its place.

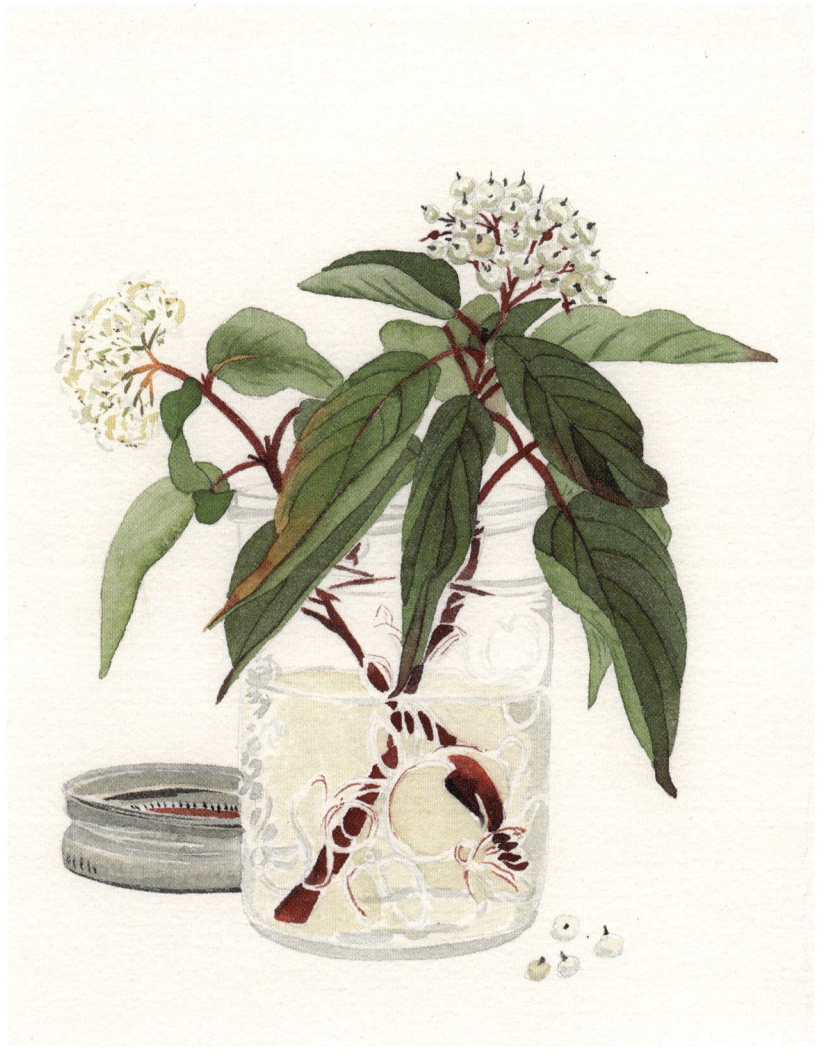

MASON JAR WITH RED OSIER DOGWOOD

2016

Wild beauty in all seasons
The osier is quiet
Unassuming in its role
As creek bank protector.

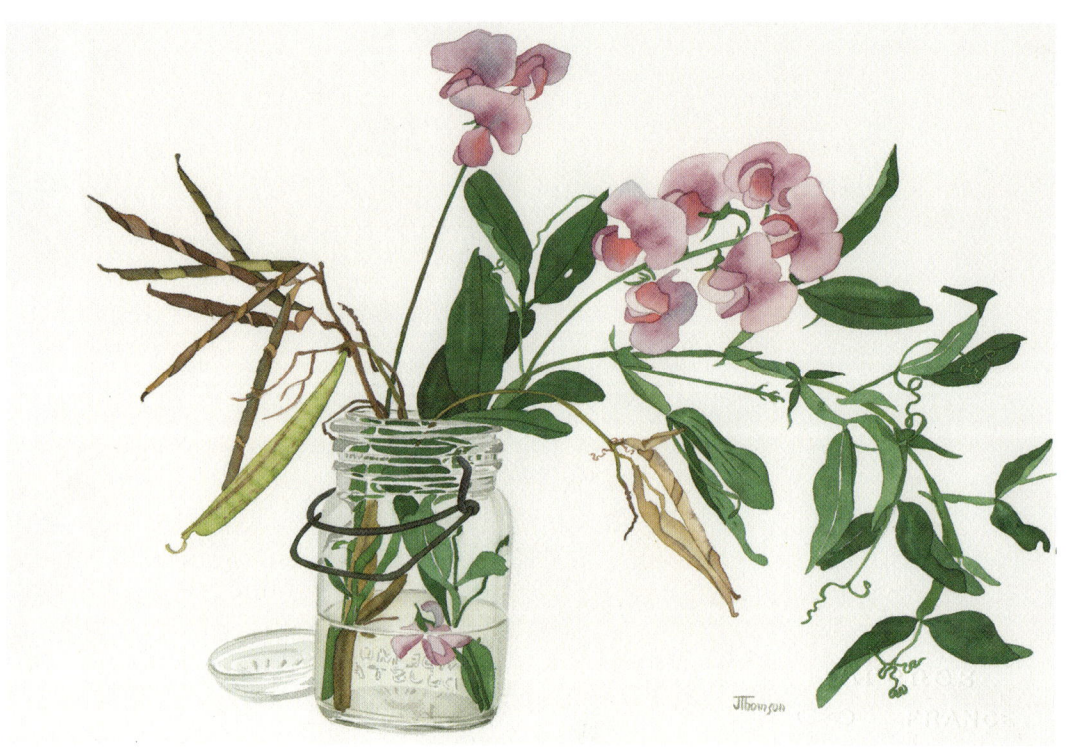

MASON JAR WITH Ditches and beaches awash with pink

BEACH PEAS Snapping pods flinging peas

2016 Summer and Fall they demand admiration.

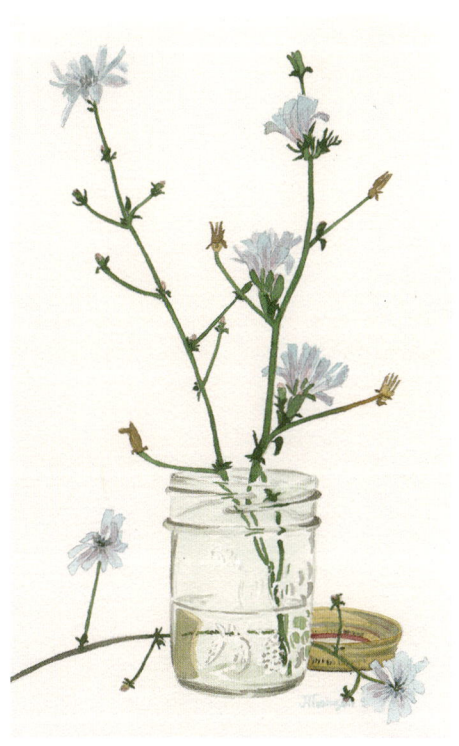
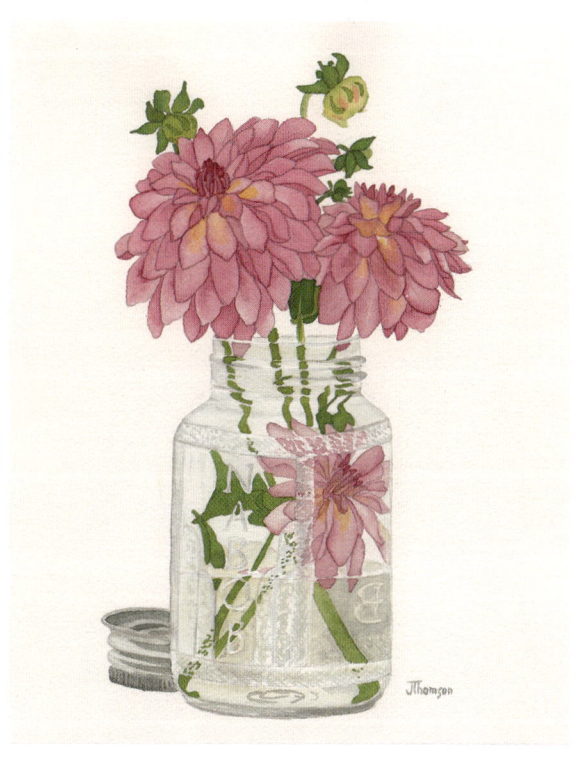

MASON JAR WITH CHICORY 2016

Roadside beauties
Bring sky to earth
Short-lived bursts
On stalks of green.

MASON JAR WITH DALIAS 2016

'Can I have a few?'
'As many as you want
It is near the end of the season.'
Frost took the rest that night.

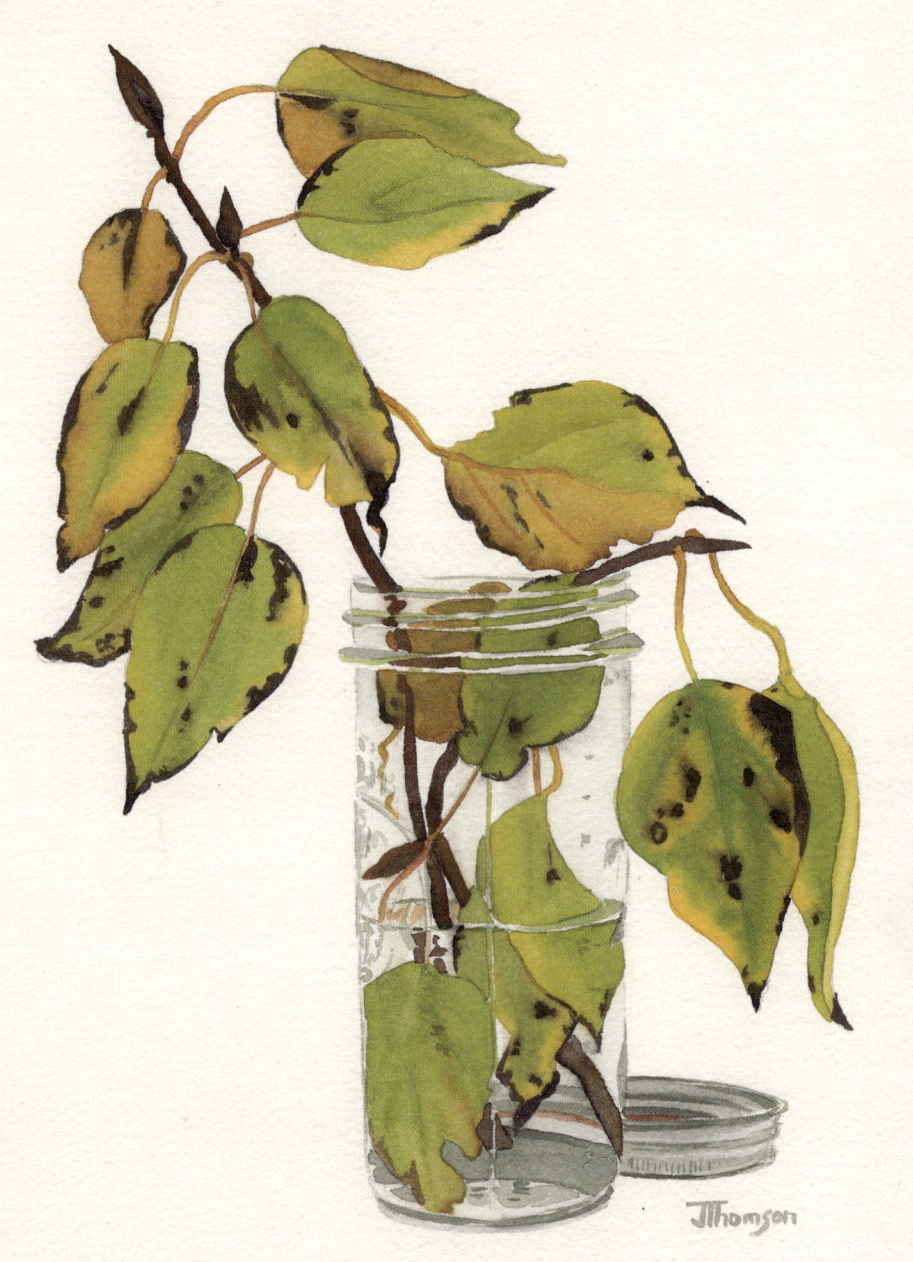

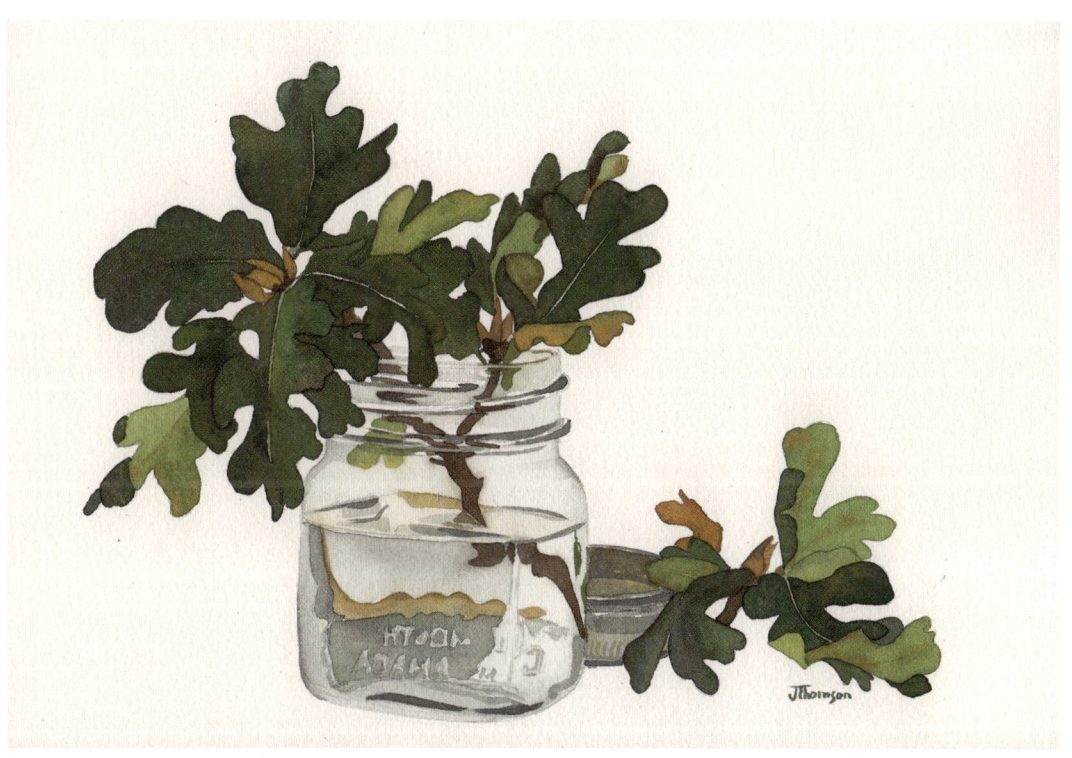

MASON JAR WITH Sweet sap of cottonwood
COTTONWOOD LEAVES Evoking springtime
2016 Twice a year.

MASON JAR WITH Twisting toward the sky
GARRY OAK Denying builders straight wood
2016 A great survival strategy.

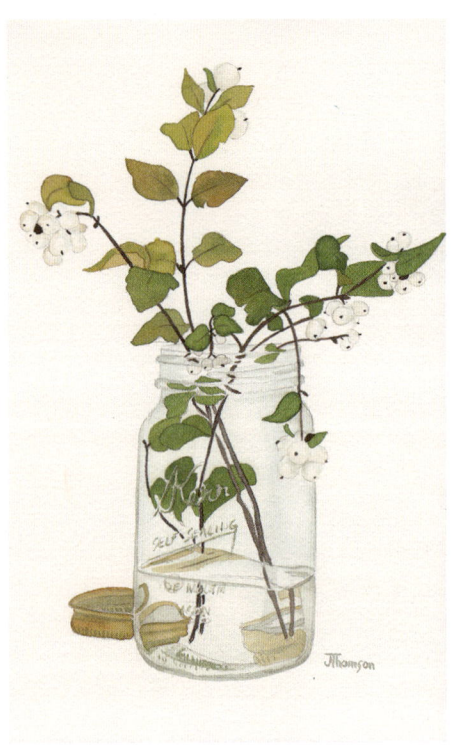

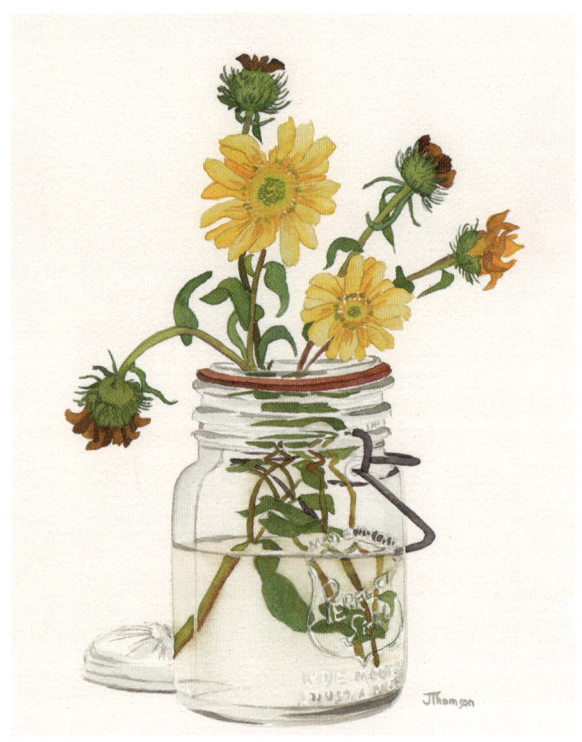

MASON JAR WITH
SNOWBERRIES
2016

Soon the leaves will fall
Leaving offerings of berries
To imitate the coming snows.

MASON JAR
WITH GUMWEED
2016

Near the ocean
Edging the salt marsh
Gumweeds pretend to be sunflowers
And claim space.

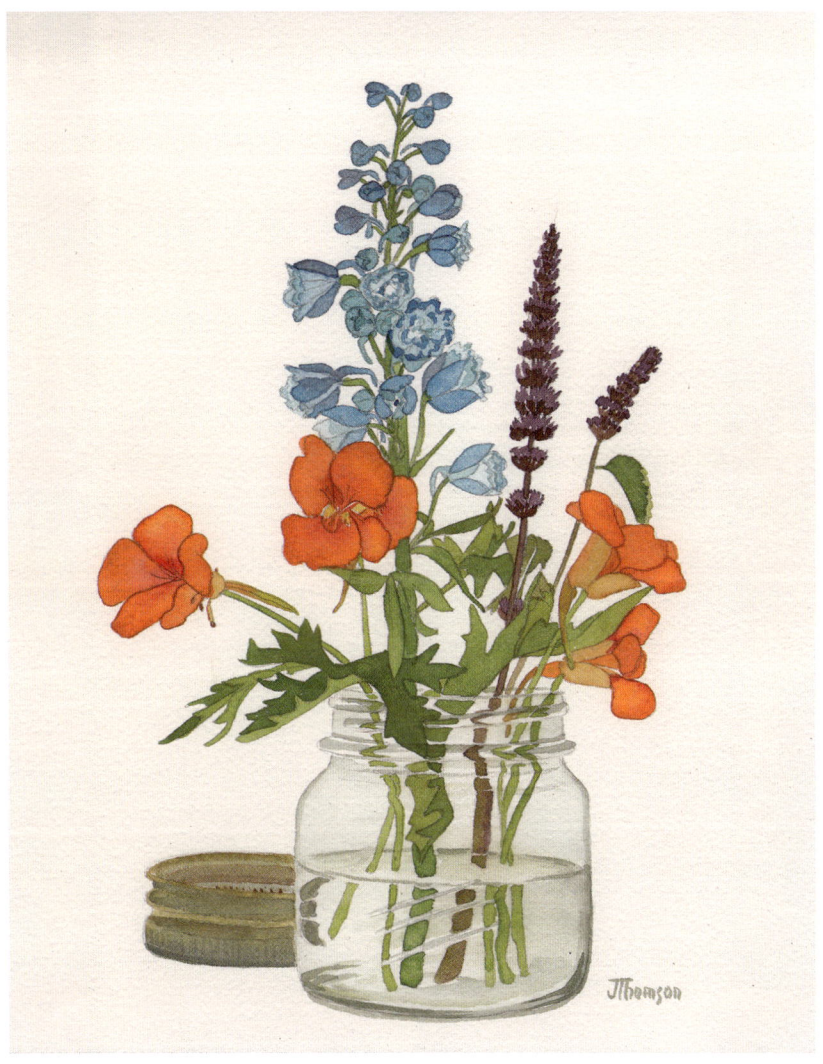

**MASON JAR WITH
END OF SEASON
FLOWERS**

2016

Delphinium snatched from deer,
Nasturtium and licorice mint
Protected by their scents.

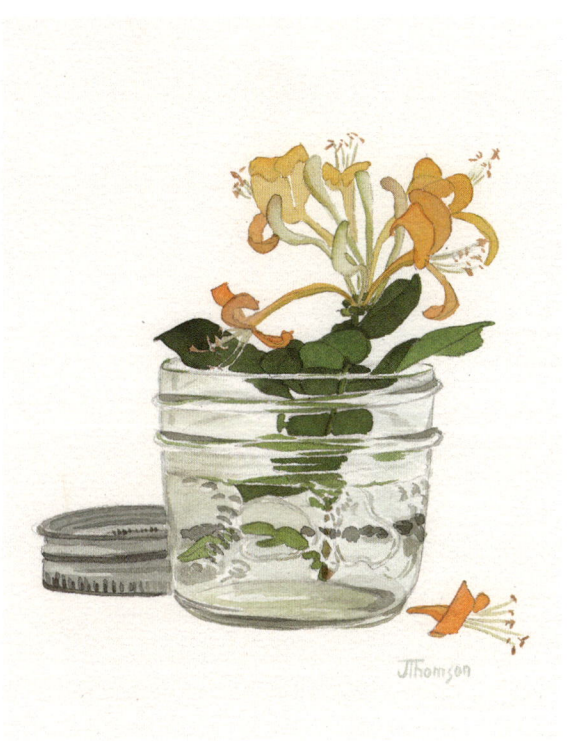

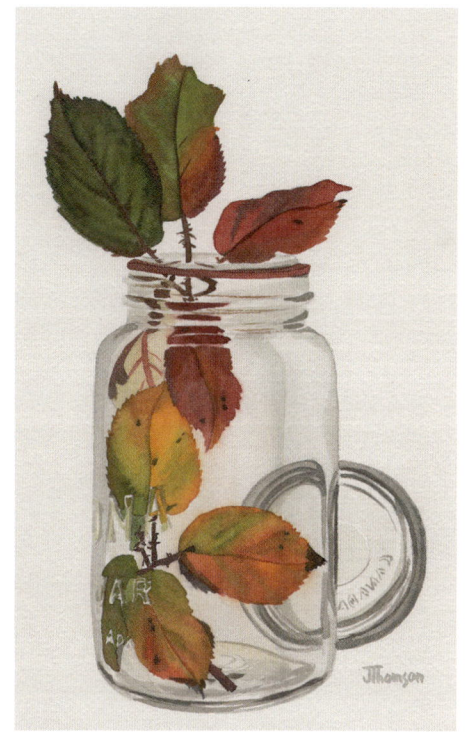

MASON JAR WITH
HONEYSUCKLE
2016

Fragrant fragile beauties
Honeysuckles weave
Support in hedges and bushes.

MASON JAR WITH AUTUMN
BLACKBERRY LEAVES
2016

The first frost brings colour
As the shock of cold
Heralds the coming of winter.

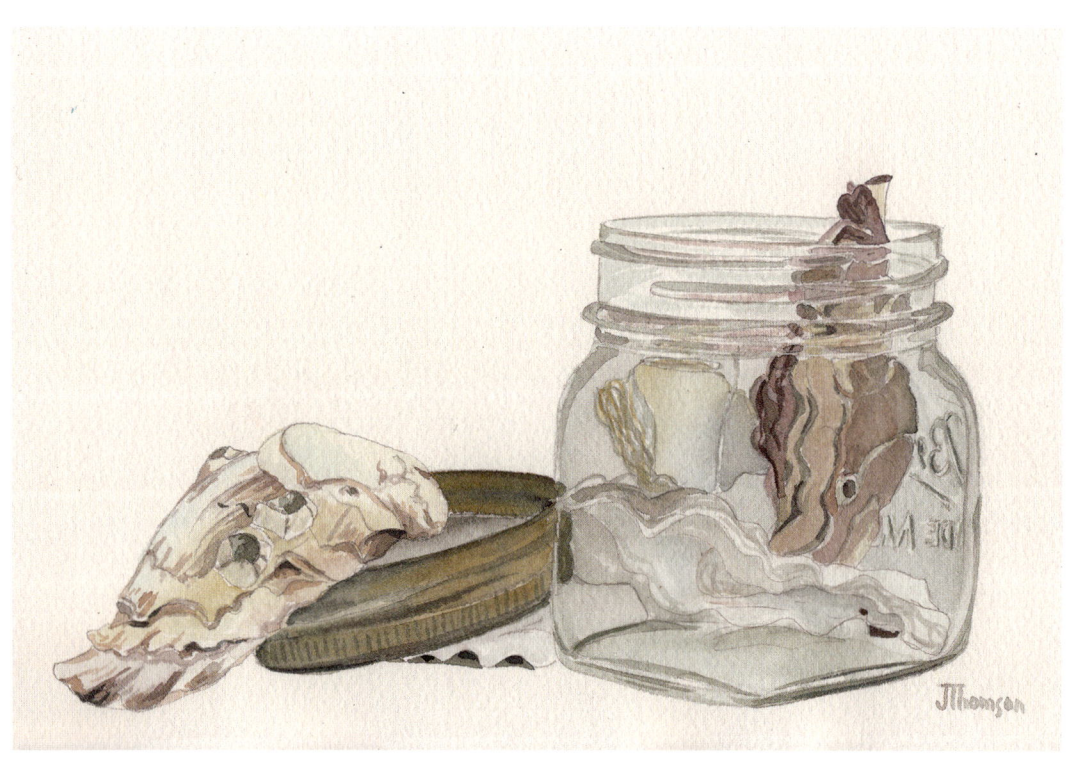

MASON JAR WITH
OYSTER SHELLS
2016

Oysters change
Male one year
Female the next
That could be a benefit to our species.

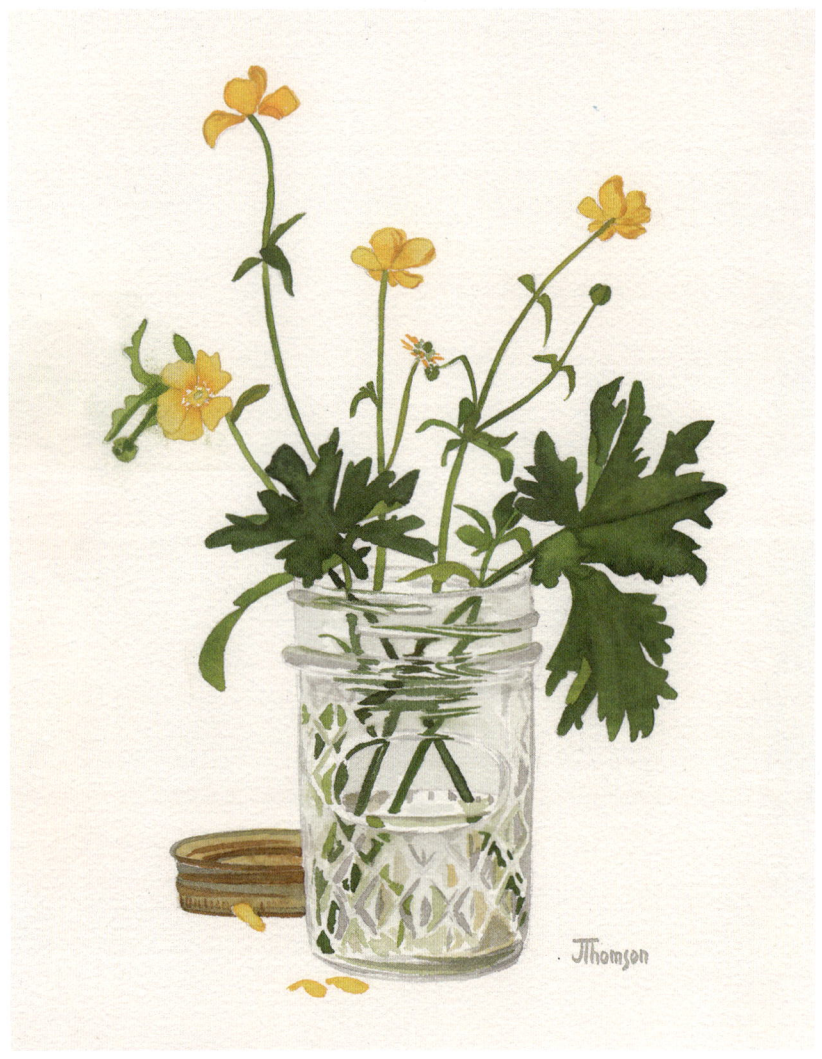

MASON JAR WITH The gardener's challenge

BUTTERCUPS Is the children's delight

2016 Please pick freely and take the roots too.

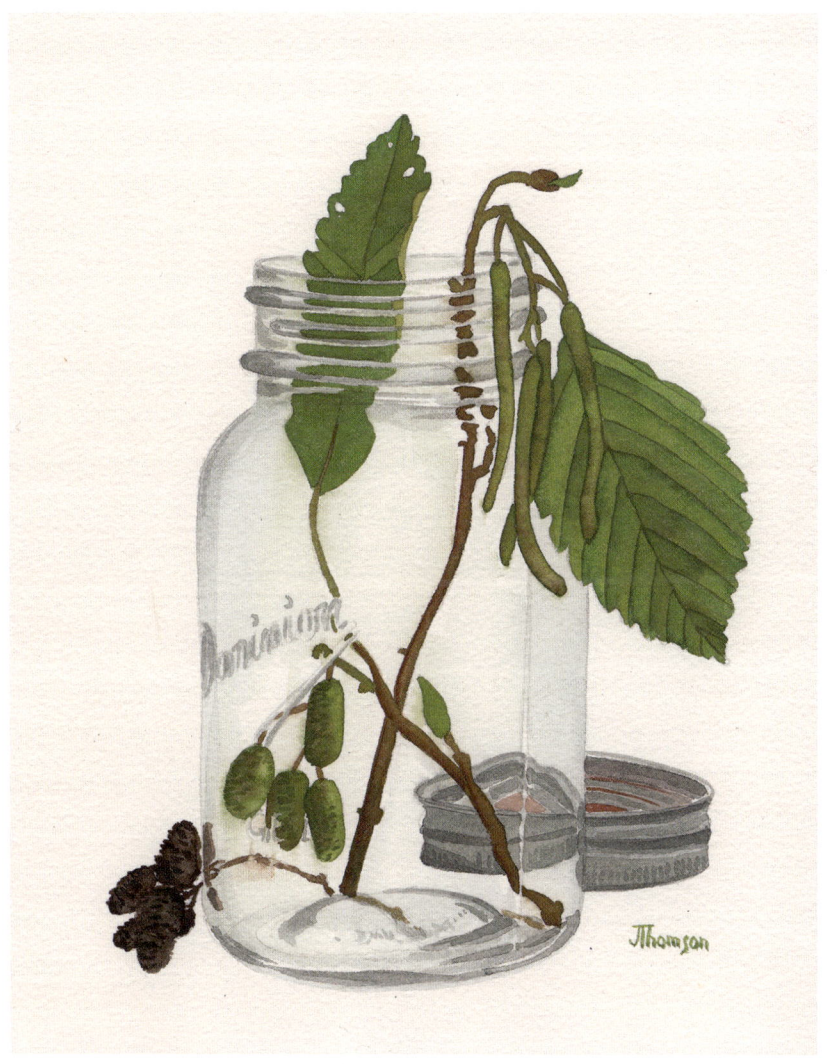

MASON JAR   More Boreal than coastal
WITH ALDER   Alder reminds me of childhood
2016   Walks in the woods on logging roads
                  Overtaken by their quick growth.

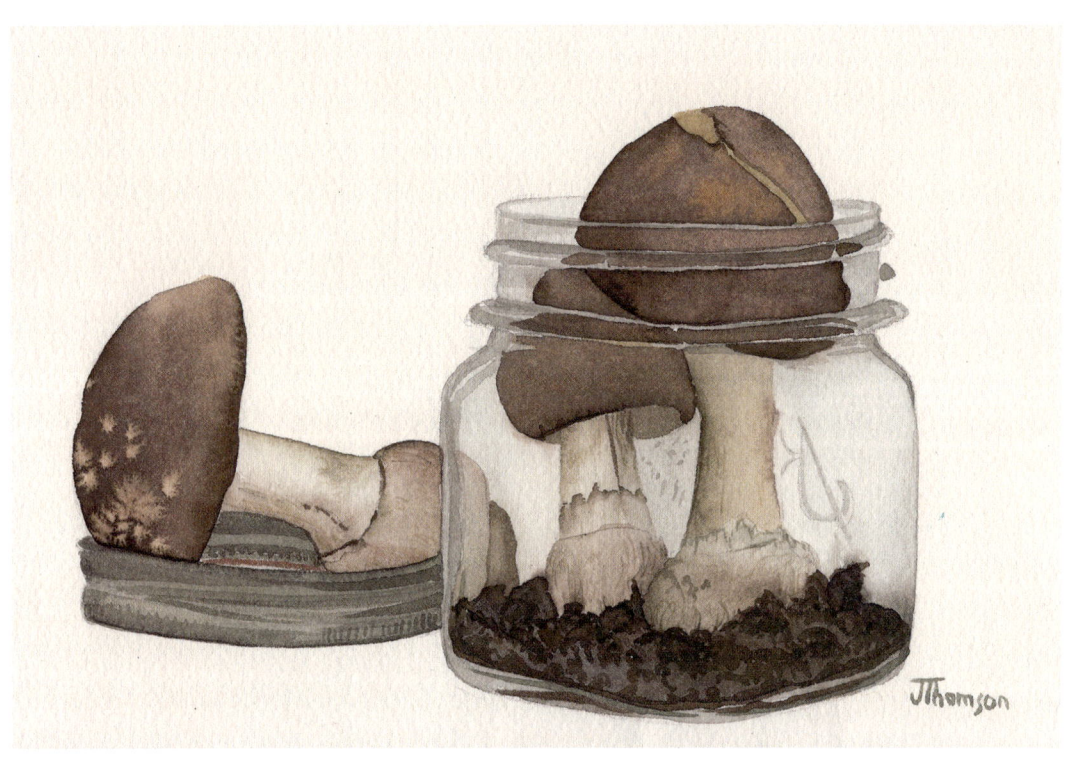

MASON JAR WITH

MUSHROOMS

2016

Not to be overlooked

Mushrooms flourish with the rains

Popping up in lawns, forests, and fields.

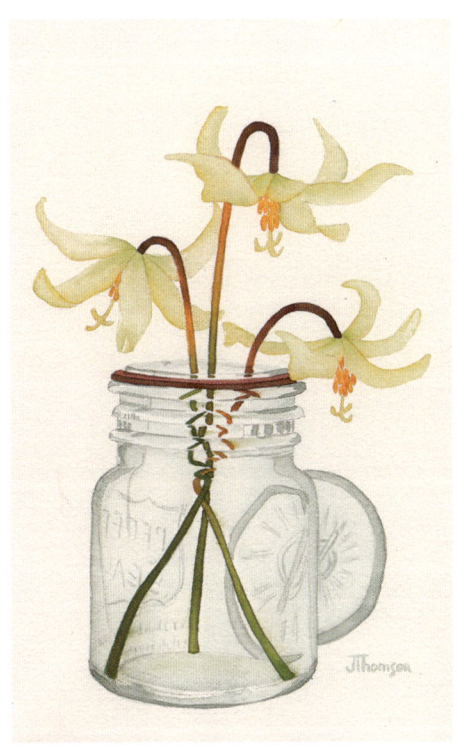

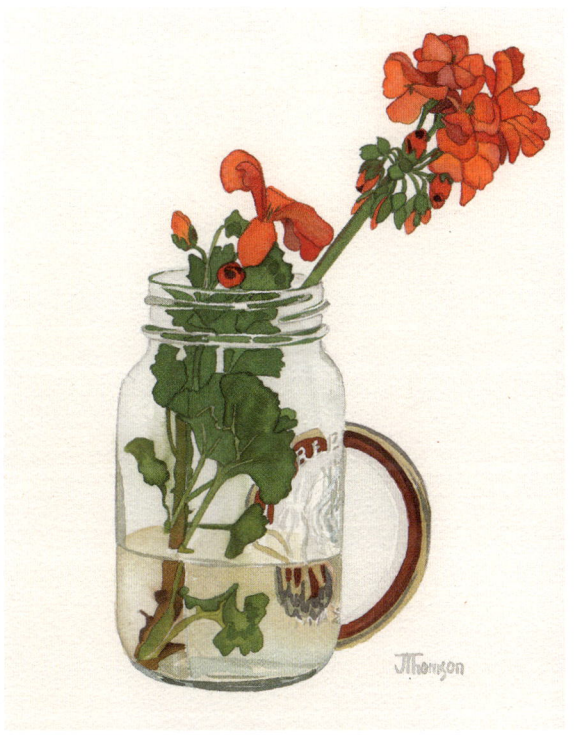

MASON JAR WITH
FAWN LILIES
2016

Three lilies imagined in a jar
Their few-ness and fragility
Protect them from harvest.
These were painted from drawings.

MASON JAR WITH
GERANIUM
2016

As frost draws near
Flowers retreat
A basement in winter
Becomes appealing.

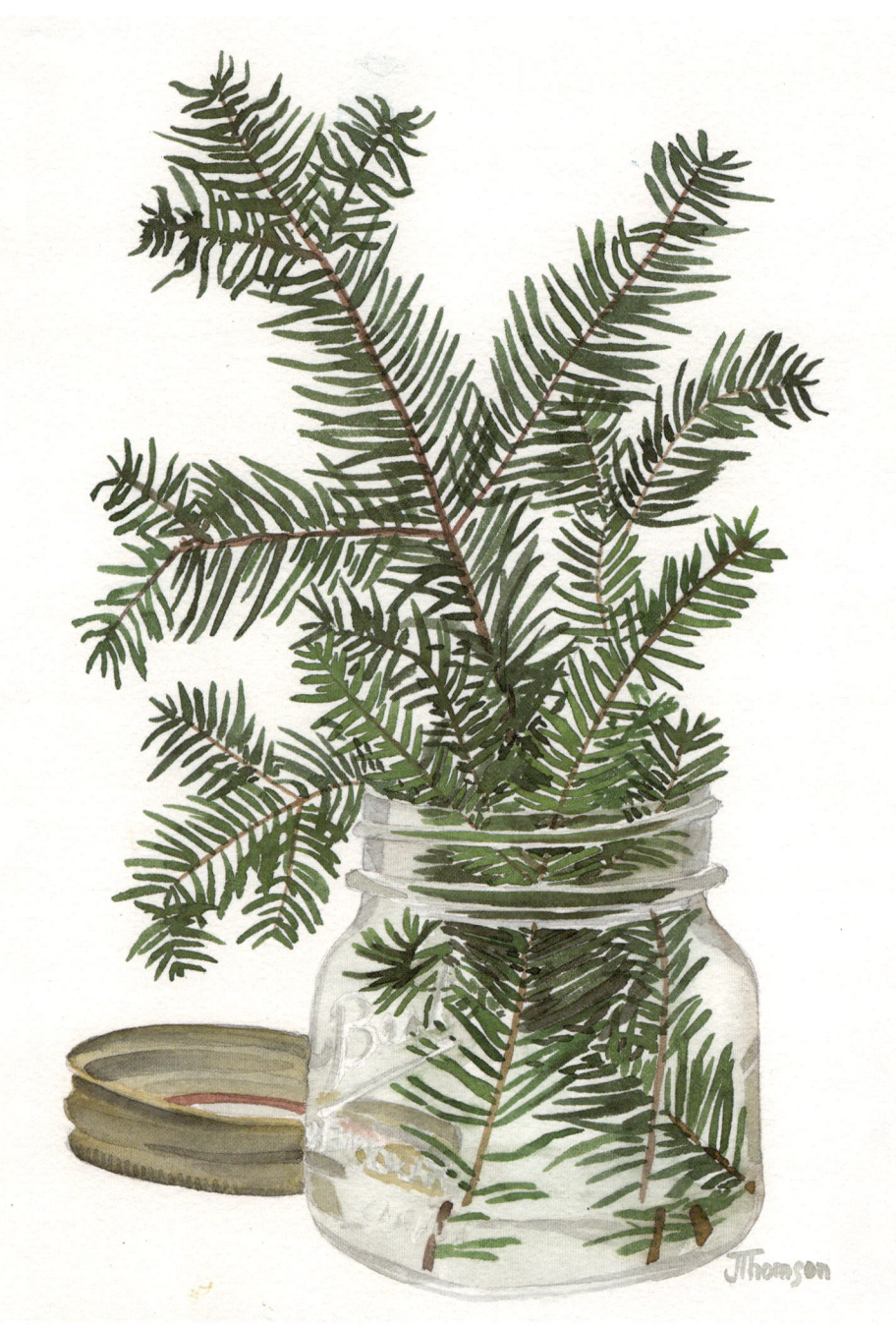

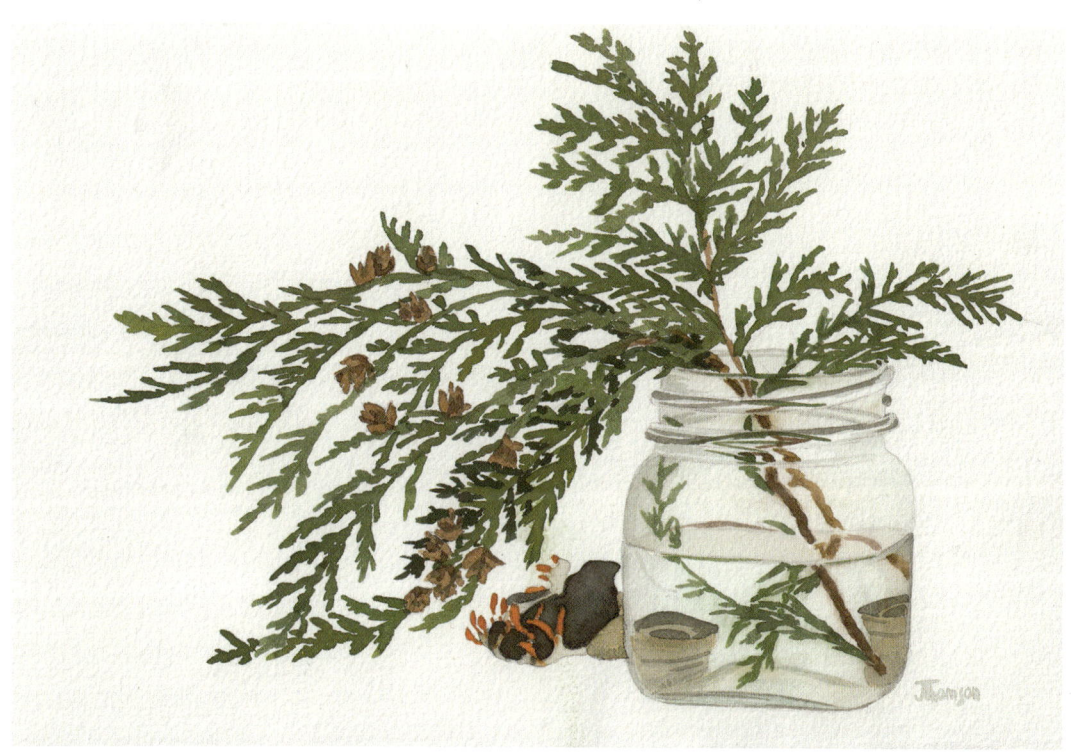

MASON JAR WITH	Moss covered forest floor
GRAND FIR	Moss-covered trunks reaching for the sky
2017	Small branches wind broken
	Land quietly.
MASON JAR WITH	Break a small bundle of green needles
RED CEDAR	Inhale the scent
2017	Return to the beginning
	Trees still reign supreme.

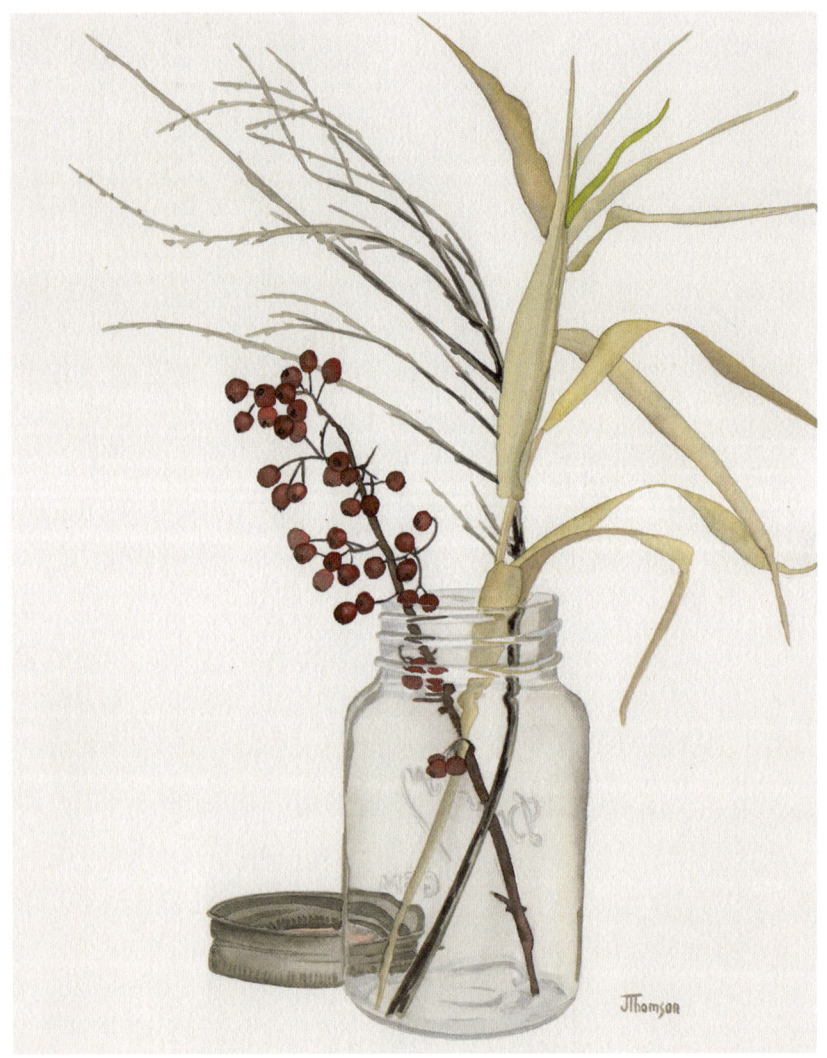

MASON JAR
WITH INVASIVES
2017

Pedigree doesn't matter
To a lover of native plants
Dried and dead these are at their best.

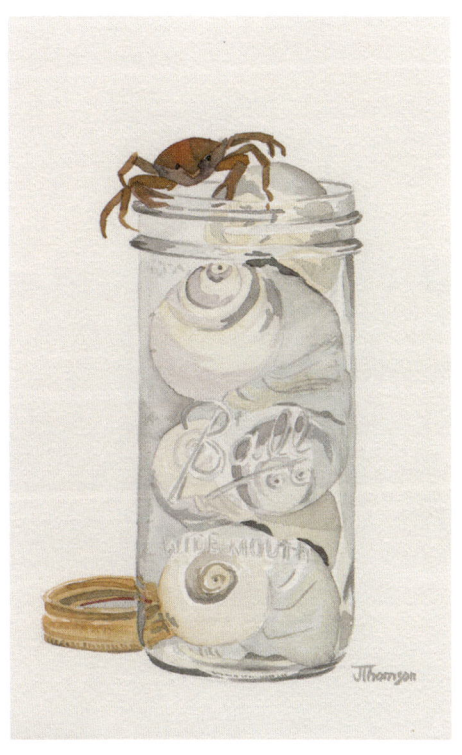

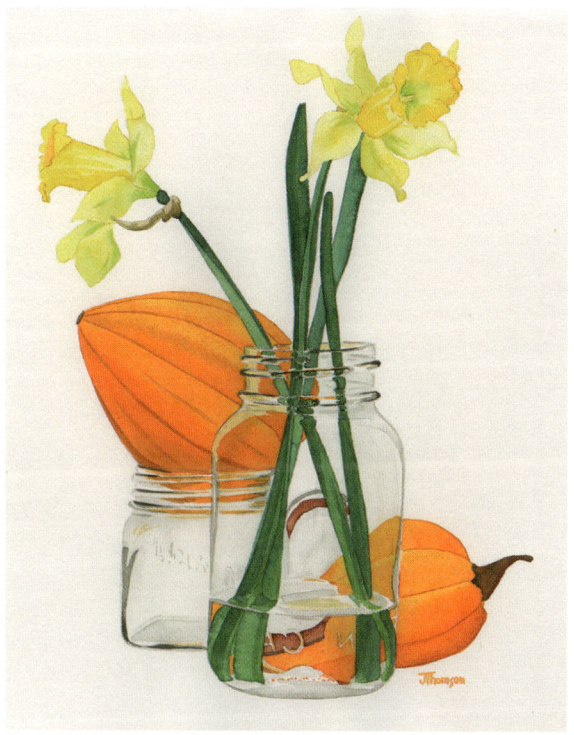

MASON JAR WITH	Memories of summer trips to the shore
MOON SNAILS	Moon snails and kelp crabs
AND KELP CRAB	Wet feet and salt water
2017	Sand between toes, and salt sticky fingers.
MASON JAR WITH	Every harvest is different
DAFFODILS AND	One year squash don't keep,
WINTER SQUASH	Another they last until Spring.
2017	They like to tease.

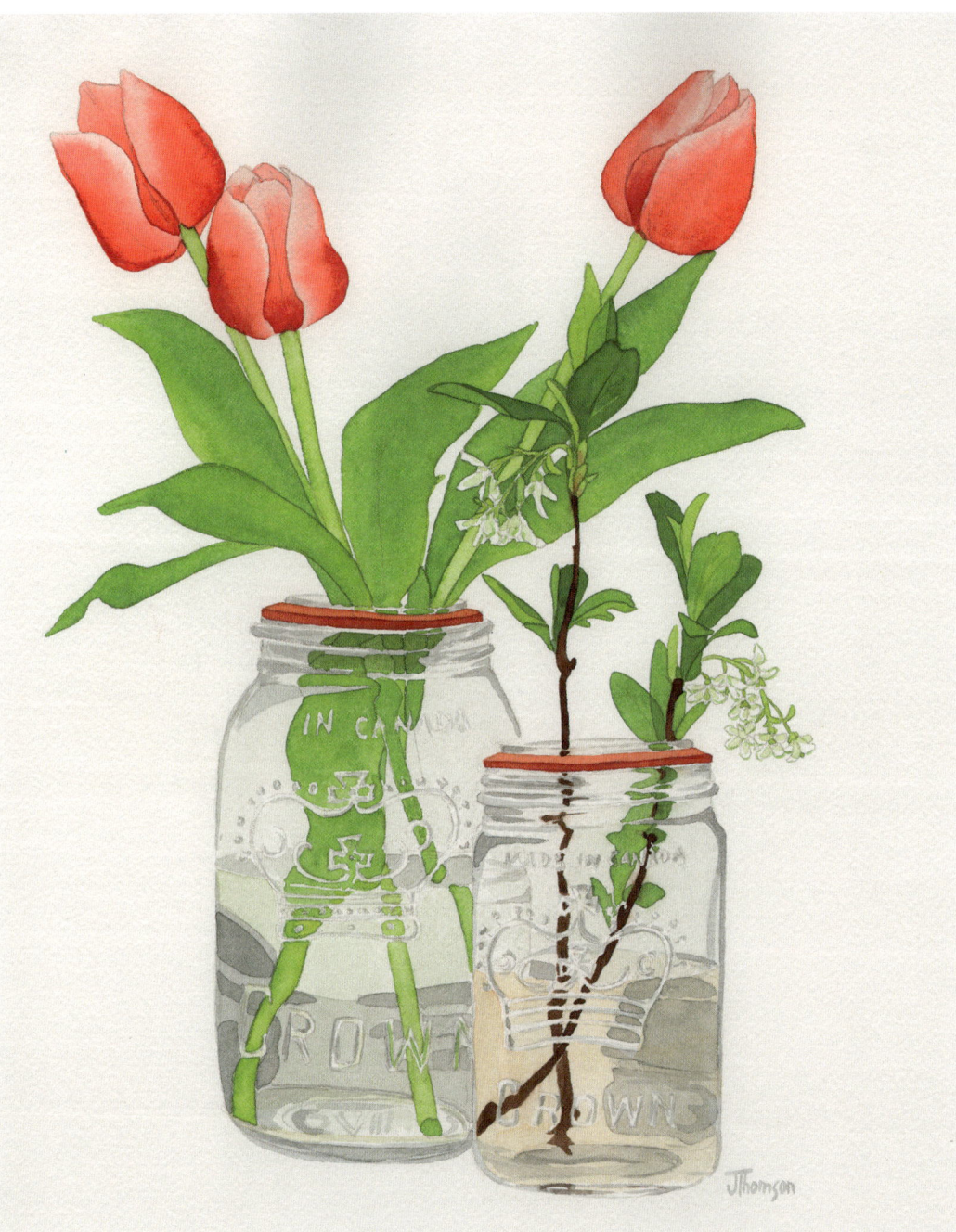

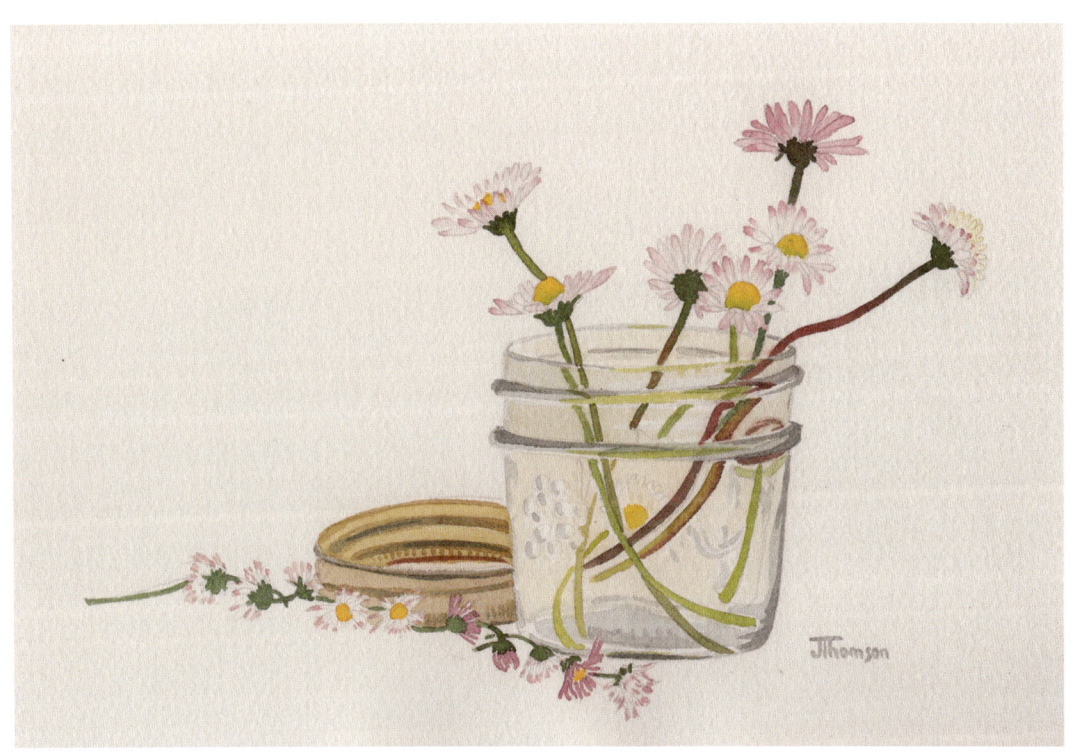

MASON JAR WITH
TULIP AND
INDIAN PLUM
2017

Domestic and Native
The flowers allow each their place
Each their beauty and uniqueness
A lesson for humanity.

MASON JAR WITH
DAISY CHAIN
2017

Memories of children
Dancing on the grass
With fairy jewels
And smiles as bright as sunshine.

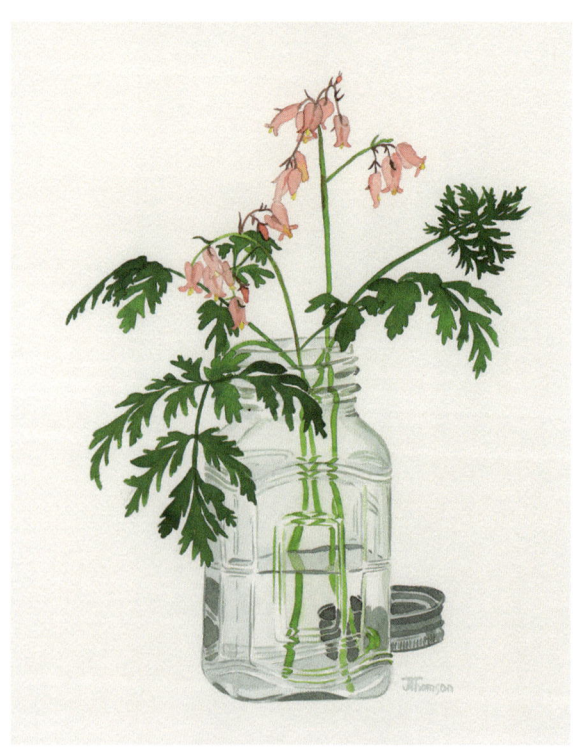
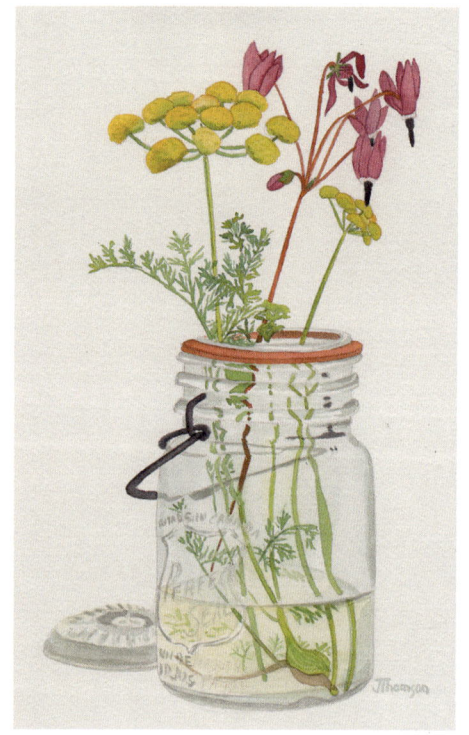

MASON JAR WITH
BLEEDING HEART
2017

Moving in the breeze
Delicate, resilient survivors
Speak of love and sorrow.

MASON JAR WITH
SPRING GOLD AND
SHOOTING STAR
2017

These sisters take turns
The meadows flash gold
Next they flash magenta
Dominance always only a year away.

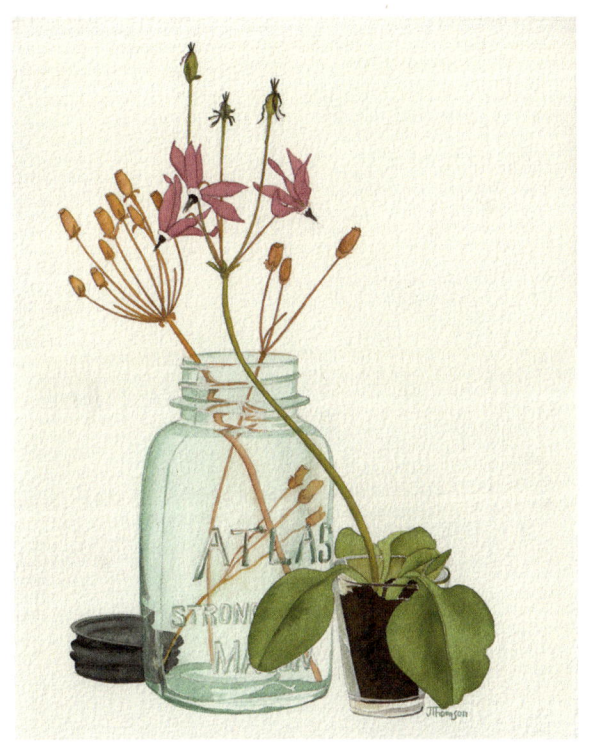

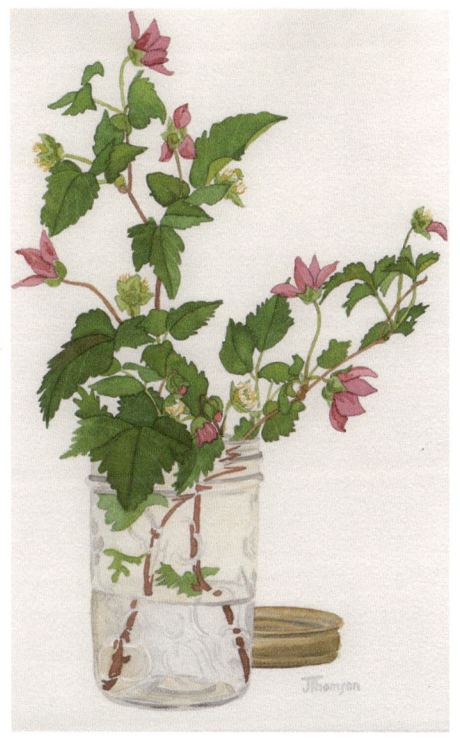

**MASON JAR WITH SHOOTING
STAR FLOWERS AND SEEDPODS**
2024

Wild seeds saved and scattered
To help the flowers survive
In places that are no longer wild.

**MASON JAR WITH
SALMONBERRY FLOWER**
2017

Petals fall onto the drab pathway
Look up, greet this springtime beauty
Friend to hummingbirds
And then to bears.

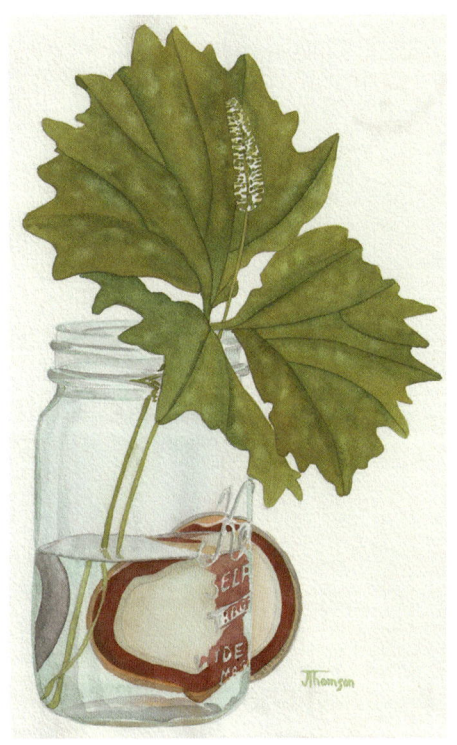

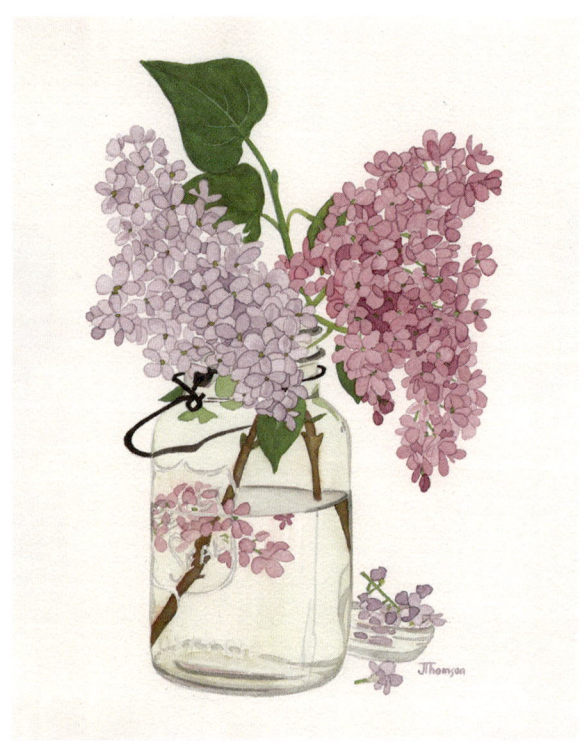

MASON JAR WITH　　Settler's bedding plant.
VANILLA LEAF　　　For sleep, not decoration.
2017　　　　　　　Their subtle scent more valued than their beauty.

MASON JAR　　　　Hardy homesteaders' companions
WITH LILAC　　　　Lilac show where hope of home
2017　　　　　　　Prospered once
　　　　　　　　　　And where lilacs prosper still.

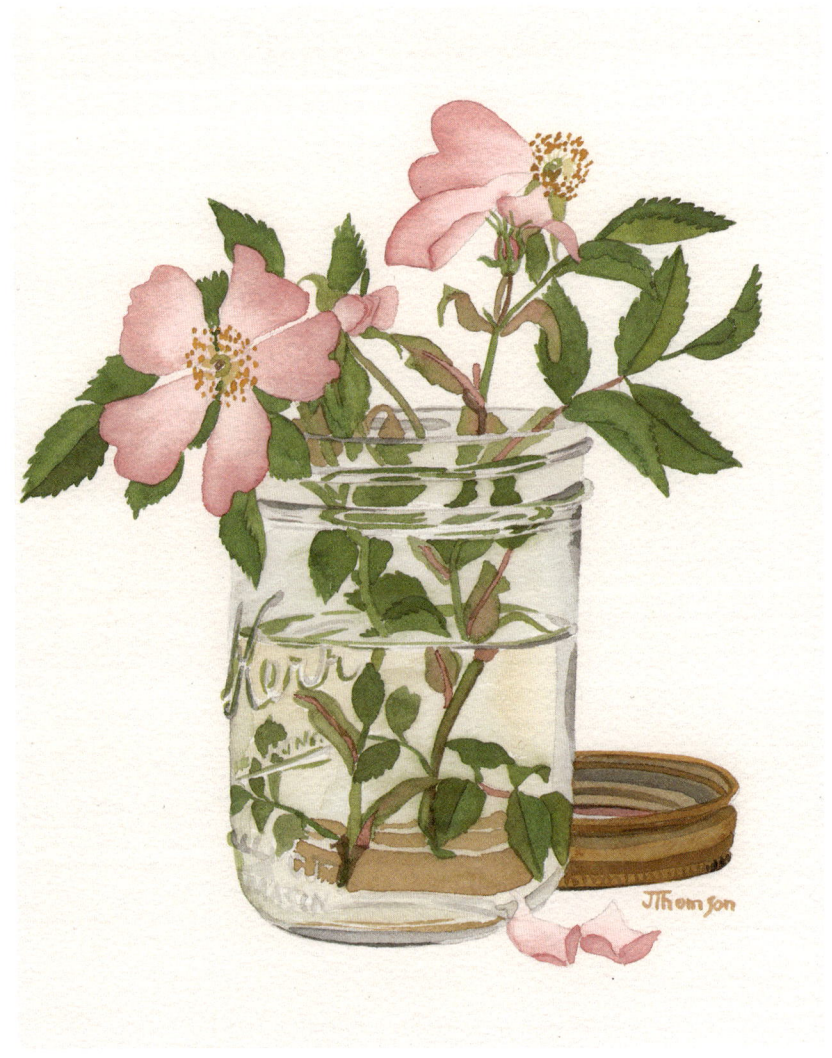

MASON JAR WITH   Every year

WILD ROSES   The scent of roses

2017   Lures me into thorny wild places.

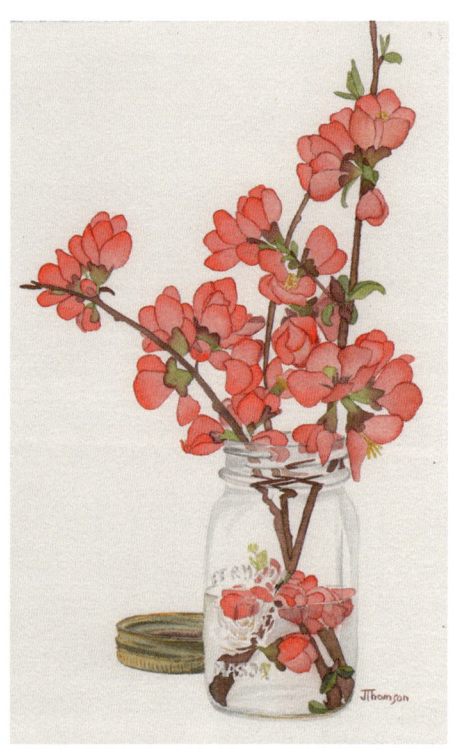
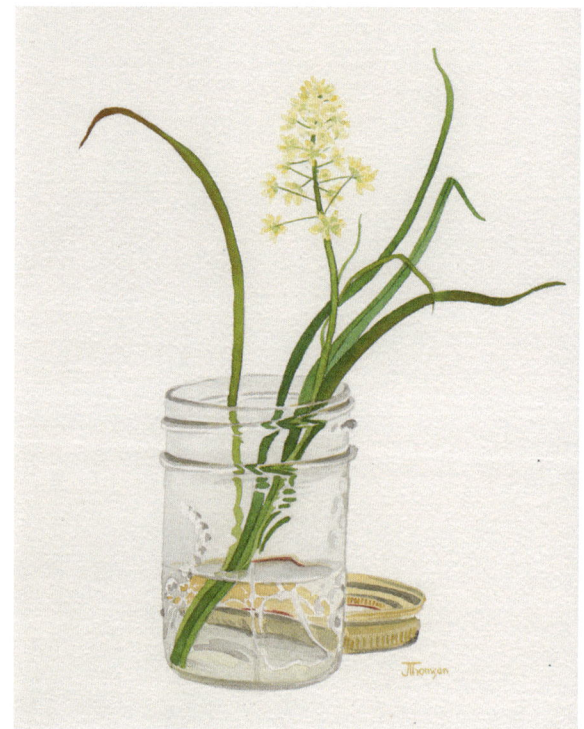

MASON JAR
WITH JAPONICA
2018

Every year the quince blossoms
Belying its plane name
Asking to be called Japonica
More poetic and matching its beauty.

MASON JAR WITH
DEATH CAMAS
2017

Not many on this coast,
Carefully culled by First Nations people
Death uninvited
Lingers on the edges of cliffs.

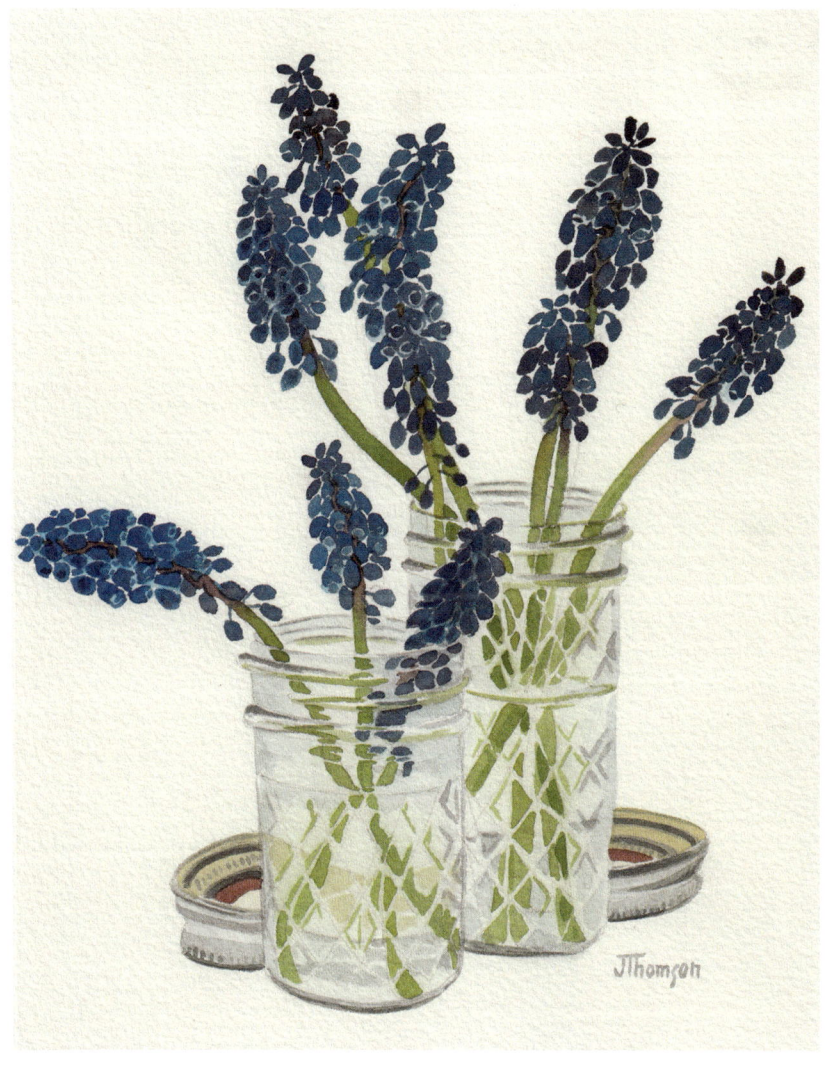

MASON JARS WITH   Every Spring they return
GRAPE HYACINTHS   Bright Blue as soon as the snow recedes
2019   Naturalized and plentiful.

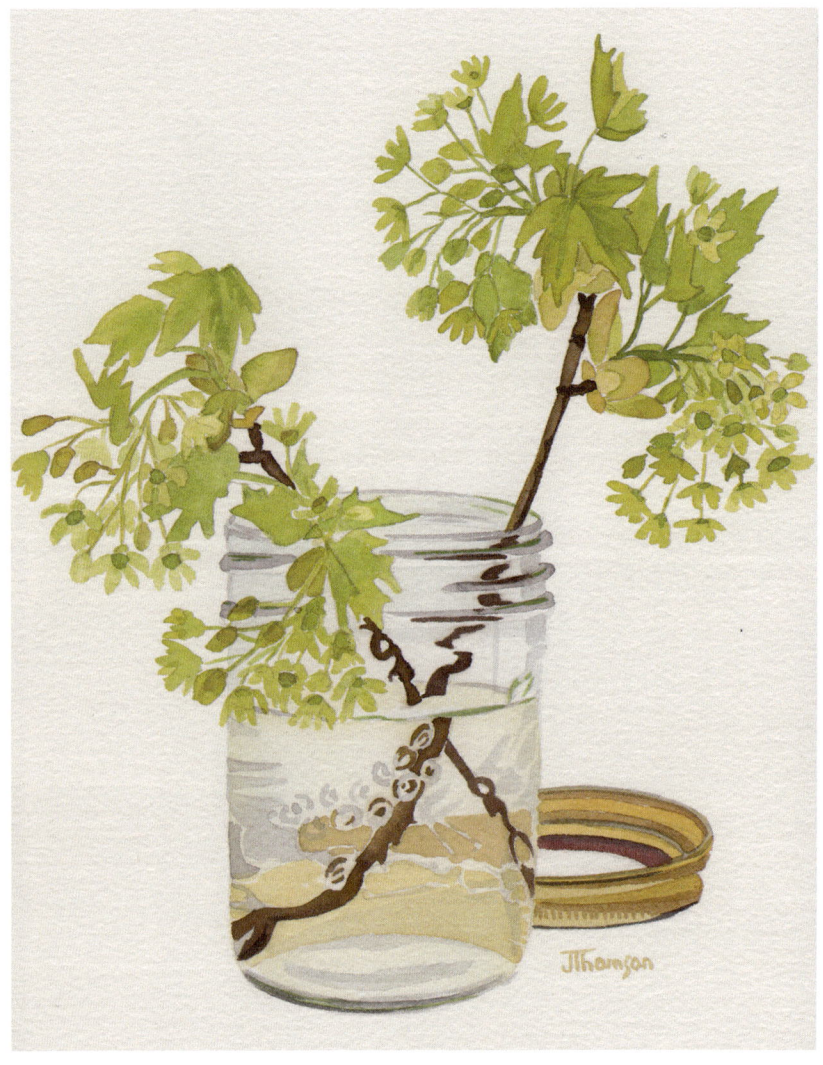

**MASON JAR WITH
MAPLE BLOSSOMS**

2019

They come and go so quickly
Pale beauties beneath new leaves
Easy to miss in Spring's exuberance.

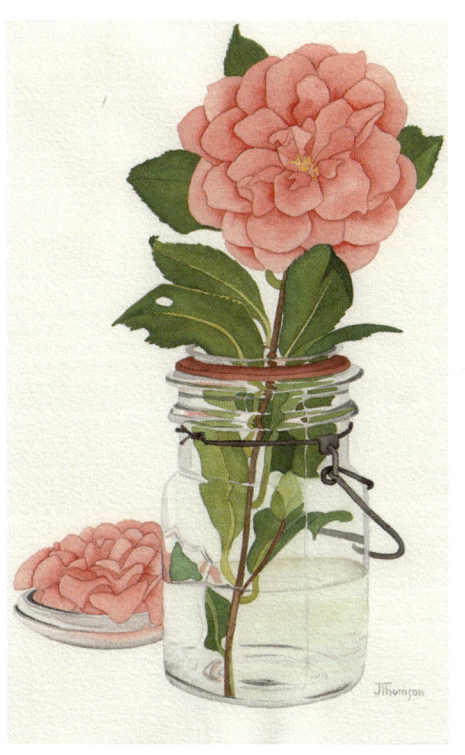

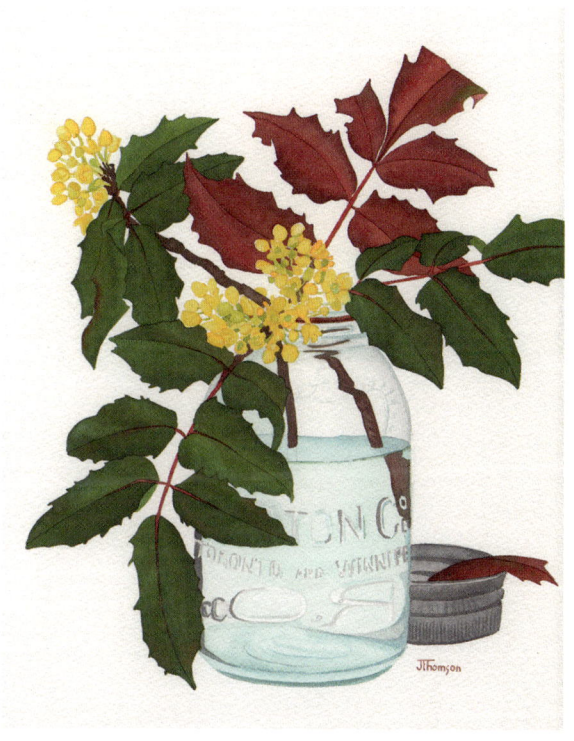

MASON JAR WITH
CAMELLIAS
2019

Foreign to this unpredictable land
Most fall to frost and rain.
A few always make it.

MASON JAR
WITH OREGON
GRAPE BLOSSOM
2019

Scenting the forest yellow
Between leaves of past and present.

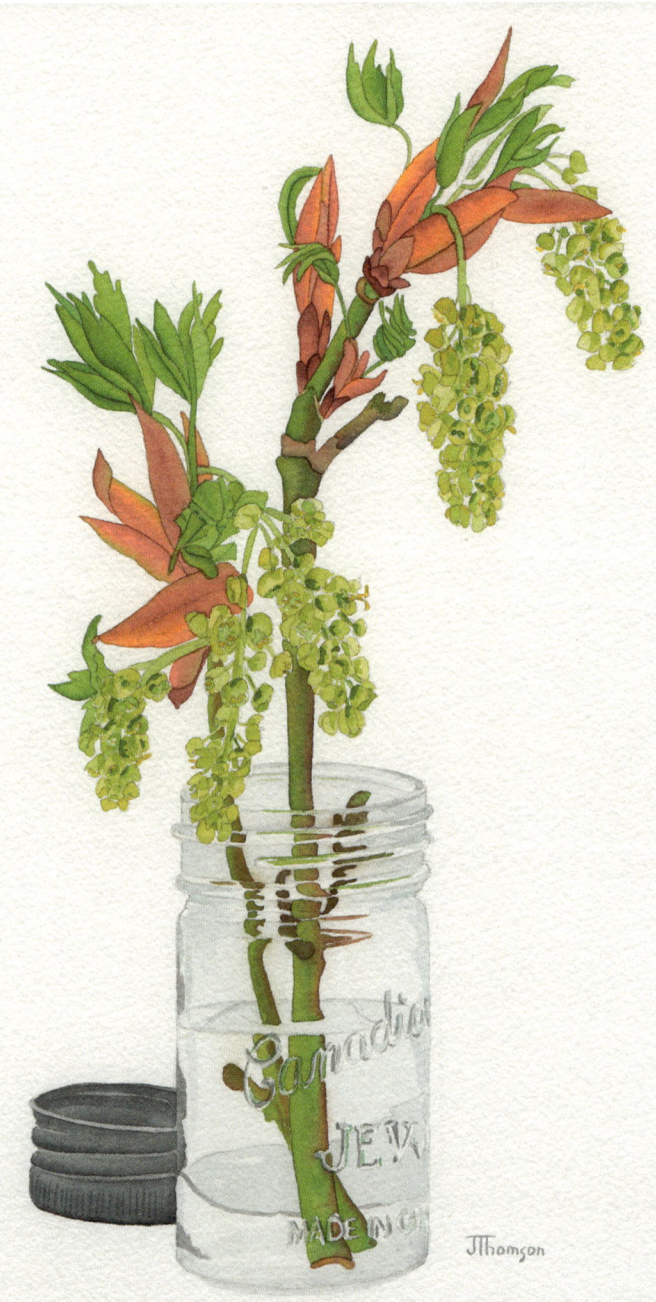

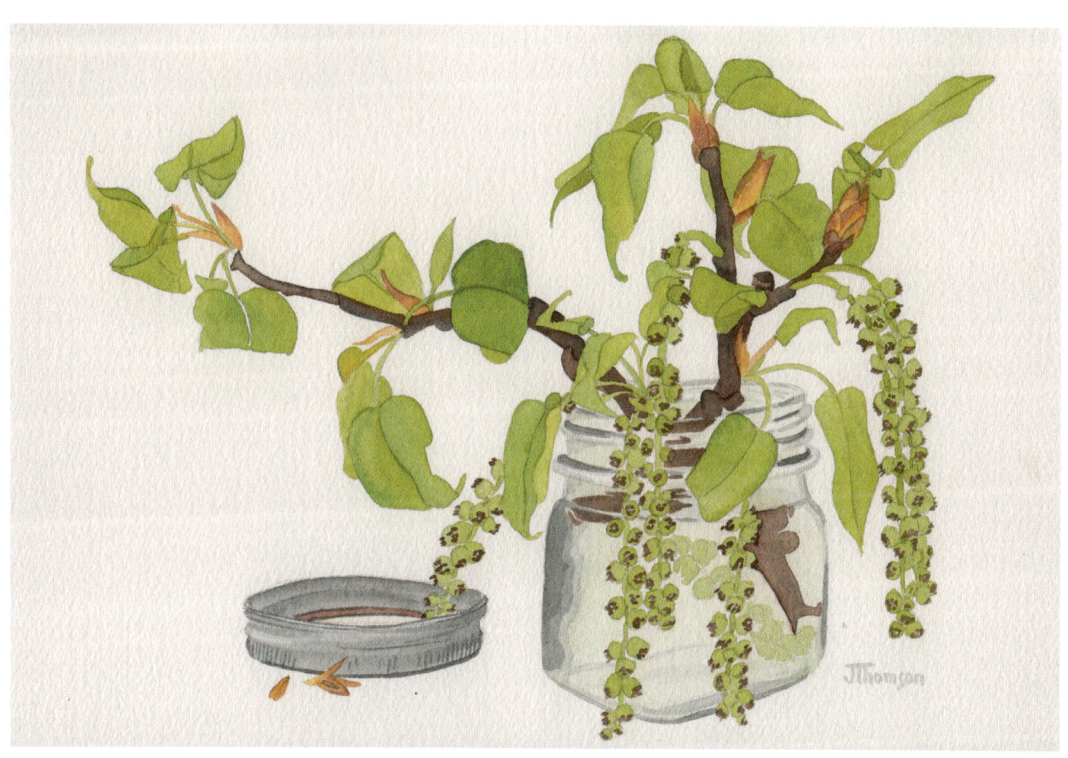

MASON JAR WITH BIG LEAF MAPLE BLOSSOMS

2019

Each year they startle me
Exuberant beauty
Hurrying out before leaves
Declaring Spring!

MASON JAR WITH COTTONWOOD FLOWERS

2019

The scent of Spring
Sticky leaves and flowers
Breathe deeply
It is gone too soon.

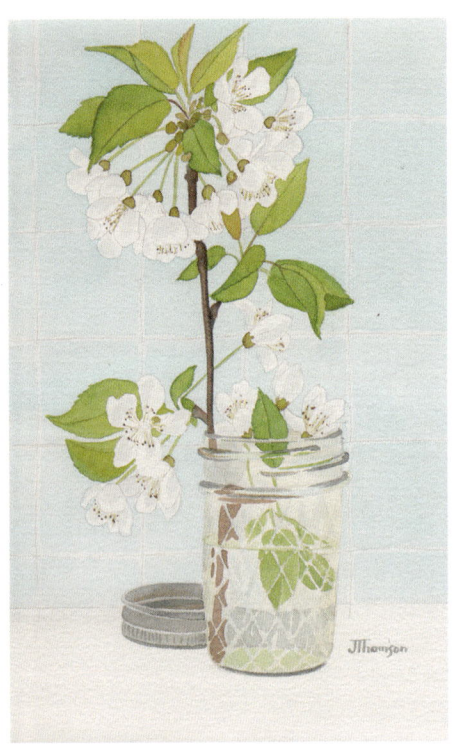 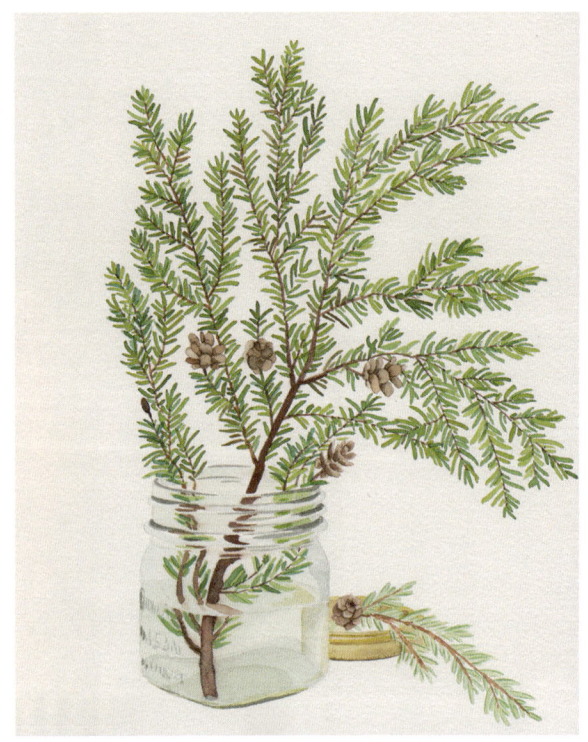

MASON JAR WITH WILD
CHERRY BLOSSOMS

2019

They used to be bright pink and oversized
Then the grafted part died.
Now they reach from shoots
Regaining their delicate beauty.

MASON JAR WITH
WESTERN HEMLOCK

2019

The naughty one
Missed the call for needles
Dressed in left overs
Modern couture before couture existed.

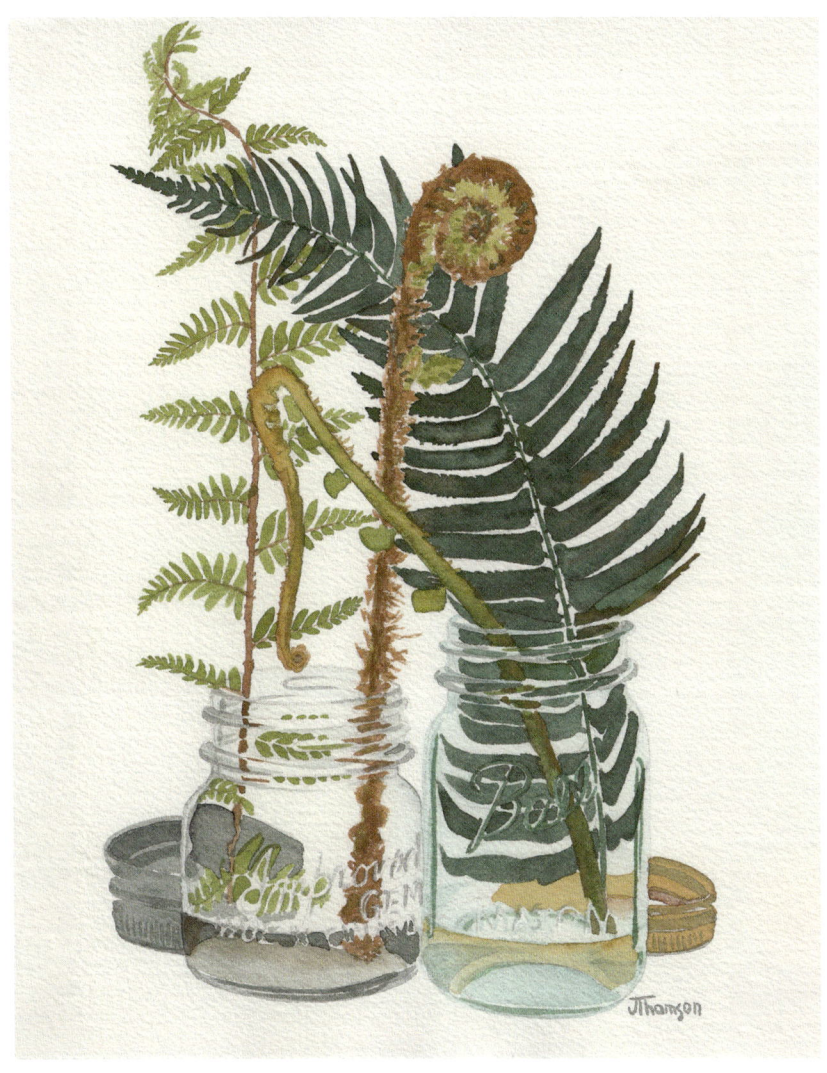

MASON JAR WITH Fiddlehead soup
FERNS UNFOLDING A rare treat
2019 Though not all ferns
Are culinary equals.

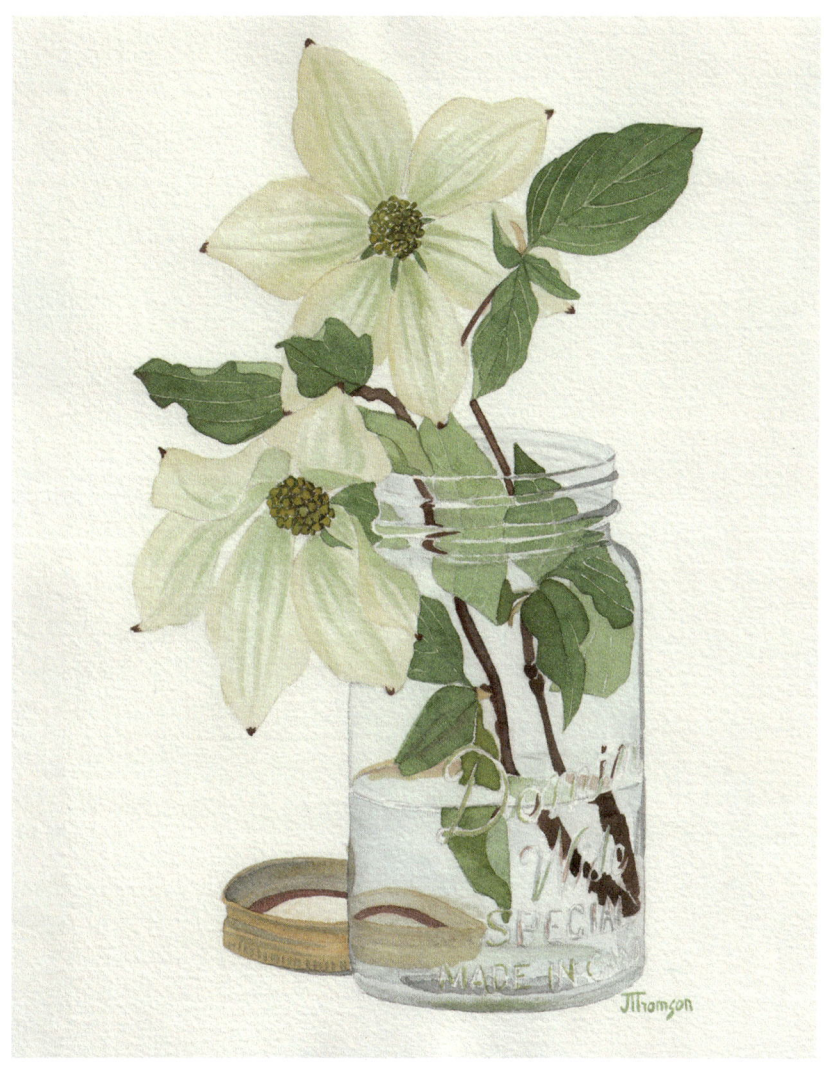

MASON JAR WITH Dogwood flowers light up the forest
PACIFIC DOGWOOD Surprising the evergreens
2019 With delicate deciduous beauty.

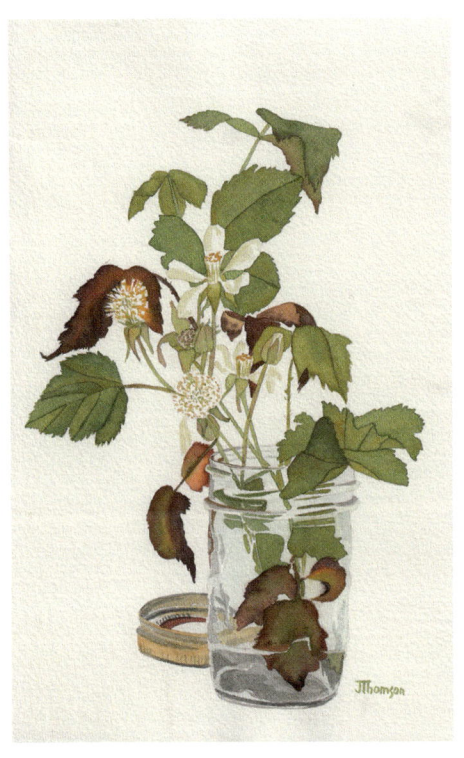

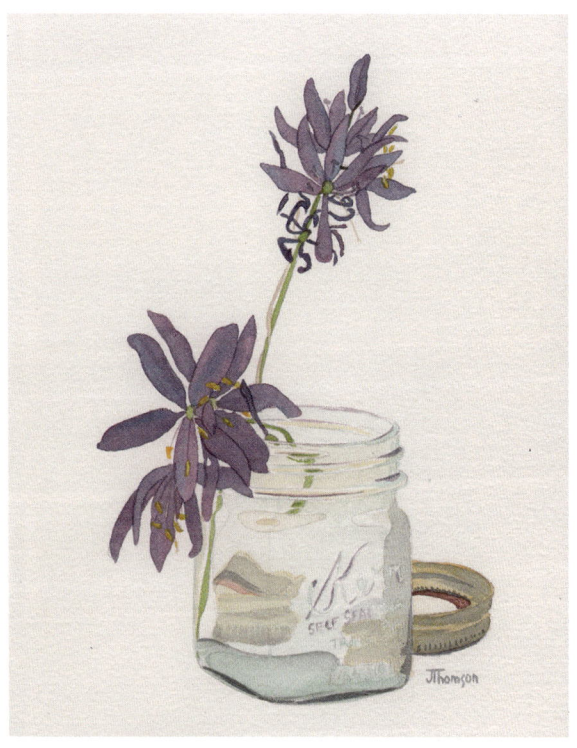

**MASON JAR WITH TRAILING
BLACKBERRY IN FLOWER**

2019

Quickly now, the light is right
Let's bloom before the grasses grow
And win the race for sunshine.

**MASON JAR WITH DOG
DAMAGED GRAND AND
COMMON CAMAS**

2019

Unleashed exuberance.
Snapped beauties.
Preserved in paint.
Interrupted propagation.
Leashes are preferable.

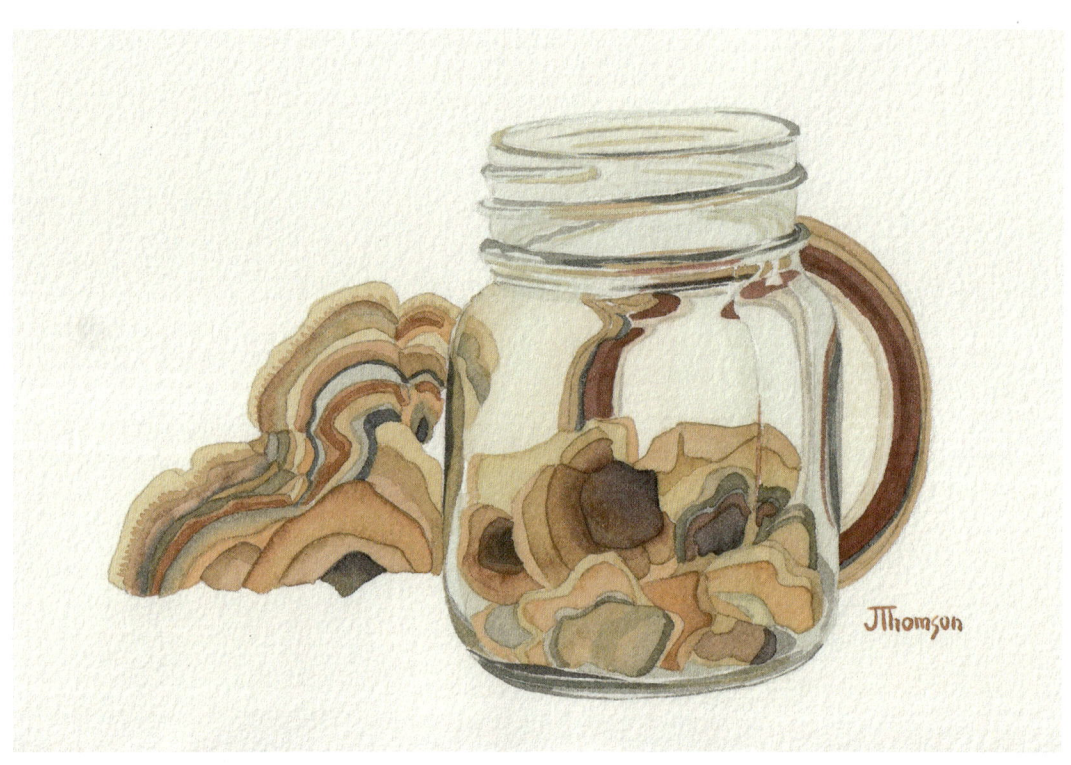

MASON JAR WITH   Colours that reflect complexity

TURKEY TAIL   Within and below

MUSHROOMS   Distilled into medicines

2019   These lovelies fight cancer.

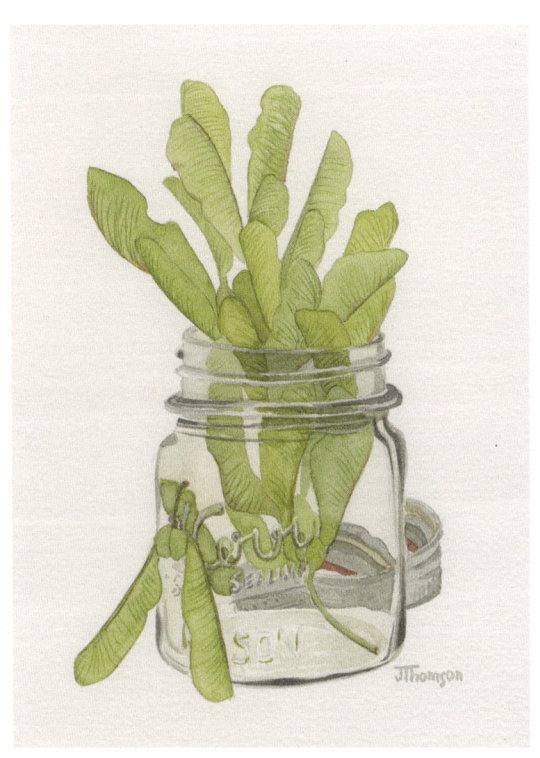

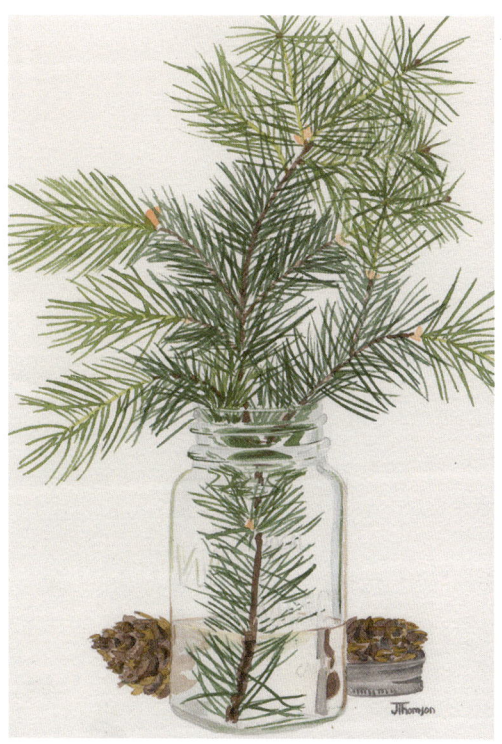

MASON JAR WITH	So many more than can ever grow
MAPLE SEEDS	They fly from the trees on the wind.
2019	Or fall in clumps and feed the squirrels.
MASON JAR WITH	New growth
DOUGLAS FIR	Storm tossed in June
2019	Salvaged for fir-tip tea
	Lovely for the home and heart.

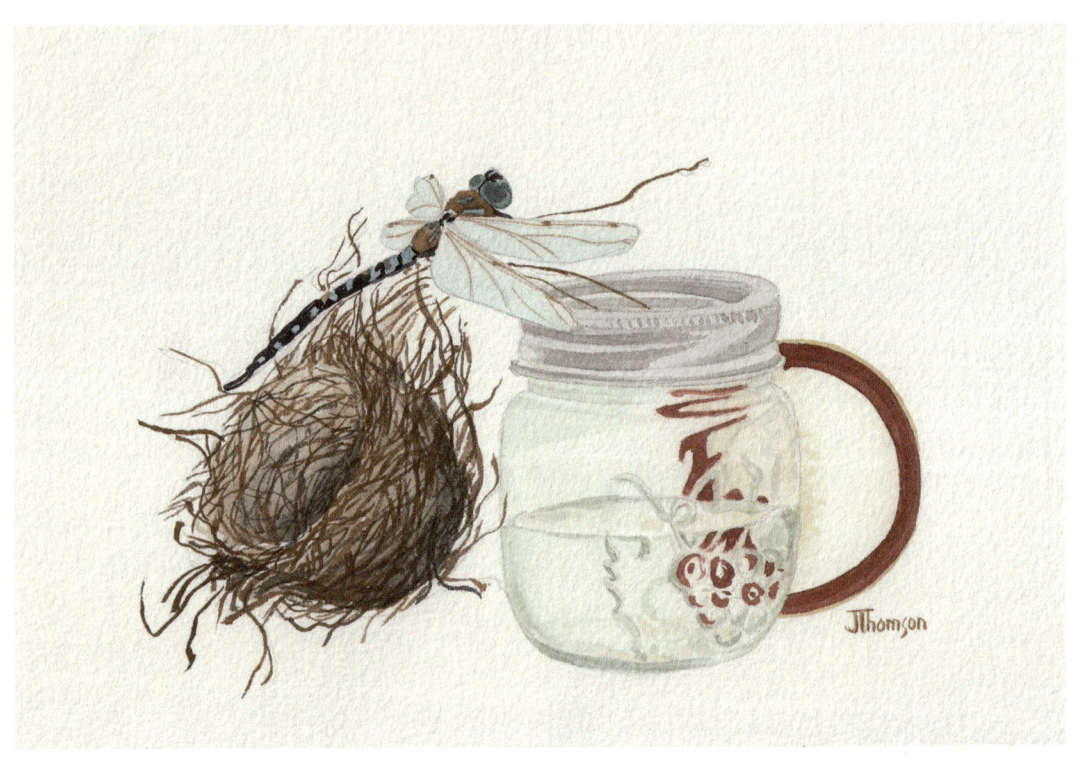

MASON JAR WITH Sometimes gifts fall from the sky
BIRD NEST AND Onto a deck
DRAGONFLY Or onto a leaf
2019 The noticing make them mine.

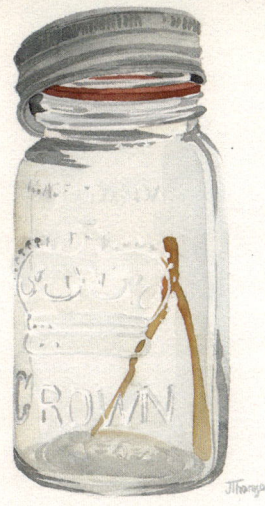
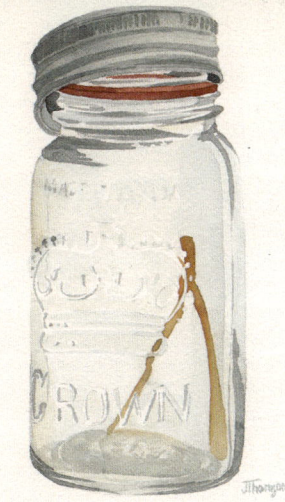
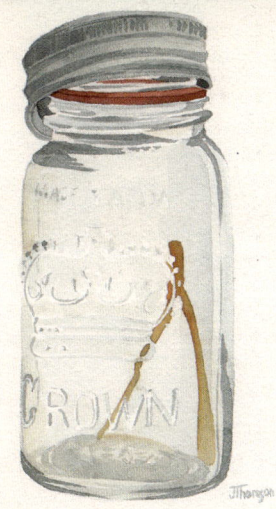
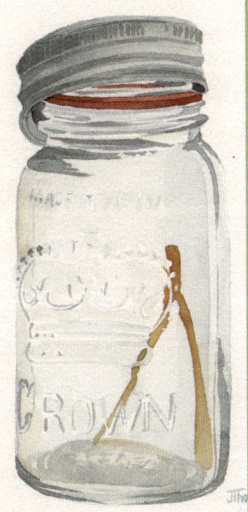
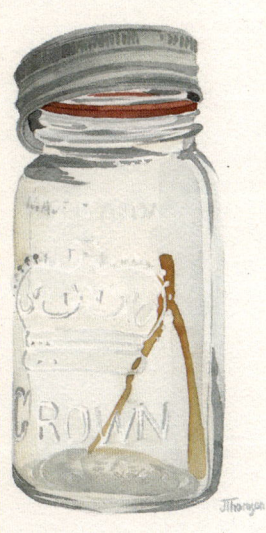

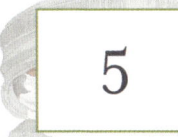

5

HEIRLOOMS AND ARTIFACTS

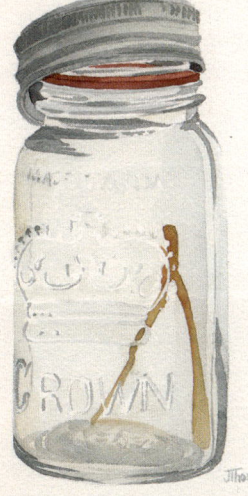
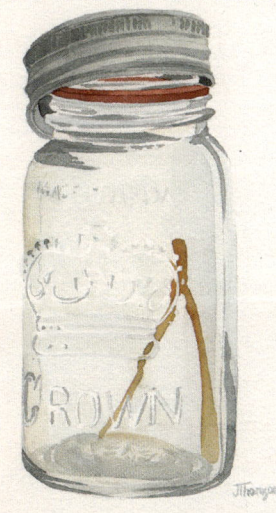
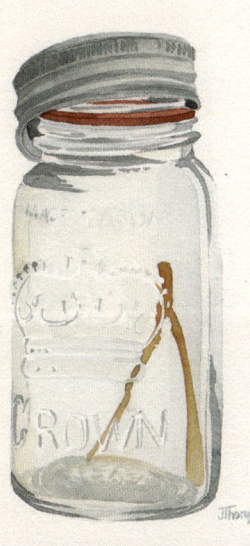

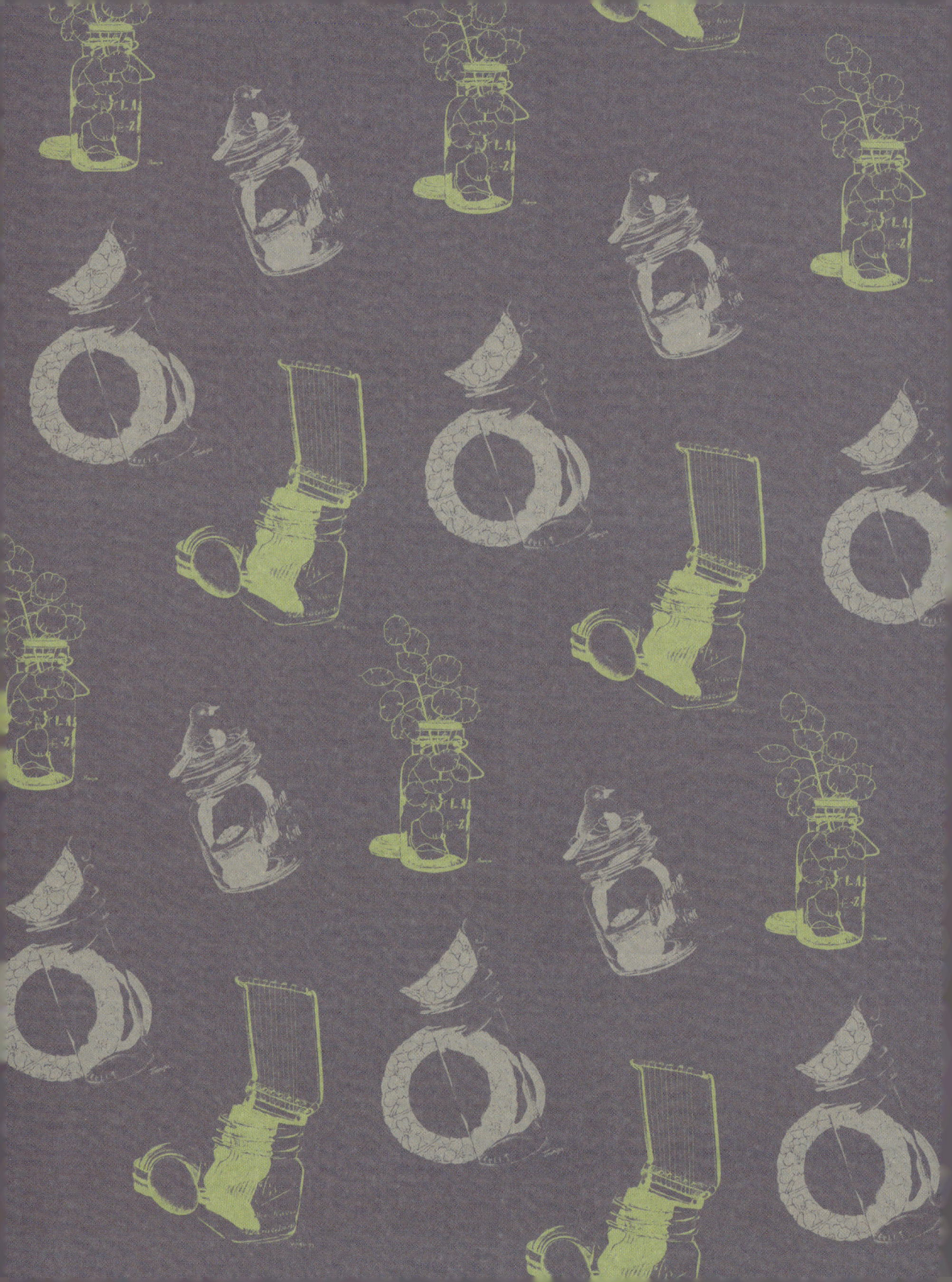

MEMORIES ARE HELD in objects. It is these memories that make them valuable.

An Avon perfume jar evokes the scent of Grandmother Thomson as she traces the lines on my palm and then smooths the hair away from my brow. Films stacked on a shelf conjure up the whirr of the projector and my father's cigarette glowing in the dark on a winter evening. A pipe cleaner bumble bee from a bouquet of flowers gifted to a girl in 1947 remembers the man who would love that girl for the rest of his life. A teacup that cost a week's wages found 60 years later in a thrift shop for one dollar allows a story to be told. An egg cutter that cut eggs for devilled egg sandwiches long before I was born speaks of picnics and school lunches. Simple, everyday objects hold stories that change with each telling, and illustrate a family heritage.

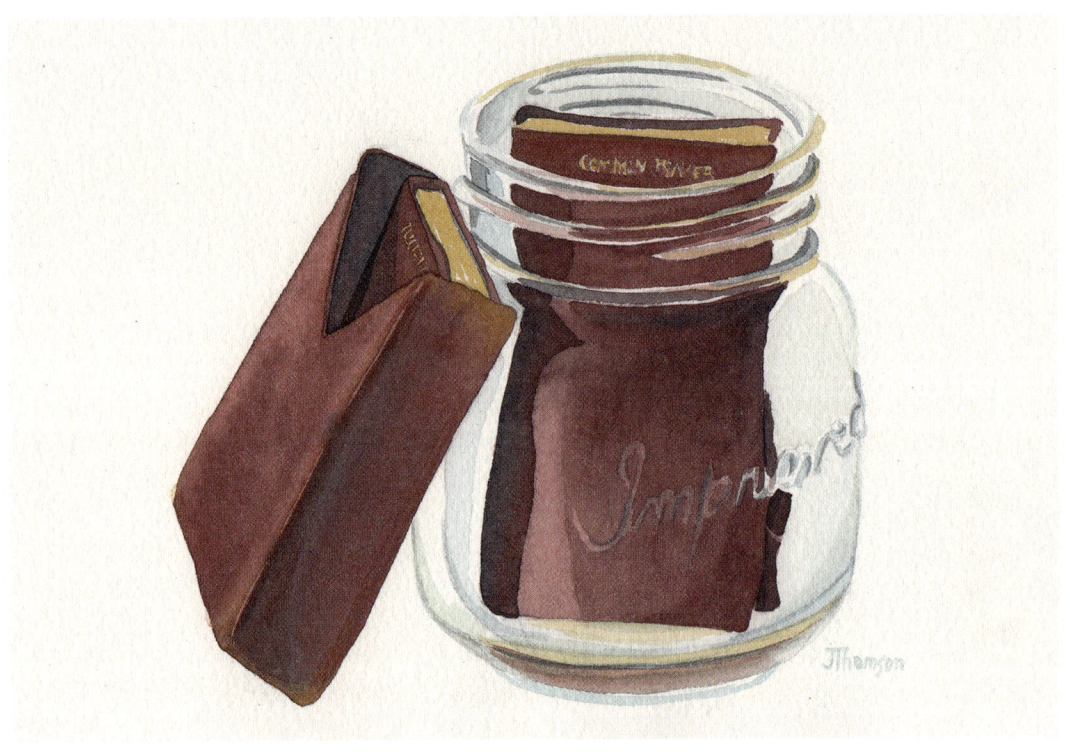

MASON JAR WITH
HYMNAL AND COMMON
PRAYER BOOK
2014

The trappings of piety
A code to live by
Anglican traditions passed down
Not always followed.

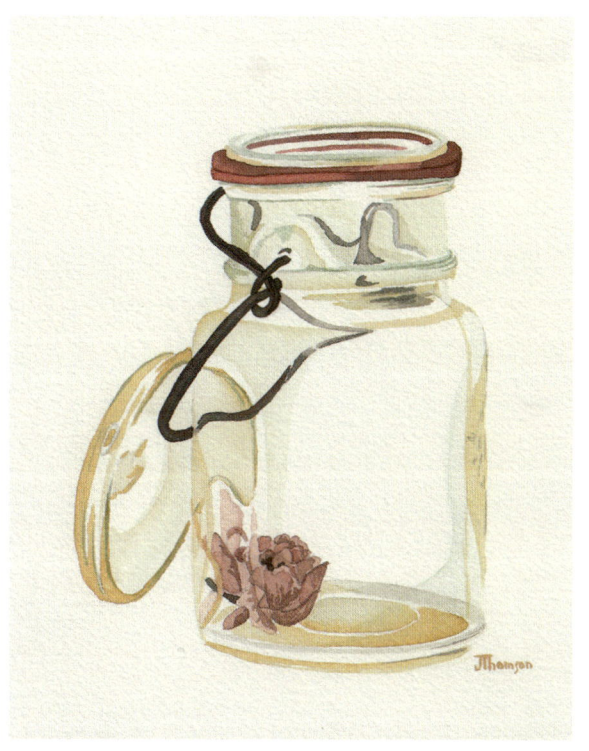 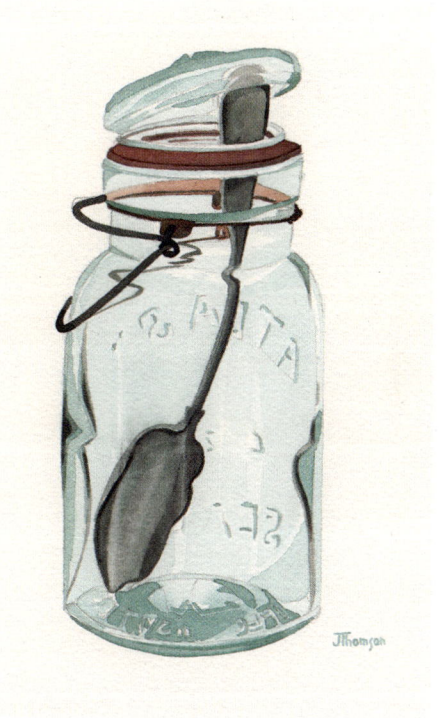

**MASON JAR WITH
DRIED ROSE**

2014

Little girl dreams of a handsome prince
Luxury and leisure
Planted disappointments
Kept safe and passed on.

**MASON JAR WITH
SILVER SPOON**

2014

"Born with a silver spoon in his mouth"
A disparaging comment, a complaint,
A desire, an envy, an ambition.
Ohhh, to have been born to wealth!

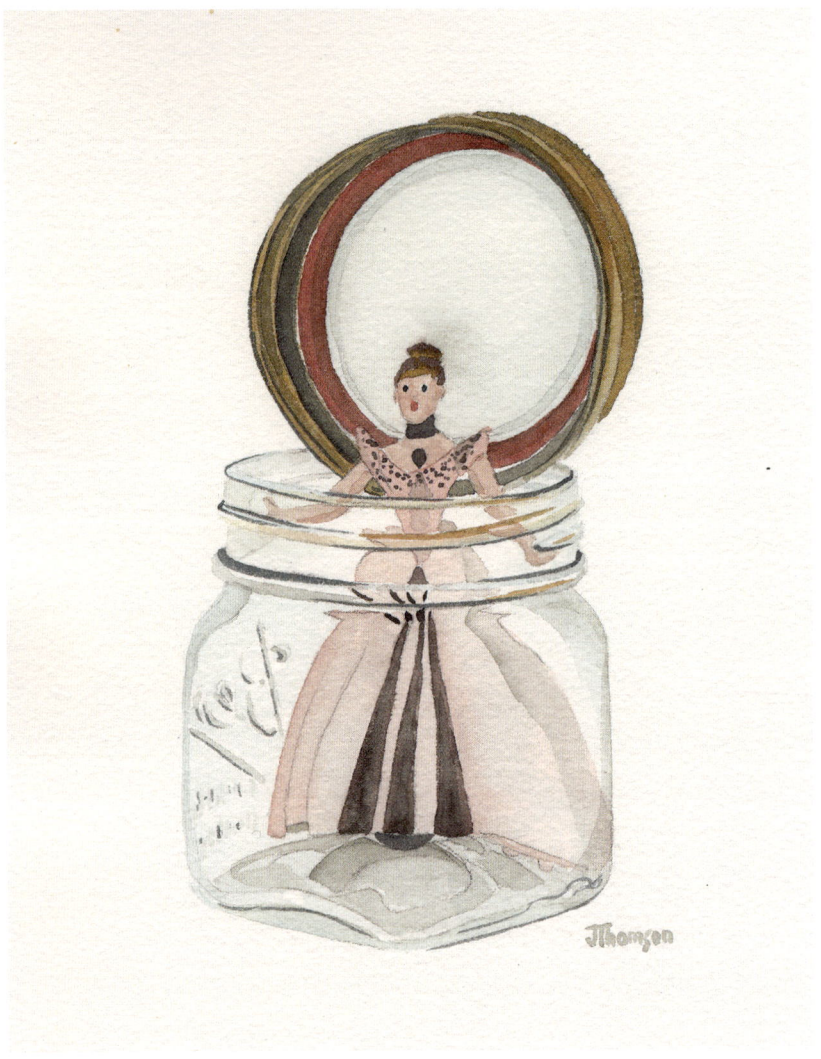

MASON JAR WITH
CINDERELLA DOLL
2014

Wind her up with a key
She will dance for you
Make your wishes come true
And release you from the past.

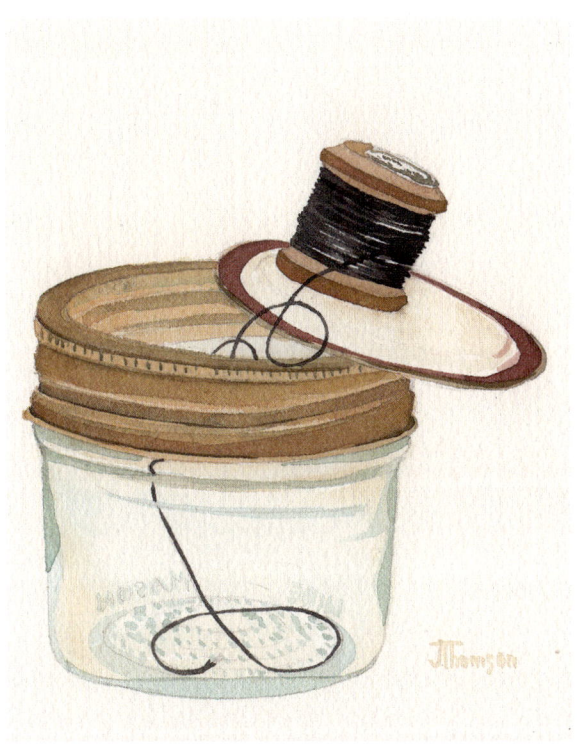

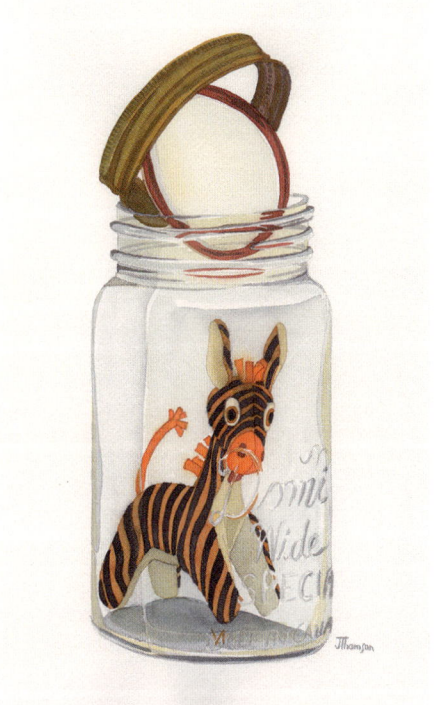

MASON JAR WITH	Wooden spool
BLACK THREAD	Coarse thread
2014	Strong repairs are sometimes needed.

MASON JAR WITH	A foreigner,
ZEBRA TOY	Different, sturdy and determined'
2014	Sticks his tongue out at those who
	Deny his belonging.

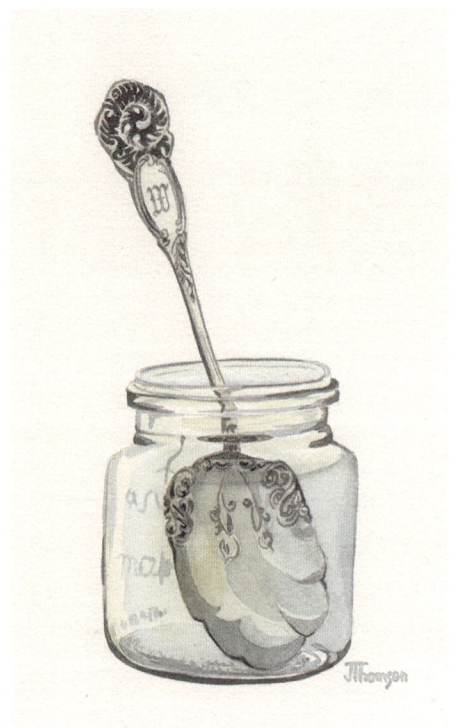

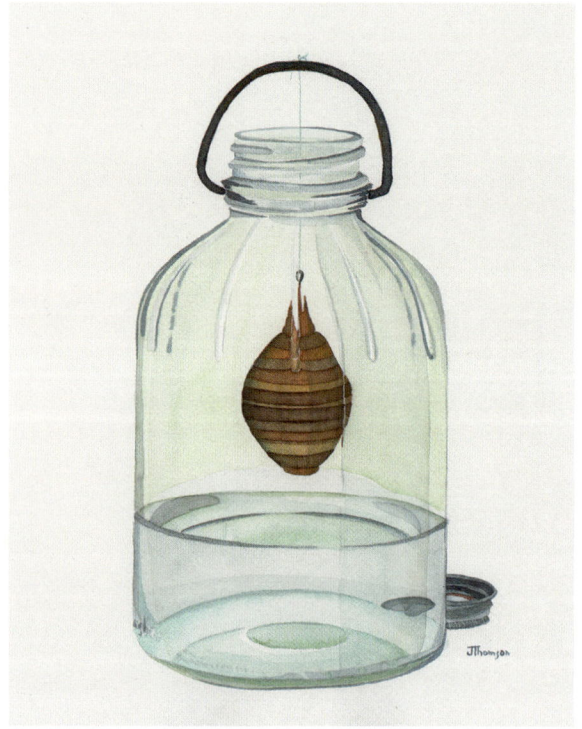

MASON JAR WITH
WILLOMENA'S
SILVER SPOON
2014

She etched a W in each one
Claiming this reminder of past glory.

MASON JAR WITH
BOINK MAKER
2014

My father's voice tells a story
His audience doubles over with laughter
Scotch and cigarettes scent the air
And the Boink Maker lives again.

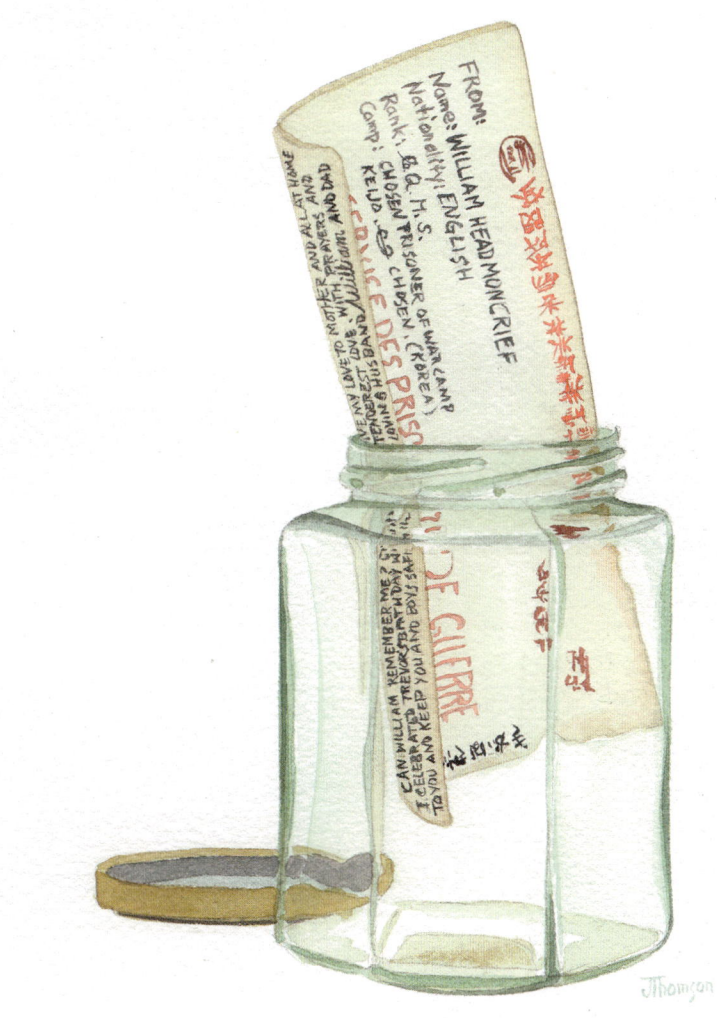

MASON JAR WITH   Letter to home

UNCLE WILLIAM'S   From prison camp in Asia

POSTCARD   Love to both my sons and you

2014   My love.

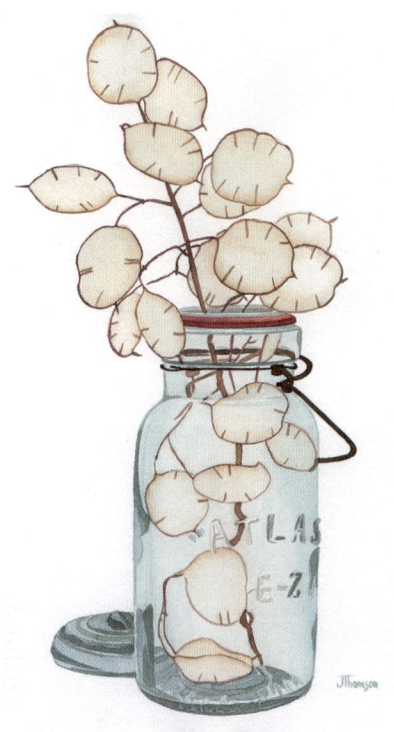

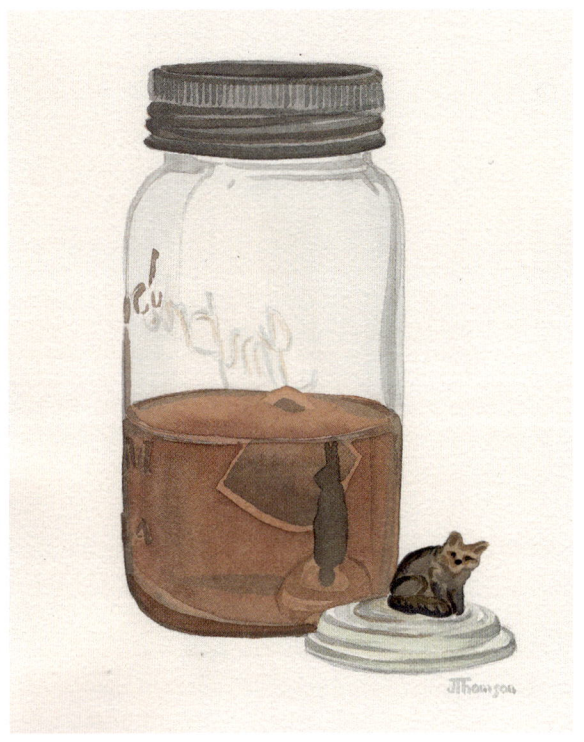

MASON JAR   If the money used in childhood games were real
WITH HONESTY   There would be fields of honesty plants
PLANT DISCS   Wealth beyond measure

2014   We would grow our food for pleasure alone.

MASON JAR WITH   Who is the hunted?
TEA AND NABOB   Who is the hunter?
TEA ORNAMENT   The fox becomes a stole.

2014

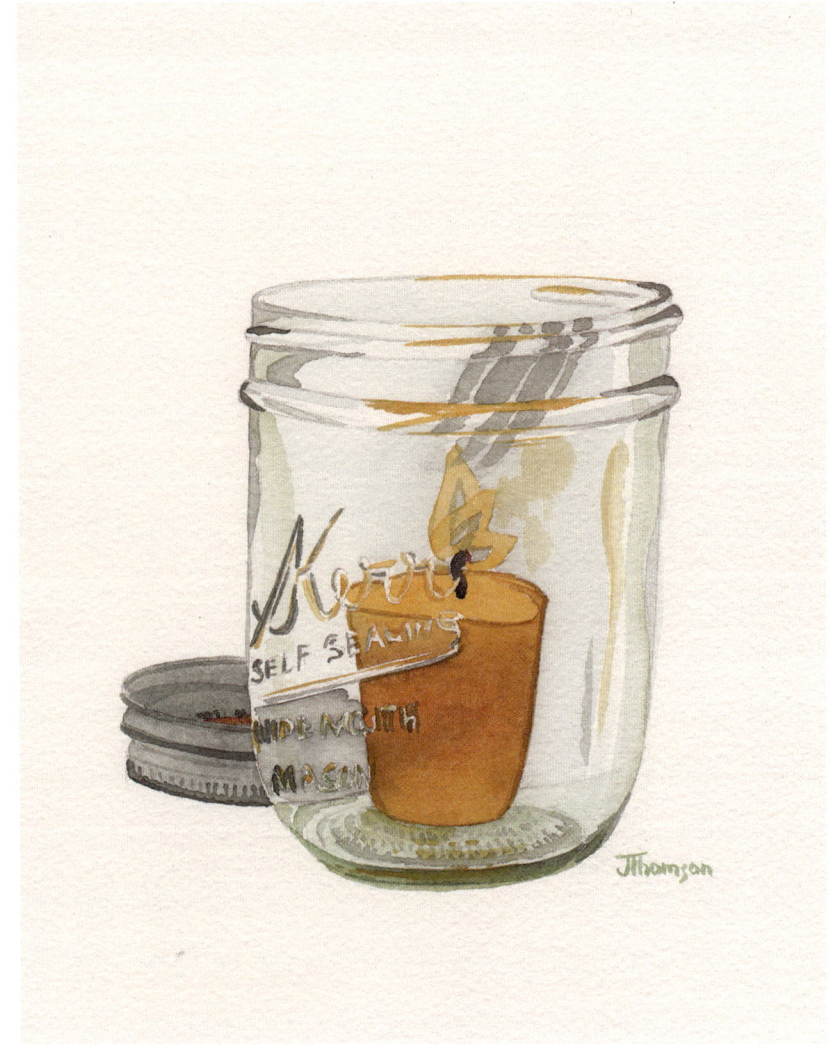

MASON JAR WITH
BEESWAX CANDLE
2014

The bees were not a success.
Flowers too few
Winters too long
Their lives were not wasted
Just cut short.

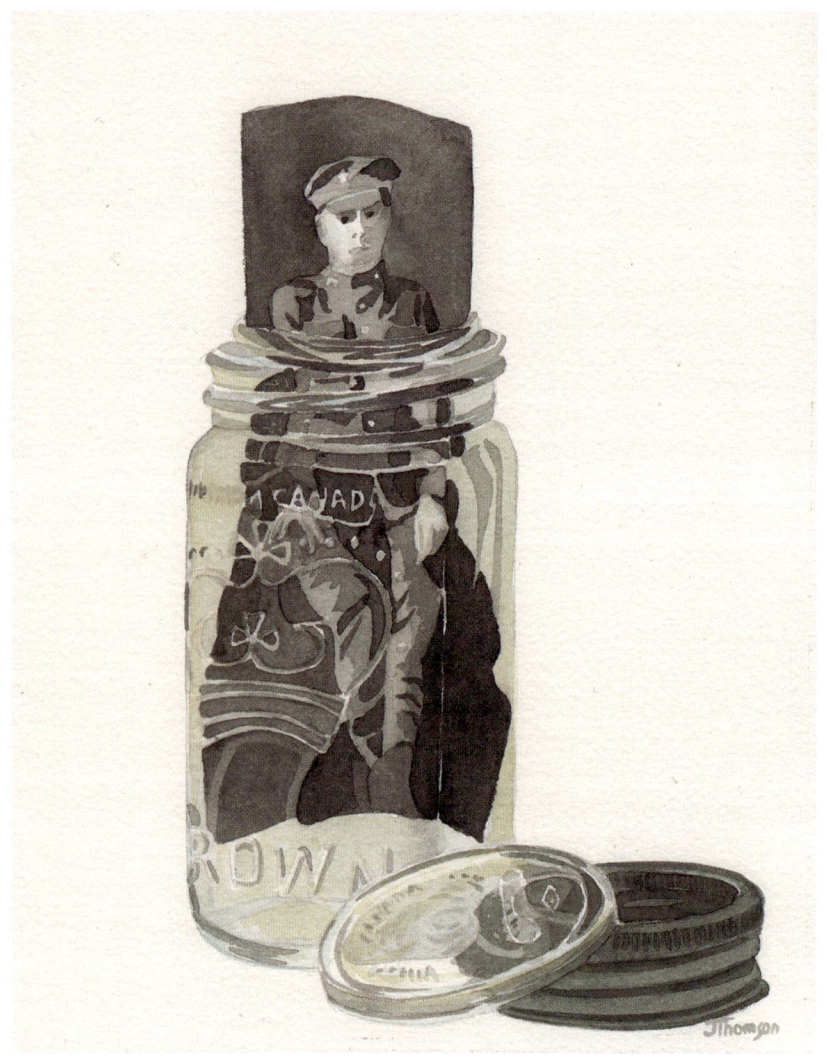

MASON JAR   German born he volunteered
WITH WERNER,   The myth dictates:
CIRCA 1917   Accepted and then discharged
2015   No time for paper work
              Just a photographic record.

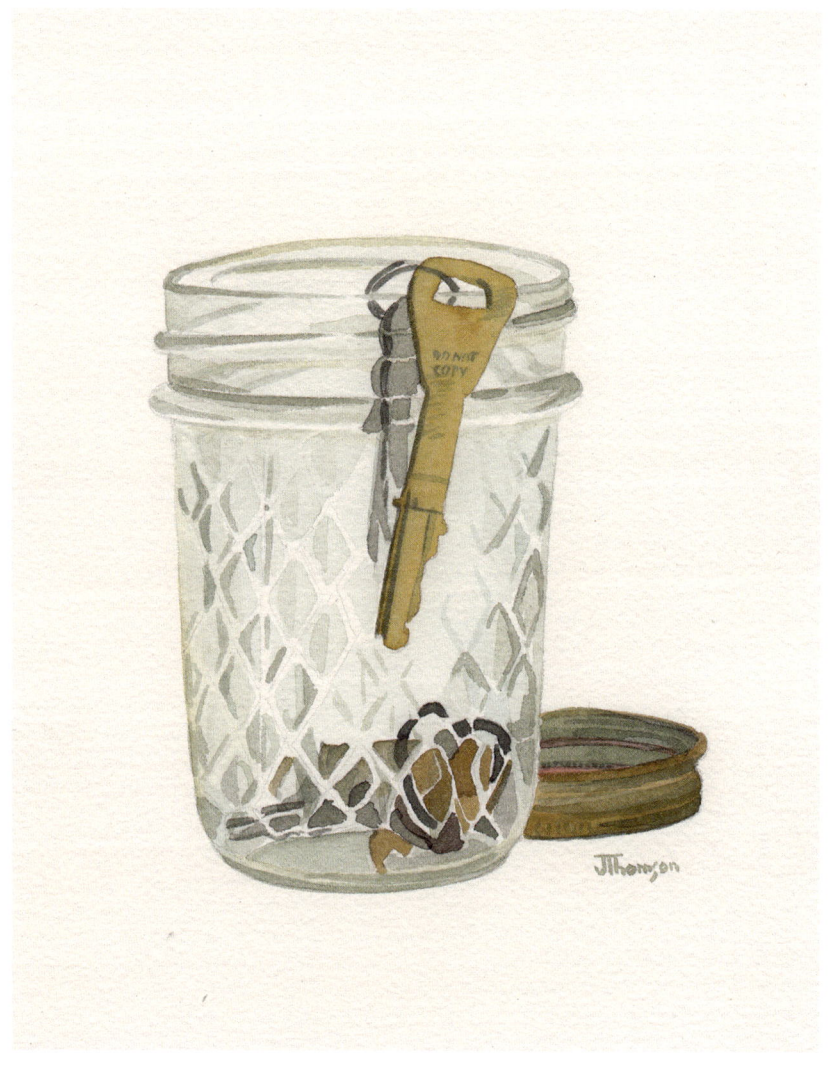

MASON JAR
WITH "DO NOT
COPY" KEY
2015

I have broken the rule
Copied the key
I have no idea what it is for
But it is now mine.

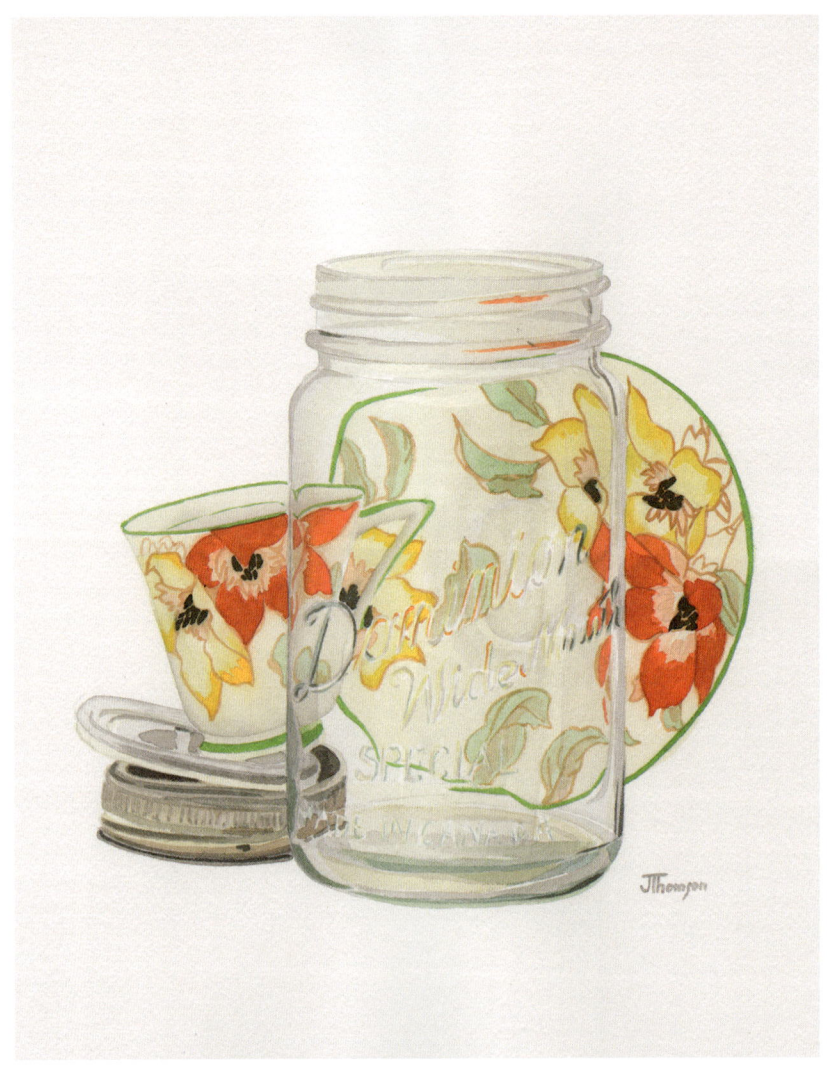

**MASON JAR WITH
ART DECO TEA
CUP AND SAUCER**

2015

If she had not wanted to be another
Had welcomed who she was
This would have been enough.

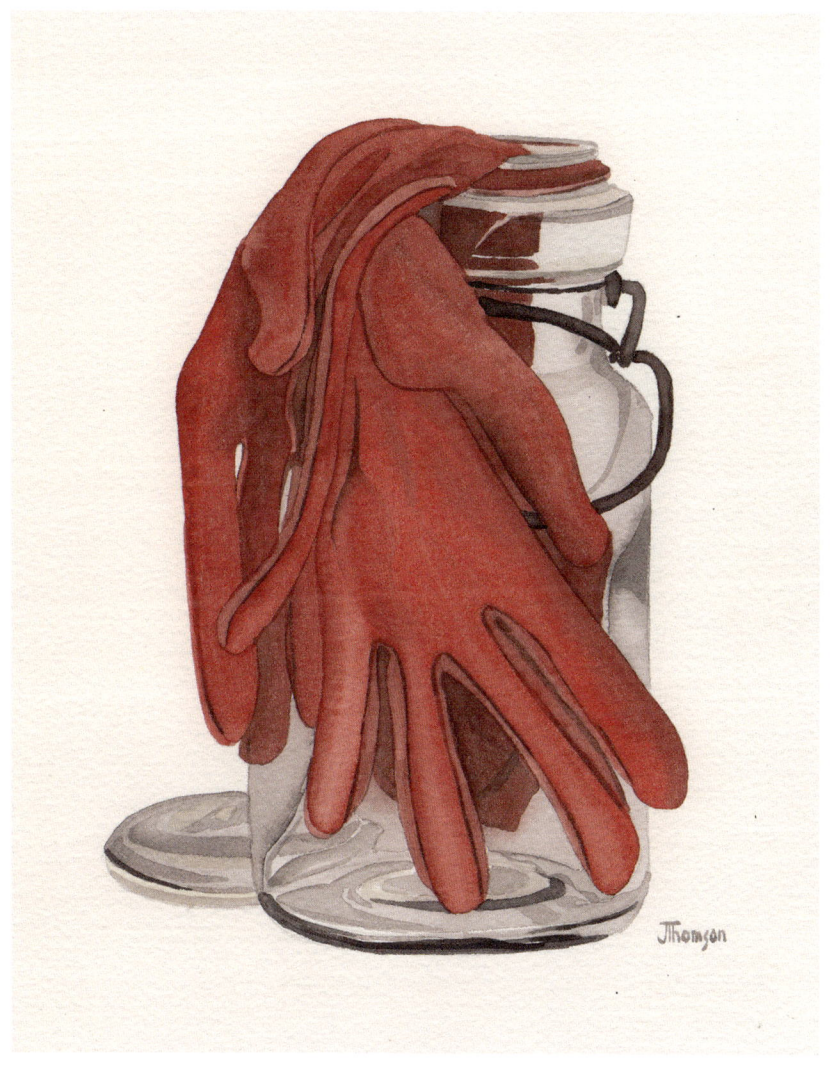

MASON JAR WITH
RED LEATHER GLOVES

2015

She wanted status, elegance, and wealth
Always wore gloves and a hat.
I wish I had given her red kid gloves
And a tall red hat with a feather.

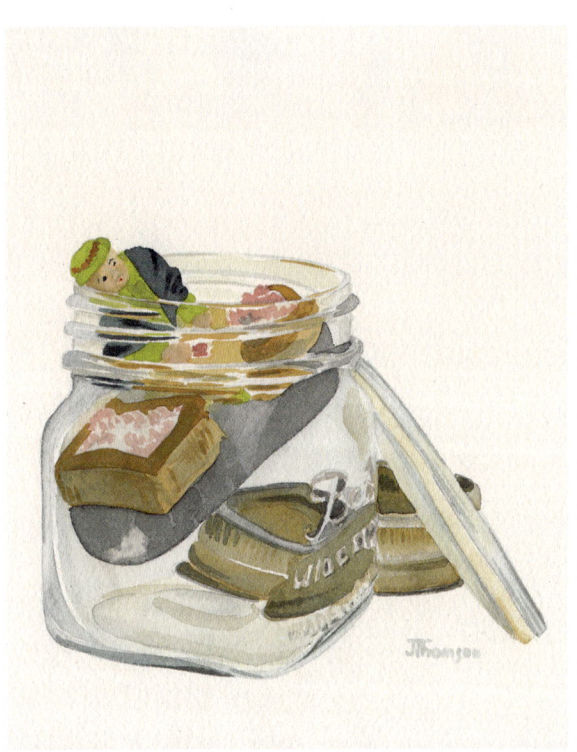

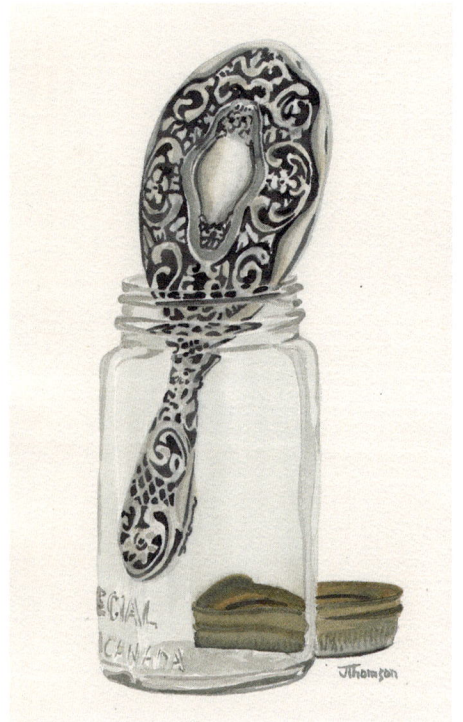

MASON JAR WITH
FLOWER SELLER
ORNAMENT
2015

She came from England
This warning,
Study and work hard
You are not guaranteed success.

MASON JAR
WITH MIRROR
2015

Sterling heritage
Best forgotten.
Remembered wealth
Brews bitterness.

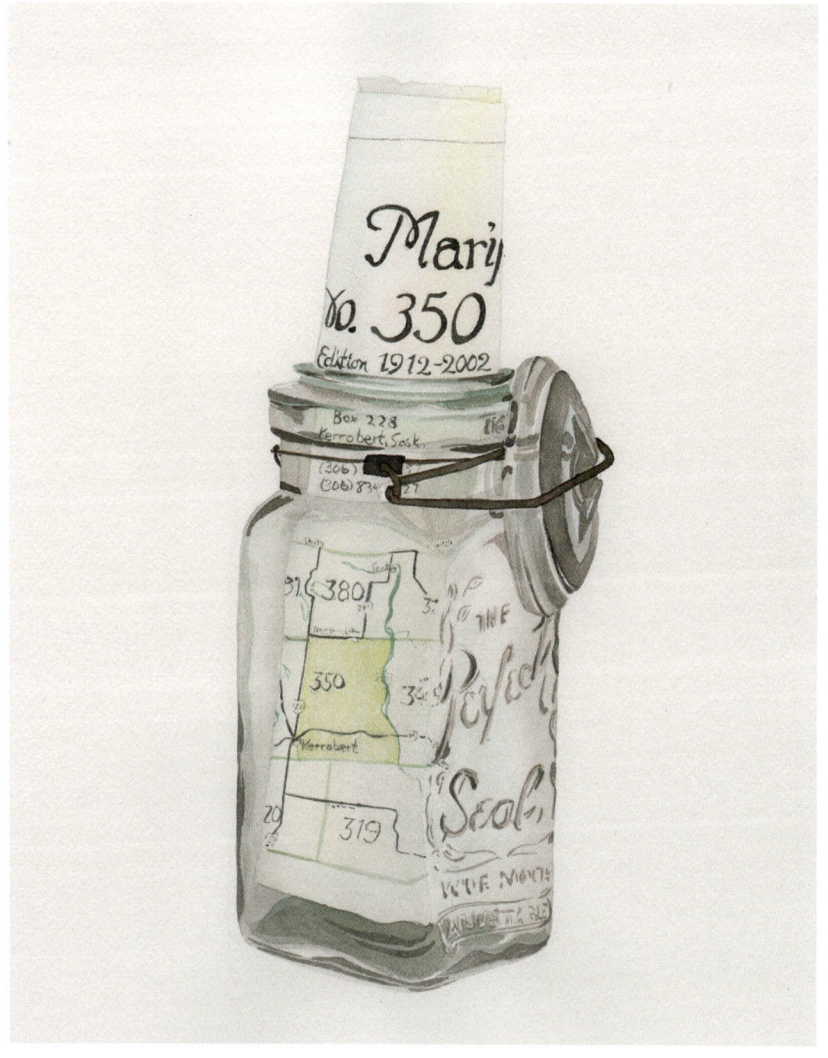

MASON JAR WITH A piece of land to call his own
MAP OF MARIPOSA Near and yet so far away
2015 Dry land that did not hold
Water enough for prosperity.

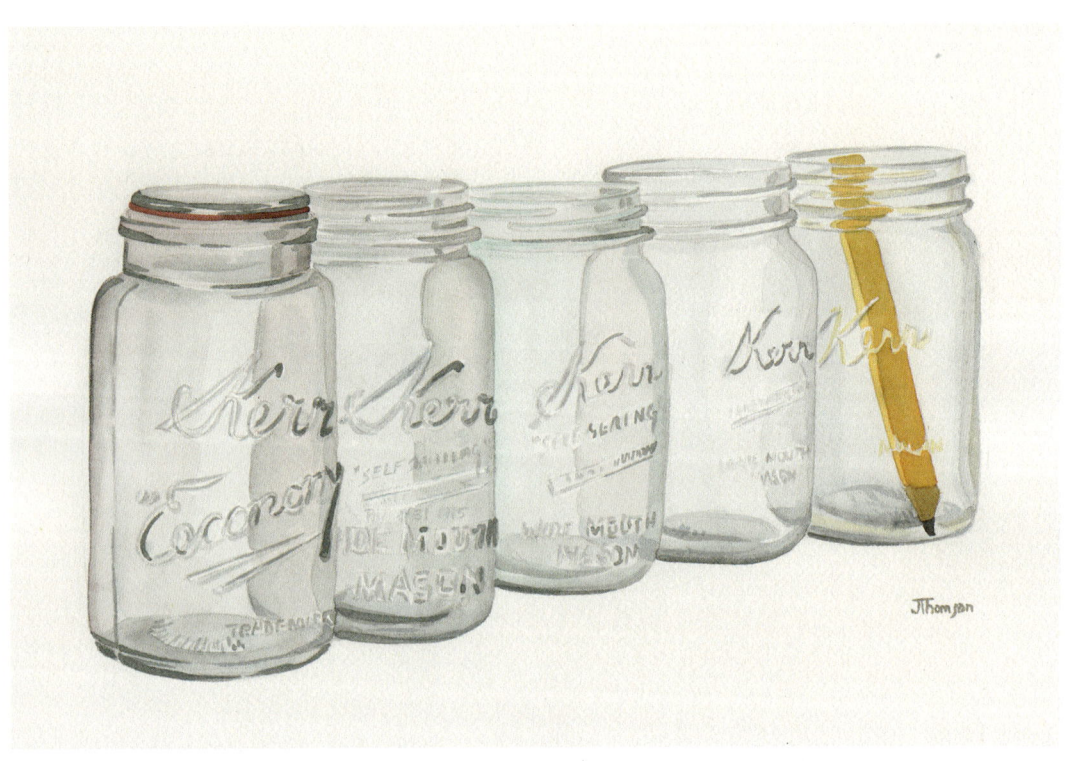

MASON JARS WITH Kerr used to be yelled out
FADING MEMORIES This is who we are,
2015 Economical, self-sealing, trademarked
The sound becomes thin and finally reflective.

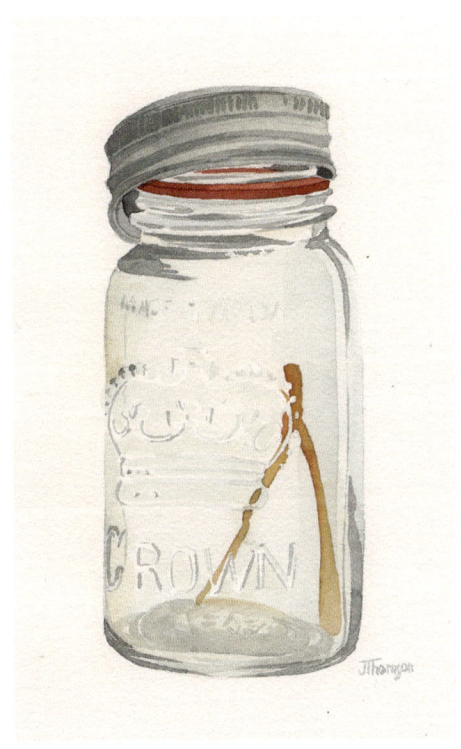
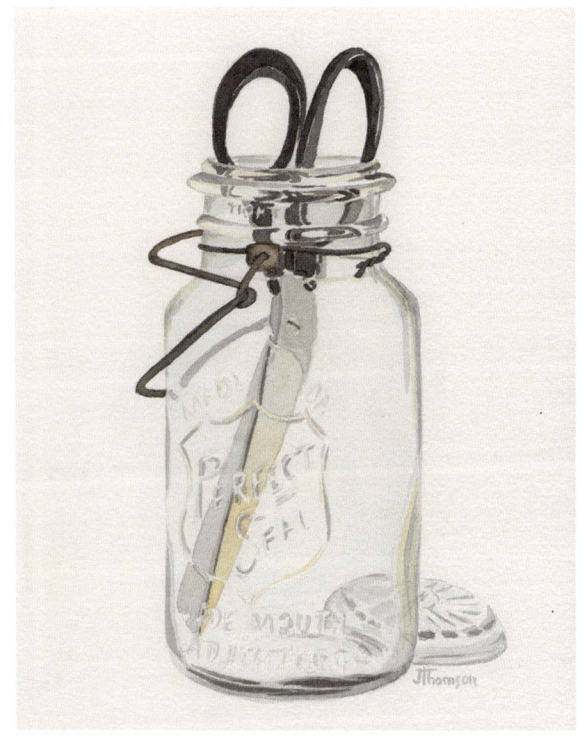

MASON JAR WITH
WISHBONE
2015

Wishes come and wishes go
Why do we wish on bone?
Breast bones of birds
That cannot fly?

MASON JAR
WITH SCISSORS
2017

Sturdy scissors
Sharpened repeatedly
Born in the Depression
Still the best in the house.

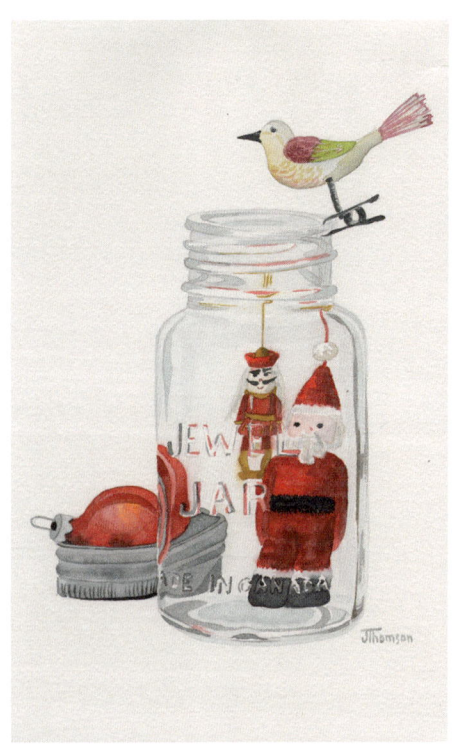

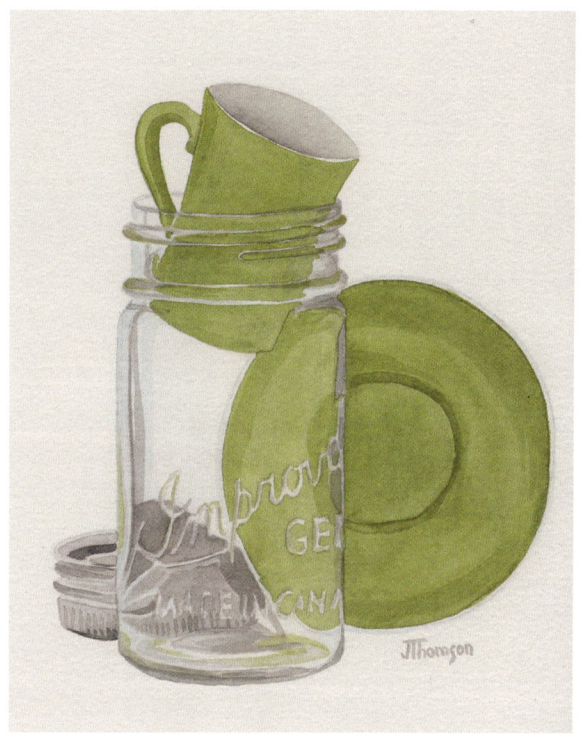

MASON JAR WITH
FOUR GENERATIONS
OF CHRISTMAS
2017

Time passes
New is made
Old fades
Together they make the story.

MASON JAR WITH
ESPRESSO CUP
2019

A tiny cup and saucer
For tiny hands and mouth
Special times with Grandma
Sugar and milk and tea.

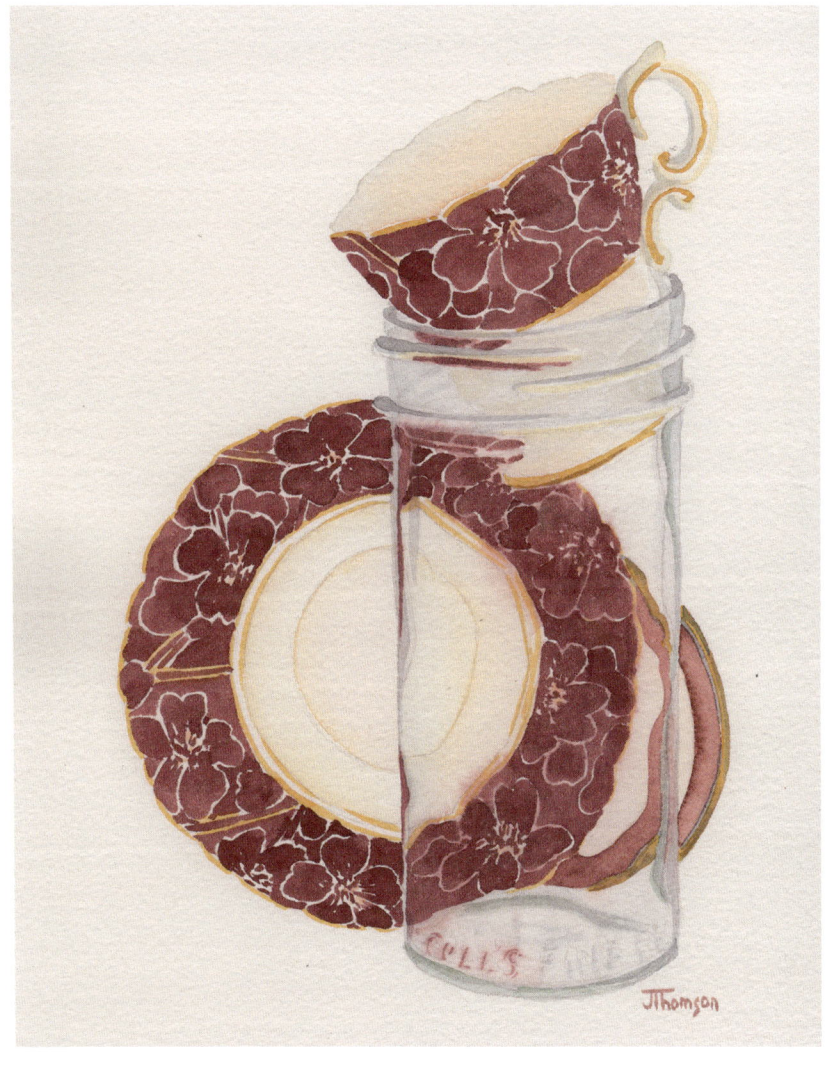

MASON JAR WITH   A week's wages for her mother-in-law

MOTHER'S DAY   Now one dollar in a thrift store

CUP AND SAUCER   Beauty undiminished

2019   Only fashion has departed.

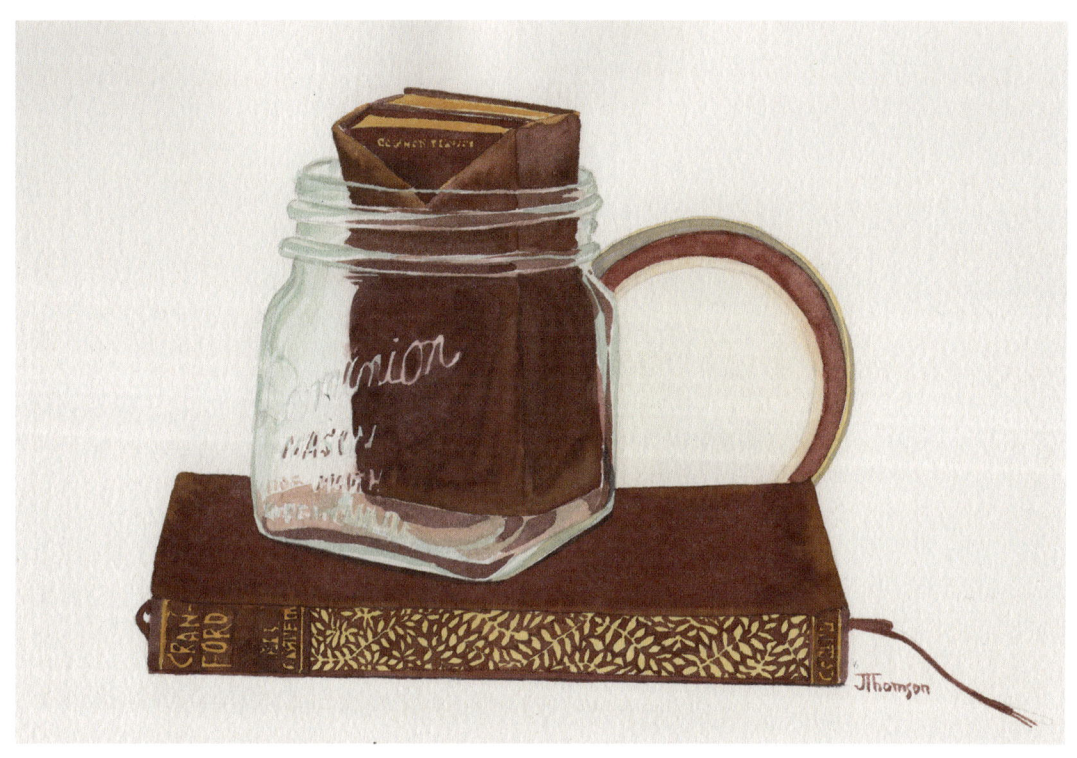

MASON JAR WITH
CRANFORD BOOK
2019

Mrs. Gaskell's story
Of genteel poverty
Moved to Canada with Eva
In this godmother's gift of 1920.

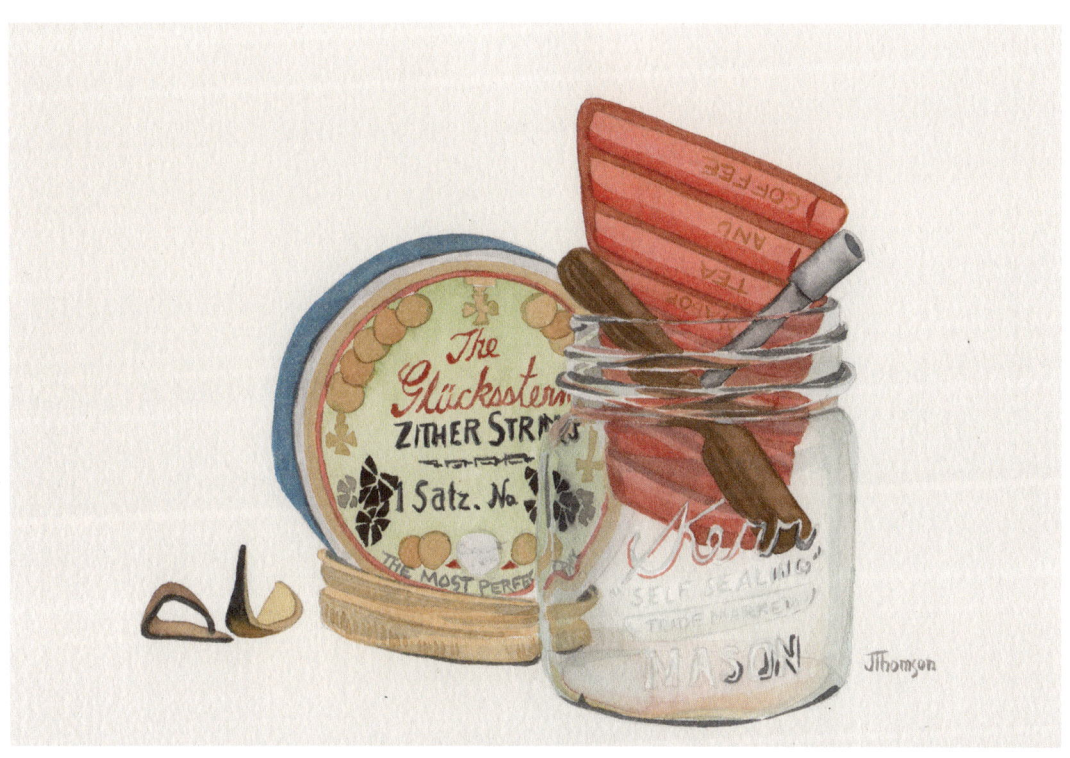

MASON JAR WITH
ZITHER STRINGS

2019

The Zither
Un-played for 70 years
Now has new strings
and hope.

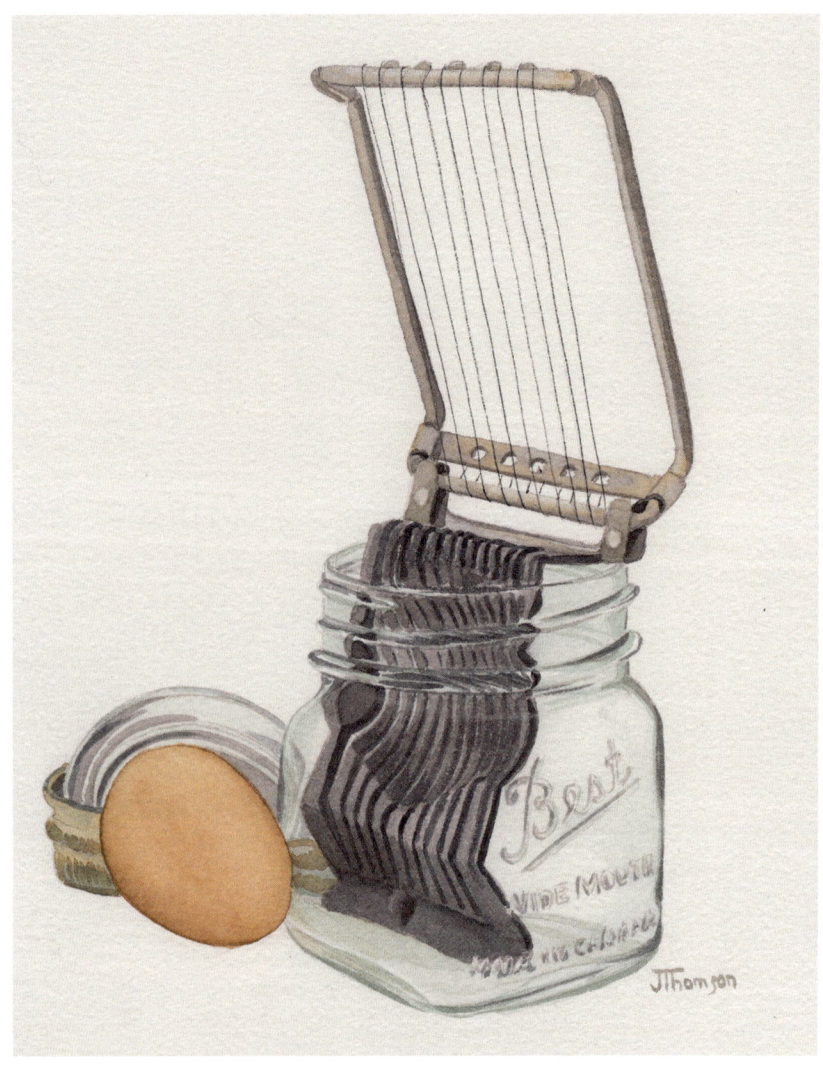

MASON JAR WITH   School lunches
EGG SLICER   Potato salads
2019   This warrior goes on and on.

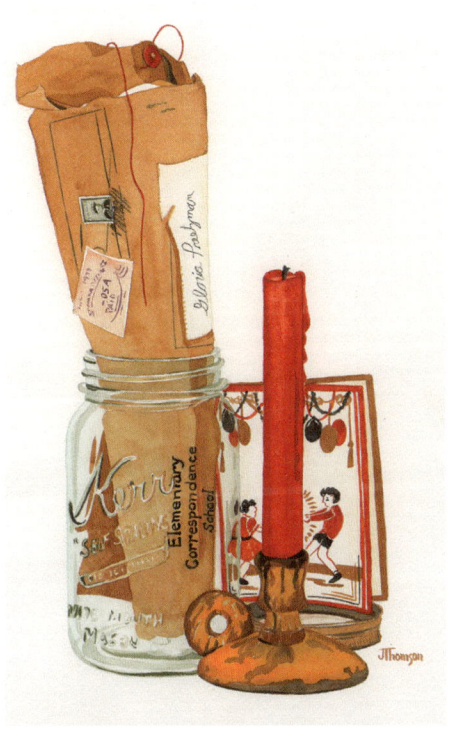

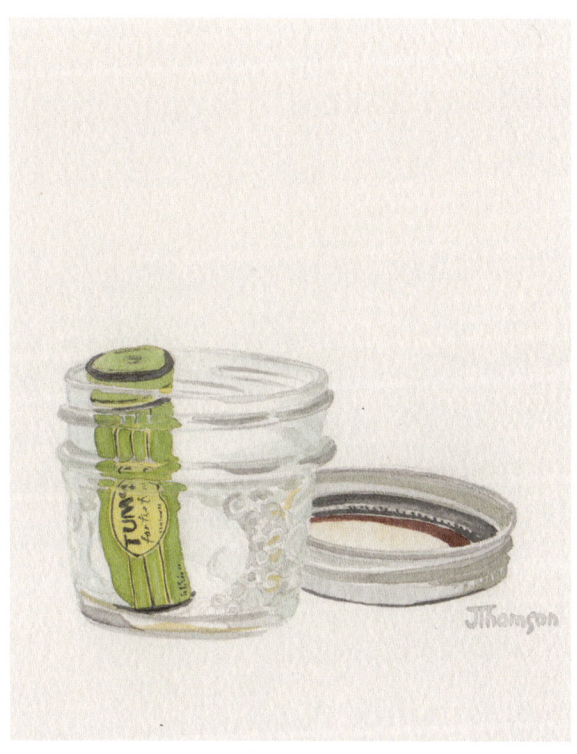

MASON JAR
WITH GLORIA'S
SCHOOL PAPERS

2019

This is the best one you have done yet!
Memories of times spent in the house
With Eva, Werner, and Jean.

MASON JAR WITH
WERNER'S TUMS

2019

He had what I have
Followed Doctor's orders
Drank milk and ate soda crackers
A suggested cure not at all suitable
For the gluten and lactose intolerant.

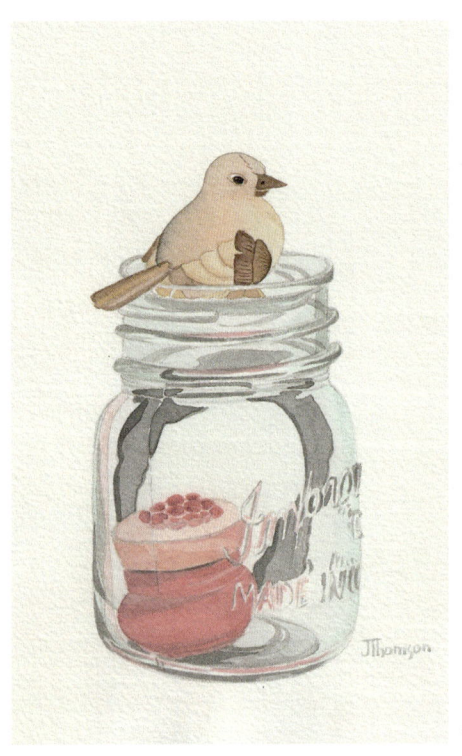

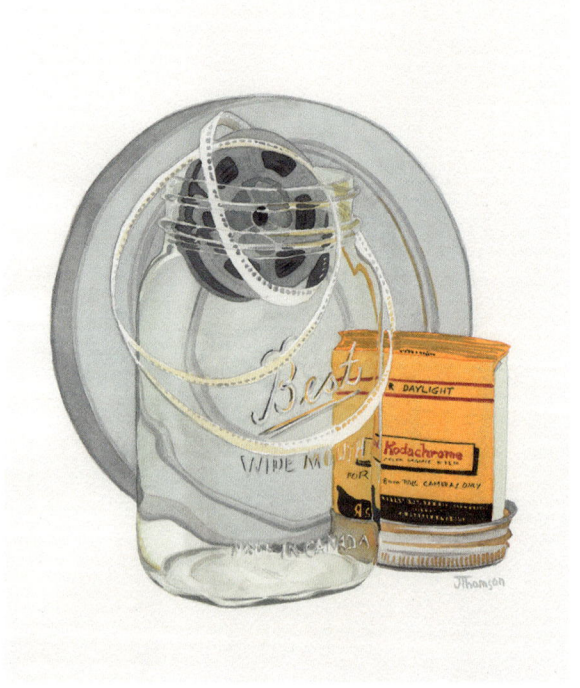

MASON JAR
WITH SCENTS
OF GRANDMA T
2019

I asked for this jar
Not voicing it was her smell I wanted.
She cleaned it out well.
Yet I can still imagine her touching my palm.

MASON JAR WITH
HOME MOVIES
2019

Winter evenings
Remembered summers
Remembered childhoods
Popcorn and snuggles.

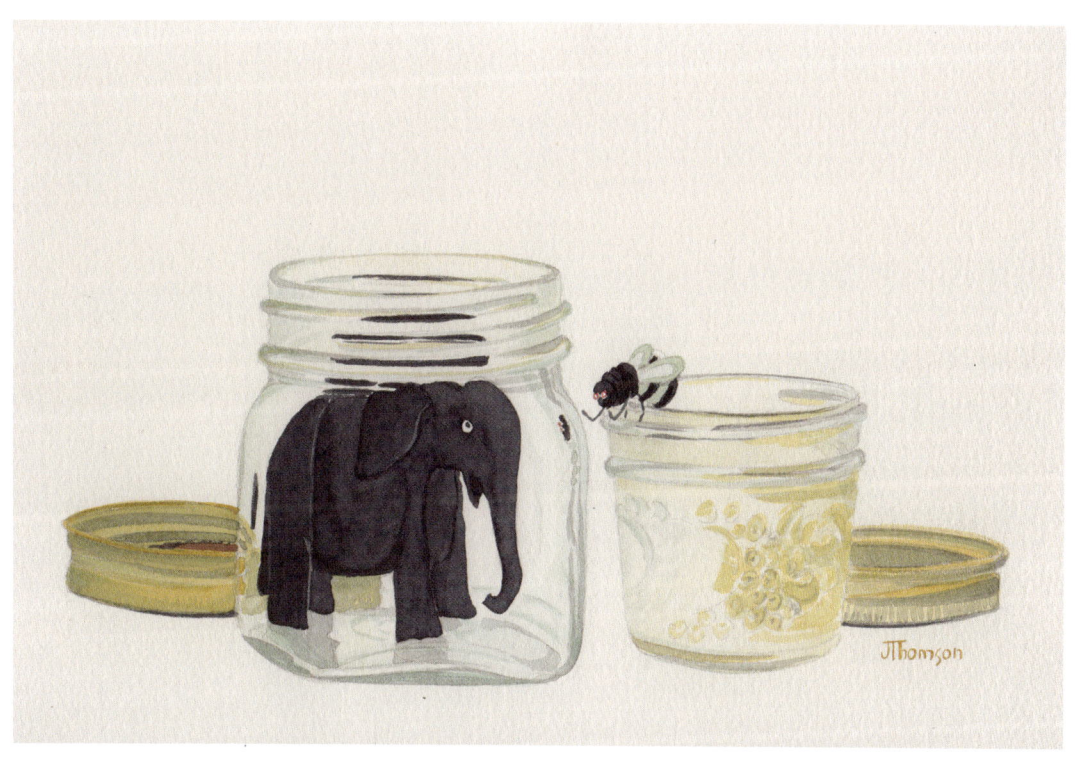

MASON JARS WITH　　It all happens in the cabinet
CHINA CABINET　　　Where past and present mingle
CONVERSATION　　　Children of generations
2019　　　　　　　　Existing in timelessness.

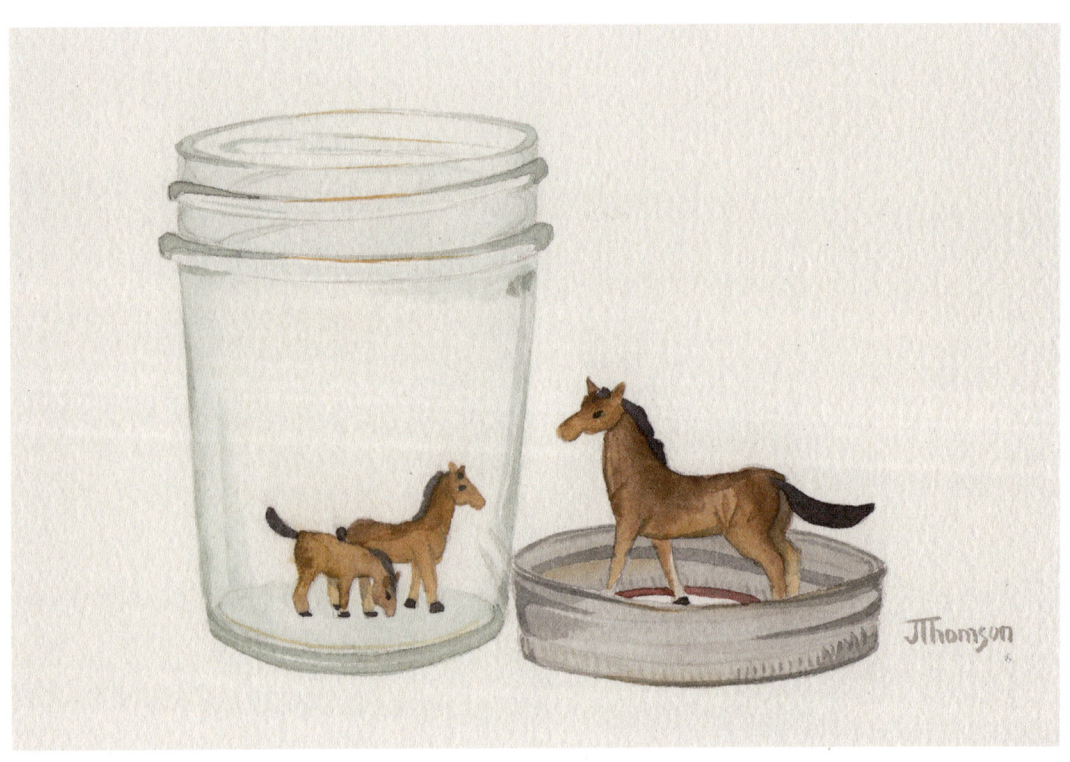

MASON JAR WITH
JAPANESE HORSES
2019

A birthday gift
So beautiful
I wanted another.
But Mom said no.

MASON JAR WITH
PRAYER PLANT
2018

When a Matriarch dies
She leaves the gift of her love
and a plant to pray for her family.

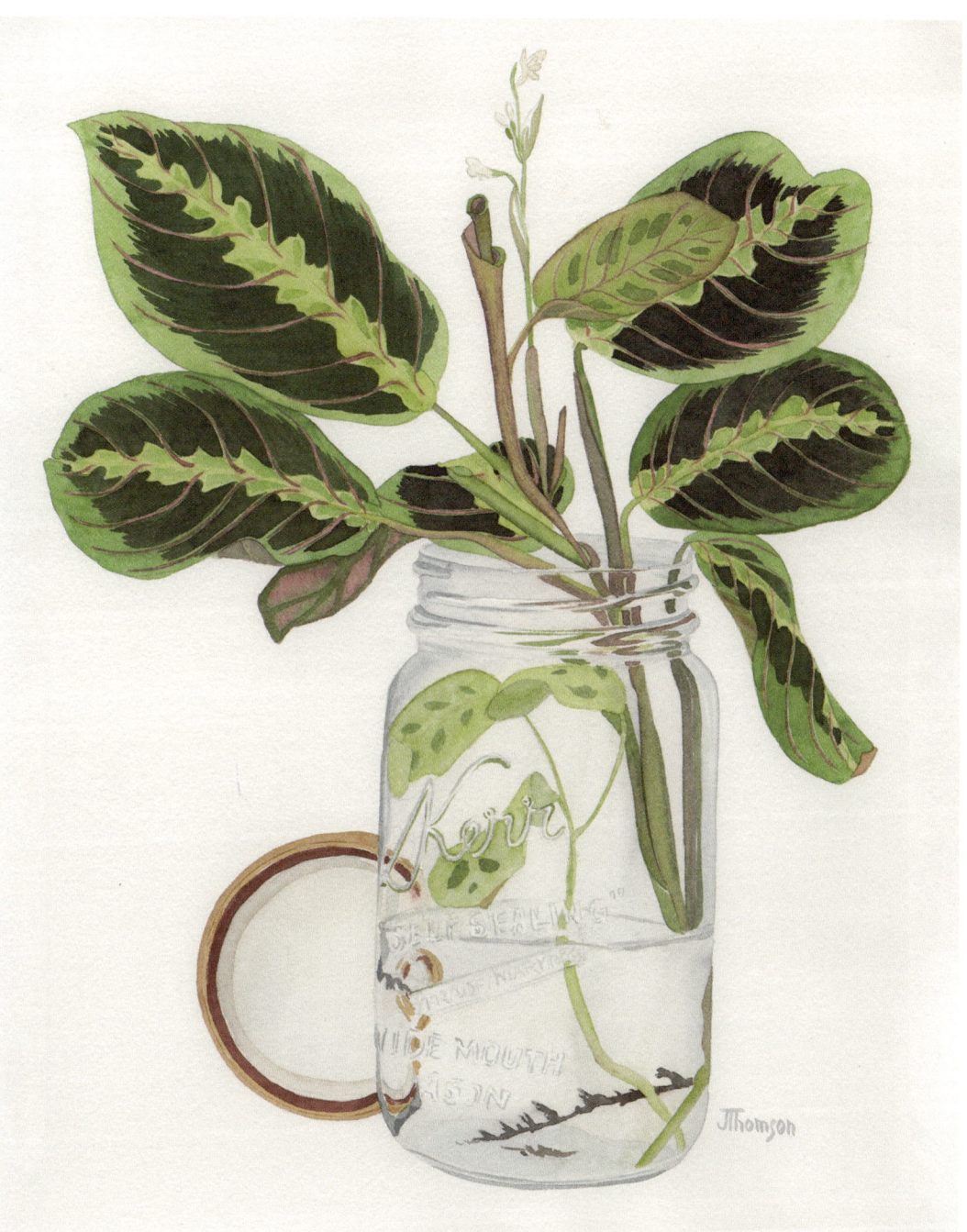

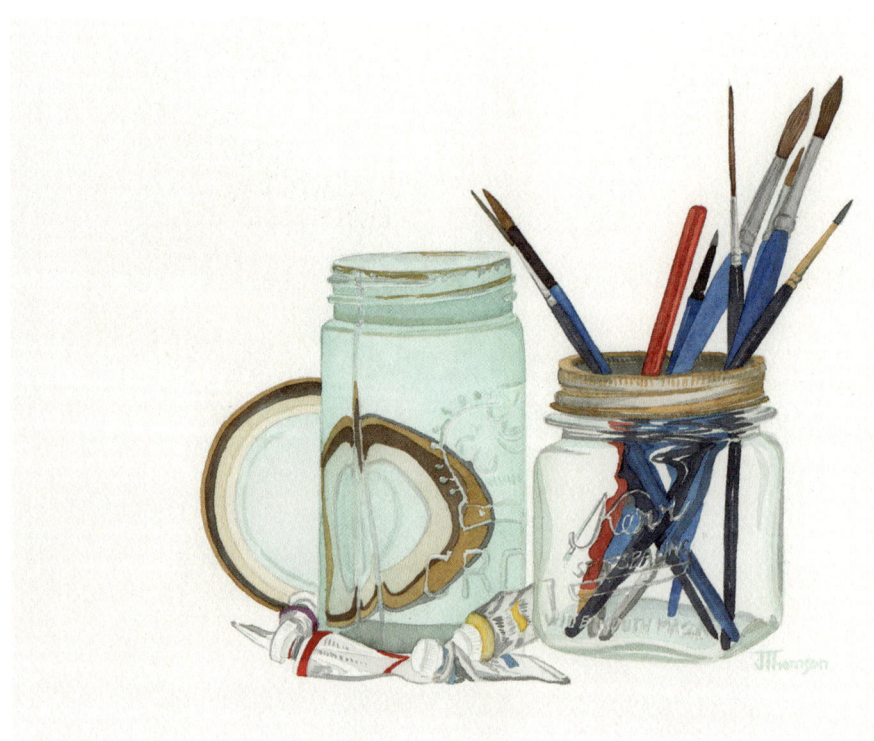

MASON JAR WITH
TOOLS OF THE TRADE
2019

This is the final painting of the Mason jar series.
A journey of moments bottled and released.
Like all the other artifacts,
These tools will go on to make more experiences.

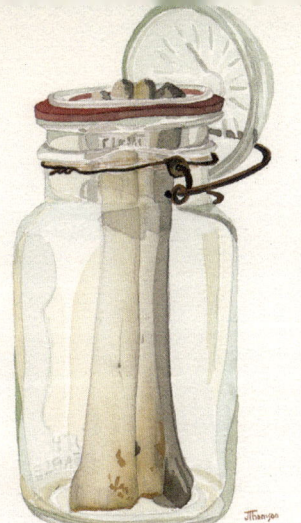
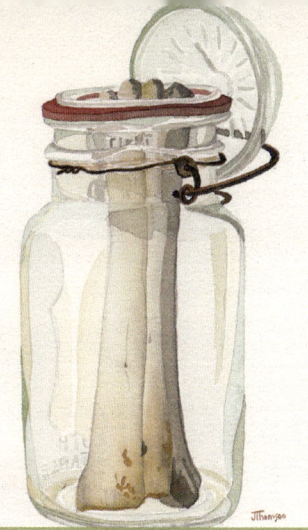
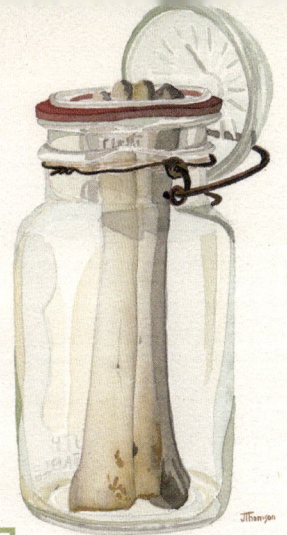
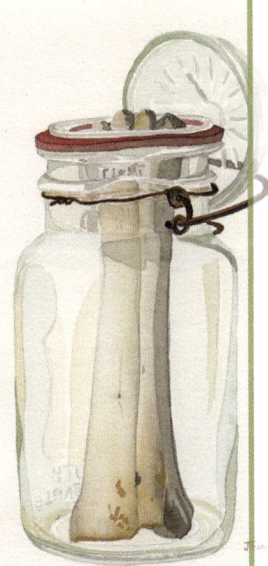
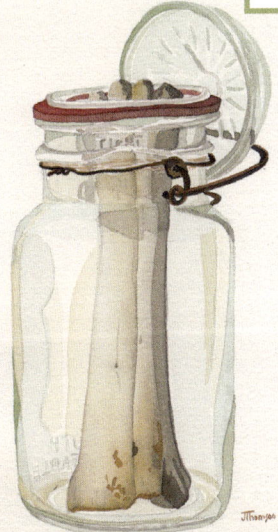
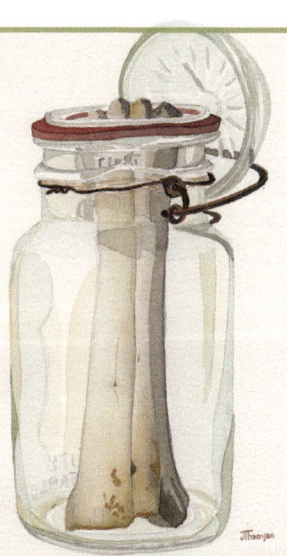
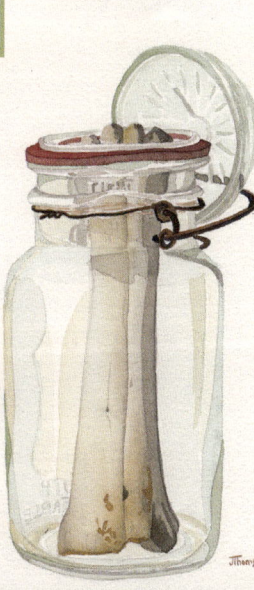

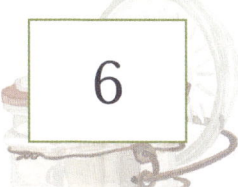

6

HIDDEN
AND
SUPPRESSED

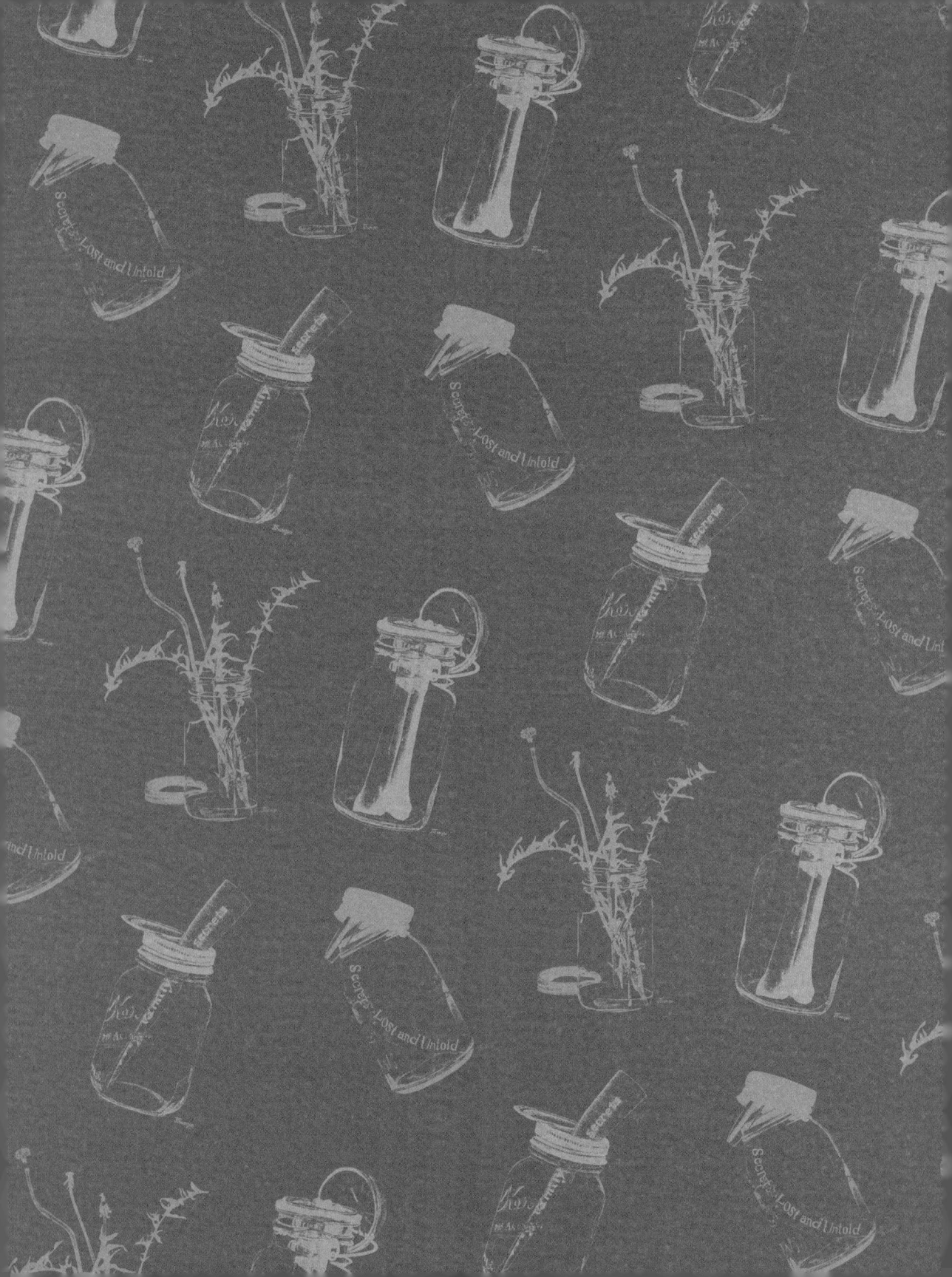

THERE ARE dark chapters in every family history. Events that are not voiced, which resonate down the generations. Our family is no different. A son born to Eva and Werner, their last child, only survived two days. A world war divided family members and saw life lost on one side and imprisoned on the other. There was a son who did not speak to or acknowledge his mother. A marital separation which led to the alienation of children from their father. Poverty and resentment of that poverty resided next to the pride in making a living off the land. Lost dreams ultimately led to a loss of hope for things to improve. There was despair, overwhelming despair, and a decision by Werner not to go on. Yet there is also a legacy of love and resilience, hard work and determination, all of which resonate through the generations with enough force to balance the light and the dark. There is an ability to find joy in simple acts, everyday interactions, nature, and good food.

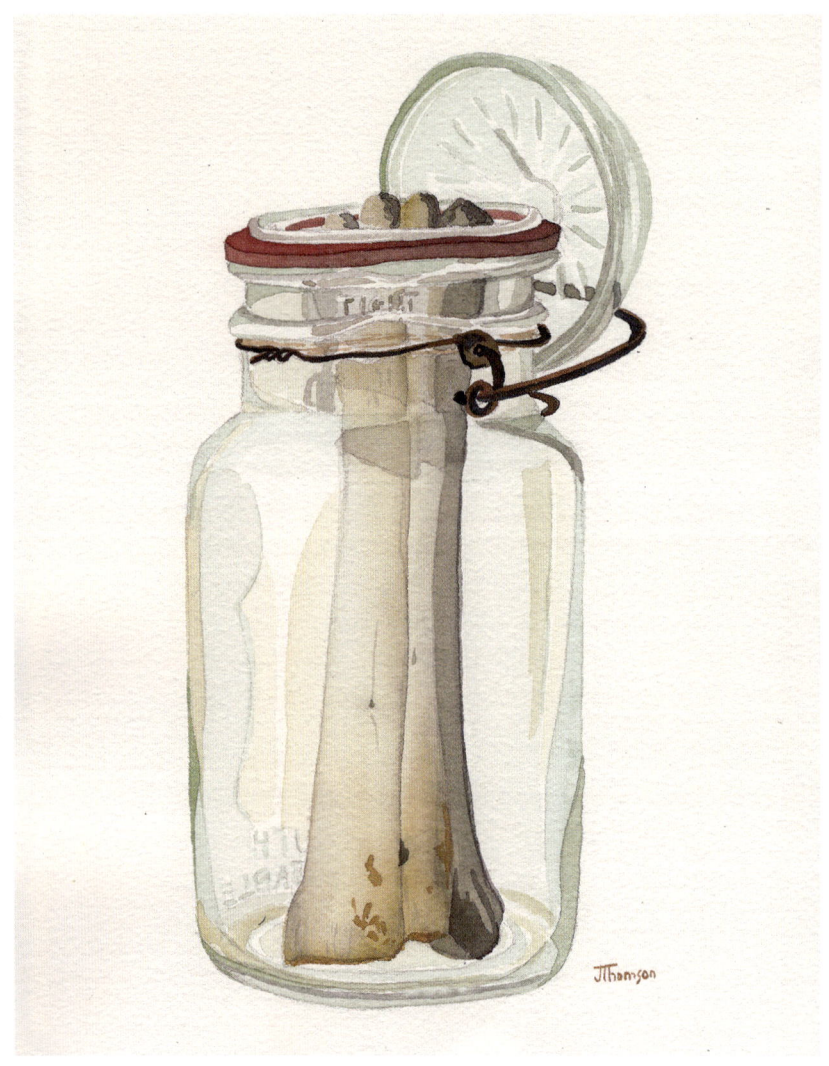

MASON JAR   Bones hold memories
WITH BONE   What they once were
2014   What they are still
   Taking longer than the soul to depart.

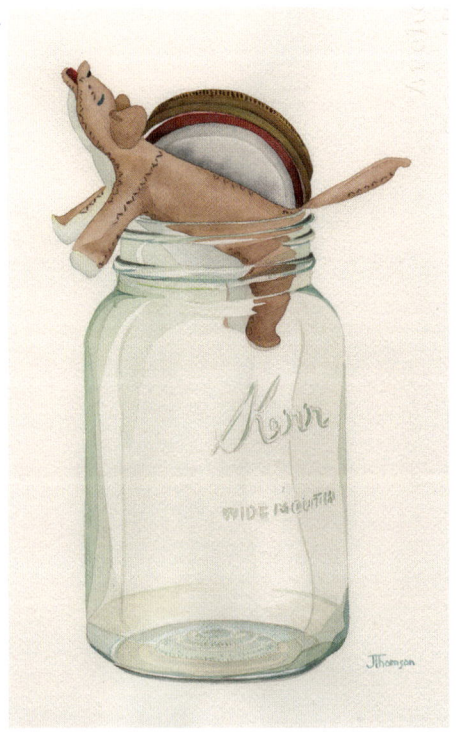

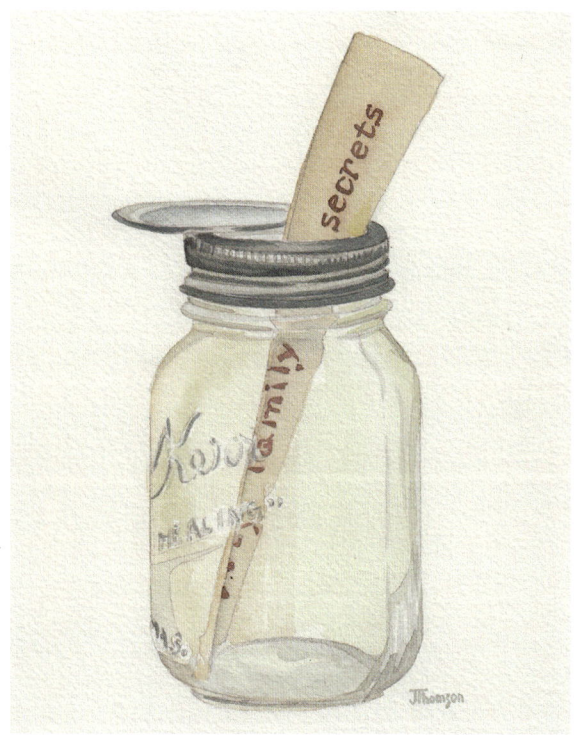

MASON JAR WITH   Wide mouth open

BARKING DOG   She barks out the family secrets

2014   Refusing to put a lid on it!

MASON JAR   The lids are off

WITH SECRETS   The secrets are out

2014   To find that secrets are shared

Everyone has them

Often the same ones.

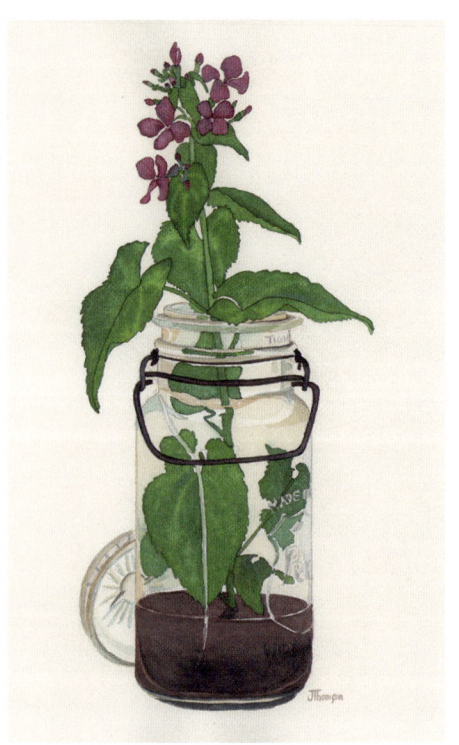

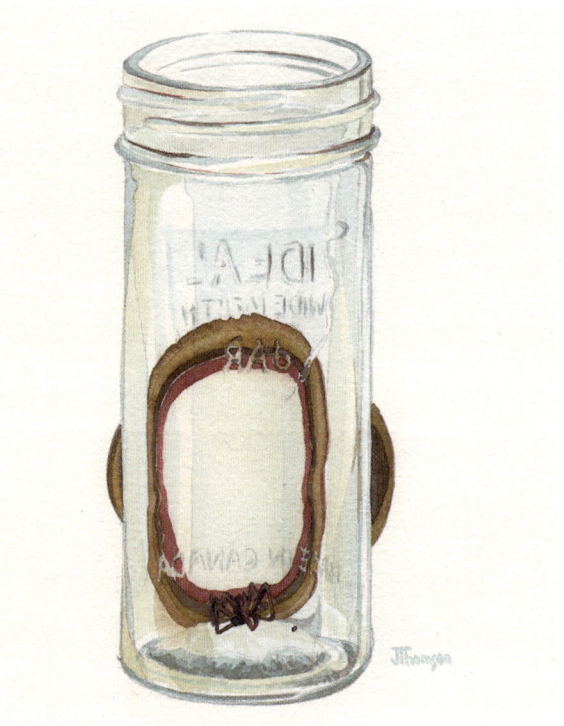

**MASON JAR WITH
HONESTY PLANT**

2014

Honest pay for honest work
Doesn't always happen.
Enjoy beauty while it lasts
If it becomes money, enjoy that too.

**MASON JAR
WITH SPIDER**

2014

Perhaps it is not safe to have the lids off all the time
Perhaps some secrets should be kept
Otherwise unexpected visitors
Fall in and meet their demise.

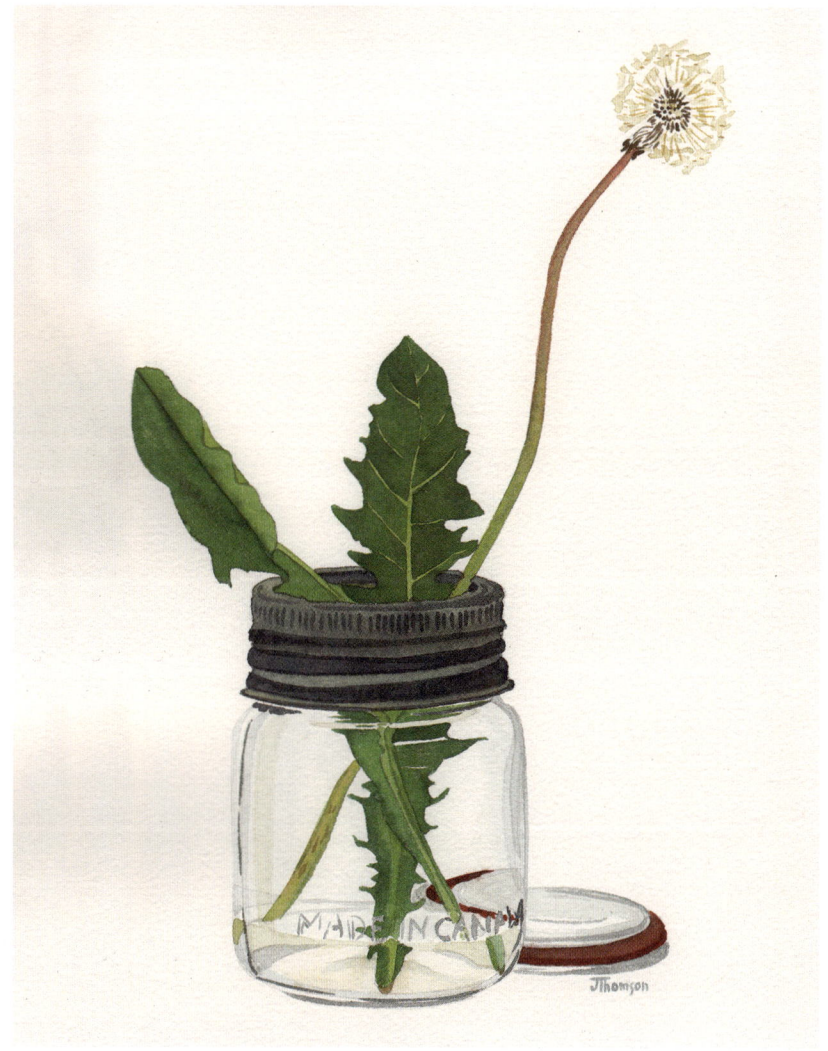

MASON JAR WITH
DANDELION WISHES

2014

A puff and they fly away
These wishes and hopes
Offered freely by children.

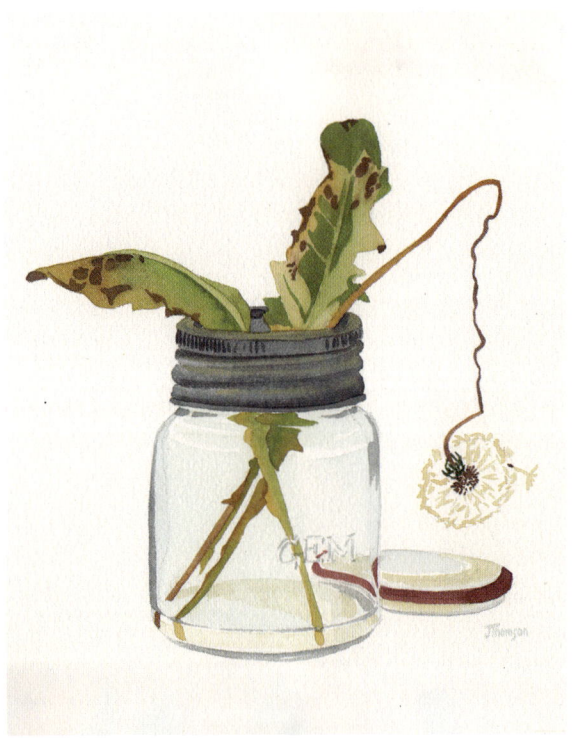

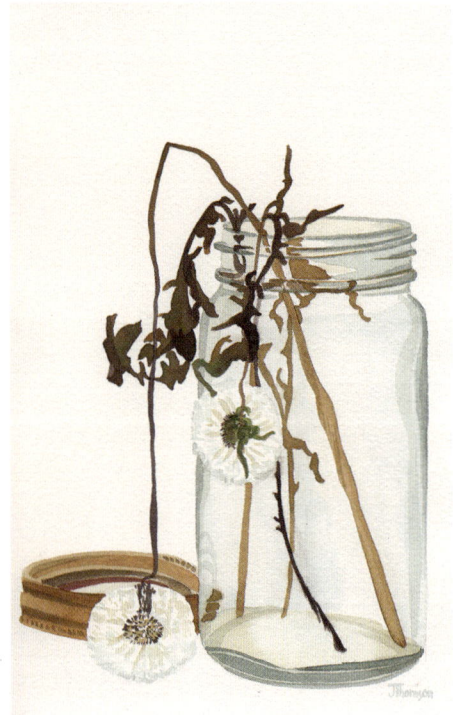

MASON JAR WITH　　We hold our wishes and our dreams
DYING DANDELION　　Even as we feel ourselves dying.
2014　　Perhaps the dreams are for others,
　　Perhaps they are ours to keep.

MASON JAR WITH　　If the dead remain
DEAD DANDELION　　They can hold onto their wishes
WISHES　　Only when they pass over
2014　　Can their wishes range free and be granted.

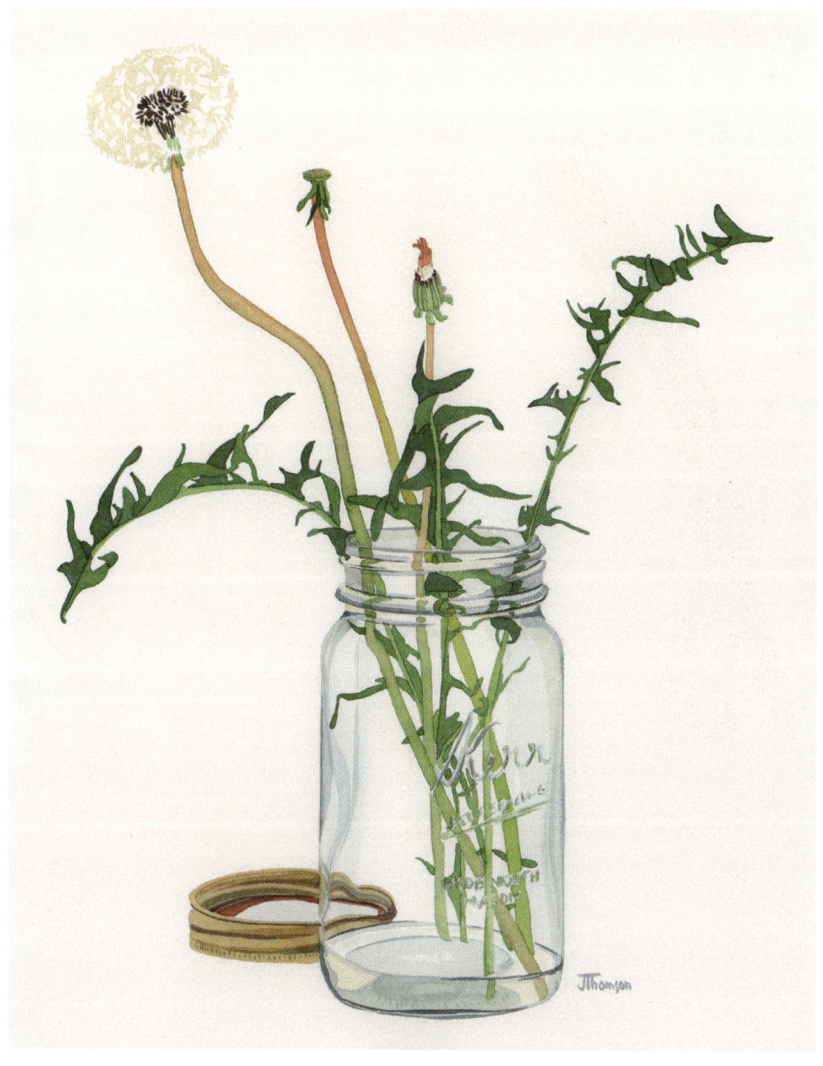

MASON JAR WITH
WISHES, COMING
AND GONE
2014

A metaphor for wishing
What we wanted,
What happened,
What didn't.

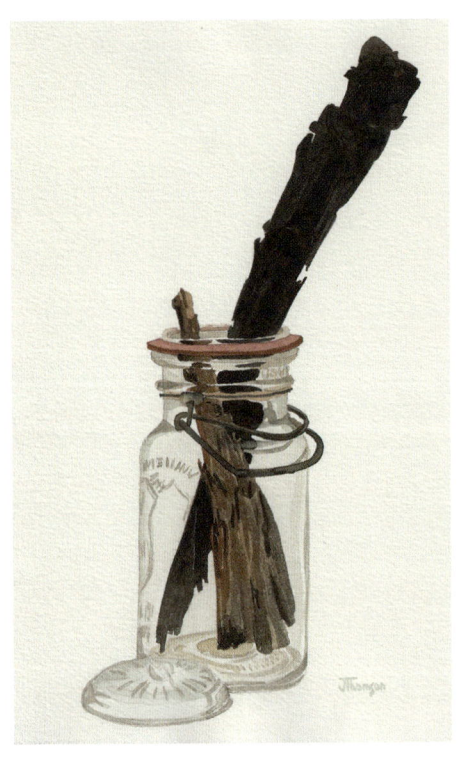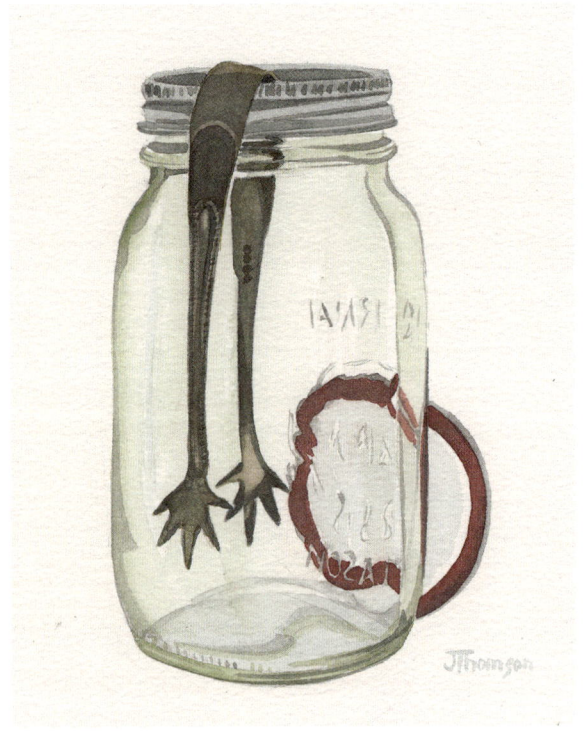

MASON JAR WITH   Buried beneath this tree
LIGHTNING   There is a boy
STRUCK WOOD   So many hopes lost
2014   It drew the lightning and burned down.

MASON JAR WITH   Tarnished dreams
SUGAR TONGS   Of elegant ladies at tea
2014   Pleasures in what was
Lost to what could have been.

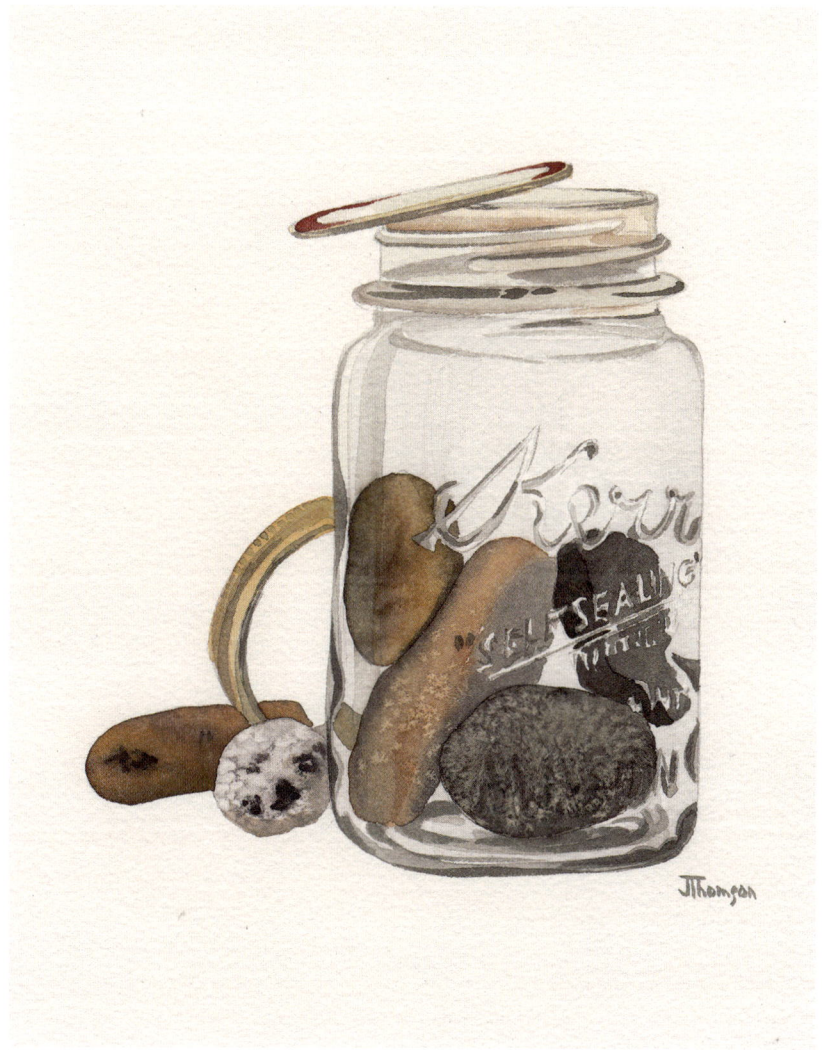

MASON JAR WITH   Here is where he last looked at rushing water

STONES FROM   Ice on the shore,

BOUNDARY CREEK   Snow between the trees

2015   He chose fire.

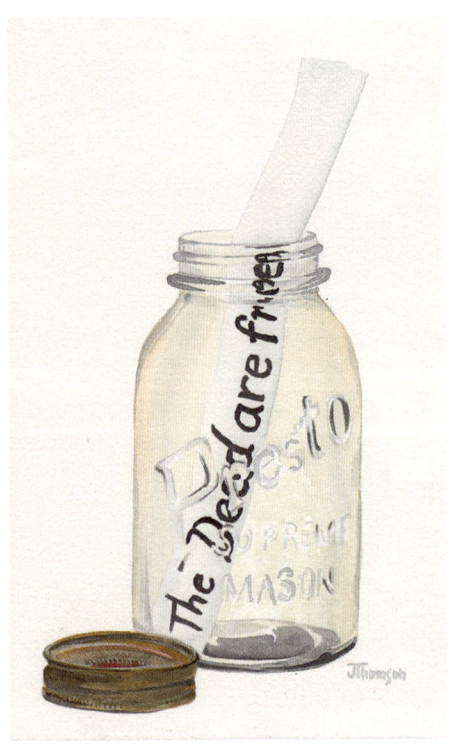

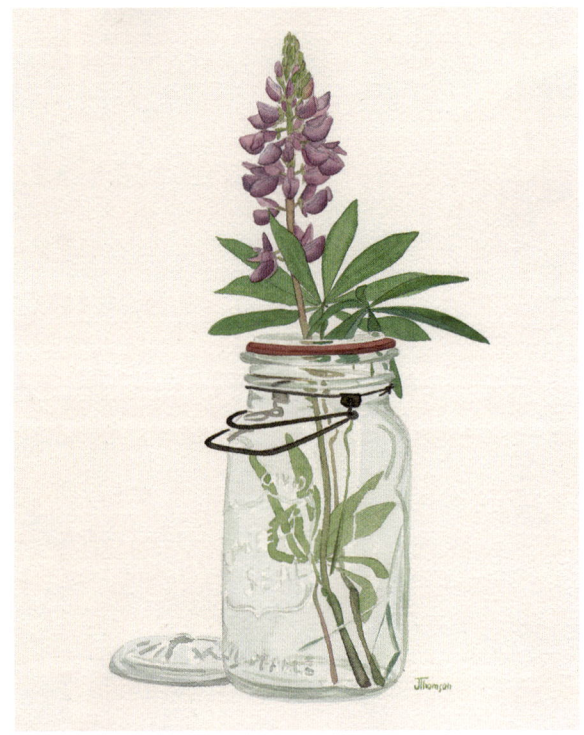

MASON JAR WITH
"THE DEAD ARE FREE"
2015

What cost are they who went before
Complete in their incompleteness.
We fools remain and try to gain
The past within the present.

MASON JAR WITH
LUPIN IN BROKEN JAR
2016

Holding her head up
In a jar that cannot hold water
This lupin will never be antique.

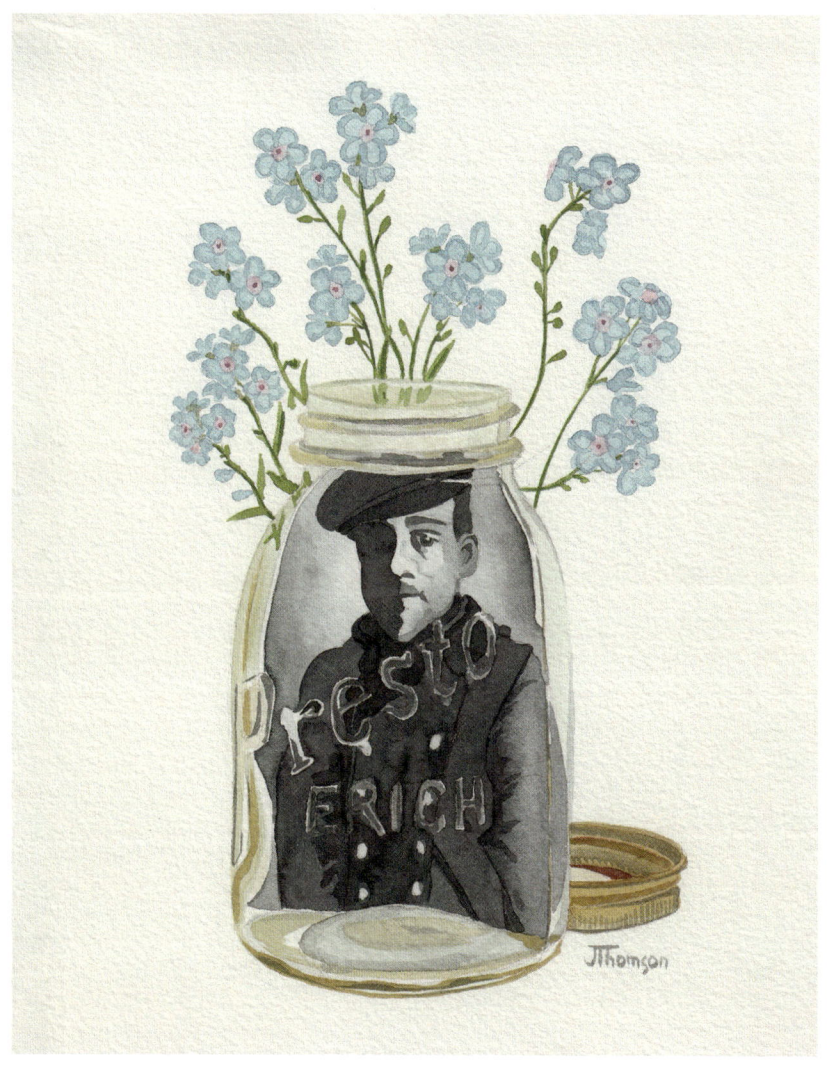

MASON JAR WITH   I never knew you,

ERICH AND   My German pilot uncle.

FORGET-ME-NOTS   I never knew your brother.

2019   I hope you both are at peace.

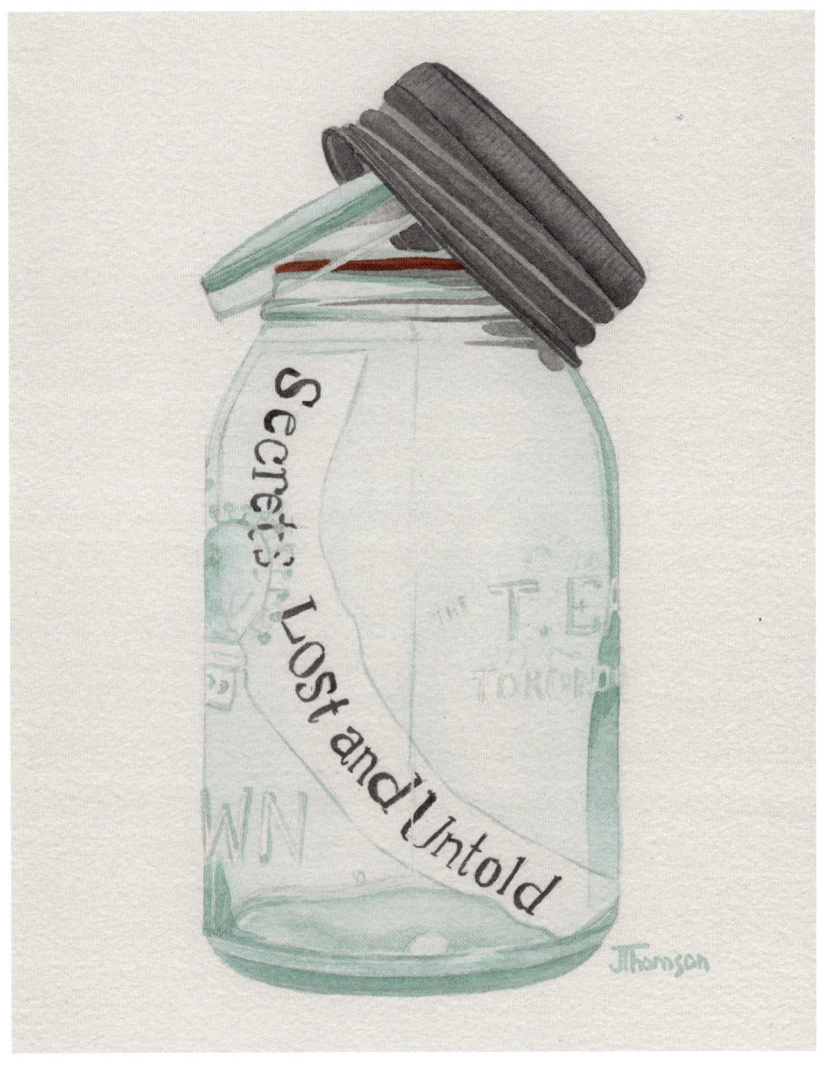

MASON JAR WITH   Stories fade to shadows

MANY SECRETS   Some will not be told

LOST AND UNTOLD   Yet freedom comes with telling

2019   Releasing those who have been held.

AFTERWORD

A BRIEF FAMILY HISTORY
IN PHOTOGRAPHS

WERNER WAS BORN WERNER THEODOR VON Preetzmann, in Wansen, East Prussia, Germany, on February 16, 1893. He was the second of five children born to Theodor Von Preetzmann and Hedwig Schwetschke. His mother was from a successful publishing family, and his father from a military family. Eva, my grandmother, was born Eva Lindsay Moncrief, in Unlock, Cumberland, England, on December 25, 1895. She was the middle child of thirteen children born to Mary Ann (née Galloway) and John Moncrief. John worked as a caster at the Whitehaven Pottery. The family lived in the "Pottery House."

Eva and Werner married in Greenwood, BC, on September 24, 1926. He was 34 and she was 30. On their wedding certificate, their occupations are listed as farmer and domestic servant. We don't know how they met. In one version, Eva met Werner in Liverpool at her brother's home when Werner was on his way to Canada. In another, she told me that the young women of her church wrote to pioneers in Canada to keep them company, and Werner asked her to marry him. Mail-order brides were common after the First World War, and I think this is likely the true version.

Jean Moncrieff Preetzman was born on November 8, 1928, and Gloria Moncrief Preetzman was born on September 26, 1930. (Yes, the spelling of Moncrief has both one and two f's; that is another story). Jean was born in Greenwood, BC, about 9 miles by horse and wagon from Kerr Creek. The area around their home was sparsely populated with bachelor veterans from World War I, each on their own 160 acres, and an occasional family. There was no electricity or running water in the home. Schooling was by correspondence, and occasionally by a school teacher when there were enough children nearby to warrant one.

Around 1945–46, the land called "up Kerr Creek'" was sold, and Eva and Werner separated. The Second World War had ended, and Werner had gone to Vancouver Island to look for a home for the family. While there, he became ill with appendicitis and was unable to return. Eva decided to sell the land and move to Salmon Arm so she could enroll Jean and Gloria in high school. Jean was able to finish grade 10 and then went to work full time as a secretary. Gloria boarded out and cared for the children of two local families. She was able to finish Grade

12 and go to nursing school in Victoria. Jean and Cyril Frank Donald Thomson (the mayor's youngest son) married on November 10, 1948, two days after Jean turned 20. They had two children, Vikki Jean, born on May 25, 1954, and me, Joanne Dawn, born May 31, 1956.

Werner passed on March 3, 1951, at the age of 58. Eva lived to be 101 years old, missing her 102nd birthday by only a few weeks. While most of the paintings in this book reference multiple memories and individuals, the following is a list inspired by specific individuals (see "Chronological List of Artwork" on page 239 for numbered titles):

Werner: 4, 5, 12, 20, 35, 42, 44–46, 55, 57, 58, 60-66, 71, 75, 85, 89, 97, 98, 100, 106, 110, 113, 124, 125, 131, 144, 153, 276, 281.

Eva: 1, 3, 4, 6, 8, 18, 89, 90, 99, 101, 115, 117, 118, 120, 121, 139, 145, 186, 237, 243, 274, 287, 291

German ancestors: 13, 241, 266, 268, 269, 273.

English ancestors: 77, 122, 143, 153–55, 241, 272, 274.

Jean: 11, 59, 92, 245, 246, 258, 277, 282, 285–86.

Gloria: 59, 280, 281, 293.

C.F. Donald: 54, 56, 248, 262, 270–71, 284, 289-90.

The Thomson grandparents: 153–55, 249, 283.

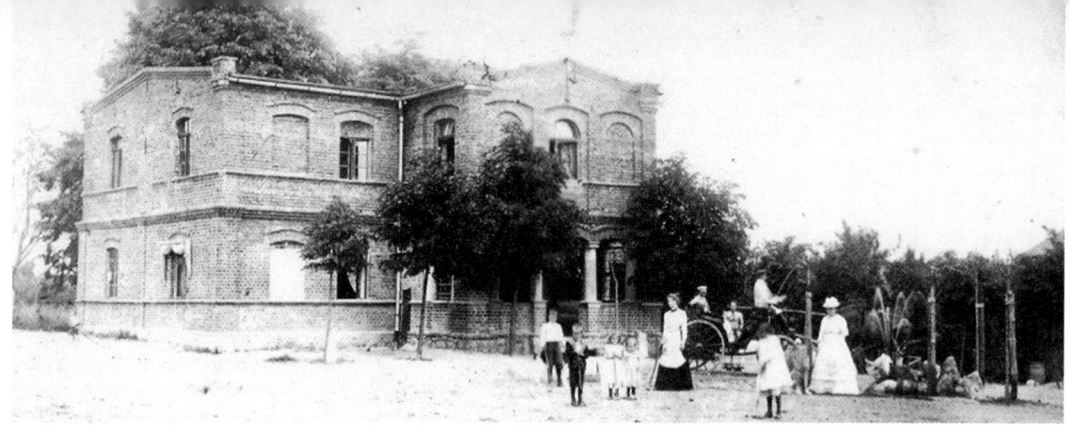

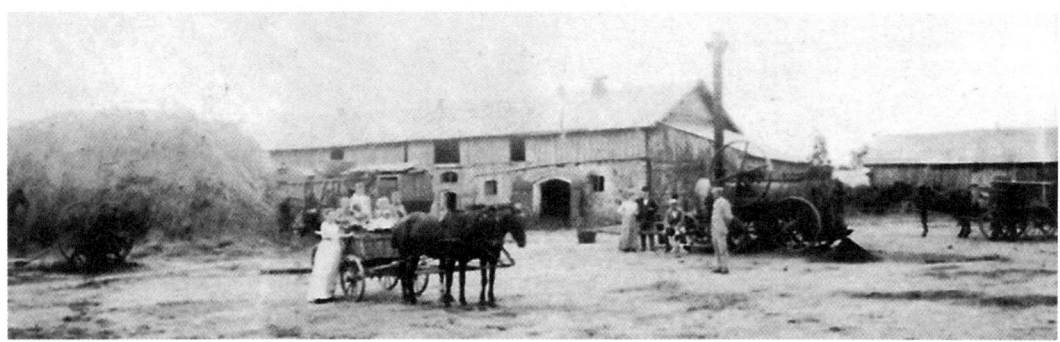

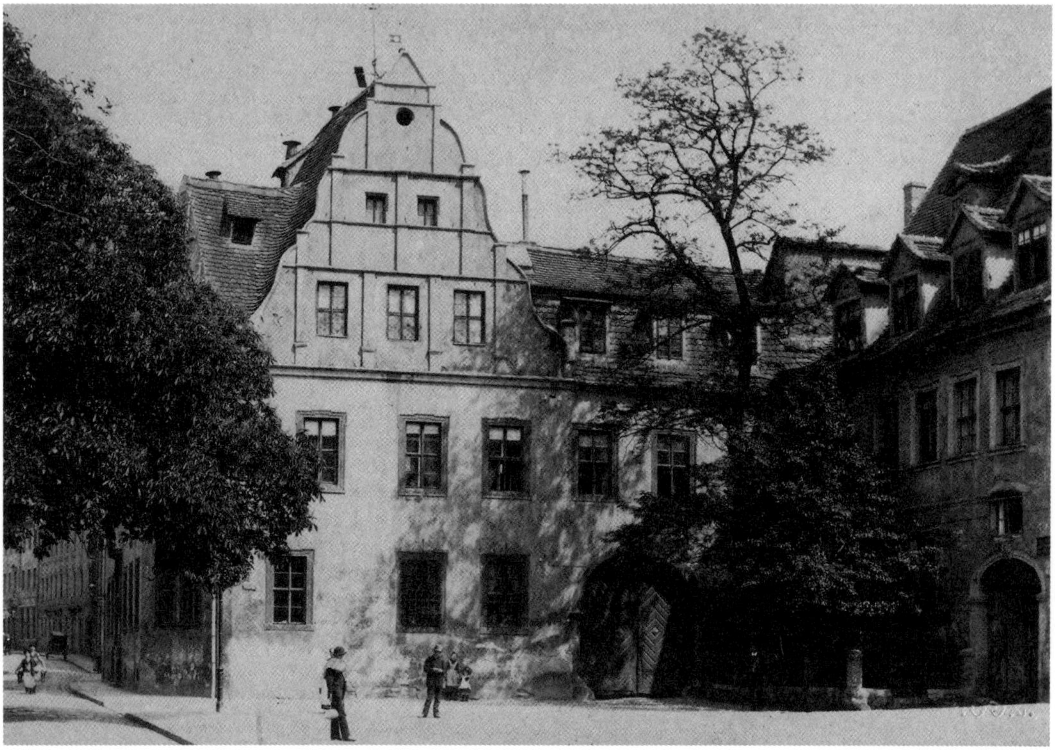

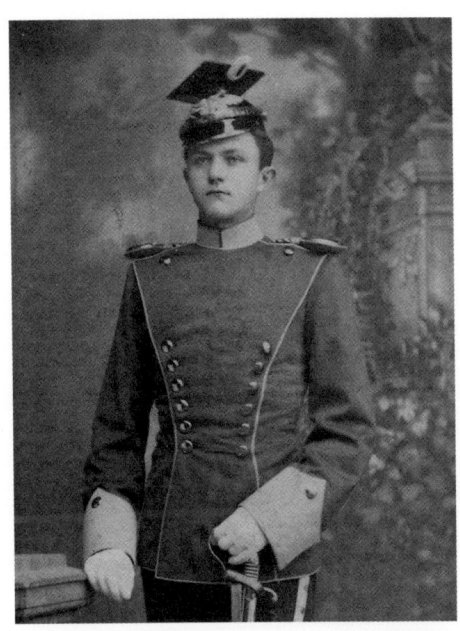

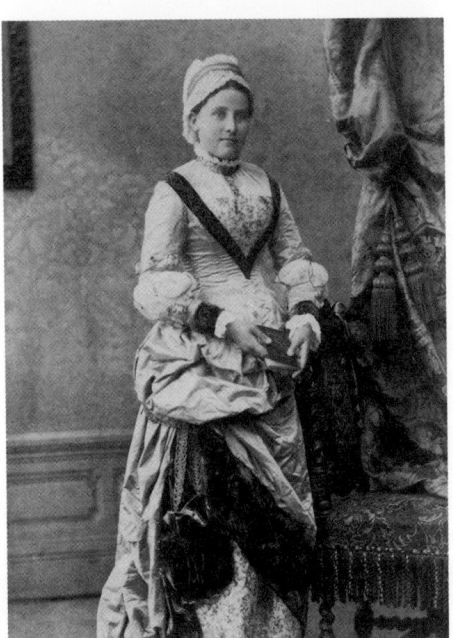

opposite, top The Von Preetzman estate in Wansen, East Prussia, with the children and their nanny in the foreground, circa 1905.

opposite, middle The Von Preetzman farm in Wansen, East Prussia, with children in the wagon and steam engine.

opposite, bottom Schwetschke house in Halle, Germany, Grosse Markenotstrasse 11, Author's great grandmother's ancestral home, now a museum.

left, top Theodor Von Preetzman, Werner's father and the author's great-grandfather.

left, bottom Hedwig Schwetschki before marriage, Werner's mother and author's great-grandmother.

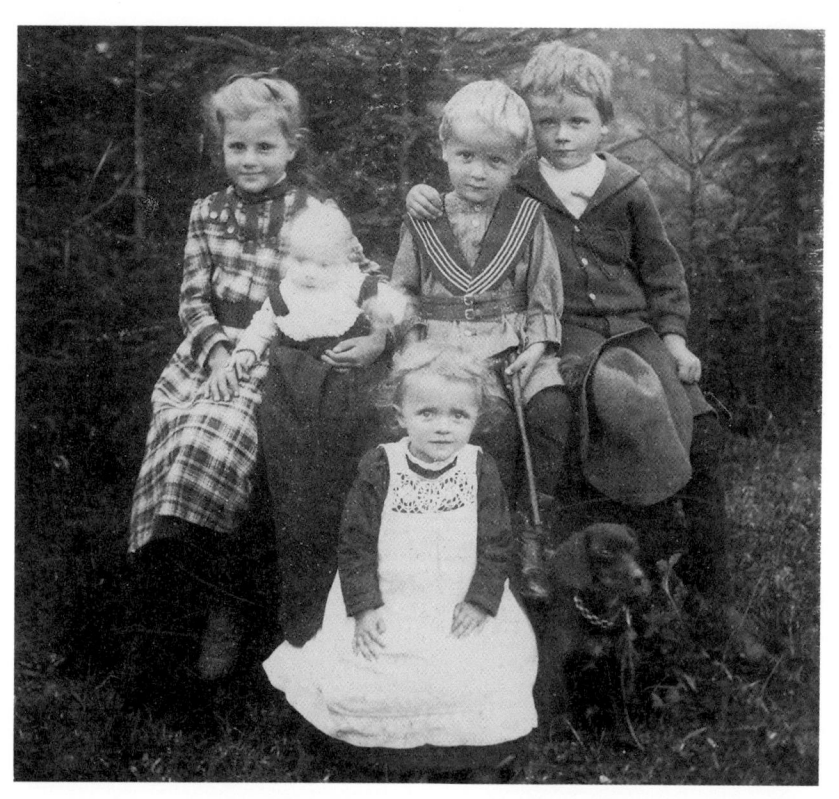

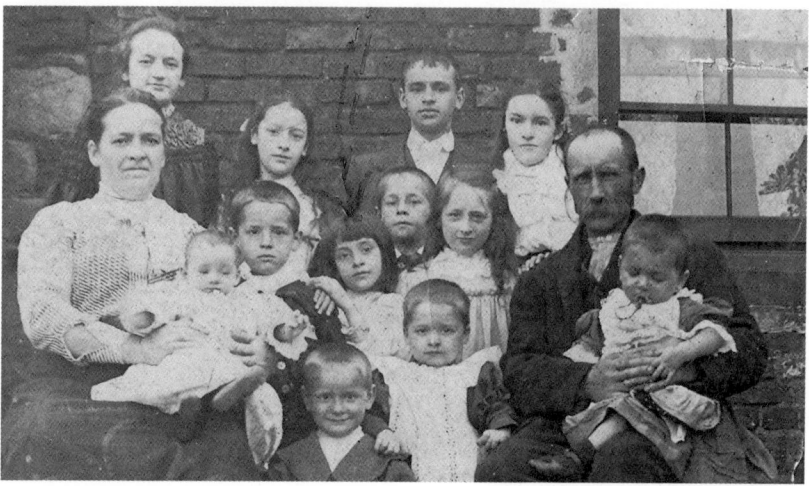

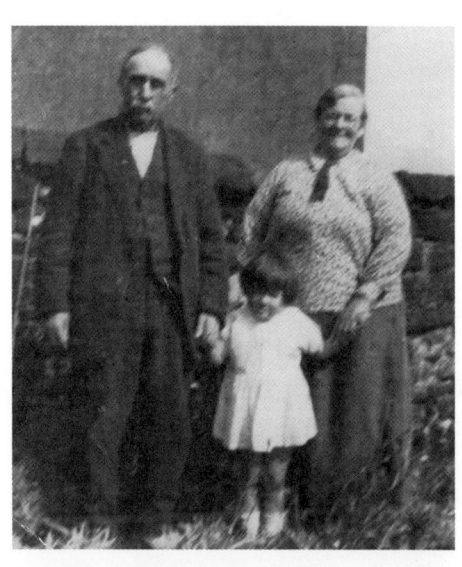

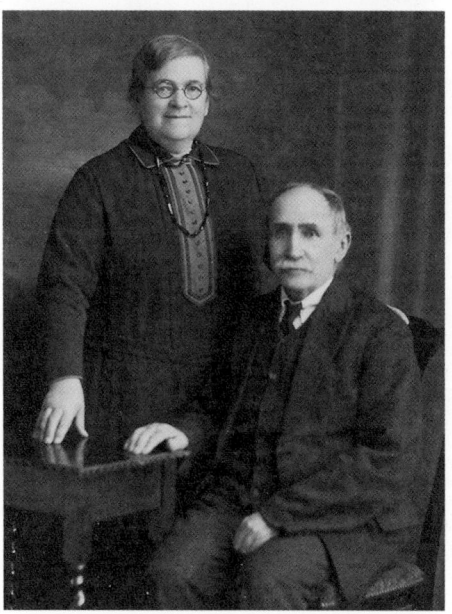

opposite, top Von Preetzmann Kinder, July 1898. Author's grandfather Werner, aged 5, far right, with his arm around Erich.

opposite, bottom Moncrief family, Whitehaven, England. Eva, the author's grandmother, was the middle child of thirteen. Eva is pictured at about 8 years, at centre. The youngest child, Mary, is not yet born.

left, top Eva's parents, Mary Anne and John, with their youngest child, Mary, in their garden. Author's great-grandparents and aunt.

left, bottom Mary Ann (Galloway) Moncrief (1865–1956) and John Moncrief (1855–1936), 50th wedding anniversary portrait.

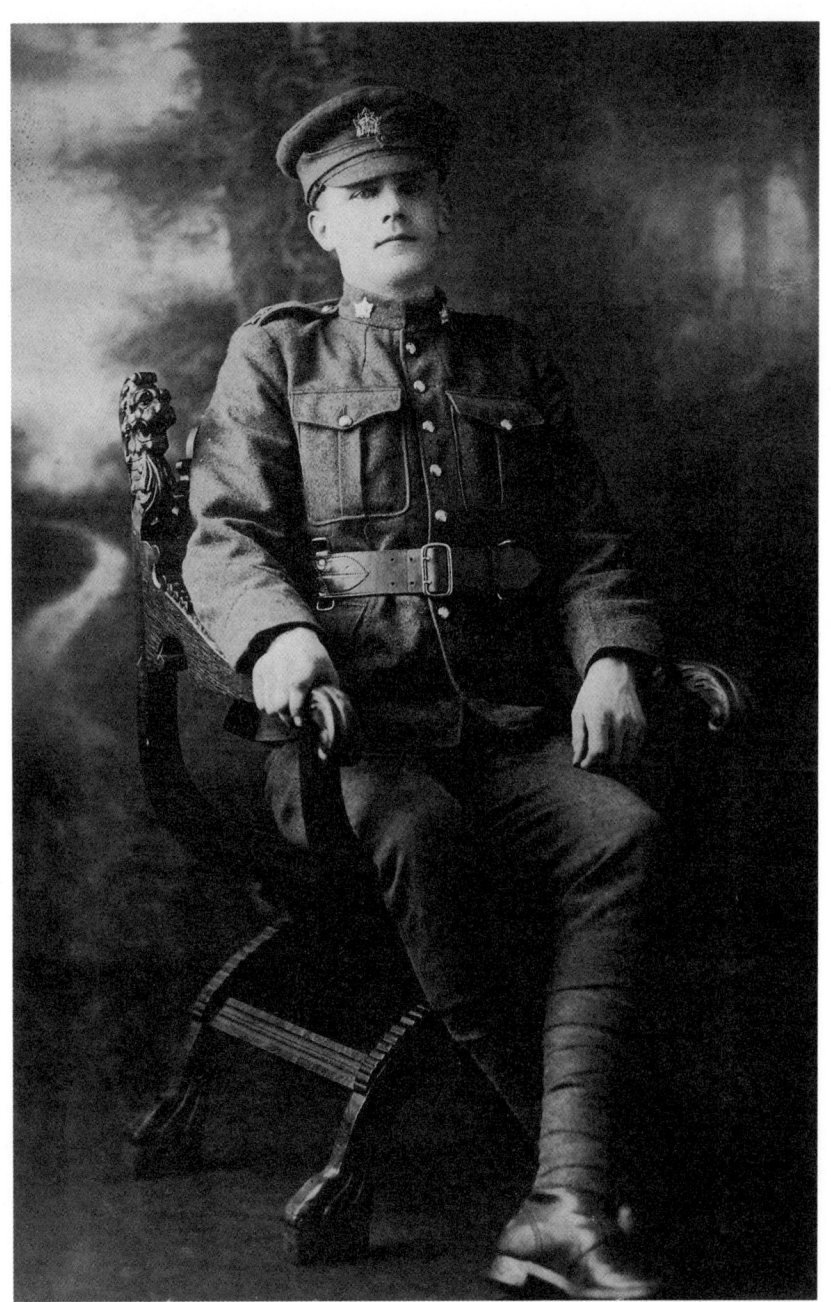

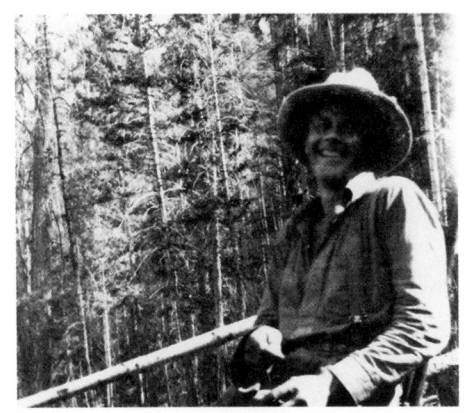

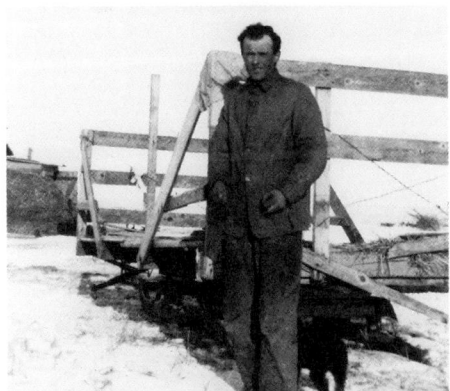

opposite Werner wearing a Canadian Army uniform 1917. This photo was taken in a studio in Kindersley, Saskatchewan, about 30 miles south of Kerrobert.

left, top Werner Theodore Preetzman, author's grandfather, at Kerr Creek near Midway, BC, circa 1925.

left, middle Werner on his first procurement just north of Kerrobert, Saskatchewan, circa 1914. He took photographs of himself with a string attached to his box camera. Later, Eva took over as photographer.

left, bottom Werner and Eva just after they married, circa 1927.

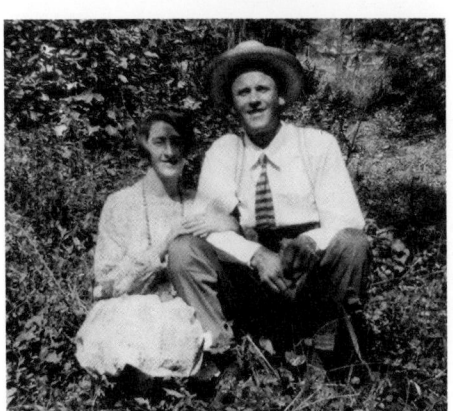

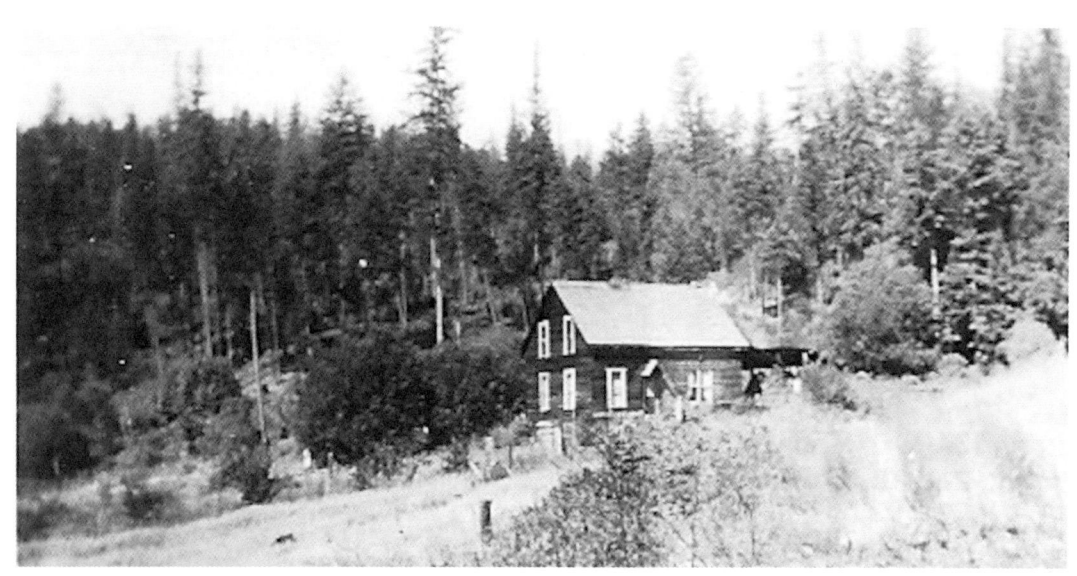

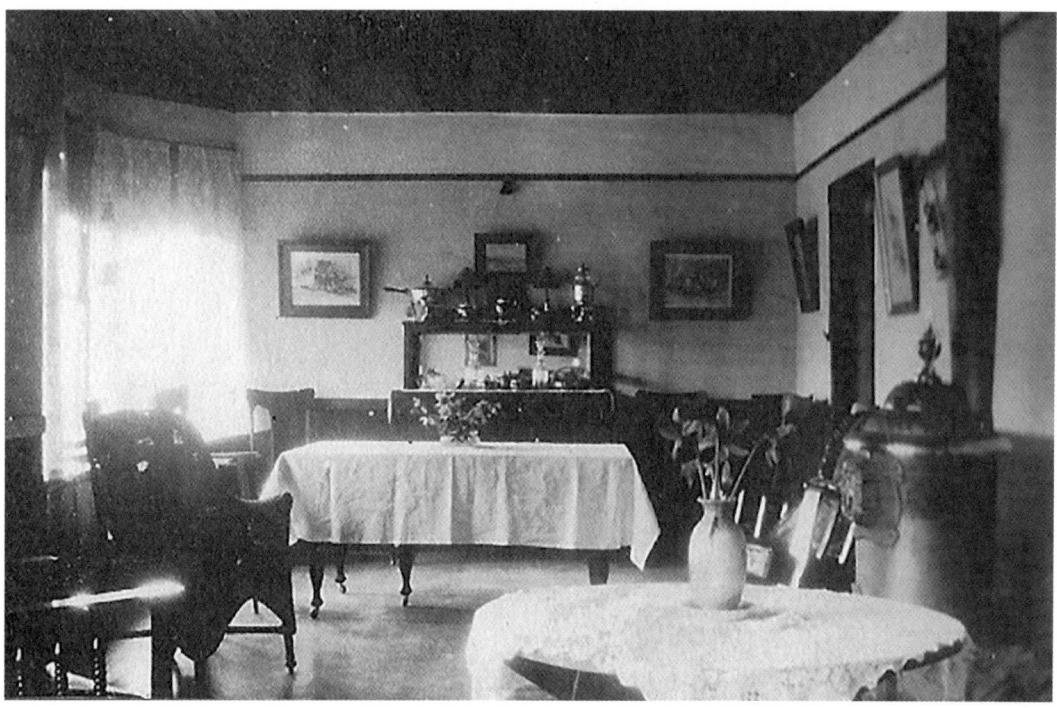

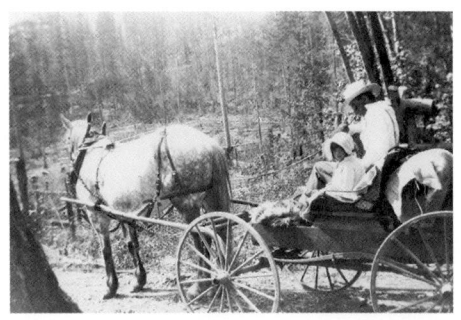

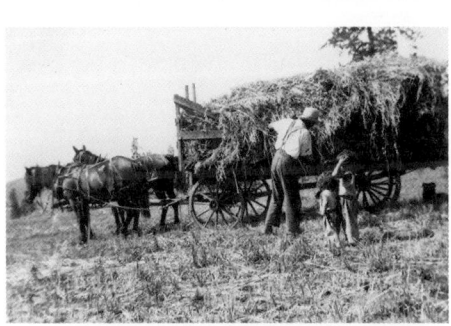

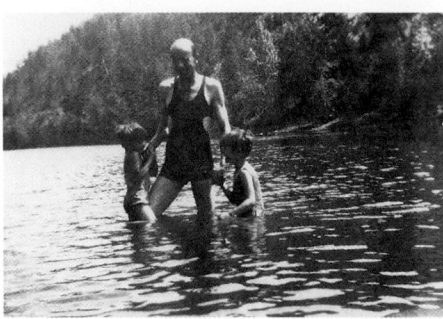

opposite, top The new Preetzman home, built by Werner at Kerr Creek. When Eva arrived, they lived in a one-room log cabin until they moved into this house after both children were born.

opposite, bottom Interior of home. Eva worked hard to make the interior elegant.

left, top Werner and Jean in the wagon going to town, circa 1930. Eva formally takes over as photographer.

left, middle Jean and Gloria posed in front of the hay wagon, circa 1932.

left, bottom Werner swimming in Boundary Creek with Gloria and Jean, circa 1933.

right, top Werner with Jean and Gloria planting the vegetable garden, circa 1934.

right, bottom Gloria walking alongside Werner as he ploughs the base for a new road, 1942.

opposite, top left Gloria and Jean posing with Werner as he saws wood for railroad ties, winter 1936.

opposite, top right Werner after a hard day's work, asleep in the new house at Kerr Creek.

opposite, bottom left Eva, Jean, Werner, Gloria Preetzman on holiday in Oliver, BC.

opposite, bottom right Eva with Jean and Gloria, circa 1939, at Kerr Creek.

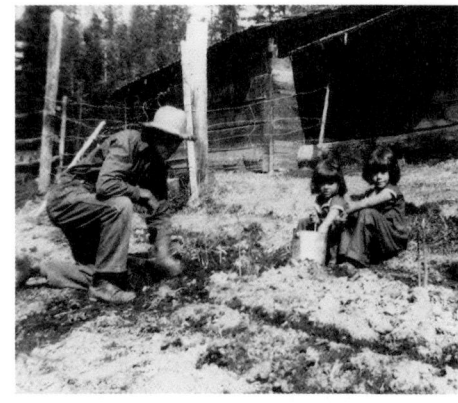

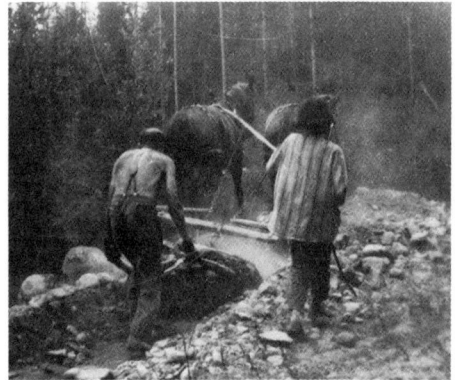

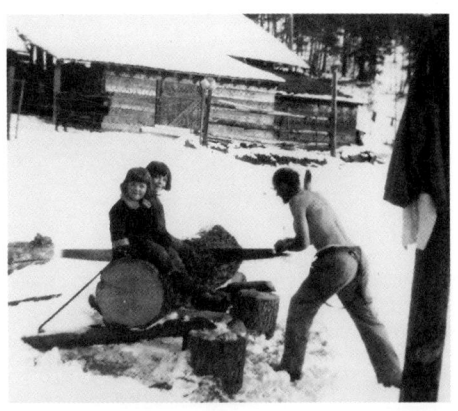
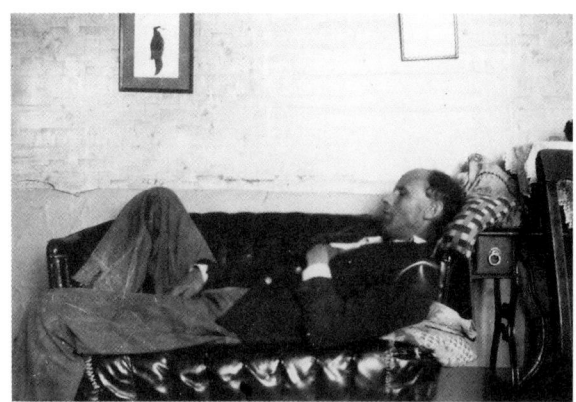
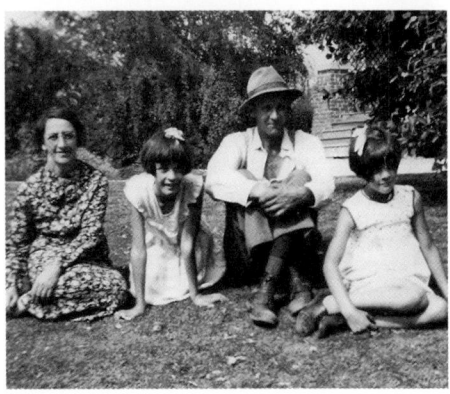
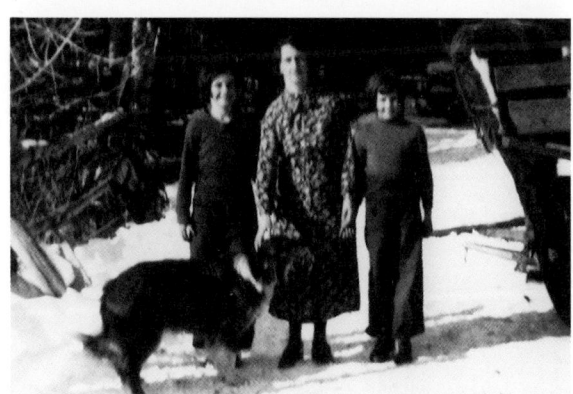

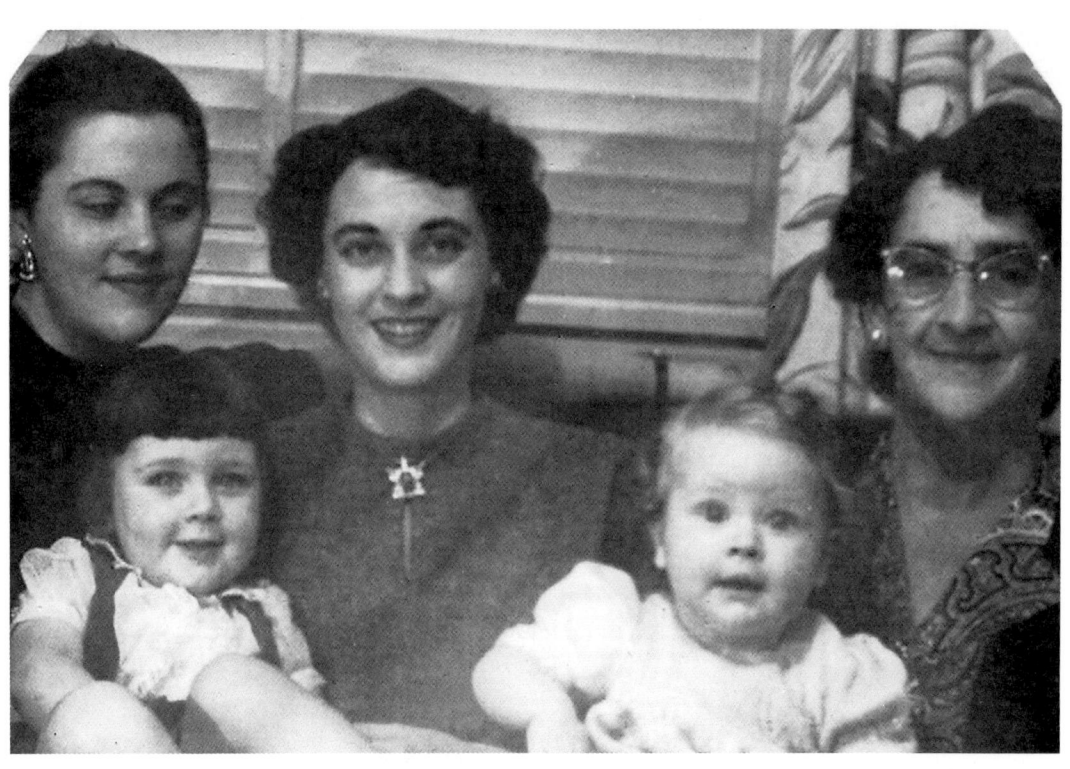

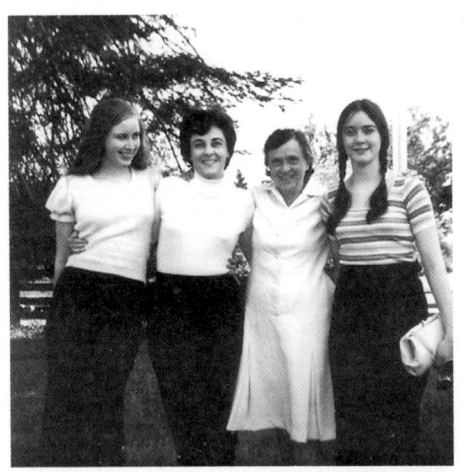

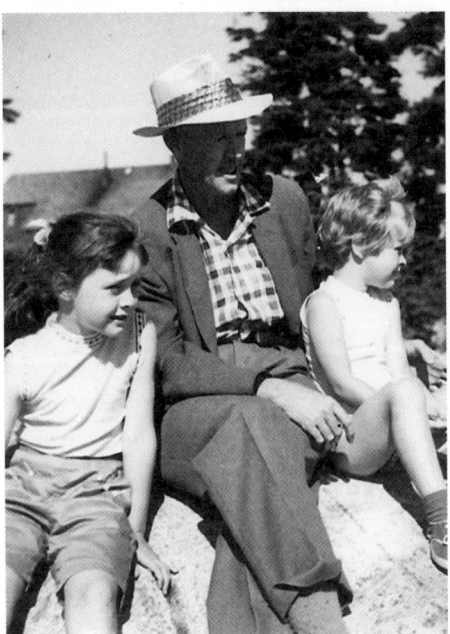

opposite Christmas 1956. *Back row from left to right:* Author's aunt Gloria, mother Jean, and grandmother Eva. *Front row left to right:* Author's sister Vikki and author Joanne.

left, top *Left to right*: Joanne, Jean, Hertha, and Vikki, circa 1970. Hertha was Werner's sister and a fantastic source of information about the German relatives. In this photo, she was visiting the author and her family in Terrace, BC.

left, bottom Don Thomson, author's father, at centre, sister Vikki at right, and Joanne at left.

CHRONOLOGICAL
LIST OF ARTWORK

1. Mason Jar with Egg, March 28, 2014
2. Mason Jar with Anjou Pear, March 29, 2014
3. Mason Jar with Knitting Needles, March 31, 2014
4. Mason Jar with Homespun Wool, April 1, 2014
5. Mason Jar with Bone, April 2, 2014
6. Mason Jar with Hymnal and Common Prayer Book, April 2, 2014
7. Mason Jar with Dried Rose, April 3, 2014
8. Mason Jar with Crochet Doily, April 4–7, 2014
9. Mason Jar with Plum Blossom, April 4, 2014
10. Mason Jar with Barking Dog, April 5, 2014
11. Mason Jar with Dragonfly, April 6–7, 2014
12. Mason Jar with Steak, April 8, 2014
13. Mason Jar with Silver Spoon, April 9, 2014
14. Mason Jar with Secrets, April 11, 2014
15. Mason Jar with Cinderella Doll, April 11, 2014
16. Mason Jar with Honesty Plant, April 13–15, 2014
17. Mason Jar with Cherry Blossom, April 15, 2014
18. Mason Jar with Crochet Hooks and Cotton for Lace, April 16, 2014
19. Mason Jar with Lemon Slices, April 17, 2014
20. Mason Jar with Dandelions, April 18, 2014
21. Mason Jar with Spider, April 19, 2014
22. Mason Jar with Yerba Buena, April 20, 2014
23. Mason Jar with Pear Blossoms, April 20, 2014
24. Mason Jar with California Poppy, April 21, 2014
25. Mason Jar with Not Canola, April 21, 2014
26. Mason Jar with Canola, April 22, 2014
27. Mason Jar with Miner's Lettuce, April 25, 2014
28. Mason Jar with California Poppies Past Their Prime, April 26, 2014
29. Mason Jar with Apple Blossoms, April 27, 2014
30. Mason Jar with Rhubarb, April 28, 2014
31. Mason Jar with Raspberry Cane, April 29, 2014
32. Mason Jar with Calypso Orchid, May 3–4, 2014
33. Mason Jar with Elderflower, May 4–5, 2014
34. Mason Jar with Saskatoon Flower, May 6–7, 2014
35. Mason Jar with Black Thread, May 7–8, 2014
36. Mason Jar with Last Year's Plums, May 9, 2014
37. Mason Jar with Wild Rose Buds, May 12–13, 2014
38. Mason Jar with Wild Rose, May 13, 2014
39. Mason Jar with Lily of the Valley, May 14, 2014
40. Mason Jar with Strawberry Plant, May 15–16, 2014
41. Mason Jar with Chives, May 17–18, 2014
42. Mason Jar with Wheelbarrow and Freshly Planted Garden, May 19, 2014
43. Mason Jar with Vetch, May 21–22, 2014
44. Mason Jar with Dandelion Wishes, May 23–24, 2014
45. Mason Jar with Dying Dandelion, May 29–June 8, 2014

46. Mason Jar with Dead Dandelion Wishes, June 8, 2014
47. Mason Jar with Wild Strawberries, June 8, 2014
48. Mason Jar with Zebra Toy, June 10, 2014
49. Mason Jar with Willomena's Silver Spoon, June 15–16, 2014
50. Mason Jar with Raspberries, June 16–17, 2014
51. Mason Jar with Indian Paintbrush, June 17, 2014
52. Mason Jar with Blackberry Blossoms, June 20–25, 2014
53. Mason Jar with Bing Cherries, June 26, 2014
54. Mason Jar with Boink Maker, June 28–July 2, 2014
55. Mason Jar with Puttee, July 2–3, 2014
56. Mason Jar with Hand Drill, July 4–19, 2014
57. Mason Jar with Canadian Army Hat Badge and Lavender, July 5, 2014
58. Mason Jar with Canadian Army Button, July 6, 2014
59. Mason Jar with Two Bits, July 10–16, 2014
60. Mason Jar with Compass, July 10–16, 2014
61. Mason Jar with Boundary Creek, July 11, 2014
62. Mason Jar with Settler's Cabin, July 11–16, 2014
63. Mason Jar with Brown-eyed Susan, July 11, 2014
64. Mason Jar with Wagon Invention, July 11–September 30, 2015
65. Mason Jar with Hay from Bauer Creek Ranch, July 11, 2014
66. Mason Jar with Staghorn Flower, July 13, 2014
67. Mason Jar with Saskatoon Berries, July 14, 2014
68. Mason Jar with Purple Vetch, July 14, 2014
69. Mason Jar with Harebells, July 15, 2014
70. Mason Jar with Pale Indian Paintbrush, July 15–16, 2014
71. Mason jar with Wishes, Coming and Gone, May 26–June 10, 2014
72. Mason Jar with Peaches, July 19–20, 2014
73. Mason Jar with Apricots, July 20, 2014
74. Mason Jar with Canned and Fresh Clingstone Peaches, July 20–21, 2014
75. Mason Jar with Bricks from Bauer Ranch, July 21–22, 2014
76. Mason Jar with Beet, July 28–29, 2014
77. Mason Jar with Uncle William's Postcard, August 12, 2014
78. Mason Jar with Corn on the Cob, September 8, 2014
79. Mason Jar with Tomatoes, September 8, 2014
80. Mason Jar with Prune Plums, September 9–11, 2014
81. Mason Jar with Nasturtiums and Capers, September 9–11, 2014
82. Mason Jar with Cucumbers, September 11, 2014
83. Mason Jar with Zucchini, September 18–19, 2014
84. Mason Jar with Windfall Apples, September 18–19, 2014
85. Mason Jar with Railroad Spike, September 22–23, 2014
86. Mason Jar with Bartlett Pears, September 24, 2014
87. Mason Jar with Hubbard Squash, September 28, 2014
88. Mason Jar with Potatoes, September 29, 2014
89. Mason Jar with Lightning Struck Wood, September 19, 2014
90. Mason Jar with Honesty Plant Discs, October 6, 2014
91. Mason Jar with Green Beans, October 6, 2014
92. Mason Jar with Ribbon Rose, October 7, 2014
93. Mason Jar with Pickles, October 8, 2014

ACKNOWLEDGEMENTS

THIS BOOK has been a personal and a public journey. I offer thanks to my patrons, students, and the lenders of Mason jars. Your enthusiastic financial and relational support and sharing allowed me to see that this journey of ancestral healing is a shared one. Thank you to my friends who stood by me as I struggled with issues the series uncovered and the death of my mother. You know who you are and that I love you.

Thank you, Eva, for documenting life "up Kerr Creek"; Jean for embracing the project as "the best work you have ever done"; Aunty Gloria for sharing personal artifacts and stories; Vikki for rescuing the Mason jars used "up Kerr Creek" so they could model in this series.

Elizabeth, my daughter, without you this book would not be. Thank you for repeatedly prodding me to publish and finding time in your busy life to spend countless hours creating a beautiful manuscript to send out to publishers.

And thank you to Lara Kordic and the team at Heritage House Publishing for such a speedy and enthusiastic acceptance of the beautiful manuscript Elizabeth put together.

I would also like to thank Annora Brown (1899–1987), who welcomed me into her home in Deep Cove in the summer of 1986, for seeing my enthusiastic, overburdened-with-rules young self. Her comment, *there are no rules*, followed by her advice to *throw away any rule that doesn't serve you*, have guided my art making ever since.

ABOUT
THE AUTHOR

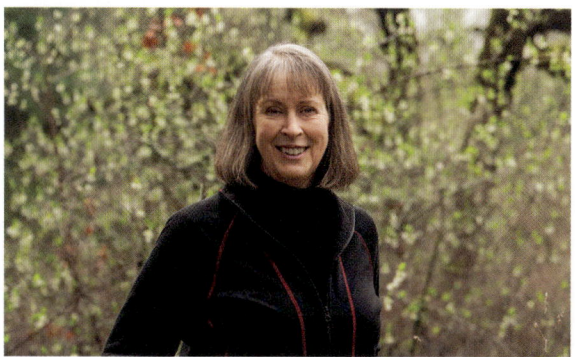

NAOMI MAYA

JOANNE THOMSON is a full-time visual artist, divides her time between fine art, illustration, and teaching. She has facilitated community art projects, including murals in Victoria, Saanich, and Terrace, BC, and was the lead painter for the Beatty Biodiversity Museum Blue Whale Project at UBC. Prior to turning to art full-time in 2004, Thomson also worked as a registered nurse in hospitals, communities, and in nursing education. She is currently an illustrator for Life and Death Matters, an independent publisher of resources for teaching palliative care. She holds and Master of Adult Education degree and lives in Victoria, British Columbia.